Promotive Activities in Technology-Enhanced Learning

European University Studies

Europäische Hochschulschriften

Publications Universitaires Européennes

Series V

Economics and Management

Reihe V Série V

Volks- und Betriebswirtschaft

Sciences économiques, gestion d'entreprise

Vol./Bd. 3359

PETER LANG

Frankfurt am Main · Berlin · Bern · Bruxelles · New York · Oxford · Wien

Christine Bauer

Promotive Activities in Technology-Enhanced Learning

The Impact of Media Selection on Peer Review, Active Listening and Motivational Aspects

PETER LANG
Internationaler Verlag der Wissenschaften

Bibliographic Information published by the Deutsche Nationalbibliothek
The Deutsche Nationalbibliothek lists this publication in the Deutsche Nationalbibliografie; detailed bibliographic data is available in the internet at http://dnb.d-nb.de.

Printed with financial support
of the Federal Ministry for Science
and Research in Vienna

ISSN 0531-7339
ISBN 978-3-631-58809-3

www.peterlang.de

Acknowledgements

Although this book is an individual work, I could never have reached the heights or explored the depths without the help, support, and guidance of a lot of people.

First I would like to thank my doctoral advisor ao.Univ.-Prof. Dipl.-Ing. Dr. Renate Motschnig-Pitrik for the support and encouragement throughout my doctoral work. You stimulated my analytical thinking, furthered my research abilities, and offered invaluable assistance, support, and guidance. Above all, you encouraged me to develop independent thinking and found the ideal proportion of guidance and self-direction. And at the perfect point in time you managed let go, enabling me to sing my song.

Special thanks go to Dr. MMag. Kathrin Figl for all the support and efforts. Throughout my work you came up with ideas, provided hints and methodical assistance – like my mentor rather than a peer.

Furthermore I would like to thank ao.Univ.-Prof. Mag. Dr. Christine Strauß for the mentoring and advice in the final phase of my work. It may have been late in my doctoral phase when we first met but in good season for the challenge that I am heading for.

Along the long and winding road through my doctoral work, there have been many people accompanying me a short or longer way. I would like to express my sincere appreciation and gratitude to those who believed in me and still do, who showed appreciation and empathy – *unconditionally*. It is you who gave me the strength to move on.

Above all I want to thank my parents and family for all their love and support. Without you I would not stand where I am – being the one who I am.

"When there's no one else
look inside yourself
like your oldest friend just
trust the voice within"

(Words & music by
Glen Ballard & Christina Aguilera,
"The Voice Within")

Abstract

Numerous studies indicate that learning is most effective in terms of persistency when it addresses the whole person rather than merely the intellect. Based on the person-centred approach to learning, a set of non-directive, promotive activities that foster significant learning have been identified and extensively researched in classroom settings.

Equally, it turned out that technology-enhanced learning settings, which thoughtfully combine online elements with learning in presence phases, have benefits compared to pure e-learning or traditional learning settings in class. For instance, a combination allows creating or making use of distinct settings according to requirements of, for example, different learning phases, activities, or styles, etc. that are most likely distinct as also the results of this work show.

Adopting the well-proven promotive activities to technology-enhanced learning environments is, though, challenging as transferring these activities to technology-enhanced settings requires appropriate media selection, adequate adaptation of activity patterns to a chosen setting, and – above all – respective media competence that allows for conveying the underlying interpersonal qualities with the respective medium. Nevertheless, as this work demonstrates, the person-centred approach with the three levels of learning and personal growth (intellect, social skills, and personality) and technology-enhanced learning complement one another and are, thus, a particularly effective combination.

The major scientific goal of this work is to investigate whether and how non-directive, promotive activities may be applied in cooperative technology-enhanced learning settings. Besides transferring existing activity patterns to the online context, this work presents – by giving practical examples – new opportunities that could only emerge with technology enhancement.

With respect to promotive activities, the main three fields of interest are: motivational aspects, the impact of media selection on peer review, and active listening with means of written online communication. By combining qualitative and quantitative methods, these aspects have been investigated in a scale of studies conducted in five distinct courses at the University of Vienna.

Four distinct courses, which implement similar but, though, different course designs, were compared with the aim to identify pedagogical elements that drive motivation. As expected, students appreciate the person-centred style. Furthermore, rewarding self-initiative and high practical relevance are qualified motivation drivers.

Investigating the impact of media selection, two case studies compared online and face-to-face peer reviews. With respect to cooperative learning, the studies explored communication and collaboration aspects. Furthermore the quality and kind of feedback were analysed. Essentially, the setting with written online peer review and the possibility to raise a query seemed highly appropriate.

Adopting the highly recognised face-to-face communication concept of *active listening* in settings with written online communication is a novel asset that had been explored in two case studies. Demanding both verbal and nonverbal skills, this way of communication improves mutual understanding by using techniques like paraphrasing. For instance, it avoids misunderstandings and in conflicts people tend to be more willing to explain in detail, which increases chances to find a joint solution. The presented studies investigate *active listening* in an educational setting using written online communication. Thereby, the focus laid on instant messaging and e-mail communication, examining both settings' capacities and differences and exploring whether *active listening* is effective in written online communication. Besides demonstrating that *active listening* is not limited to an oral setting, these studies aimed at investigating students' media competence. Interestingly enough, students' report scepticism although analysis of their communicative behaviour provides evidence that students are able to overcome the difficulties of the respectively used media (instant messaging and e-mail) and can, hence, apply the concept accordingly. While, naturally, there are limitations to expressing empathy in online settings, the latter were found to offer valuable opportunities that face-to-face conversations tend to lack. For instance, it appears that instant messaging tools leave control with the person who expresses his or her thought. This allows this person to completely verbalise his or her thought before responding. Analysis reveals that the benefits can already be observed with newcomers to the concept.

Finally, the work draws up general recommendations concerning promotive activities in technology-enhanced learning settings in higher education targeted at students of business informatics and computer science. Findings do not only give direction to educators but do, moreover, provide indication for tool designers, what they need to take into consideration when developing tools that support whole person learning.

Contents

I. Figures 15

II. Tables 17

III. Abbreviations 19

1 STARTING POINT 21

1.1 Aims – this work's gains 22

1.2 Research question 23

1.3 Relevance 24

1.4 Book structure 25

1.5 Remarks 25

2 THEORY AND BACKGROUND 29

2.1 Learning 29
2.1.1 Traditional learning paradigms 29
2.1.2 Technology-enhanced learning and its current research directions 32
2.1.3 Person-centred learning 34
2.1.3.1 The person-centred approach 34
2.1.3.2 The three Rogers variables 37
2.1.3.3 The three levels of learning and personal growth 40
2.1.3.4 Person-centred e-learning 44

2.2 Communication and media 46
2.2.1 Communication theories and models 47
2.2.1.1 The transmission model of communication by Shannon & Weaver 47
2.2.1.2 The linguistic model of communication by Eco 49
2.2.1.3 The interpersonal communication by Watzlawick 50
2.2.1.4 The sociopsychological model of communication by Schulz von Thun 52
2.2.2 Characteristics of media 54
2.2.3 Media choice theories 56
2.2.4 Communication for collaboration in technology-enhanced environments 62
2.2.4.1 Media requirements for collaborative settings 63
2.2.4.2 Eligibility of selected media for particular tasks 73

2.3 Excursus: Development of social skills 76
2.3.1 Acquisition and development of social skills 77
2.3.1.1 Developing social skills in a technology-enhanced environment 78
2.3.1.2 Using social skills (acquired in online situations) in a face-to-face context 80
2.3.2 Acquiring social skills in addition to intellectual knowledge 83

3 FACTORS AFFECTING MEDIA'S ELIGIBILITY FOR PARTICULAR EDUCATIONAL SETTINGS 87

3.1 Learning factors 89

3.2 Human factors 91
3.2.1 Variables of both learners and educators 91

3.2.2 Learner specific variables 92
3.2.3 Educator specific variables 93
3.3 Learning environment factors 94

4 PROMOTIVE, NON-DIRECTIVE ACTIVITIES 97

4.1 Facilitating learning by providing resources 100
4.1.1 Material learning resources 100
4.1.2 Persons as learning resources 103
4.2 The four dimensions of comprehensibility 106
4.3 Thinking processes 108
4.4 Furthering a beneficial working process 116
4.4.1 Learning to know the task personally 117
4.4.2 Professional elaboration and investigation of subtasks 119
4.4.3 Finalising, exploiting and / or applying work 122
4.5 Working in teams 123
4.6 Learning contracts 126
4.7 Living together in a good group 131

5 METHODS 135

5.1 Research strategies in social sciences 135
5.2 Research strategies in business informatics 139
5.3 Quantitative and qualitative methods 144
5.4 The research design 146
5.4.1 The case study as a research strategy 148
5.4.2 The case study design 152
5.4.3 The case study selection 155
5.4.3.1 Case 1. Motivational aspects in technology-enhanced learning settings 156
5.4.3.2 Case 2a. Differences of face-to-face and written online peer reviews 158
5.4.3.3 Case 2b. Evaluating peer review settings with different media combinations 162
5.4.3.4 Case 3a and 3b. Active listening in technology-enhanced learning settings 165
5.5 Quality of research 169
5.5.1 The classic quality criteria in quantitative research 170
5.5.2 Quality criteria in qualitative research 171
5.5.3 Quality criteria for case study research 173

6 MOTIVATIONAL ASPECTS IN TECHNOLOGY-ENHANCED LEARNING SETTINGS 179

6.1 Theory and background 180
6.1.1 The ARCS model of motivational design 182
6.1.2 The SuperMotivation model 187
6.1.3 The time continuum model of motivation 189

6.2 Measuring motivation 191
6.3 The research questions 193
6.4 The case design 193
6.4.1 Course designs 193
6.4.1.1 Course descriptions 193
6.4.1.2 Overview over pedagogical elements 196
6.4.2 Implementation of the study 199
6.4.2.1 Data collection and methods 199
6.4.2.2 The sample 201
6.5 Results 201
6.6 Conclusion 210

7 THE IMPACT OF MEDIA SELECTION ON PEER REVIEWS 213

7.1 Theory and background 214
7.1.1 Peer assessment 214
7.1.2 Peer review in writing classes and language courses 215
7.1.3 Peer review in scholarship 216
7.1.4 Peer review in software development 218
7.1.5 Positive effects of peer reviewing in educational context 224
7.1.6 Terminology 225
7.1.7 Online versus face-to-face peer reviews 226
7.2 Case 2a. Differences of face-to-face and written online peer reviews 227
7.2.1 The research questions 227
7.2.2 The case design 228
7.2.2.1 Description of the setting 228
7.2.2.2 Implementation of the case 229
7.2.2.3 Data collection and methods 235
7.2.3 Results 236
7.2.3.1 Differences in the number of words and statements 236
7.2.3.2 Differences regarding the type of peer reviews 238
7.2.3.3 Differences in activities 242
7.2.3.4 Workload distribution in teams 245
7.2.3.5 Work efficiency and review quality 246
7.2.3.6 Suggestions for improvement 248
7.3 Case 2b. Evaluating peer review settings with different media combinations 248
7.3.1 The research questions 248
7.3.2 The case design 249
7.3.2.1 Description of the setting 249
7.3.2.2 Implementation of the case 250
7.3.2.3 Data Collection and methods 255
7.3.3 Results 256
7.3.3.1 Impact of the online peer review activity on students' learning's 256
7.3.3.2 Difficulties in reviewing other papers 259
7.3.3.3 Quality of received peer reviews 259
7.3.3.4 Appropriateness of particular media combinations for peer reviews 261
7.4 Conclusion 265

8 *Active listening* in technology-enhanced learning settings 269
8.1 Theory and background 270
8.1.1 The listening modes 270
8.1.2 Active listening 275
8.1.2.1 Techniques in and for active listening 278
8.1.2.2 The benefits of active listening 279
8.1.2.3 Difficulties in active listening 282
8.2 The research questions 284
8.3 The case design 284
8.3.1 Description of the setting 285
8.3.2 Implementation of the cases 286
8.3.3 Data collection and methods 289
8.4 Case 3a. Active listening in written online communication 289
8.4.1 The sample 289
8.4.2 Results 289
8.5 Case 3b. Online active listening and media competence 294
8.5.1 The sample 294
8.5.2 Results 294
8.6 Comparison and Conclusions 298
8.7 Achievements, limitations, and further work 301
9 Conclusions and recommendations 303
10 Summary and outlook 313
10.1 Summary 313
10.2 Suggestions for future research 315
11 References 319
Appendix 351
Appendix 1. Questionnaire concerning motivational aspects 352
Appendix 2. Questionnaire for comparing online and face-to-face peer reviews 357
Appendix 3. Questionnaire investigating media enhancement for peer reviews 361

I. Figures

Figure 1.	Cooperative learning as a central process	23
Figure 2.	Book structure and dependencies among sections	26
Figure 3.	The three levels of learning and personal growth	41
Figure 4.	The iceberg metaphor	42
Figure 5.	The transmission model of communication by (Shannon & Weaver, 1949/1963)	48
Figure 6.	The basic model of interpersonal communication	53
Figure 7.	The recipient with four ears	53
Figure 8.	Media requirements for collaborative settings	64
Figure 9.	General media requirements for collaborative settings	65
Figure 10.	Task-related media requirements for collaborative settings	67
Figure 11.	Social media requirements for collaborative settings	70
Figure 12.	Environmental factors	72
Figure 13.	Conditions for developing social skills	78
Figure 14.	Factors influencing media choice in technology-enhanced learning settings	88
Figure 15.	Promotive and non-promotive person-to-person activities	99
Figure 16.	Learner-supplied resources on the website for the course on *PROJECT MANAGEMENT –BASICS AND TECHNIQUES*	103
Figure 17.	The four dimension in comprehensible writing and optimal ratings	108
Figure 18.	Kinds of thinking processes	110
Figure 19.	UML activity diagram for the teaching method brainstorming and reflection	115
Figure 20.	Web-supported team building	126
Figure 21.	UML activity diagram for WELL learning contracts	128
Figure 22.	Structure of WELL contracts	129
Figure 23.	UML activity diagram for the blended evaluation scenario as used for the learning contracts	130
Figure 24.	Motivational orientation due to various factors regarding the course style for a typical course (*expectation*) compared with the course on *PROJECT MANAGEMENT – BASICS AND TECHNIQUES* (*perception*), n=15	131
Figure 25.	Frequency of research method use in business informatics	143
Figure 26.	Key concepts for learning motivation	180
Figure 27.	Levels of motivation	182
Figure 28.	The ARCS model of motivation	183
Figure 29.	Motivational aspects in various courses (scale from 1 to 5), Part 1	202
Figure 30.	Motivational aspects in various courses (scale from 1 to 5), Part 2	203
Figure 31.	Items without significant differences	204
Figure 32.	High motivation in the course on *SOFT SKILLS*	206
Figure 33.	Positive effects of the person-centred style	207
Figure 34.	Low scores for *WEB ENGINEERING* in motivational items closely linked to facilitators	209
Figure 35.	Peer review formality spectrum	220
Figure 36.	The flexibility and discipline dimensions in peer review	221

Figure 37. UML activity diagram illustrating the process of the peer review activities 231
Figure 38. The interface for registering deficiencies 233
Figure 39. List of reported deficiencies 235
Figure 40. Example of questionnaire item 236
Figure 42. Chronological order of tasks in the course *BASICS OF SCIENTIFIC WRITING* 253
Figure 43. UML activity diagram of the peer review process in the course *B ASICS OF SCIENTIFIC WRITING* 254
Figure 44. General feedback on the peer review activity (mean +/- sd), n=38 256
Figure 45. The influence of the online peer review activity on students' learning's (mean +/- sd), n=38 257
Figure 46. Feedback on writing the peer reviews (mean +/- sd), n=38 258
Figure 47. Difficulty of assessing various review criteria (mean +/- sd), n=38 259
Figure 48. Feedback on receiving the peer reviews (mean +/- sd), n=38 260
Figure 49. Perception of qualities of received reviews (mean +/- sd), n=37 261
Figure 50. Ratio of positive and negative annotations concerning media combinations for peer reviews 263
Figure 51. Comparison of listening modes according to the models by (Weisbach, 1999) and (Weissglass, 1990) 275
Figure 52. UML activity diagram of the case study *Active listening with instant messaging* 287
Figure 53. UML activity diagram of the case study *Active listening with e-mail and instant messaging* 288
Figure 54. Aspects to consider for promotive activities 304

II. Tables

Table 1. Characterisation of selected media and their capabilities 62
Table 2. Media eligibility for collaboration 74
Table 3. Media eligibility for task types 75
Table 4. Top eight expectations and individual fears in the course on *PROJECT MANAGEMENT – BASICS AND TECHNIQUES* 111
Table 5. Relevant situations for different research strategies 137
Table 6. The methodical spectrum in business informatics 141
Table 7. Characteristics of quantitative and qualitative research 145
Table 8. A schematic comparison of case study with experimental and survey approaches 149
Table 9. Case study tactics for assuring the quality of a research design 174
Table 10. Pedagogical elements potentially influencing motivational aspects 199
Table 11. Sample size and response rate 201
Table 12. Common criteria for the scientific peer review 217
Table 13. Number of words and statements in peer reviews 237
Table 14. Positive and negative feedback 239
Table 15. Types of negative feedback 242
Table 16. Differences of activities in online and face-to-face peer reviews 246
Table 17. Results of one-tailed Student's t-tests concerning work efficiency and review quality of online and paper reviews 247
Table 18. Online peer review form 252
Table 19. Students' perceptions concerning the suitability of different settings of peer reviews 262
Table 20. Detailed figures on positive and negative annotations concerning media combinations for peer reviews 264
Table 21. Active listening techniques 279
Table 22. Summary of reflections' analysis concerning active listening with instant messaging 291
Table 23. Summary of findings concerning active listening with e-mail and i nstant messaging 296
Table 24. Overview of issues raised in both case studies on active listening 299

III. Abbreviations

CIS	Course Interest Survey
df	degrees of freedom
ECTS	European Credit Transfer System
EPS	Education Participation Scales
f2f	face-to-face
ICT	information and communication technologies
IMMS	Instructional Materials Motivation Survey
IT	information technology
LaTeX	Lamport TeX
OD	Organisational Development and Business Processes
PCC	Person-Centred Communication
PCL	person-centred learning
PhD	Doctor of Philosophy (latin: Philosophiæ Doctor)
PHP	PHP: Hypertext Pre-processor (recursive backronym, originally: Personal Home Page Tools)
p.	page
pp.	pages
RLO	reusable learning object
sd	standard deviation
SS	Soft Skills
UML	Unified Modeling Language
VoIP	voice-over-IP, voice over Internet Protocol
Vol.	Volume
vs.	versus
WE	Web Engineering
XML	Extensible Markup Language

1 Starting point

Globalisation, innovation dynamics, and the potential of the information and communication technologies (ICT) established new basic conditions for collaboration and learning.

With the first Internet hype – both in business as well as in higher education – organisations tried to make full use of this innovation. Virtual teams, whose members never meet on site (or as it is called, they do not meet face-to-face), were established. Often team members originate from different organisations, are located at various places around the globe, and sometimes – due to time zones – do not even work at the same time. In educational settings, distance learning (or later referred to as e-learning) developed. Students do not meet each other or the educator in class but learn – interconnected or not – via their computers.

Later, so-called technology-enhanced learning (also referred to as blended learning) emerged, when it turned out that the blended aspect has benefits compared to pure e-learning or pure traditional learning settings in class.

Research has shown that learning is most effective in terms of persistency when it addresses the whole person rather than merely the intellect. Consequently, we intend not to impart factual knowledge only but rather aim to further whole person learning.

This approach to learning provides a wide range of opportunities. It will, however, only be effective if it is implemented accurately and professionally. For instance, the facilitator has to be capable of imparting social skills to students.

Carl R. Rogers' person-centred approach (Rogers, 1959, pp. 68-70) with the three levels of learning and personal growth (intellect, social skills, and personality) and technology-enhanced learning are a particularly effective combination.

Still, it is a challenging task in educational scenarios, how interpersonal qualities can be transformed into promotive actions in technology-enhanced environments. (Tausch & Tausch, 1963/1998) have identified and extensively researched a set of activities that tend to be promotive for learners – or, in other words, foster significant learning. While they considered pure face-to-face settings, the primary goal of this work is to illustrate in which ways these and related promotive activities can be lived in technology-enhanced environments. By giving practical examples and students' perceptions from courses we conducted at the University of Vienna, we hope to inspire interested readers to apply learning technology in ways that promote significant learning in both learners and facilitators.

1.1 Aims – this work's gains

This book aims to deliver results in following fields:

- First, the research relates findings with the three levels of learning and personal growth (intellect, social skills, and personality), which is a concept that is not only accepted in education but is also highly supported in business, with technology-enhanced learning, and aims to show that the use of technology can in a way be consistent with this concept.
- Second, this work shows how these enhanced values of learning (i.e. simultaneously addressing all three levels: intellect, social skills, and personality) can be achieved in specific situations in technology-enhanced learning settings.
- Third, with the discussion of case studies it delivers a thorough documentation of implementation and can, thus, build the basis for attempts to reproduce and further develop these enhanced values of learning in similar situations.
- Fourth, results give tool designers an indication, what they need to take into consideration when developing tools that support whole person learning.

The research is interdisciplinary in its core. It considers requirements in business (business administration & economics) for specialists in business informatics (computer science) with respect to learning (educational sciences and psychology) in groups (social sciences) with various media (communication science).

Figure 1 illustrates the interdisciplinary scope of cooperative learning, as it is a central process combining and targeting various areas and disciplines. Essentially, cooperative learning combines technology and soft sciences. The two big intersecting arrows illustrate that the borders of these areas are easily blurred. Each of the disciplines research, knowledge management, development, and applications and industry influences all the other disciplines, which is illustrated by double-headed arrows interconnecting all these fields.

It targets at people working in the field of academic and vocational education (scholars, educators, etc.) as well as management staff development. Results shall be considered as guidelines, open for further improvement in the educational context and spinning off to business – thus, to another context.

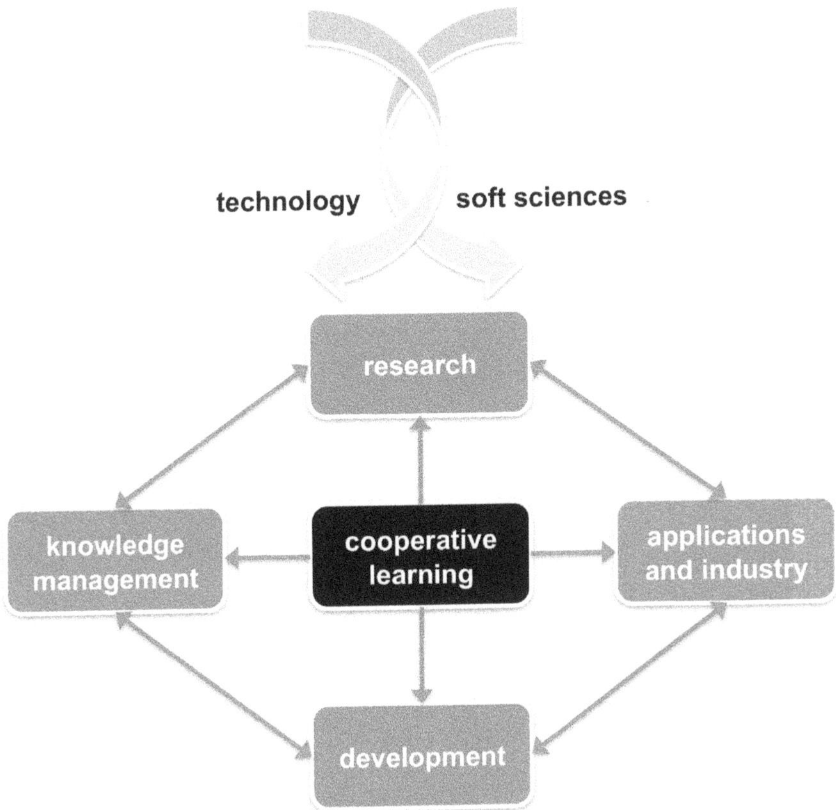

Figure 1. Cooperative learning as a central process

Source: (Motschnig-Pitrik, 2003, (adapted))

1.2 Research question

Based on the concept of whole person learning, this work aims to show that mixing the forms of expression (face-to-face, online, oral, written, collocated, at distance, etc.) can enhance learning in context of cooperative learning in university courses targeted at students of computer science and business informatics. This implies that this work aims to explore how the three levels of learning and personal growth (intellect, social skills, and personality) can be particularly furthered with respect to promotive activities when learning takes place in a blend of complementary activities in presence as well as online phases (technology-enhanced learning) compared to settings where learning takes place either only in present courses or only online in e-learning settings. How can promotive activities be implemented in technology-enhanced learning settings in order to enhance cooperative whole person learning with mixing the forms of expression and why?

1.3 Relevance

This book has three target groups: scholars, educators, and people working in the field of human resources development.

Scientific relevance

As this research project is part of an action research process pursued at the Research Lab for Educational Technologies at the University of Vienna, findings are of particular significance for ongoing research in this research lab.

Since the field of technology-enhanced learning is still a young discipline, research is dominated by case studies. Field of interest are studies comparing two or more cooperation technologies. This approach has its roots in communication theory. However, analyses dedicating to the person-centred approach are yet a novelty.

Promotive activities, which have its roots in the person-centred approach, are well researched in traditional learning settings. Combining those findings to the technology-enhanced learning environment bring new insights to the person-centred community as well as to the technology-enhanced learning community.

Since the research field is interdisciplinary, results are relevant to researchers in business administration & economics, computer science, communication science (in particular media studies), social science, educational sciences, and psychology.

As teamwork in an academic setting and in business shows many overlapping characteristics and requirements, it will be of particular interest to test whether the findings are valid also in the business field, thus in another context.

Practical relevance

Since pedagogical scenarios (teaching methods) are analysed, this research is of significance for people working in the field of academic and vocational education (scholars, educators, etc.). As the empirical study is carried out in an academic setting, it is of particular interest for scholars and facilitators at universities, although findings will also be valuable to educators outside academic settings.

Furthermore, it targets at people in the field of human resources development, in particular management staff development. In business, teamwork (and, thus, cooperative learning) plays a prominent role, particularly in business informatics projects. Findings will help to develop adequate staff development measures.

1.4 Book structure

Figure 2 outlines the structure of this book. Arrows connect sections with other sections they depend on. A straight-lined arrow indicates a strong connection; a dashed-line arrow represents a weak connection. Generally the dependencies among sections are transitive, which means that Section 7 is not only strongly connected to Section 6 but also to Section 5. If a connection to an earlier section is particularly important, this is emphasised with an extra arrow.

Basically Figure 2 illustrates the sections' interdependencies in terms of train of thoughts (i.e. ideas and elaborations of one section flow into another). However, these dependencies are not intended to convey mandatory reading instructions, but rather to guide the reader through the work.

The appendix includes the questionnaires used in this research. Questionnaire items are given in German, as they were used in the studies, with English translations (Appendix 1, Appendix 2, and Appendix 3).

1.5 Remarks

- Words and phrases in *italics* indicate emphasis. Proper names that may be confused with common English terms are also printed in italic font (instead of using quotes which are reserved solely for citations in this work).
- For transparency reasons, *COURSE TITLES* and c u r r i c u l a t i t l e s have their particular style accentuation within the text. QUESTIONNAIRE ITEMS are highlighted with small capitals.
- Throughout the text, all headings (top-level headings as well as all lower heading levels) are referred to as *Sections*.
- Footnotes are used for additional information – predominantly for acknowledgments –, whereas none of the additional information in footnotes is required for following the discussion. This should contribute to making the text more readable.

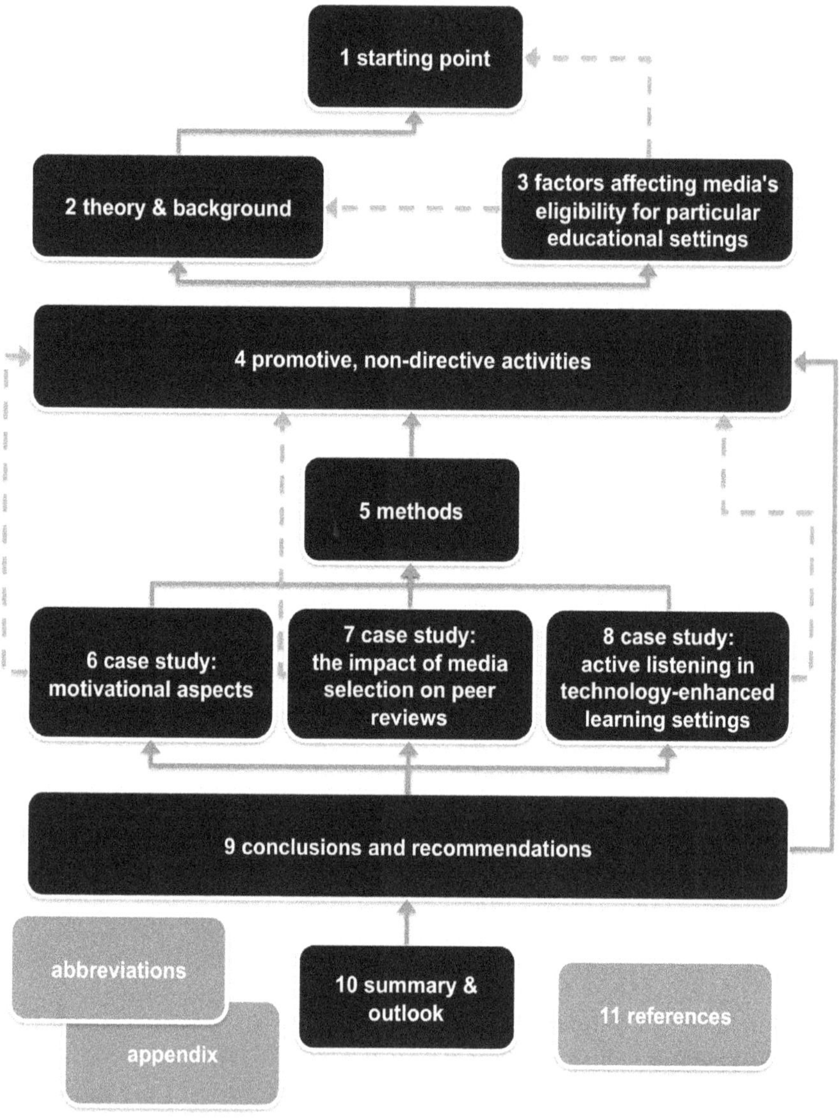

Figure 2. Book structure and dependencies among sections

- References are cited by author name(s) and year of publication within the text, usually at the end of a train of thought. Ideas, block citations, sentences, or concepts originated by other authors are cited within quotes (" ") – if longer passages are referred to, they are cited stand-alone and indented. Concepts that are put in a dense form here are referenced using *cf.* (=confer), meaning that the cited source contains more details and interested readers should consult the original sources. *Cf.* is also used to reference to sections within this work. Usually, citations include page numbers (either single or a range of pages), which allows readers to exactly locate what is referenced in the source. If whole concepts are referenced, the sources as such (without page numbers) are given.
- At the bottom right of every figure or table, information is provided regarding its source. This holds true for all figures and tables in this work, except for those that were produced totally independently from any source.
- *Excerpts, quotes and phrases* from the data source used to back up arguments in qualitative analysis are given within quotes (" ") and in *italics*. Besides the accentuation, context will make it easy to distinguish such statements from literal citations originated by other authors as the latter are preceded or succeeded by a respective reference to the source. For anonymity reasons, names are generally changed within such excerpts from the data source; instead fictional names are used, which are given in squared brackets ([ ]).
- Meeting the he / she problem, this work uses the plural form (which is gender-neutral in English language) or refers to both, *him or her*. Work may not be completely consistent in gender-neutrality in this aspect, but it tries to remedy that situation as best as possible while keeping the text readable.
- Although this work is an individual work, it is embedded in the research endeavours of the Research Lab for Educational Technologies at the University of Vienna and, naturally, every single research activity takes from and gives to the other: interrelations and interdependencies are manifold. In particular qualitative analysis requires more than just one researcher in order to allow and increase inter-subjectivity. Hence, collaboration is essential. Consequently, throughout the text this work will use the first person plural (e.g., *we* investigate, *our* research) in order to express this community, interplay, and cooperation.

2 Theory and background

This Section introduces the essential terms and definitions. Basically, it provides a literature review on learning (Section 2.1) as well as on communication and media (Section 2.2). Finally, this section closes with an excursus to the development of social skills (Section 2.3).

2.1 Learning

Naturally, over time many approaches and theories about learning emerged and changed. Most of them give their own notions of what learning is and how it can and should be initiated and supported. The following sections aim to:

- provide an overview of prominent learning paradigms,
- discuss technology-enhanced learning and its current research directions, and
- present the approach of person-centred learning, for which its application in traditional and technology-enhanced learning settings will be considered.

2.1.1 Traditional learning paradigms

In any case, learning and instruction (teaching) is based on a learning paradigm, whether implicitly or explicitly stated by the educator (cf. e.g., Baumgartner, 1997). The three dominant learning paradigms, which provide different perspectives on how learning occurs, are *behaviourism*, *cognitivism*, and *constructivism* (e.g., Baumgartner, Laske, & Welte, 2000; Derntl, 2005, p. 8).

- *Behaviourism*. In the twentieth century, behaviourism was one of the dominant learning paradigms. It is a worldview that operates on a principle of stimulus and response. It propositions that all behaviour is caused by external stimuli and can be explained without the need to consider internal mental states. It concentrates on behaviour as something perceptible and measurable. In context of learning this means that a learner is essentially passive, responding to stimuli of the environment. Every learner starts off with a clean slate (i.e. tabula rasa) and during lifetime behaviour is shaped through positive and negative reinforcement. In other words, learning is described in terms of stimuli and corresponding reactions, based on conditioning. According to behaviourism, learning is, thus, defined as a change in behaviour in the learner. Interestingly, lots of early behaviourists worked with animals (e.g., Pavlov's dogs, Premack worked with rats and apes, Thorndike with cats) and generalised findings to humans. Important contributors to behaviourism include John B. Watson, Ivan P. Pavlov, David Premack, Burrhus F. Skinner, and Edward L. Thorndike, to mention a few (cf. e.g., O'Donohue & Kitchener, 1999; Zimbardo & Gerrig, 2004, pp. 14-15, 242-277).

- *Cognitivism.* In the 1960's, cognitivism revolutions behaviourism as the main learning paradigm. In contrast to behaviourism, it is based on the claim that the inner mental processes – such as thinking, memory, knowing, and problem solving – cannot be ignored when researching human learning. It, thus, focuses on the inner mental activities postulating that opening the *black box* of the human mind is valuable and necessary for understanding how people learn. Essentially, cognitivists regard learners in a more interactive role within their learning environments and not just as a reactor to environmental stimuli (as behaviourists do). According to cognitivism, learning is, thus, regarded as a process of knowledge acquisition by integrating new information into existing cognitive structures. With the changing paradigm and the move towards a process-orientated view of learning, also the role of the educator changes; an educator is no longer seen as just the instructor but rather an enabler of the learning process. Key players in cognitivism were Jean Piaget, Edward C. Tolman, Lev S. Vygotsky, and George A. Miller (cf. e.g., Zimbardo & Gerrig, 2004, pp. 15-16, 282-288; Mergel, 1998).
- *Constructivism.* As reaction to didactic approaches like behaviourism and cognitivism, constructivism states that learning is an active, contextualised process of constructing knowledge rather than acquiring it. According to this worldview, learning is neither seen as a pure stimulus-reaction sequence as in behaviourism, nor as solely driven by cognitive processes as in cognitivism. Instead, constructivism postulates that knowledge is constructed based on personal experiences and hypotheses of the environment. Learners continuously test their hypotheses through social negotiation. Consequently, each person has a different interpretation and construction of the knowledge process. Put differently, every learner constructs his or her own understanding of his or her environment based on prior experiences and on reflections of current and past situations. In that sense, educators are considered as facilitators who further learners in the process of knowledge construction (cf. e.g., Mergel, 1998; Baumgartner, 1999, p. 4). A common misunderstanding of constructivism is that facilitators should never tell students anything directly, as this would impair them in constructing knowledge for themselves. This does, however, not hold true since constructivism as learning paradigm assumes that all knowledge is constructed from the learner's previous knowledge, regard-

less of how one is taught. Hence, activities like listening to a lecture also involve active attempts to construct knowledge.

Based on these paradigms a host of derived learning theories have evolved, such as anchored instruction (cf. The Cognition and Technology Group at Vanderbilt, 1990), the situated learning theory (cf. Lave & Wenger, 1991), or the social development theory (cf. Vygotsky, 1978).

This work builds on the person-centred learning approach, discussed in Section 2.1.3, which takes a constructivist view. Many traits inherent to person-centred learning are, though, not unique to constructivism alone but shared by other learning strategies like, for instance, situated cognition or cognitive apprenticeships (cf. Maharg, 2000). However, there are clear similarities between what the person-centred learning approach advocates and the constructivist understanding of the learning process (Maharg, 2000):

- Both approaches question the value of direct teaching.
- Both stand up for *self-discovered, self-appropriated learning*.
- Both advocate the replacement of didactic instructional strategies with the *facilitation of significant learning*.
- Both rely on an epistemology, which emphasises the *learning process* (the process of knowing) rather than the content (object of knowledge) to be learned.
- Both constructivists and advocates of the person-centred approach would agree that educational theory has to take account of epistemological method and construct. (The person-centred approach's support of epistemology is grounded less in theory but rather in experience and practice, as is constructivist learning design. Constructivism considers epistemology because of the felt need to return to the fundamental question of what constitutes learning.)

Although there are differences between the constructivist educational practice and the person-centred approach – in methodology as well as in practice –, we can perceive a similar move to enquire at a deep level into the nature of understanding and the status of knowledge, followed by a movement from epistemological enquiry to translating the results of this enquiry into promotive learning activities in educational context (Maharg, 2000).

Accordingly, the person-centred learning approach can be said to take a constructivist view.

2.1.2 Technology-enhanced learning and its current research directions

When seeking for a clear definition of *e-learning*, you will soon be disappointed by the fact that there is no. There rather coexist several definitions that adumbrate the term but leave space for ambiguity. Moreover, up to now there is no unambiguous notation that could win recognition; hence, one equally comes across spellings like *eLearning*, *e-Learning*, *E-Learning*, or *e-learning* (Baumgartner, Häfele, & Häfele, 2002, p. 4; Minass, 2002, pp. 23, 27).

Basically, we can distinguish two groups of understanding the term e-learning: a technologic-organisational interpretation and an etymologic-psychological interpretation (Dichanz & Ernst, 2001).

With respect to the *technologic-organisational interpretation*, e-learning refers to information packages for continuing education (learning), which are provided to individual learners, either via an electronic medium as online product or via CD-ROM, and which are available independent from time and place. In the interoffice context, also particular forms of organisation and support like, for instance, internal programmes, hotlines, etc., are part of the assistive elements of the e-learning arrangement (Dichanz & Ernst, 2001).

The *etymologic-psychological interpretation* of the term e-learning emanates form the term itself: e-learning. This could mean (Dichanz & Ernst, 2001):

- easy learning,
- effective learning,
- entertaining learning,
- elaborated learning,
- electronic learning, etc.

In most cases it connotes to electronic learning. Again, it raises the question, what this means in particular cases. Frequently, commercial suppliers of e-learning platforms and courses seem to want us make believe in their advertising that e-learning has a bit of everything: easy learning, effective learning, and naturally effective learning. These promises are, however, neither sound nor scientifically demonstrated on such a generic basis (Dichanz & Ernst, 2001).

Although the definitions of e-learning partly diverge in detail, they seem to share a uniform structure with common characteristics (e.g., systems that enable learning and present learning content, spatial independence, etc.) (Minass, 2002, pp. 23-24). Aspects that are not uniformly defined, primarily refer to following fields (Minass, 2002, pp. 24-27, 31):

- synchronity or asynchronity,
- degree of technology use (technology supported learning), and
- whether only learning components are deployed or if supplementary functionalities (e.g., communication) are additionally implemented.

According to (Kovacs, 2004), definitions touching the field of ICT largely orientate at current technical possibilities, which finally results in this multitude of definitions that we are confronted with. Indeed, in its early days, the term e-learning referred to electronically supported learning (satellite supported learning, learning via interactive TV, CD-Rom, video, etc.), while in the course of the Internet hype in the late 1990s, this term was mainly used for web-supported learning. In the early years of the new millennium, *e-learning* increasingly established as umbrella term for any kind of media supported learning. Hence, it included both, learning with locally installed software as well as learning with the Internet (Baumgartner, Häfele, & Häfele, 2002, p. 4).

Additionally to e-learning, the term *distance learning*, which goes back to a time long before the Internet, is still in use. Basically, distance learning refers to formalised instructional learning, where time and geographic constraints are bridged over such that the learner does not have to share the same location with what is being learned nor does it require in-person contact of student and facilitator (cf. King, Young, Drivere-Richmond, & Schrader, 2001). While in its early days, books were shipped and educators contacted students, for instance, via radio communication, ICT found its way into distance learning and seems – due to its advantages – to be the new foundation of distance education. Hence, the terms distance learning and e-learning are no longer distinct.

However, *e-learning* is actually just one side of the coin; on the other side it needs e-teaching. They are both part of a reciprocal process called *e-education*. However, *e-education* does no only involve these two sides of the coin, which are both often constrained to a *purposeful* process, but allows – derived from Humanities' tradition – a more open, not only purposeful interpretation (Baumgartner, Häfele, & Häfele, 2002, pp. 4, 6).

In practice, these terms are frequently mixed up and interchanged. Nevertheless, one should keep the differentiation between and the interplay of *learning*, *teaching*, and *education* in mind (Kovacs, 2004, p. 7).

2.1.3 Person-centred learning

The person-centred approach to learning was a radically new approach to education. It is rooted in psychotherapy (Rogers, 1951), and draws also on such diverse sources as Otto Rank, John Dewey, William Heard Kilpatrick, Søren Kierkegaard, Martin Buber (cf. Reimer, Eckert, Hautzinger, & Wilke, 1996/2007, p. 236; Thorne, 1992/2003, pp. 7, 9, 24).

With respect to these origins, it is crucial to explain the core of the person-centred approach, which is done in the subsequent Section (2.1.3.1). Thereafter, the three Rogers variables, which are significant factors in this approach, are outlined in detail (Section 2.1.3.2).

With respect to learning, we discuss the three levels of learning and personal growth (Section 2.1.3.3). And finally, the last Section is dedicated to person-centred e-learning, which essentially is the application of the person-centred approach to technology-enhanced learning settings (Section 2.1.3.4).

2.1.3.1 The person-centred approach

The person-centred approach has been developed by the American psychologist Carl R. Rogers and has its roots in psychotherapy (person-centred therapy) (Rogers, 1951). The entire theory is built on a single assumption, which is called the *actualising tendency*. Basically, it can be defined as a constructive tendency present in any living organism that drives it to strive towards developing its potentials to the fullest extent possible and making the best out of its own existence (Boeree, 1998/2006; Damásio, 1994, 1999). Interestingly, the concept and findings of (Damásio, 1994, 1999) appear to match and, hence, confirm the theories of personality and behaviour of (Rogers, 1951). Damásio's theory can be complemented and enriched by Rogers' insights that particular attitudes (in Damásio's terminology *non-automated devices*) have been proven to bring people closer to their own optimum (in Damásio's terminology *perfection*) and also to the optimal being of their peers (principle of reciprocity) (Motschnig-Pitrik & Lux, 2008, p. 289). More precisely, this means that "Rogers's theory complements Damásio's in supplying the psychological and social preconditions that are necessary and sufficient for the development and maintenance of a trustworthy self as the base for the organisation of feelings and meanings" (Motschnig-Pitrik & Lux, 2008).

According to (Rogers, 1959) the actualisation tendency can unfold itself best in an atmosphere that is characterised by three attitudinal conditions (also known as the three *Rogers variables*). Essentially these dispositions are (cf. Rogers, 1961):

- *congruence* (realness, genuineness, authenticity), which connotes honesty with a client without putting on any facades or masks.
- *acceptance* (respect, positive regard), which means unconditional positive regard towards a client, and
- *empathy* (understanding), which is the ability to feel and understand what a client feels from his or her perspective.

These three dispositions have to be held and lived by a person, and reciprocally be perceived by the other person at least to some degree for allowing the actualisation tendency to be most effective (cf. Section 2.1.3.2). Altogether, these are the necessary and sufficient conditions for establishing the most constructive atmosphere in a relationship (e.g., Rogers, 1961, 1983).

Rogers' theory is not only constrained to person-centred therapy but was found to be applicable in other domains where people interact and communicate. The ideas from client-centred therapy flow into the more general person-centred approach, which is, for instance, applied in counselling (e.g., Heist, 2006; Rogers, 1970, 1980), conflict, peace resolution (which resulted in a Nobel Prize nomination) (cf. Kirschenbaum & Henderson, 1989, pp. 436-504), and educational settings (e.g., Cornelius-White, 2007; Rogers, 1983; Tausch & Tausch, 1963/1998).

Rogers' theory of person-centred learning was a radically new approach to education (Rogers, 1983). This approach, which is also known as experiential learning,

> "is based on the hypothesis that students who are given the freedom to explore areas based on their personal interests, and who are accompanied in their striving for solutions by a supportive, understanding facilitator not only achieve higher academic results but also grow with respect to their personal values, such as flexibility and self-confidence" (Motschnig-Pitrik & Derntl, 2002, p. 2).

In person-centred learning, the role of the instructor becomes that of a *facilitator* of learning, who does no longer act as an instructor but provides a learning climate that supports students in their striving for solutions. Again, the facilitator has to hold and live the three Rogers variables and students have to perceive all these three conditions at least to some degree.

In general, the person-centred learning approach aims towards (Rogers, 1983, p. 3):

- a climate of trust, in which curiosity and the desire to learn can be nourished and enhanced,
- participation of students and facilitators in all aspects of learning and decision-making,
- helping students to build their confidence and self-esteem,
- uncovering the excitement in self-initiated discovery, which leads students to become life-long learners,
- developing in facilitators the attitudes that are most effective in facilitating learning (as research has shown),
- helping facilitators to personal growth, finding satisfaction in their interaction with learners, and
- an awareness that the good life is within and not something, which is dependent on outside sources.

According to (Rogers, 1983, p. 20), purely cognitive instruction by assignment – as today still is the most widely practised approach in higher education – is incapable of producing significant learning effects since students are merely passive information recipients in such settings. In contrast, whole-person learning is meaningful, significant learning (therefore it is frequently also referred to as significant learning or experiential learning), which is characterised by (cf. Rogers, 1983, p. 20):

- *personal involvement* of students as whole persons including both feelings and cognitive aspects in the learning activity,
- *self-initiated learning* that is driven by an desire coming from within (even if the stimulus comes from outside),
- *pervasive learning* as it alters behaviour, attitudes, and personality of the learner,
- being *evaluated by the learner* in the sense that every person knows him or herself what she wants to know, and
- *personal meaning* to the student for the elements to be learned.

We can summarise that according to this approach, learning is most effective when it involves the whole person, i.e. intellect, feelings, intuitions, meanings, goals, involvement, etc. Basically, person-centred learning is based on the hypothesis that students who are given the freedom to solve authentic problems, and who are supported by a resourceful, understanding facilitator not only achieve higher academic results but also grow with respect to their personal values and social skills (Motschnig-Pitrik & Derntl, 2002, p. 2; Motschnig-Pitrik & Mallich, 2002, pp. 1-2; Rogers, 1983).

2.1.3.2 The three Rogers variables

As we have already outlined in Section 2.1.3.1, the actualisation tendency can unfold itself best in an atmosphere that is characterised by three attitudinal conditions (Rogers, 1959), which are also referred to as the three *Rogers variables*: congruence, acceptance, and empathy.

Various studies (e.g., Derntl & Motschnig-Pitrik, 2004; Motschnig-Pitrik, 2004b; Motschnig-Pitrik & Derntl, 2003; Motschnig-Pitrik, Derntl, & Mangler, 2003) could reveal that despite all opportunities that e-learning technology offers, the facilitator's attitudes and values still have a highly significant influence on most aspects of students' motivation to learn.

While these three variables can best be described in their original meaning in the context of psychotherapy and counselling relationships by referring to Rogers' original definitions (cf. Rogers, 1961), these descriptions will be amended by discussing their meaning particularly in educational settings (cf. Derntl, 2005, pp. 33-34).

Congruence (realness, genuineness, authenticity)

> "I have found that the more that I can be genuine in the relationship, the more helpful it will be. [...] Being genuine also involves the willingness to be and to express, in my words and my behavior, the various feelings and attitudes, which exist in me. [...] It is only by providing the genuine reality which is in me, that the other person can successfully seek for the reality in him." (Rogers, 1961, p. 33).

In other words, a person has to be real and honest in the relationship with the other, be the person he or she is without using any masks or facades in communication.

In learning settings, congruence is characterised by giving the opportunity to solve authentic problems, which are in line with their personal interests. While in conventional, assignment-based settings, the educator predetermines topics and tasks, person-centred scenarios give students a certain degree of freedom to propose their own topics of interest. Certainly, these proposals have to be within a certain context that is supplied by the educator or predetermined by curricular requirements. Provided with such freedoms, students tend to dedicate more time for elaborations (Motschnig-Pitrik, Derntl, & Mangler, 2003), tend to achieve better results (Motschnig-Pitrik, 2001; Aspy, 1972), and also tend to perceive the course mode and the whole course as more appealing (Derntl & Motschnig-Pitrik, 2004, 2005).

A further way of transporting authenticity and transparency in a course is to further constructive, open feedback giving students the opportunity to express their particular desires and needs. There are several options for collecting feedback. For instance, students can be asked to express it verbally after presentations by their peers. The introduction of written reaction sheets is another option; these may be collected for single course units, particular learning activities, whole courses, or for a combination of these. With this practice, students are offered the opportunity to reflect on their personal experiences and to transparently convey it to the educator and their peers (Derntl, 2005, p. 33).

Although it seems evident that being real is not always easy, it is basic to a person who wants to become a facilitator of learning (Rogers, 1983, pp. 121-123).

Acceptance (respect, positive regard)

> "I find that the more acceptance and liking I feel toward this individual, the more I will be creating a relationship which he can use. By acceptance I mean a warm regard for him as a person of unconditional self-worth, of value no matter what his condition, his behavior, his feelings. It means a respect and liking for him as a separate person, a willingness for him to possess his own feelings in his own way." (Rogers, 1961, p. 34).

Essentially, acceptance implies that a person accepts and respects the whole personality of the other and feels basic trust in his or her constructive tendency, striving for solutions in his or her own, personal way. Acceptance is an operational expression of a person's essential confidence and trust in the capacity of the human organism. The significant part of this description is that a person is approached with *unconditional* positive regard and, hence, accepted *unconditionally*.

In learning settings, acceptance basically means facilitating students in their own actualisation tendency. A facilitator may have students participate in decision-making processes and in designing course goals and processes according to personal interests. Similarly, one may provide them with a high degree of freedom without imposing freedom on them. Generally, the diversity of students' perspectives has to be taken into account (Derntl, 2005, p. 34).

In particular, behaviour patterns of being acceptant towards students can be derived almost straightforward from the central characteristics of the person-centred learning approach (Derntl, 2005, p. 33). The participatory mode involving students in elaborating and setting overall and specific course expectations as well as considering personal learning objectives is a way of demonstrating acceptance. Letting participants solicit concrete proposals within a topic frame that is supplied by the facilitator according to curricular requirements, is another option of being acceptant in educational settings. When having part in the decision-making process, students will perceive topics and problems that have been selected according to their personal interests as real and meaningful for their personal learning (Motschnig-Pitrik, 2004a). Even when the stimulus comes from outside, this mode is capable of inducing self-initiated learning (Rogers, 1983, p. 20).

Project-based learning scenarios and collaboration in small teams foster students' active involvement allowing them to develop social skills while co-constructing knowledge in a constructivist manner (cf. Chou, 2001). Furthermore, project-based learning scenarios and learning contracts are viable tools to provide students with a significant degree of freedom to work and self-direct their learning while preserving the ability to comply with curricular requirements (Rogers, 1983, p. 149). Here, the facilitator can be acceptant by demonstrating basic trust in students and allowing them to take self-responsibility in their learning endeavours.

Empathy (understanding)

> "[...] I feel a continuing desire to understand – a sensitive empathy which each of the client's feelings and communications as they seem to him at that moment. Acceptance does not mean much until it involves understanding. It is only that I understand the feelings and thoughts which seem so horrible to you, or so weak [...] – it is only as I see them as you see them and accept them and you, that you feel really free to explore [...] your inner and often buried experience. [...] There is implied here a freedom to explore oneself at both conscious and unconscious levels." (Rogers, 1961, p. 35).

Summarising, empathic understanding is the ability to listen with the goal to understand the meanings as well as feelings from the other person's point of view, respectively from inside.

Every individual has a personal history. Throughout lifetime, everyone undergoes a continuous process of learning, which already starts as an unborn foetus. All the learning, impressions, feelings, the environment, and other influences form a person's weltanschauung. Reactions and behaviour is to be ascribed to a person's history. Empathic understanding means understanding an individual from the individual's point of view, and not from one's own. (Rogers, 1983, pp. 125-126) points out that understanding simply signifies understanding – not evaluating, not analysing, not judging. Only when listening actively (cf. Section 8.1.2) to individuals, one will understand their questions, motivations, intentions, and their communication's meanings.

Showing empathic understanding in learning settings requires facilitators to try at their best to be aware of students' perspectives without judging them. Although empathy is an essential facilitative attitude in any kind of communication and interaction between facilitator and student, (Rogers, 1983, p. 126) acknowledges that being empathic sometimes needs to be traded for being authentic; if a facilitator has little understanding of a student's inner world and feels dislike for particular students or their behaviour, "it is almost certainly more constructive to be *real* than to be pseudoempathic" (Rogers, 1983, p. 126).

2.1.3.3 The three levels of learning and personal growth

Numerous scientific studies (e.g., Aspy, 1972; Motschnig-Pitrik & Derntl, 2002; Motschnig-Pitrik & Mallich, 2002; Nykl & Motschnig-Pitrik, 2002; Rogers, 1983) have revealed and proven that learning is most effective in terms of persistency if it addresses the whole person rather than merely the intellect. This kind of learning is also referred to as whole person learning or experiential learning (Rogers, 1983, pp. 19-20).

Recent research and educational policy in the European Union as well as in the United States strongly support this whole person view on learning since it appears to be qualified for facilitating lifelong learners who can appropriately cope with the complex, dynamic, and unpredictable problems of today's world (Claxton, 1998).

The left hemisphere emphasises the parts (the details) that make up the whole. It tends to function in logical and linear ways accepting what is sure and clear. It deals in ideas and concepts. The right hemisphere emphasises the essence before it understands the details. It operates in metaphors and is creative and intuitive rather than logical (Rogers, 1983, p. 20).

(Rogers, 1983, p. 20) claims:

> "Significant learning combines the logical *and* the intuitive, the intellect *and* the feelings, the concept *and* the experience, the idea *and* the meaning. When we learn in that way, we are *whole*, utilizing all our [...] capacities."

Hence, at its best, learning involves the whole person: the intellect, feelings, intuitions, attitudes, meanings, goals, social skills, practical skills, involvement in learning communities, etc. (cf. Motschnig-Pitrik & Derntl, 2002, p. 2).

The three levels of learning and personal growth (Figure 3) have been introduced by (Nykl & Motschnig-Pitrik, 2002) as a result of uniting Carl R. Rogers' (cf. Rogers, 1961, 1983) and Lev S. Vygotsky's theories of personality and learning (cf. Vygotsky, 1978). According to this concept, personal growth – thus learning – ideally addresses the whole person. They have identified the three levels intellect, social skills, and personality, which have to be addressed in order to substantially alter attitude and motivation (Figure 3).

Integration of all the three levels brings us a step closer to the nowadays eminently respectable success factor of lifelong learning. However, traditional teaching tends to address either the level of intellect only or occasionally the three levels in a strictly separated way.

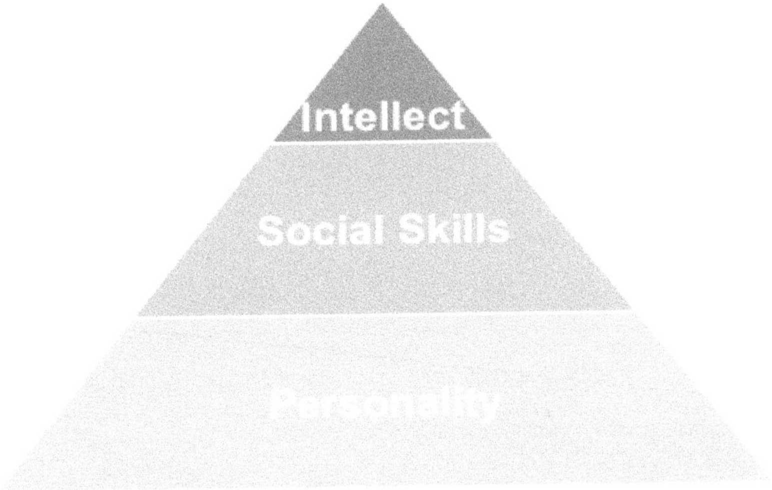

Figure 3. The three levels of learning and personal growth

Source: (Motschnig-Pitrik & Mallich, 2002, (adapted))

The project *getProfile* (Motschnig-Pitrik, Karasek, & Zelger, 2003), carried out in Austria from 2002 to 2003, highly supports the concept of *learning on three levels*. The survey's respondents (representatives of economy including IT providers, IT users as well as personnel consultants) pinpoint that social skills (including communication skills, cooperation and coordination skills, team(work) skills, as well as conflict management skills) are regarded as highly important factors in professional life.

However, university education generally fails to accurately address this learning level.

Rogers' person-centred learning approach claims that learning is most effective when it involves the whole person – thus all three levels of learning.

The iceberg metaphor (Figure 4) seems to be suited to illustrate the visibility and influenceability within the model of the three levels of learning and personal growth.

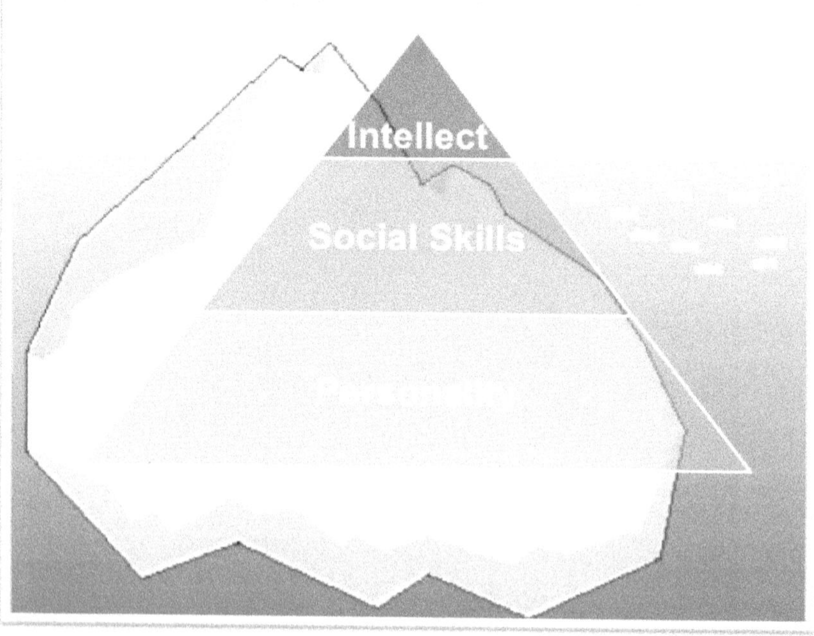

Figure 4. The iceberg metaphor

Above the water line is the intellect, which is explicit and visible. Intellectual knowledge is testable. In our information and knowledge culture, we have established measures for the intellect level. With a history of focusing on intellect going back many years, we are even sensitised for this level, such that it is clearly visible to us.

At the water line is the transition zone, where the observer has to be more alert: now *you see it, no you do not*. Social skills are considered at the waterline. It is difficult to measure social skills. They surface only when they are required in cooperation. Sometimes a lack of social skills in a situation when they are needed strike more rather than their existence would attract positive attention in the same situation.

Below the water line lies the personality level. It is hidden. Personality subsumes habits, assumptions, understandings, values, judgments that we know but do not or cannot articulate. It usually does not occur to you to question or explain those feelings. It takes time until a person gets sensitised for his or her own personality. It is even harder for another person to measure it. Changes in personality will usually take longer periods of time. Measuring changes may be even more difficult.

We suggest that personality highly influences the levels of social skills and intellect. Personality shapes a person's ability to develop social skills. Egocentrics will have to change personality in order to broaden their social skills, while an inherently sociable personality may merely lack of specific social skills and instruments for development can be directly targeted at the social skills level. The impact on the intellect level can be seen in similar perspective. Attitudes like, for instance, reluctance to learn or aversion to others' approaches to a topic lie deep in personality and affect a person's ability to develop as regards the intellect level.

More than being valued in presence phases, the three levels of learning are still relevant in online settings.

The Internet can be considered as a social space where people can communicate and interact in diverse ways. Hence, these activities obviously require and at the same time determine a multitude of learning experiences as well as these evoke socialisation processes and foster personal growth.

It is a widely adopted misapprehension that learning only takes place where people state explicitly that learning is their aim or motivation of utilisation (for example, downloading of study material, etc.). When people read novels, join a political party, or set up a separate family, they will hardly associate their activities with the motivation of learning something new. Nevertheless, these events and activities are highly learning intensive, may change personalities and attitudes and even induce specific occasions for learning (for example, teaching children how to swim, etc.) (Döring, 1997/2000).

Acquiring Internet skills does not only involve the acquisition of technical skills and utilisation competence (hardware, software). Moreover, cognitive competence (e.g., evaluation of information, problem-orientated thinking), media competence (e.g., media choice, efficient use) as well as social skills (learning of the netiquette, Internet policy) play an eminent role (Döring, 1997/2000, pp. 447-450).

The Internet itself is highly demanding on its users' learning. Hence, motivation for self-initiated learning processes and mutual help and support is highly stimulated (Döring, 1997/2000, pp. 447-450).

What has been said so far in this Section indicates that learning in online settings involves and affects all three levels of learning as concerned in whole person learning – the intellect, social skills, and personality. Thus, the three levels of learning hold also in online situations.

2.1.3.4 Person-centred e-learning

While the benefits of the pure person-centred learning approach have been proved in numerous field studies and seem to be well documented in literature (e.g., Rogers, 1983; Cornelius-White, 2007; Tausch & Tausch, 1963/1998), its combination with information and communication technology is a rather novel asset developed by Renate Motschnig-Pitrik at the University of Vienna (cf. e.g., Motschnig-Pitrik, 2001, 2002; Motschnig-Pitrik & Holzinger, 2002). Enrichment of Rogers' person-centred learning with elements of e-learning, while emphasising the three levels of learning and personal growth, results in an approach they call *person-centred e-learning*. (Originally they called it student-centred e-learning, but in later work they switched to terming it person-centred learning as all persons in a learning scenario – including the facilitator – are involved and centred.) However, despite the 'e' in this approach's labelling, it is rather a technology-enhanced learning solution than a pure e-learning approach.

Essentially, person-centred e-learning aims at combining the benefits of the person-centred approach by (Rogers, 1983) with the opportunities that technology has to offer for learning in order to make the whole approach more effective as concerns the improvement of learning processes and time efficiency aspects (cf. Motschnig-Pitrik & Holzinger, 2002; Motschnig-Pitrik & Mallich, 2002).

Basically, also in the technology-enhanced version of person-centred learning, the facilitator is required to hold the three person-centred dispositions (congruence, acceptance, and empathy; cf. 2.1.3.2) and has to be able to communicate these towards the students. One of the major propositions of person-centred e-learning is that students are given the opportunity to direct their own learning, which is eventually achieved by providing them with sufficient learning resources and simultaneously leaving them a significant degree of freedom to activate their inner curiosity and personal interest according to the self-actualising tendency (Motschnig-Pitrik, 2002; Derntl, 2005, p. 29).

As the person-centred course style is characterised by a high degree of flexibility in courses, it is more demanding with respect to preparation time and resource provision on the side of the facilitator than conventional courses since facilitators continuously adjust to student needs and evolving situations. (Motschnig-Pitrik & Mallich, 2002) hypothesise that the use of information and communication technologies, in particular of the Internet, can reduce some of the overhead caused by the person-centred course style. They claim that these technologies can, for instance, simplify the provision and distribution of learning material (including artefacts produced by students). Furthermore, they assume that communication, in particular concerning organisational issues, can be handled more efficiently. Time and resources that are set free can, in turn, be fruitfully used to enrich learning in presence phases in terms of depth and scope (cf. Motschnig-Pitrik & Holzinger, 2002; Motschnig-Pitrik & Mallich, 2002).

Illustrating, how information and communication technology has the potential to reduce a main part of the overhead while retaining the benefits of the person-centred style, (Derntl, 2005, p. 29) provides following examples:

- Making learning resources available on an e-learning platform as well as linking to sources on the Internet relieves facilitators from having to prepare comprehensive collections of material right before the beginning of a course. Instead it may be supportive to provide an anchor for students to start with. Subsequently the repository can be filled. A facilitator should not necessarily do this alone. Rather students are given the opportunity to complement sources as well as to explore the material in their own ways independent of time and location.
- Many activities of the person-centred approach to learning are suitable to be conducted online, e.g., communication with peers and facilitators, peer reviews, evaluation, providing feedback, reflective activities, student proposals, learning contracts, etc. (cf. Section 4). Besides having a positive impact on learning outcomes, the deployment of technology for such activities can significantly reduce organisational overhead. However, although technology can be an enabler for learning with regard to many aspects (cf. Section 4), limiting activities to the online setting is not sufficient; rather a combination of activities in the online environment and a face-to-face setting offers considerable benefits (cf. Sections 7 and 8).

Finally, it shall be mentioned that also research benefits from employing technology for learning. Without any extra effort, information about student behaviour, attitudes, reactions, etc. are available digitally, mostly in written form. Consequently, data can be used for analysis with less effort than when having to bring information into an analysable form beforehand (e.g., having to transcribe course units).

2.2 Communication and media

We can consider communication as basic module for any kind of collaboration (e.g., Spieß & Winterstein, 1999, p. 51; Wendel, 1996, pp. 22, 24). Hence, when investigating cooperative learning, it is essential to define the meaning of communication. Even more so in technology-enhanced learning settings, communication plays a significant role as in the online phases learners are merely connected by means of communicative ties.

However, a unique understanding of the term communication is still lacking as scientific disciplines stretch it differently.

Although this work is dedicated to communication in technology-enhanced learning settings, it is important to first define interpersonal communication in general, as it constitutes the basis for communication in learning settings.

In particular, it is to be emphasised at this place that this work is concerned with interpersonal (i.e. human-to-human) communication but does not particularly investigate human-computer interaction. Even though learners make use of some form of medium, interpersonal communication – in face-to-face as well as in online environments – keeps in the spotlight.

For collaborative activities learners, naturally, make use of some kind of media in order to communicate and collaborate. While each communication setting is distinct, they show characteristics that are similar for several media. Based on these characteristics, media serve different purposes in varying degrees. Research on media choice investigates the factors that drive people to choose a particular medium for a certain task.

In educational settings, learners are frequently not free to choose their most favourable medium since they are bound to those that are offered in the particular learning setting or even to one that is imposed by the educator. In order to be able to appropriately design learning scenarios and courses, educators are required to be aware of media's strength and weaknesses with respect to particular tasks and situations.

Considering these issues, this Section is organised as follows. First, it presents communication theories and models (Section 2.2.1). Section 2.2.2 provides an overview of the basic characteristics of media, which makes it easier to understand the media choice theories that are discussed in Section 2.2.3. Building on all these beforehand-discussed theories and models, Section 2.2.4 is dedicated to communication for collaborative activities in technology-enhanced environments.

2.2.1 Communication theories and models

In the scope of communication research, a scale of different definitions and models of communications were developed (e.g., Wendel, 1996, p. 22). The following sections present selected models from distinct perspectives that are relevant to this work. First, Section 2.2.1.1 is dedicated to the transmission model of communication by (Shannon & Weaver, 1949/1963), which considers communication from a information theory viewpoint and constitutes one of the main sources out of which communication studies have grown. Section 2.2.1.2 briefly describes the linguistic model of communication by (Eco, 1972/1994). Section 2.2.1.3 focuses on interpersonal communication, which is an important perspective in cooperative learning and interaction. This Section presents the prominent model by (Watzlawick, 1976) that considers communication from a sociological viewpoint. Finally, Section 2.2.1.4 presents the socio-psychological model by (Schulz von Thun, 1981/2003), which builds upon communication models from several disciplines and is well-known in the German-speaking area.

2.2.1.1 The transmission model of communication by Shannon & Weaver

In communications engineering, communication is considered as a process transmitting information. The transmission model by (Shannon & Weaver, 1949/1963) is widely accepted and constitutes one of the main sources out of which communication studies have grown.

Originally, this model goes back to (Shannon, 1948), who worked as a research scientist at Bell Telephone Company. He aimed at achieving maximum telephone line capacity with minimum distortion, which resulted in his mathematical theory of signal transmission (Shannon, 1948), for anything but telephones. Only later Warren Weaver joined Shannon's concept of information loss, which finally lead to the popular communication model (Shannon & Weaver, 1949/1963) as we now know it (Chandler, 1995/2000).

Although they were principally concerned with communication technology, their work contributed in computer science, led to valuable insights in work on redundancy in language. In making information measurable, it gave birth to the mathematical study of information theory. Furthermore, many practitioners and researchers claim that their model has a much wider application to human communication than a purely technical one (Chandler, 1995/2000).

The original model by (Shannon, 1948) consists of essentially five parts:

- an *information source*, which produces a message or sequence of messages to be communicated,
- a *transmitter*, which encodes the message into signals,
- the *channel*, which is the medium used to transmit the signal from transmitter (sender) to receiver,
- the *receiver*, which decodes (reconstructs) the message from the signal, and
- the *destination*, which is the person (or object) for whom a message is intended, i.e. where the message arrives.

The dysfunctional factor *noise* is a sixth element, which refers to any interference with a message along its transmission (Shannon, 1948; Shannon & Weaver, 1949/1963).

Essentially this model represents the path of a message from sender to receiver (Figure 5). A message is selected or created from a source. A transmitter decodes the message and forwards it via a channel to a receiver. There, the received signals get decoded and directed to the destination. On the path of transmission, inferences may occur, which may lead to the signal received being different from that sent (Shannon, 1948; Shannon & Weaver, 1949/1963).

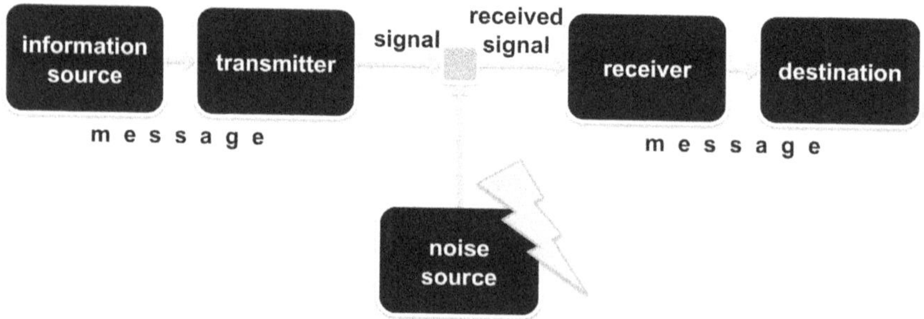

Figure 5. The transmission model of communication by (Shannon & Weaver, 1949/1963)

Source: (Shannon, 1948, (adapted))

(Shannon & Weaver, 1949/1963) mention three levels of problems that can occur in communication:

- a *technical* problem: How accurately can the message be transmitted?
- a *semantic* problem: How precisely is the meaning conveyed to the destination?
- an *effectiveness* problem: How effectively does the decoded and received meaning affect behaviour?

When the model is applied to interpersonal communication, speaker and listener would strictly be source and destination rather than transmitter and receiver. In discussions, however, the communicators are commonly referred to with the terms sender and receiver. This misuse is, incidentally, not specific to the model by (Shannon & Weaver, 1949/1963) but inherent to the general transmission model (according to this model, communication consists of a sender passing a message to a receiver), which it reflects (Chandler, 1995/2000). The reader has to be aware of not to confuse terms and definitions in the particular context.

The strengths of this model lie in its simplicity, generality, and quantifiability. These advantages made it attractive to several disciplines. As it also drew serious academic attention to human communication and information theory, it gave rise to further research and theory in this field (Chandler, 1995/2000).

(Chandler, 1995/2000) argues that no serious communication theorist would still accept (Shannon & Weaver, 1949/1963)'s transmission model due to its oversimplification as regards interpersonal communication and missing aspects that later research could meanwhile reveal. Nevertheless, it has undoubtedly been the most influential model of communication that has yet been developed. It is the best-known informational approach to communication, which reflects a commonsense understanding of what communication is (Chandler, 1995/2000).

2.2.1.2 The linguistic model of communication by Eco

Semiotics is the term for the scientific investigation of objects and functionality in communication processes (Wendel, 1996, p. 22; e.g., Picot, Reichwald, & Wigand, 2001, pp. 89-90). Although it is not originated by Umberto Eco, he made a wider audience aware of this concept by various publications (e.g., Eco, 1972/1994, 1987/1991). Semiotics as linguistic model of communication is, though, commonly attributed to him.

Semiotics distinguishes essentially three levels of communication: syntax, semantics, and pragmatics (e.g., Eco, 1972/1994).

- *Syntax* determines the formal relation of signs or signals of communication to each other.
- *Semantics* defines the relation of signs to each other in formal structures. Put differently, it outlines the meaning of signs.
- *Pragmatics* signifies the signals' impact on the communicators. In other words, it determines the relation between signs and their users in a particular context.

These three levels of communication cannot be looked at completely separately as they build on each other and overlap (Wendel, 1996, p. 22; e.g., Picot, Reichwald, & Wigand, 2001, pp. 89-90).

2.2.1.3 The interpersonal communication by Watzlawick

According to (Watzlawick, Beavin, & Jackson, 1969/2000, p. 50), communication denotes not only a domain but is, moreover, a term for a unit of behaviour. In other words, these authors orientate their concept of communication to human behaviour.

A single message is referred to as *one* communication, while the reciprocal interchange of messages between two or more persons is termed *interaction* (Watzlawick, Beavin, & Jackson, 1969/2000, pp. 50-51).

(Watzlawick, Beavin, & Jackson, 1969/2000, p. 51) emphasise that communication is not limited to words but includes, for instance, paralinguistic phenomena (e.g., voice intonation, rate of speech, pauses, laughs, sighs) and body language (e.g., gesture, mimics, posture) within a particular context. In a nutshell, according to this pragmatic approach, any kind of behaviour is communication (Watzlawick, Beavin, & Jackson, 1969/2000, p. 51).

As behaviour has no counterpart (there is no anti-behaviour) (Watzlawick, Beavin, & Jackson, 1969/2000, p. 51) and behaviour is put on the same level with communication, this induces the first of the five pragmatic axioms of this approach: *One cannot not communicate* (Watzlawick, Beavin, & Jackson, 1969/2000, p. 53).

The second axiom implies that *every communication has both, a content and relationship aspect*. It is not only about, *what* somebody says but also *how*. This means that apart from the plain words, a communication includes information about how the talker wants the message to be understood and how he or she sees the relation to the listener. Hence, the relationship aspect determines the content aspect and is therefore meta communication (i.e. communication about communication) (Watzlawick, Beavin, & Jackson, 1969/2000, pp. 53-56).

The third axiom says that *the nature of a relationship depends on how both parties punctuate the communication sequence* (Watzlawick, Beavin, & Jackson, 1969/2000, p. 61). As mentioned before, the reciprocal communication process is called interaction. During interaction emerges a string of behaviour that gets structured due to punctuations. Talker and listener, though, structure the communication flow differently. Therefore, communicators interpret their own behaviour merely as reaction on the other's behaviour (i.e. every communicator believes that the other one is the cause of a particular behaviour). Consequently, human communication cannot be dissolved to plain causation and reaction strings, behaviour is both, cause and reaction; thus, communication appears to be rather cyclic (Watzlawick, Beavin, & Jackson, 1969/2000, pp. 57-61).

The fourth axiom explains that *human beings communicate both digitally and analogically.* If speech is used for the transmission of information, we speak of digital communication. Analogue communication includes all information but spoken words (e.g., pictures, rate of speech, accentuation). While digital communication can convey a main part of information, relations are better expressed analogously (Watzlawick, Beavin, & Jackson, 1969/2000, pp. 62-68).

In the fifth axiom (Watzlawick, Beavin, & Jackson, 1969/2000, p. 70) postulate that *interpersonal communication processes are either symmetric or complementary, depending thereupon whether the relationship of the communicators is based on equality or difference.* With this axiom, the relationship aspect is particularly emphasised. Symmetric relationships mirror equality in behaviour, while complementary relationships show a superordinate and a subordinate. These terms, however, are not to be associated with good and bad or strong and week. Rather, complementary relationships are based upon cultural or societal context like, for instance, mother and child or physician and patient (Watzlawick, Beavin, & Jackson, 1969/2000, p. 70).

According to (Watzlawick, Beavin, & Jackson, 1969/2000, p. 50), these five axioms are the simplest characteristics of communication. They argue that the formulation of those is on a provisional basis and the list is not intended to be exhaustive. These axioms, however, have not substantially changed although a scale of studies and further developments are based on this model.

Despite the wide adoption, work by (Watzlawick, Beavin, & Jackson, 1969/2000) is also criticised for methodical and logic errors (e.g., Girgensohn-Marchand, 1992/1996; Retter, 2000). (Girgensohn-Marchand, 1992/1996, pp. 16-17, 20-21, 22-23) claims that the conceptual approach would be insufficient as (Watzlawick, Beavin, & Jackson, 1969/2000) does not adhere to the common terms and definitions in communication psychology but transfers conclusions from various disciplines (e.g., mathematics, cybernetics) into psychology. The major critique addresses the fact that (Watzlawick, Beavin, & Jackson, 1969/2000) had based all further research on the five axioms and has, thus, in this respect not met his very own scientific requirements. (Retter, 2000, p. 551) claims that the theory shows fundamental methodical and logic insufficiencies that cast a part of the basic assumptions into doubt.

2.2.1.4 The sociopsychological model of communication by Schulz von Thun

(Schulz von Thun, 1981/2003) tried to break the rather one-dimensional psychological view of communication. His work builds upon communication models from several disciplines. The main sources of his eclectic approach are the communication models by (Shannon & Weaver, 1949/1963) and (Watzlawick, Beavin, & Jackson, 1969/2000), which both have been presented before. A further significant model inspiring (Schulz von Thun, 1981/2003)'s work is the *organon model* by (Bühler, 1934/1999), which differentiates three functionalities of linguistic symbols: representation (of objects and content), expression (of reactions or sensitivities of the sender), and appeal (to the person for whom a message is intended) (Schlag, 1995/2004, p. 67).

(Schulz von Thun, 1981/2003) manages to integrate these sophisticated theoretic backgrounds into a clear, illustrative model (Schlag, 1995/2004, p. 68).

In his model, (Schulz von Thun, 1981/2003, pp. 26-30) claims that every communication contains four messages (aspects): content, appeal, self-revelation, and the relation between the actors.

- The *content* aspect relates to the transmission of facts.
- The *relational* aspect delivers the starting point for interpretation of the content (e.g., whether it is praise or blame).
- With a communication the speaker wants to achieve a particular effect, which (Schulz von Thun, 1981/2003, pp. 29-30) summarises as *appeal* aspect.
- The *self-revelation* aspect considers that with communication people reveal themselves intentionally – but also unintentionally.

Figure 6 helps to understand the basic process of interpersonal communication. A sender sends a message to a recipient. The recipient recognises the message and interprets it.

Figure 6. The basic model of interpersonal communication

Source: (Schulz von Thun, 1981/2003, p. 45, (adapted))

A listener reacts to these four aspects of communication with *four ears* (Figure 7). As a message contains four messages (aspects), the recipient has to process and interpret each of these. Most people, though, are particularly respondent to one aspect of a message (Schulz von Thun, 1981/2003, p. 47).

Figure 7. The recipient with four ears

Source: (Schulz von Thun, 1981/2003, p. 45, (adapted))

(Schulz von Thun, 1981/2003, pp. 79-80) explains that a recipient is basically self-responsible for the reactions on a message. Giving ear to all four aspects of a message on a balanced basis is the major goal in the advancement of being a good communicator. Providing feedback gives chance to improve communication, particularly if it contains a high degree of self-revelation.

Interferences of communication are unavoidable if speaker and listener interpret communication differently. Such conflicts can only be resolved by communicating how messages are to be understood (meta communication). Only then communicators can advance to the underlying message.

Although the sociopsychological model of communication by (Schulz von Thun, 1981/2003) is an eclectic approach and also incorporates work by (Watzlawick, Beavin, & Jackson, 1969/2000), it is hardly criticised. However, many of the points raised criticising the approach of (Watzlawick, Beavin, & Jackson, 1969/2000) (cf. Girgensohn-Marchand, 1992/1996; Retter, 2000), will also apply for the model by (Schulz von Thun, 1981/2003).

In contrast to other communication models, (Schulz von Thun, 1981/2003) makes use of a rather popular scientific presentation as his books are written in a form predominantly targeting at commonality rather than solely a scientific audience. Regardless of language use, the model seems to build on a scientifically sound basis as it integrates work by (Bühler, 1934/1999), (Shannon & Weaver, 1949/1963), and (Watzlawick, Beavin, & Jackson, 1969/2000) into a illustrative model (cf. Schlag, 1995/2004, pp. 67-68).

2.2.2 Characteristics of media

Literature often refers to keywords like e.g., online communication, face-to-face-communication, online learning, presence courses, or traditional learning settings. Actually these terms are not accurately defined. Learning and communication settings, whether or not enhanced by information and communication technologies, hold a wide range of characteristics. These characteristics may or may not fulfil a certain purpose in the learning and communication process. An overview of characteristics is provided below (e.g., C. Bauer & Kovacs, 2004; Duarte & Snyder, 2001; Lipnack & Stamps, 1997):

- *Synchronous – asynchronous*. Media can basically be divided in synchronous and asynchronous ones. While in synchronous settings people interact simultaneously, using asynchronous applications they interact at different points in time.
- *Same place (collocation) – distributed (distance)*. Learning can take place in presence phases (participants meet) or people learn distributed (e.g., collaboration via the Internet, self-paced learning at home).

- *(Computer-)mediated communication.* As soon as communicators are not collocated, communication takes place by means of some additional medium (e.g., a computer, a telephone, etc.).
- *Push system – pull system.* From the learner's perspective, in push systems information is delivered or retrieved automatically. Pull systems demand the learner to get the information actively.
- *Oral – written.* The oral medium is the most traditional communication system of the human evolution. People retain what they are communicated orally in their individual memories only, not in the communication medium that links them; speech evaporates (Lipnack & Stamps, 1997). The invention of writing gave new directions in communication. Although written interaction is slower and cognitively more demanding than oral communication, it offers the ability to capture communication and make messages explicit, public, and permanent (Lipnack & Stamps, 1997; Duarte & Snyder, 2001), which leads to a further characteristic: permanence.
- *Permanence.* Permanence is the degree to which a medium is capable of creating and / or keeping a record of messages / information (Duarte & Snyder, 2001). For instance, a book or a discussion by e-mail have permanence because inputs are saved and are available at later points of time, whereas an oral lecture often does not have permanence, unless the lecture is recorded or someone takes detailed notes. Permanence is of prime importance for reusable learning objects (RLOs).
- *Communication channels.* Communication channels describe whether the communication flow is one-way or two-way. Furthermore, they determine how many people can communicate with each other (e.g., one-to-one (1:1), one-to-many (1:n), many-to-one (n:1), many-to-many (n:m)).
- *Channel width.* This characteristic refers to the number of hints and cues (e.g., voice, body language, social context) that can be simultaneously processed via various communicative channels.
- *Self-paced – collaboration.* Media may or may not support self-paced learning (e.g., book, CD-ROM) or collaboration with co-learners (e.g., expert discussion via chat).
- *Potential for interactivity.* According to media synchronicity theory (Dennis & Valacich, 1999; Dennis & Kinney, 1998; Dennis, Fuller, & Valacich, 2008), a medium's potential for interactivity is the higher, the more it makes an immediate response possible. We speak of potential instead of degree because it depends on the communicators if they make use of a medium's possibilities (since there is a gap between what people make out of a medium and what is technically possible).

Every setting can be qualified by the above-mentioned characteristics. For exemplification, the following tries to match characteristics with communication settings:

- Face-to-face communication within a team: synchronous, collocation, direct communication (not computer-mediated), push system, oral, no permanence, two-way, n:m, all ways of expression, collaboration.
- E-mail correspondence from facilitator to a course's participants: asynchronous, distance, computer-mediated, pull system, written, permanence, two-way, 1:n, textual expression, collaboration.
- Instant messaging or chatting between two students (e.g., by using ICQ, MSN Messenger, Skype): asynchronous (depending on the setting: short lag only or long-term asynchronity), distance, computer-mediated, push system, written, permanence, permanence, two-way, 1:1, textual expression, collaboration.
- Writing of an online reaction sheet: asynchronous, distance, computer-mediated, pull system, written, permanence, one-way, 1:n, textual expression, self-paced.

2.2.3 Media choice theories

Research in the field of media choice basically investigates the eligibility of different media for specific communicative processes and tasks. The most influential theories follow a technological deterministic view, which is premised on an assumption of rationality and predictability (e.g., Sørnes, 2004, pp. 36-37). Put differently, these theories are based on the concept of rational media choice: A user decides on a particular medium by weighting costs and benefits and selects the medium, which seems to best suitable for a particular communicative activity (Nohr, 2002). Further media choice theories include factors like the influence of the social environment, individual experiences and attitudes as well as aspects of group dynamics (cf. e.g., Schwabe, 2001).

The most prominent media choice theories based on rational media choice are the social presence theory (Short, Williams, & Christie, 1976), the reduced social cues theory (Sproul & Kiesler, 1986), the media richness theory (Daft & Lengel, 1986), and the media synchronicity theory (Dennis & Valacich, 1999; Dennis & Kinney, 1998; Dennis, Fuller, & Valacich, 2008). The theoretical framework presented here covers these fundamental media choice theories, with particular attention to those means of communication, which are vital for the case studies as presented in the Sections 7 and 8 (face-to-face, e-mail, and instant messaging / chat).

While the social presence theory and the media richness theory are sketched briefly, the focus lies on the description of the media synchronicity theory, as this concept details most precisely how the use of media can enhance cooperative processes in group settings (cooperative learning).

Social presence theory (Short, Williams, & Christie, 1976)

Despite predating many networked information and communication technologies and the Internet in particular, this theory has been one of the most influential early approaches to explain the use of information and communication technologies (Sørnes, 2004, p. 38). Basically, social presence is referred to the subjective feeling that others are involved in a communicative process (Köhler, 1999). The basic principle of the social presence theory defines social presence as the extent to which a medium is perceived as transmitting the genuine physical presence of communicators. Hence, social presence can also be attributed to a medium. Media, though, create a sense of social presence in varying degrees only. (Short, Williams, & Christie, 1976) argue that the more communication channels a medium has (e.g., nonverbal, emotion, feedback, cues about the social context), the more the communicators will sense the other's presence. While face-to-face meetings are considered to score highest in social presence, e-mail communication is concluded to have considerably less.

The medium with highest social presence is, however, not necessarily the most appropriate one. Different activities require different levels of social presence. While resolving a conflict may demand for rather high social presence, the mere exchange of factual information will need less. (Short, Williams, & Christie, 1976) hypothesise that the users of any given medium are in some sense aware of its degree of social presence. Consequently, they tend to avoid using a medium for interactions requiring a higher degree of social presence than they perceive the medium to have.

The social presence theory has been controversial and subsequent research criticised its presuppositions (Sørnes, 2004, p. 40). Empirical research could not provide consistent support for this theory as the test subjects themselves assessed social presence, even though social presence is considered a media inherent quality. While some studies have proved to be partially supportive and built the basis for further theorising (e.g., Daft & Lengel, 1986), others have offered only partial support (e.g., Markus & Robey, 1988).

Reduced social cues theory *(Sproul & Kiesler, 1986)*

This theory postulates that when people use information and communication technologies instead of face-to-face communication, they have to deal with the absence of *social cues*. Simply put, social cues are nonverbal and contextual symbols that complement human interaction. These cues can be subdivided into static and dynamic cues. Information that relates to place, position, and person are referred to as static cues as these do not alter during a conversation. Dynamic cues, in contrast, can usually be drawn from people's behaviour (e.g., facial expression); these cues evolve and rapidly change rapidly in the course of a communication process.

According to (Sproul & Kiesler, 1986) a face-to-face conversation conveys the highest degree of social context cues in communication, while computer-mediated communication is considered to transmit considerably less social context. The reduced social cues theory distinguishes following four features that illustrate the lack of social context cues of information and communication technologies compared to face-to-face communication: absence of regulating feedback (lack of cues like e.g., smiling, nodding), dramaturgical weakness (lack of cues not intentionally given for the purpose or regulating feedback like tone of voice and facial expression), few social-status cues, and social anonymity (Kiesler, Siegel, & McGuire (1984) as cited in Sørnes, 2004, pp. 41-42).

An implication of the reduced social cues theory is that a given medium's reduced social-context cues will regulate social interaction as it reduces the social-cues information about communicators. (Sproul & Kiesler, 1986) believe that the lack of this type of information will hinder communicators to form impressions that are necessary to establish relationships. Consequently, they regard this as an absolute limitation of information and communication technologies. (Walther, 1992), though, argues and shows in a series of studies (e.g., Walther, 1992, 1995, 1996, 1997; Walther & Burgoon, 1992) that information and communication technologies are capable of carrying these cues as face-to-face communication does; but it happens differently than in face-to-face situations and usually it takes more time.

While the reduced social cues theory has been influential in identifying the effect of reduced social cues that media may show, it is heavily criticised for underestimating the social and psychological power of information and communication technologies (e.g., Sørnes, 2004, p. 43).

Media richness theory ***(Daft & Lengel, 1986)***

In contrast to the social presence theory, the media richness theory determines media's suitability for specific communicative activities in a more differentiated way and focuses on the communicative richness of media. It determines a medium's communicative richness according to following four characteristics: its capacity for immediate feedback, the number of cues and channels available (e.g., voice, body language, etc.) (symbol variety), language variety, and the degree of personal focus (i.e. whether communicators are anonymous or identifiable).

Similar to the social presence theory and the reduced social cues theory, also the media richness theory ranks the face-to-face setting above all other forms of communication.

The richest medium is, again, not always the appropriate choice. Too rich a medium tends to make issues more complicated than necessary, as medial richness can be distracting; consequently it may even increase insecurity rather than reducing it. The low degree of personal contact and lack of feedback of lean media may lead to oversimplification, which renders impossible to develop a common understanding (Reichwald, Möslein, Sachenbacher, & Englberger, 1998).

In general, complex, equivocal tasks require communicators to elaborate a common understanding. For such tasks, media richness theory suggests rich media (e.g., face-to-face meeting). Nonetheless, in some cases it may be more appropriate to use media which can convey a lot of information (e.g., e-mail) (Nohr, 2002).

While the media richness theory had gained recognition for a rather long time period, over the years it has been critiqued and further developed by other theoretical views on the use of information and communication technology (e.g., Dennis & Kinney, 1998; Dennis & Valacich, 1999; Sheer & Chen, 2004).

Media synchronicity theory (Dennis, Valacich, Speier, & Morris, 1998; Dennis & Valacich, 1999; Dennis, Fuller, & Valacich, 2008)

Criticising media richness theory for being one-sided, finally gave rise to the development of the media synchronicity theory. (Dennis & Valacich, 1999) argued that is not sufficient to solely define media choice by the specific properties of a communicative task as the media richness theory suggests. As a consequence they developed the media synchronicity theory, which distinguishes communication media for their interactivity. Synchronicity is thereby defined as "the extent to which individuals work together on the same activity at the same time" (Dennis & Valacich, 1999).

Apart from the two poles, synchronicity and asynchronicity, there are further five factors influencing media choice in communicative processes, which are described below (cf. Schwabe, 2001):

- *Feedback immediacy*. This factor describes how quickly feedback can be given with the respective medium (e.g., interacting simultaneously instead of waiting for answers).
- *Symbol variety*. This factor is a reminiscent of the media richness theory, defining the number of hints that can be simultaneously processed via various communicative channels. While some activities need only little symbol variety, others require additional cues like, for instance, non-verbal cues, pictures, voice, etc.
- *Parallelism*. Essentially, the term *parallelism* refers to two characteristics of communication processes. On the one hand, it specifies how many communicators can participate in a communication process at the same time. On the other hand, it describes how many communicative processes can take place simultaneously with a given medium. The more simultaneous conversations are possible, the more difficult coordination naturally gets.
- *Rehearsability*. If a medium permits the sender to revise a message before it reaches the recipient, we can speak of a high degree of rehearsability. Generally, it is easier to compose messages with the intended meaning using media with high rather than low rehearsability.
- *Reprocessability (permanence)*. Essentially, this factor describes whether a message can be reused at a later point in time. It allows a receiver to re-examine a message as many times as he or she needs to understand it.

Basically, there are two communicative processes, which concern a medium's synchronicity: conveyance and convergence.

- Conveyance (divergence) is about delivering as much information as possible to as many recipients as possible. For group decisions, for instance, this is most critical, since accumulating a large amount of information positively influences decisions. Ambiguity and insecurity are to be reduced, for which media with low synchronicity are eligible. Hence, for the exchange of information – sending much information to several receivers – media with low synchronicity can and should be used.
- In convergent processes, communicators are about developing a common understanding and joint interpretation of information. In such

cases, it is rather counterproductive if too much information is available; rather, contents need to be condensed in order to reduce ambiguity. Hence, media with high synchronicity seem appropriate.

Both types of communicative processes emerge during group processes. Hence, depending on the stage in the group building process and the specific situation different media may be appropriate. According to (Dennis & Valacich, 1999), groups that have just started to work together demand for higher synchronicity in their communication. The degree of synchronicity can then be gradually reduced as the group building process progresses and people know each other better. Furthermore, (Dennis & Valacich, 1999) argue that for conflict situations and problem solving activities a high level of synchronicity is beneficial. The execution of assigned tasks, in contrast, demands for media with low synchronicity.

Support and evidence for the media synchronicity theory could be found in a scale of studies (e.g., DeLuca & Valacich, 2005; Watson, Keats, & Yoong, 2005).

Media characterisation

Adhering to the presented media choice theories, Table 1 compares face-to-face meeting, e-mail communication, and instant messaging according to the categorisation scheme by (Weigle & Krcmar, 2000). Only those media were selected that are essential in the empirical part of this work and which seemed to best cover the whole possible spectrum of communication in technology-enhanced cooperative learning environments, allowing the reader to get as broad a picture as possible.

Face-to-face conversation is a communication form, which is considered to have high media synchronicity due to offering immediate feedback and low parallelism.

E-mail communication, in contrast, conveys slow feedback and high parallelism and, hence, provides little media synchronicity.

Instant messaging (chat) provides medium feedback and parallelism and, thus, less media synchronicity than a face-to-face conversation but more than e-mail communication.

Concerning the level of synchronicity, calls via phone or voice-over-IP (VoIP) range between face-to-face meetings and instant messaging; these media provide immediate feedback and low parallelism but rather low symbol variety and communicative richness.

Table 1. Characterisation of selected media and their capabilities

	FACE-TO-FACE CONVERSATION	E-MAIL	INSTANT MESSAGING / CHAT	VOICE-OVER-IP / PHONE
transmission velocity	high	low-medium	medium-high	high
time aspect	synchronous	asynchronous	asynchronous (short or long intervals)	synchronous
parallelism	medium	high	low-medium	low
symbol sets (symbol variety)	few-many	few-medium	few-medium	few
ways of expression	all	textual	textual	only voice
rehearsability	low	high	medium	low
reprocessability / permanence	low	high	medium-high	low
information transmission	fast	slow	medium	fast
information processing	low	high	low-medium	low
space aspect	dependent	independent	independent	independent
social presence	very high	low	low	medium
communicative richness	high	low	low	medium
synchronicity	high	low	medium	medium

Source: (Dennis, Fuller, & Valacich, 2008, (adapted and supplemented))

2.2.4 Communication for collaboration in technology-enhanced environments

The discussion of media choice theories (cf. Section 2.2.3) already elucidated that different media serve different purposes. In collaborative settings, the kind and the level of difficulty that accrue from a particular task, determine media's appropriateness. While each problem definition is unique as regards its specific content, this does not hold for abstracted forms of tasks. (Hollingshead & McGrath, 1995, pp. 51-54) distinguish four basic kinds of tasks), to which each specific task can be put down to:

- to generate ideas or plans,
- to choose a correct answer or a preferred solution,
- to negotiate conflicting views and interests, and
- to execute a tasks to rivalry opponents or external execution standards.

Considering these basic kinds of tasks, which have been validated in (Straus, 1999), (C. Bauer, 2002) developed a catalogue of requirements, which media ideally have to comply with in order to serve the tasks' purposes. Although it was developed in view of teams collaborating in business environments, this abstraction complies with cooperative learning settings. First, the typology by (Hollingshead & McGrath, 1995) describes tasks according to their nature and characterisation, irrespective of the context of application. Second, media used for communication in business teams are the same as used in cooperative learning. Third, team tasks of students are frequently very close to tasks in business environments, particularly when students are given the opportunity to work on *real problems* in the educational setting.

Emphasising the significance of appropriate media selection and punctuating the particular impacts of various media characteristics, Section 2.2.4.1 will introduce the framework by (C. Bauer, 2002). Naturally, particular attention is attributed to communication in cooperative learning environments. Section 2.2.4.2 provides an overview of how selected media meet the requirements as described in the framework.

2.2.4.1 Media requirements for collaborative settings

As displayed in Figure 8, (C. Bauer, 2002) structures media requirements for collaborative tasks by four headings: general requirements, social requirements, task-related requirements, and environmental factors.

General requirements

General requirements refer to factors that are beneficial for group effectiveness, irrespective of the particular task that is to be fulfilled. Group effectiveness is, basically, potential effectiveness minus process losses plus process surpluses.

Process surpluses comprise those attributes of group activity, which make group achievements superior to individual ones. Process losses comprise those aspects of group activity that reduce task effectiveness. Such attributes are, for instance, dominance of a subgroup, inhibition among team members with low status, or conformity pressure that may lead to a insufficient solution alternatives due to the fact that a problem is not dealt with properly (Walther, 1996, p. 6).

As can be seen from Figure 9, general requirements cover following fields: cost, appropriate flow of information, permanence, distraction / attention, democratisation, flexibility, and time context (C. Bauer, 2002, pp. 19-25).

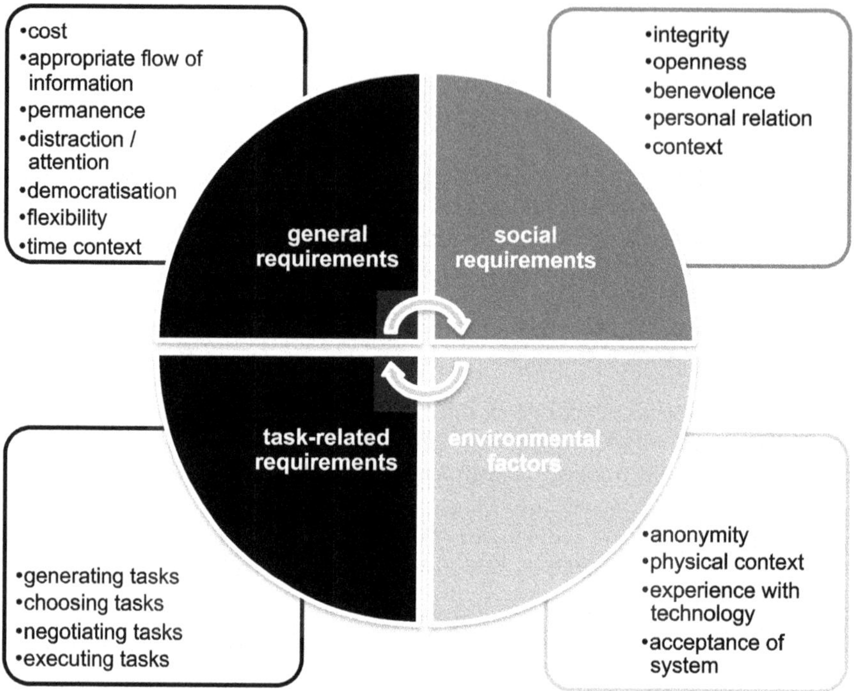

Figure 8. Media requirements for collaborative settings

- *Cost.* A communication system should not be more demanding or costly as its deployment's benefits since a medium is not pivotal but rather a vehicle for communication. Thus, the cost-benefit ratio is to be minimised. Similarly, mastering a task is demanding. Hence, the deployment of a particular medium should ideally not be (cognitively) demanding as energy could better be dedicated to the task itself. The simple handling and usability of a tool is advantageous and effectuates learning effects more quickly in the early phases of its deployment. Eventually, remaining all other factors at the same level, the time exposure for communication shall be kept low. Put differently, a communication system that requires less time for sending the same information (in quality and richness) is to be favoured.
- *Appropriate flow of information.* Media are called upon to provide exchange of information to an adequate degree. More information is, however, not always beneficial since additional information has to be scrutinised for relevance, which takes extra time and may possibly

also interfere with workflows (Wendel, 1996, p. 92). Deploying a medium that facilitates a free expression of opinion provides communicators with a higher amount of information, which mostly is information relevant to a task but also includes irrelevant information (Frey, 1999, pp. 33-34; Hollingshead & McGrath, 1995, p. 74; Ishaya & Macaulay, 1999, p. 150; Sassenberg, 2000, p. 107). Moreover, time constraints hinder a free flow of relevant information (Duarte & Snyder, 2001, p. 166). Furthermore, media are required to allow a short response time since this enables communicators to integrate newly acquired information immediately (Walther, 1992, p. 81) and reduces the risk that someone continues work with out-dated information (C. Bauer, 2002, p. 22).

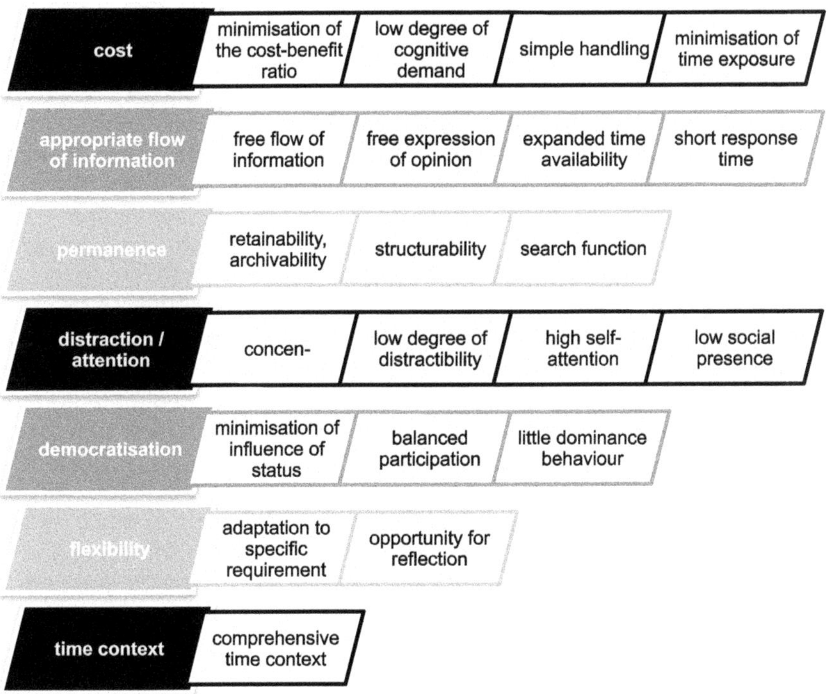

Figure 9. General media requirements for collaborative settings

Source: (C. Bauer, 2002, p. 20, (adapted))

- *Permanence*. Retainability and archivability allows permanent access to available information. It, thus, reduces the risk that important information sinks into oblivion. A high degree of permanence is, though, only advantageous if this collective memory is well structured and provides adequate search functions. Otherwise, people may not be able to refer to information due to being overloaded with its unstructured complexity (Duarte & Snyder, 2001, p. 29).

- *Distraction / attention.* As learning and fulfilling a particular task are in the foreground, supportive media are required to direct a user's attention to the task (Boos, Jonas, & Sassenberg, 2000, p. 84). Communication with low social presence shows high rationality. This implies a strong orientation to the task while content is emphasised and social impact is minimised. As a consequence, media ideally further a high self-attention and convey low social presence.
- *Democratisation.* Social status impacts communication partners' ideas and expectations whereupon they adapt their behaviour (Frey, 1999, p. 33). When communicating with someone of higher status, the way of speaking gets more formal and people tend to subordinate and let the person with higher status dominate a conversation. However, dominant behaviour is not limited to status. Some people try to control and command others (Walther, 1995, pp. 192, 196-197; Walther & Burgoon, 1992, p. 74), take the floor and tend to angle for attention (C. Bauer, 2002, p. 24). If a medium furthers democratisation in communication, participation will be equally distributed and divergent opinions may coexist (C. Bauer, 2002, p. 24).
- *Flexibility.* Being able to adapt the processing of information to one's requirements reduces the stress factor (Frey, 1999, p. 31) and workflows and thinking processes are not disturbed (Duarte & Snyder, 2001, p. 42; Walther, 1992, p. 81). Furthermore, complex tasks and learning processes demand for reflection, which should ideally be supported by media (C. Bauer, 2002, p. 25).
- *Time context.* If a medium does not allow immediate feedback, the sender has to anticipate potential questions and provide answers beforehand and without knowing the context, in which the message is picked up. Limited time context may also negatively impact the understanding of the message on the recipient's side (Adams, Toomey, & Churchill, 1999; Herrmann, 1991, p. 75). Conveying time context is thus a beneficial characteristic of a medium.

Task-related requirements

As already mentioned above, (Hollingshead & McGrath, 1995, pp. 51-54) distinguish four basic kinds of tasks, which demand for different aspects in communication and collaboration. The following briefly describes these kinds of tasks and outlines the respective, specific media requirements (Figure 10).

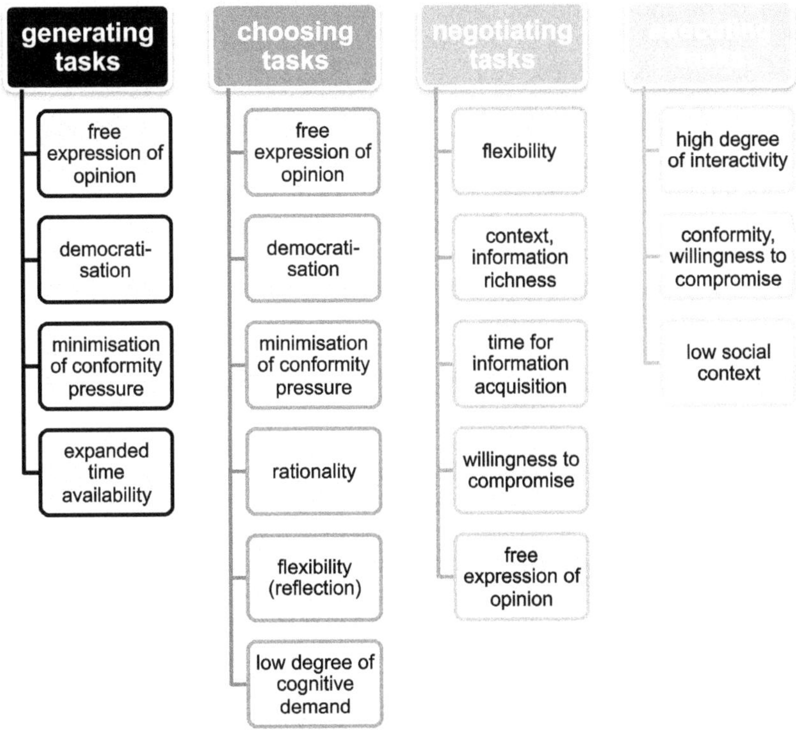

Figure 10. Task-related media requirements for collaborative settings

Source: (C. Bauer, 2002, p. 26, (adapted))

- *Generating tasks.* This task type subsumes planning and creativity tasks for the generation of ideas. While planning is a repetitive process of work design, creativity refers to both the divergent gathering of data and brainstorming as well as the convergent integration of ideas (Hollingshead & McGrath, 1995, pp. 53-54; Lipnack & Stamps, 1997, p. 216). In order to generate qualitative ideas and plans, it is important that a variety of opinions and arguments gain recognition (Duarte & Snyder, 2001, p. 35). Therefore, deployed media for this task type ideally minimise the conformity pressure and further democratisation and a free expression of opinion. Additionally, time constraints limit the plurality of ideas and plans that come up within this time frame (Duarte & Snyder, 2001, p. 166). Thus, a medium ideally also supports the expanded time availability.
- *Choosing tasks.* Basically, choosing activities are necessary for intellective (often scientific) tasks, where a correct solution exists but has

yet to be found and for decision-making tasks, where several solutions exist and one is to be chosen (Hollingshead & McGrath, 1995, p. 54; Lipnack & Stamps, 1997, p. 216). This task type is the cognitively most demanding one and requires both individual thinking and groupthink (Lipnack & Stamps, 1997, p. 216). Since choosing tasks task are cognitively demanding, the medium itself should only have a low degree of cognitive demand and allow enough time for reflection (C. Bauer, 2002, p. 28). Similar to generating tasks, choosing activities call for a free flow of information (free expression of opinion, democratisation). A conformity pressure would facilitate to find a uniformly accepted solution quickly but risks that the rationality, which is required for finding the correct or ideal solution, fades (C. Bauer, 2002, p. 28).

- *Negotiating tasks*. This task type refers to cognitive conflicts where divergent views or motives are in opposition to each other and conflicts of interests have to be solved (Hollingshead & McGrath, 1995, p. 54; Lipnack & Stamps, 1997, p. 216). Similar to generating tasks, an unequivocal correct solution does not exist. Correspondingly, people have to be flexible and creative (Lipnack & Stamps, 1997, p. 216) and people have to be willing to compromise (Duarte & Snyder, 2001, p. 37), which should ideally also be facilitated by deployed media. Furthermore, when mastering negotiating tasks, people need enough time to gather relevant information concerning alternatives and to reflect them; this also furthers willingness to compromise (Duarte & Snyder, 2001, p. 163). Particularly when (interpersonal) conflicts are involved, context is required, which is best conveyed with rich media. An efficient conflict management demands for a free expression of opinion since conflicts must not be suppressed (Duarte & Snyder, 2001, p. 37).
- *Executing tasks*. This task type refers to executing activities that require cooperative course of action often in competitive situations or for psychomotor performances (Hollingshead & McGrath, 1995, p. 54; Lipnack & Stamps, 1997, pp. 216-217). Usually, executing tasks produce a tangible product like, for instance, a data analysis or a technical design (Duarte & Snyder, 2001, p. 160) and require both individual activities as well as group action (Lipnack & Stamps, 1997, pp. 216-217). Since executing tasks require cooperative course of action, conformity is basically beneficial (Hollingshead & McGrath, 1995, p. 54; Lipnack & Stamps, 1997, pp. 216-217). Alternatively, conformity can be produced artificially with a high degree of willingness to compromise (C. Bauer, 2002, p. 30). Accordingly, media are required to facilitate this atmosphere. In contrast to negotiating tasks, an environment with low social context allows to work more efficiently and objectively

on executing tasks than in settings with full context (Grove, Hallowell, & Molloy, 2001).

Social requirements

Although technology is omnipresent, we must not forget learning is all about people. And people act in a social system. In technology-enhanced cooperative settings, trust plays a substantial, integrative role. Particularly when people rarely meet, it is trust that offers coordination. (Handy, 1995) pints out, "Virtuality requires trust to make it work: Technology on its own is not enough". Communication plays a crucial role in the process of trust development since it allows the development of shared values and the exchange of important information (Köszegi, 2000, p. 63). The correlation of trust and high performance has been proven in several studies (e.g., Ishaya & Macaulay, 1999, pp. 146, 151).

Based on the five dimensions of trust in virtual settings (Ishaya & Macaulay, 1999, p. 152) complemented by factors furthering the development of trust (Jarvenpaa & Leidner, 1999), (C. Bauer, 2002, pp. 32-38) developed a set of social media requirements (Figure 11), which are outlined below.

- *Integrity*. For determining a person's trustworthiness, integrity counts among the most crucial characteristics. Compared to face-to-face settings, the effect of negative, not accepted behaviour potentiates in an online environment; while in face-to-face situations inconsistent behaviour can often be explained through context, this is frequently impossible in online interaction (Duarte & Snyder, 2001, p. 141; Ishaya & Macaulay, 1999, p. 153). Integrity comprises honesty, loyalty, engagement, and sense of duty, which is, for instance, demonstrated with timely replies. Ignored inquiries and unfulfilled obligations disadvantageously impact the trust building process spoiled (Ishaya & Macaulay, 1999, pp. 150-152). However, trust does not only refer to interpersonal relationships per se. If you cannot trust in a peer's competence, you can neither rely on this person nor on his or her work results. Hence, integrity is also characterised by continuing competence and consistency in personal expectations. As soon as reliability and expectations vary over time, trust is likely spoiled (Ishaya & Macaulay, 1999, pp. 150-153; Lipnack & Stamps, 1997, pp. 226-227). While competence is a basic condition for the emergence of trust, it is – in its core sense – not a media requirement as it is a purely human quality. Nevertheless, media facilitate continuity in differing degrees, which includes the continuing demonstration of abilities (C. Bauer, 2002, pp. 33-34).

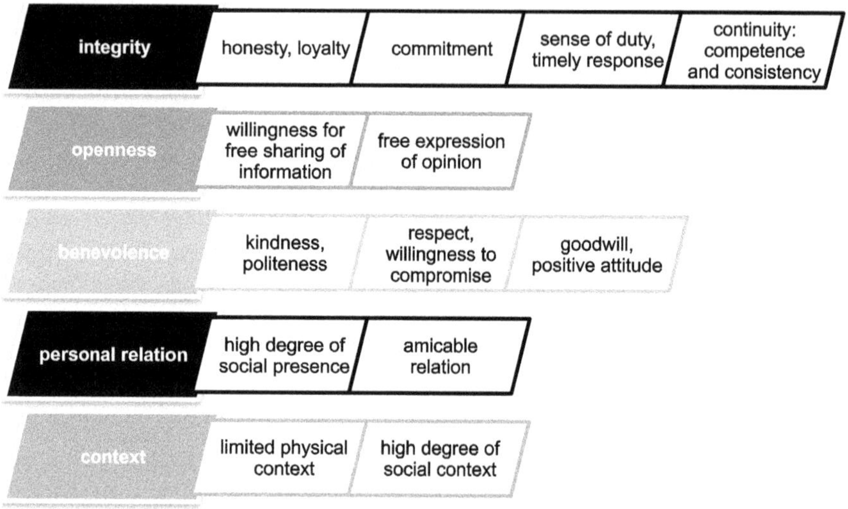

Figure 11. Social media requirements for collaborative settings

Source: (C. Bauer, 2002, p. 32, (adapted))

- *Openness*. Caginess retards and hampers the trust-building process. Therefore, media are challenged to further openness, which is characterised by the willingness to share ideas and information freely. With respect to honesty, this openness also includes free expression of opinion. And in conjunction with benevolence, open communication in a trusty atmosphere also expresses by giving positive feedback and apologising publicly (Ishaya & Macaulay, 1999, p. 152).
- *Benevolence*. Besides politeness and kindness, benevolence expresses by respect towards peers, which is demonstrated, for instance, by the willingness to compromise. Hostile and insulting communication (flaming), in contrast, hinders trust to emerge (Ishaya & Macaulay, 1999, pp. 150-152). In non-personal communication settings, flaming is more likely to occur. Thus, media choice contributes to how benevolent a learning climate is.
- *Personal relation*. Trust can never be impersonal; it always calls for personal relation and social presence. Every human communication targets – directly or indirectly – social goals like, for instance, social acceptance or the development of relationships. Even a task-orientated person will always show interpersonal tendencies (Walther, 1992, pp. 64, 69). Although relationship management claims time and effort, it is crucial for the cohesion in cooperative settings (Walther, 1996, p.

6). Furthermore, honesty and trust is rather demonstrated towards friends rather the strangers (Handy, 1995, pp. 44, 46; Valley, Moag, & Bazerman, 1998, p. 222). Media facilitating an amicable relation are, thus, advantageous (C. Bauer, 2002, p. 35).

- *Context.* People have to express their involvement more explicitly when interacting in an online environment than in face-to-face settings (Ulijn, Lincke, & Karakaya, 2001) in order to compensate for the lack of context. While in full context people sometimes implicitly assume involvement when it does not exist, the explicit expression of involvement in low-context settings proves its actual existence. With regard to this, media conveying limited context seem advantageous (C. Bauer, 2002, p. 37). Social context, in contrast, beneficially contributes to solicitousness among peers and avoids flaming to occur (Duarte & Snyder, 2001, p. 154; Ishaya & Macaulay, 1999, p. 150), which would speak for media conveying a high degree of social context. As these requirements are contradictory, the importance of factors for specific situations is to be weighted accordingly.

Environmental factors

Not only media themselves influence the efficiency of communication. Rather it is people themselves and the environment, in which they interact, that impact communication to a high degree. The following exemplifies environmental factors related closely to media and technology: anonymity, physical context, experience with technology, and media acceptance (Figure 12).

- *Degree of anonymity.* According to the wide-accepted notion, anonymity in communication describes the degree, to which one can identify a person as the author of a message (e.g., Lewe, 1995, p. 106). Although it is an environmental factor, it can also be directly attributed to media. While one can artificially create anonymity with some electronic communication systems (e.g., e-mail or forum), media conveying auditory signals make it difficult to create anonymity and those media that allow communicators seeing each other even eliminate any possibility for anonymity (e.g., face-to-face communication, video conference) and those. (C. Bauer, 2002, pp. 39-40). Anonymity reduces conformity tendencies (groupthink) and decreases the influence of status such tat minority opinions get recognition more frequently than in non-anonymous settings. Although this openness gives rise to conflicts, these tend to be issue-related rather than interpersonal conflicts and help to improve work results (Diehl & Ziegler, 2000, p. 94).

- *Physical context.* This factor describes whether a communication partner's appearance is known. If physical context is completely eliminated, it is not possible to draw conclusions concerning race, age, and look (Frey, 1999, p. 33). This induces that communication with limited physical context is less susceptible to prejudice (C. Bauer, 2002, p. 42). On the other hand, (Walther, 2000, p. 23) could show that the deployment of body images positively affect the trust building process and convey security. However, if a picture is provided only in a later phase of collaboration, it may be disappointing (Walther, 2000, p. 23) since people tend to perceive people they have never seen before as more physically attractive than communication partners they know physically (Döring, 1997/2000, p. 33).

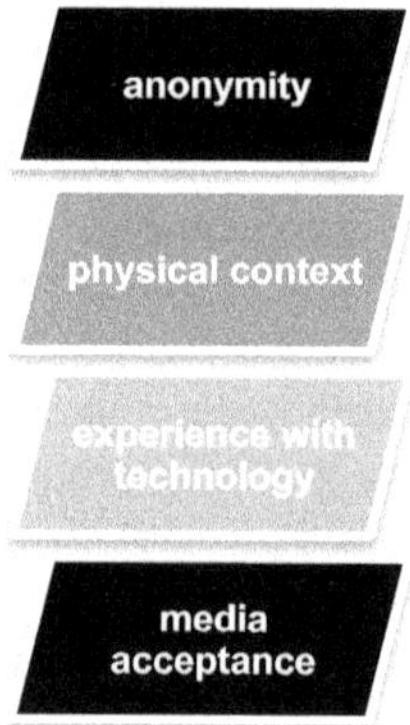

Figure 12. Environmental factors

- *Experience with technology.* The more experienced people are with a particular medium, the better they know about its strength and weaknesses and will be able to adapt to it and to use it efficiently (media competence) (e.g., Duarte & Snyder, 2001, p. 30; Foulger, 1990; Limayem & Hirt, 2000; Walther, 1992, pp. 53, 76-77).
- *Media acceptance.* Technology is not for everyone. Some people are convinced that they could and would not do learning and cooperation without the face-to-face setting with all its social presence and information richness (Duarte & Snyder, 2001, p. 23). Any attempt to make these people use other media for learning will meet with opposition (C. Bauer, 2002, p. 44). People have different preferences and experiences that, in turn, influence preferences (Borghoff & Schlichter, 1995, p. 151; Lewe, 1995, p. 111). If users do not accept a certain medium, they will hardly use it; and if they do use it, they will do it with

the corresponding negative attitude that affects behaviour and expectations (Hollingshead & McGrath, 1995, p. 76). (For technology acceptance models see (e.g., Degenhardt, 1986).)

2.2.4.2 Eligibility of selected media for particular tasks

Based on the insights by (C. Bauer, 2002), this Section provides a brief overview of how selected media (face-to-face conversation, e-mail, instant messaging, and voice-over-IP) meet the requirements for cooperative learning settings. As already indicated in the previous Section, some requirements seem contradictory. For instance, in order to minimise distraction low social presence is basically advantageous, while for building personal relations a high degree is advisable. For cost reasons, a medium should generally further rather low time efforts; generating tasks, however, call for expanded time and also for negotiating tasks, people will yield better results when having considerable time available for information acquisition. Hence, it basically depends on the specific setting (aims, people, circumstances) what medium best serves the purpose. An ideal medium does not exist.

Table 2 interrelates these selected media with the framework's general and social requirements.

The face-to-face setting meets general requirements to a high degree. The absence of permanence and the low flexibility are, though, disadvantageous. Furthermore, due to the awareness of social status and the strong presence (and dominance) of opinion leaders, a face-to-face discussion may suffer from a limited democratisation in conversation. With regard to social requirements, this medium is highly appropriate although it shows drawbacks in the factor of openness due to the same reasons why democratisation is low.

Email, in contrast, ranks rather low as concerns social aspects. Still, people tend to behave more open in such conversations over distance. Especially powerful is e-mail concerning its high permanence and the low degree of distraction. Insufficient is the limited time context. The appropriate flow of information is not particularly furthered by the medium itself but depends on people's discipline.

Interestingly, instant messaging shows a rather medium rank in most of the factors. While this indicates that it does not best support most factors, it also implies that this medium does not show extremely disturbing factors. Thus, it may be a good compromise for many purposes.

Similar to the face-to-face setting, conversations via phone or voice-over-IP meets social requirements to a high degree, although it bears certain drawbacks in context and openness. The lack of permanence as well as the limited flexibility and democratisation may impair the cooperative learning environment.

Table 2. Media eligibility for collaboration

		FACE-TO-FACE CONVERSATION	E-MAIL	INSTANT MESSAGING / CHAT	VOICE-OVER-IP / PHONE
GENERAL REQUIREMENTS	cost	low	medium	medium	low
	appropriate flow of information	medium-high	low-high	high	high
	permanence	none	high degree	medium degree	none
	distraction / attention	high degree of distraction	low degree of distraction	medium degree of distraction	medium degree of distraction
	democratisation	limited	high	high	limited
	flexibility	low	high	medium	low-medium
	time context	full	limited	high degree	high degree
SOCIAL REQUIREMENTS	integrity	high	low	high	high
	openness	medium	high	high	medium
	benevolence	high	medium	medium-high	high
	personal relation	high	low	medium	high
	context	high	low	medium	medium

Table 3 provides an overview of media's appropriateness for the presented task types.

The face-to-face setting is particularly efficient for negotiating and executing tasks. For these task types, face-to-face contact is superior to the other three media. For generating and choosing tasks, this medium does, however, not seem efficient since it ranks low in most of the required factors.

Out of the considered media, e-mail is the most efficient communication system for generating tasks as it meets all requirements. Furthermore, it is suitable for choosing tasks. For negotiating and executing tasks it is, however, advisable to switch to other media.

Table 3. Media eligibility for task types

		FACE-TO-FACE CONVERSATION	E-MAIL	INSTANT MESSAGING / CHAT	VOICE-OVER-IP / PHONE
GENERATING TASKS	free expression of opinion	limited	high	high	limited
	democratisation	limited	high	high	limited
	minimisation of conformity pressure	very high	low	low	medium
	expanded time availability	very limited	very high	medium	limited
CHOOSING TASKS	free expression of opinion	limited	high	high	limited
	democratisation	limited	high	high	limited
	minimisation of conformity pressure	very high	low	low	medium
	rationality	low	high	medium-high	medium
	flexibility (reflection)	low	high	medium	low
	low degree of cognitive demand	low degree	high degree	high degree	medium
NEGOTIATING TASKS	flexibility	low	high	medium	low
	context, information richness	very high	low	medium	high
	time for information acquisition	little	much	medium	little
	willingness to compromise	high	low	low	medium
	free expression of opinion	limited	high	high	limited
EXECUTING TASKS	high degree of interactivity	very high	low	medium	high
	conformity, willingness to compromise	high	low	low	medium
	low social context	very high degree	low degree	low degree	high degree

Instant messaging is – similar to e-mail – considered as an efficient means of communication for generating and choosing tasks but not very suitable for negotiating and executing tasks. However, for the first two task types, instant messaging does not even come close to the eligibility as e-mail does. For the latter two tasks types, though, instant messaging tends to be better suited compared to e-mail.

Interaction via phone or voice-over-IP tends to be suited for executing tasks. For choosing and negotiating tasks it does neither show outstanding nor particularly bad results. And for generating tasks it ranks by far lowest compared to the other three considered media.

2.3 Excursus: Development of social skills[1]

Although the hypotheses raised in this Section *cannot* be addressed or even answered within the scope of this book, this excursus is the right place:

- to provide the respective background information that helps the reader to understand the underlying issues and
- to raise hypotheses to be answered by future investigations[2].

Before we can discuss how social skills may be developed, we first have to define what we refer to.

Social skills

Literature and research on social competence exist abundantly (Argyle, 1969; Engelberg & Sjöberg, 2004). In spite of the encompassing discussion on this topic, (Schuler & Barthelme, 1995) argue that due to its complexity a precise definition is still lacking. However, they themselves deliver an approach, which meanwhile seems to have been widely adopted.

According to (Schuler & Barthelme, 1995), social competence is a construct, which can be divided in two kinds of characteristics: interpersonal abilities and social skills.

According to this approach, interpersonal abilities build the basis for social competence and explain the emergence of socially competent behaviour. This group involves following abilities:

1 Addressing the topic of social skills development, this Section tries to contribute to the reader's understanding of the underlying issues. Still we are aware that what is expressed in this excursus is just one perspective and a vast field with a lot more sophistication.

2 For investigating issues concerning social skills it seems crucial that research is undertaken by scholars with deep background and expertise in disciplines such as psychology, educational science, communication science, or sociology – ideally in joint effort.

- empathy,
- sensitiveness,
- the ability to assert oneself, and
- situative flexibility (ability to adapt one's behaviour to changing situations. and environmental factors).

Social skills include aspects of social competence bearing upon concrete behaviour. One can directly observe these skills when people are interacting. This category includes:

- communication skills,
- cooperation and coordination skills.
- team(work) skills, as well as
- conflict management skills.

According to (Schuler & Barthelme, 1995), interpersonal abilities can hardly be trained or even acquired since they form part of personality. However, in addition to the delivery of knowledge on behaviour on an intellectual basis, social skills can be trained to a certain degree.

(Fühles-Ubach, 2000) suggests:

- Training of specific behaviour patterns is more promising for strengthening social skills than practice of general principles.
- Enhancement of already existing strengths is more likely to meet with success than the attempt to eliminate great deficits.
- Strength of learning effects depends on personality.

After this brief definition of social skills, the next Section is devoted to social skills development. Finally, we will have a look on the aspect how social skills can be acquired in addition to intellectual knowledge in the context of learning on three levels.

2.3.1 Acquisition and development of social skills

Social skills pertain to what is referred to as behavioural knowledge. While factual knowledge is the one-way passage of facts and procedural content links action steps (or information) together to a formal process (linear path), behavioural knowledge can be considered a multipath process (Anderson, 2000).

Every kind of behavioural knowledge has to be practiced. Therefore, interaction with other people is fundamental. (Skills and behaviour can be tried out in a risk-free environment.) Moreover, changes of circumstances are important, since each situation offers and requires different possibilities for the multipath. Reinforcing the knowledge that a learner already has is also helpful as is adopting that knowledge to new circumstances (Anderson, 2000).

Irrespective of the above-mentioned conditions, it seems fundamental that a person conveys a sufficient degree of interpersonal capacities in order that social skills may emerge and develop.

Figure 13 provides an overview of conditions for developing social skills and illustrates their interplay. Having this in mind, following paragraphs deal with the development of social skills with special regard to the technology-enhanced context.

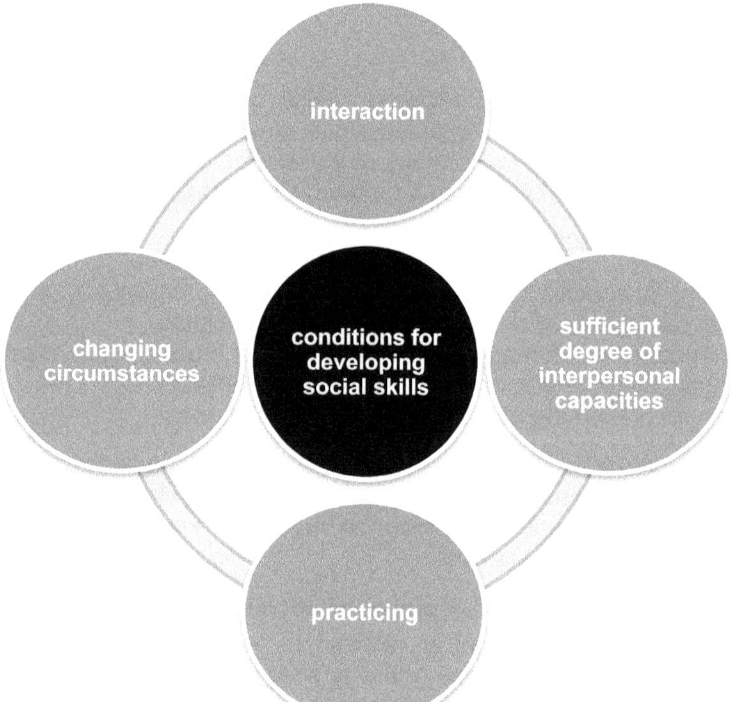

Figure 13. Conditions for developing social skills

2.3.1.1 Developing social skills in a technology-enhanced environment

As already mentioned above, (Fühles-Ubach, 2000) suggests that training of specific behaviour patterns is more promising than practice of general principles. Some truth of this rather behaviouristic statement can be seen when considered, for instance, in a business context. It may be efficient – in terms of time and money – to invest in employees' particular training of behaviour patterns in order to achieve positive results in specific situations rather early. However, when it comes to new situations (i.e. situations that than the trained situations) people may not be able to apply these trained patterns. When practicing general principles, in contrast, skills will be widely applicable (i.e. independent from situations). It will, though, take more time until skills evolve.

Either way, it appears beneficial to exercise[3] online behaviour in an online context. Computer mediated communication is different to face-to-face interaction; this is a matter of fact (e.g., Ishaya & Macaulay, 1999; Sarbaugh-Thompson & Feldman, 1998; Walther, 1992, 1995, 1996, 1997, 2000; Walther & Burgoon, 1992). However, there is no valuing within this phrase. Neither computer-mediated communication nor face-to-face interaction is praised as being superior to the other. Different does not mean better, it does not mean worse – different means different!

Research revealed that the use of some kind of online communication encourages people saying things they would not dare in face-to-face situations. In other words, they tend to engage in an abusive style (flaming) (e.g., Frey, 1999, pp. 33-34; Hollingshead & McGrath, 1995, p. 74; Ishaya & Macaulay, 1999, p. 150; Sassenberg, 2000, p. 107). During initial phases, communication might be more aggressive in computer-mediated context than in face-to-face settings (Walther & Burgoon, 1992, pp. 72-73).

Since the same people with the same social skills developed seem to behave differently in online and in face-to-face settings, it is evident that what has been learned and developed face-to-face over years does not fully hold in context engaging technology.

These observations could lead to the following hypothesis: Either social skills required for online interaction can only be developed and learned online, or they cannot at all be developed (thus, flaming would always be inherent part of computer-mediated communication).

Fortunately, the continuing revolution in human kind does not stop with online communication. Experiments and field studies give evidence that

3 Here *exercising* refers to *experiencing* and to *receiving training* respectively.

people adapt to corresponding media (media competence) and that attitudes and skills evolve and are applied irrespective of used media (Ulijn, Lincke, & Karakaya, 2001; Walther, 1992, 1995, 1996, 1997, 2000; Walther & Burgoon, 1992).

Though initial interactions in computer-mediated communication might appear more aggressive than face-to-face conversations, the studies of (Walther, 1992, pp. 192, 196-197) and (Walther & Burgoon, 1992, pp. 59, 72-73) reveal the reciprocal for later phases; later online interactions are more relaxed and composed and less tense and aroused. Many relationships become more relaxed as they develop. (Annotation: Under both conditions – computer-mediated as well as face-to-face communication – greater composure and relaxation had been experienced as groups continued interaction.)

The development from aggressiveness and tenseness in computer-mediated communication in initial interaction to more relaxed and less tense and aroused communication in later phases outlines that social learning takes place online. Face-to-face situations and online context make different demands on participants' social skills. Certainly, a great deal of social skills that we develop face-to-face throughout our lifetimes (from baby age onwards...) still apply in online context. However, these social skills acquired in face-to-face interaction seem not to be sufficient in online situations; further skills have to be developed.

Having this discussion in mind, we consider that experiencing the differences between computer-mediated communication and face-to-face interaction is beneficial with respect to the appropriate development of social skills in both contexts. From a behaviouristic point of view, it appears important to train behaviour patterns in such distinct contexts in order that people are able to apply the trained patterns in these contexts. From a rather constructivist perspective, the benefit lies rather in experiencing the two contexts such that people exercise general principles in both settings.

2.3.1.2 Using social skills (acquired in online situations) in a face-to-face context

In the previous Section, we discussed social skills in online context and its special requirements. Since skills developed in face-to-face context do not seem sufficient for online situations – thus, have to be adopted and further developed –, the question arises if skills acquired in the online context render advantageous in face-to-face situations.

The following two scenarios shall illustrate the potential of social skills developed online – and at the same time encourage further research.

Sense of success gathered online – example democratisation

In middle-size groups it comes naturally, that some few people dominate the discussion. They tend to seize everything – ideas, coordination, planning, etc. Others are eclipsed (e.g., Frey, 1999, p. 33; Hollingshead & McGrath, 1995, p. 61; Ulijn, Lincke, & Karakaya, 2001; Walther, 1996, p. 7).

Reasoning behind this behaviour is multifarious. Analysing all these areas is beyond the scope of this excursus. Therefore, the issue of democratisation is exemplified on a general basis.

Face-to-face contact allows for forcing attention (Brill & de Vries, 1998). For instance, clothing and body language provide social and situational clues, which give information about social status or hierarchy level (Frey, 1999, p. 33). Computer-mediated communication does not always supply this information (Brill & de Vries, 1998, p. 15; Frey, 1999, p. 33). And even if status and hierarchy level are known, the noticeable distance of communication at distance with low social presence seems to be perceived as protective barrier; thus, people tend to articulate what they would not dare in face-to-face situations (Frey, 1999, pp. 33-34; Hollingshead & McGrath, 1995, p. 74; Ishaya & Macaulay, 1999, p. 150; Sassenberg, 2000, p. 107).

(Walther & Burgoon, 1992, p. 74) reveal that, while face-to-face groups display a quadratic development in dominance over time, dominance declines in computer-mediated situations. Participation on discussion tends to be more balanced in computer-mediated context than in face-to-face settings; everyone seems to get a word in edgeways (Frey, 1999, p. 33; Hollingshead & McGrath, 1995, p. 61; Ulijn, Lincke, & Karakaya, 2001; Walther, 1996, p. 7).

These findings raise following hypothesis:

H 1. If people who seldom get a word in edgeways in face-to-face situations but do in online context, their sense of success experienced in the latter situation encourages them to assert themselves also in face-to-face context. Thus, social skills developed in online context hold also in face-to-face situations.

Aha experience – opening dazzlers' eyes

The above-described scenario is also suitable to explain the aha-experience for dazzlers.

Dominating behaviour does not only occur with people of high status. Moreover, it can be observed with people who attempt influence (Frey, 1999, pp. 33-34; Walther, 1995, pp. 192, 196-197; Walther & Burgoon, 1992, p. 74). Some people constantly attempt to seize conversation. Dazzlers are to be found almost everywhere. They need the feeling of being treasured. They always want to take centre stage. They want people to look up to them. – And they would do almost everything to get what they want.

Unfortunately, it is not uncommon that really good people with great ideas bow and scrape – sometimes only to avoid heavy conflicts. Innovation comes slowly since good issues are not raised due to dazzlers dominating behaviour. Furthermore, it is often seen that dazzlers take credit of other people's ideas, which leads to frustration and anger (Frey, 1999, pp. 33-34; Walther, 1995, pp. 192, 196-197; Walther & Burgoon, 1992, p. 74).

Research has shown that participants of conversations in computer-mediated settings tend to stand up for their opinions, which, moreover, tend to be multifarious. Generally, computer-mediated communication encourages advancing extreme opinions; analyses have shown that fewer opinions are introduced into face-to-face discussion than into computer-mediated conversations (Frey, 1999, pp. 33-34; Hollingshead & McGrath, 1995, p. 74; Ishaya & Macaulay, 1999, p. 150; Sassenberg, 2000, p. 107). (Diehl & Ziegler, 2000) qualify that information, which is known to all participants, dominates face-to-face discussions. Information, which is not shared, does have little chance only to be considered.

Though not sufficient, this discourse suggests that computer-mediated communication may encourage some people to resist dominating behaviour. At the same time, dazzlers experience resistance that would not or rarely occur in face-to-face situations. They undergo an aha-experience, which leads to the following hypothesis:

H 2. People who dominate face-to-face conversations and experience resistance online change their attitude in later face-to-face discussion towards democracy.

2.3.2 Acquiring social skills in addition to intellectual knowledge

As already mentioned in Section 2.1.3.3, traditional teaching tends to address the three levels of learning (Figure 3, page 41) strictly separated. Especially in university context, mainly the intellect level tends to be addressed, while the other two levels seem to be underrepresented or even ignored (e.g., Motschnig-Pitrik & Derntl, 2002; Motschnig-Pitrik & Holzinger, 2002).

As already mentioned, experience shows that the person-centred approach, which addresses all three levels, is more demanding on the facilitator's time than conventional courses, while the deployment of ICT is expected to reduce some of the *overhead*, which is required following the person-centred style (e.g., Motschnig-Pitrik & Mallich, 2002). This Section reflects on possibilities how the social skills level may be addressed in addition to the intellectual level without demanding more of the facilitator's time in the longer term.

Considering the conditions for developing social skills presented above (cf. Figure 13), the variety of learning methods can be listed as follows. Development of social skills needs interaction and practicing. Interaction, in turn, needs people. Following settings, meeting those needs, are conceivable:

- Interaction takes place in a face-to-face setting (group discussion, group work) guided by a facilitator.
- Students are assigned with a particular homework, which has to be carried out in small teams. In this setting, students can choose for themselves how to communicate, coordinate, etc.
- Students are asked to stick to a certain online platform for carrying out their group work. (Contributions on the platform are traceable. However, additional face-to-face communication can neither be prohibited nor controlled.)

Since social skills requirement vary with situations, changing circumstances are necessary in order to develop a rich variety of social skills appropriate for those situations. Artificially creating changing circumstances in any of above-mentioned settings, implicates careful preparation – in other words, much time and effort. However, when combining the three settings, changing circumstances come naturally. Assuming that coordinating a mixture of settings involves less effort than the creation of different circumstances within one setting, a blended solution seems appropriate.

Although the potential of the support of information and communication technology for learning communities and social knowledge construction had already been recognised, in the first attempts of transferring the person-centred approach to technology-enhanced learning settings, activities primarily targeting social skills were allocated more strongly to the presence phases (e.g., Motschnig-Pitrik & Mallich, 2002). However, the demand for diversity is met by offering students the possibility to experience working with various colleagues in teams of various sizes. This attempt to combine different methods including presence and online phases had been a first step towards a thoughtful combination of media. Clearly, the kind of content to be delivered at the intellectual level plays a prominent role in deciding which blend is appropriate (Jank & Meyer, 1991). However, due to this issue's complexity there are not yet patterns established providing constructive guidelines. Research, though, has made significant advancements concerning media choice and combinations while addressing all three levels of learning (e.g., Figl & Motschnig-Pitrik, 2007; Figl, Motschnig-Pitrik, & Derntl, 2006; Motschnig-Pitrik & Figl, 2007).

In case that information and communication technology takes over significant parts of the transfer of the intellectual knowledge, more room is left for addressing the social level in presence phases (Motschnig-Pitrik & Mallich, 2002). Other way round, if addressing the social level is provided by homework to be carried out in groups (whether by deploying technology or not), presence phases can focus on the intellectual level. It is, however, questionable if addressing the intellect needs richer social presence than addressing the social level.

For example, for factual and procedural knowledge, a method allowing for self-paced learning is more appropriate than interactive methods. Since students learn at different rates, the possibility to proceed at the learner's own pace (slowing down or even skipping sections if appropriate) must be convenient for learners of these types of content (Anderson, 2000). In these cases, leaving the intellectual part to non-interactive media (e.g., textbooks) seems appropriate. Consequently, students can determine their individual learning tempos on their own. Accordingly, social skills issues can be addressed in interactive settings (whether face-to-face or in online settings) without demanding much of the facilitator's extra time.

In case that an elaborative method (experiential learning) is chosen for the intellectual part, usually the social level is addressed at the same time since group interaction always includes – to some extent – the development of social skills. However, the question arises if social skills could better be developed if experienced difficulties and findings are shared face-to-face in the group due to the fact that experiences are expressed, improved, and internalised.

> *H 3. Discussing difficulties and findings concerning social skills, which have been experienced within an online context, with a group in a face-to-face setting, will contribute positively to the further development of skills compared to the situation that experiences are not shared, due to an improved understanding and further elaborated.*

It is to be emphasised at this place that discussion alone is not sufficient and further practice is needed. Still, we expect that sharing experiences has an effect on further practice and development of social skills.

3 Factors affecting media's eligibility for particular educational settings[4]

As could be demonstrated in the precedent Sections, enhancing traditional classroom teaching with learning approaches making use of information and communication technologies is a major concern in current educational research. Although experiences have been made with concepts of technology-enhanced learning, the question how one can assess to which degree a course should consist of traditional learning and e-learning elements is still to be answered.

Previous work (e.g., Attwell, Dirckinck-Holmfeld, Fabian, Kárpáti, & Littig, 2003) could identify a wide scope of relevant factors influencing an optimal mix of media. General rules for balancing could, however, not yet be revealed.

Optimally balancing the manifold opportunities for communication and learning as regards media selection seems to be a challenge, which has to be met *for each specific setting separately*. Although suggestions are to be abundantly found, practitioners are overburdened with what to consider for their specific needs as they still lack a convenient framework guiding them to find a reasonable mix.

Most research does not contemplate the whole picture but, instead, focuses on some influencing factors. Consequently, educators base the choice concerning the mix of media in their technology-enhanced courses primarily on their personal experiences and / or on case studies and experiments in very specific settings. Actually, acquiring knowledge, experience, and a sense of which media may be suitable for what kind of learning activities is a complex task and cannot be achieved within one or two application cycles (Derntl & Motschnig-Pitrik, 2004). Obviously, there is a need for an appropriate methodical framework. Notwithstanding practitioners' needs for such a generic guideline, this narrowing down to a selection of factors enables researchers to go into particular detail as concerns the chosen topics.

Due to this problem's complexity, this book cannot provide the long-desired ultimate answer with a simple model. Nevertheless, this work meets the challenge and tries to design a framework on a conceptual basis, to

4 The current Section relies mainly on work published in (C. Bauer & Kovacs, 2004).

which this Section is dedicated. Essentially, it draws from precedent findings, flavours them with own conceptions, and puts all into a new whole.

Figure 14 provides an overview of relevant factors influencing the mix in technology-enhanced learning settings. The presented factors included in the model were found to have an impact on the didactical decision what kind of media to select for a particular learning scenario. However, as several factors are inherent in a certain scenario, this may lead to demands on media that seem contradictory. In such cases, media shall be chosen that best suit the scenario. Consequently, in order to make an appropriate decision what kind of media to apply, it is not sufficient to consider only one of these inherent factors.

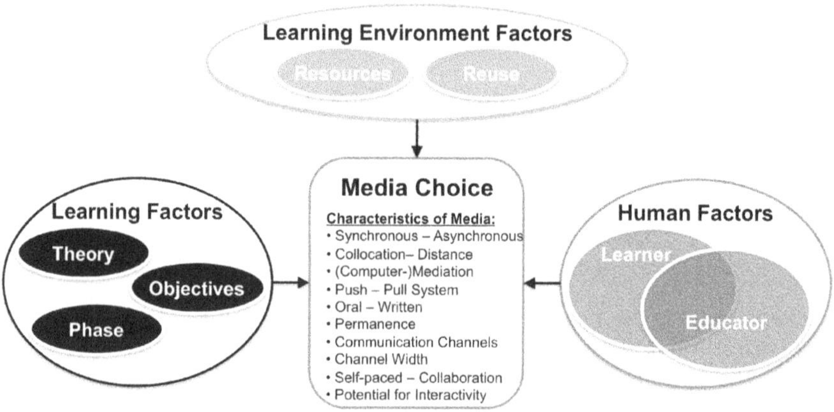

Figure 14. Factors influencing media choice in technology-enhanced learning settings

Source: (C. Bauer & Kovacs, 2004, (adapted))

It is to be emphasised that the presented framework does not claim to be a thorough model, but is an attempt to put precedent findings and own conceptions into an integrated whole. Still, it may miss further influential factors that need to be included. Nevertheless, in its current state it provides a sound basis for further development and enhancement.

Although not being complete, the framework illustrates the complexity of educational settings, particularly with respect to determining media's eligibility for learning efforts and accordingly choosing an adequate medium for a certain learning activity.

For the purpose of this work, conflating findings from previous investigations and existing concepts on a generic basis had been essential in order to be able to position endeavours as it provides the required overview of the environment, into which research is embedded. Although the discussion of promotive activities (cf. Section 4) does not directly reference particular factors presented in this Section, it naturally considers the framework and its implications as a whole. Furthermore, the presentation of the issue's complexity gives direction concerning appropriate methods for further investigation, outlined in Section 5.

The following presents the factors to be considered, having in mind that the list of factors is not exhaustive.

3.1 Learning factors

The term *learning factors* subsumes relevant factors concerning learning and the learning process in their core. Learning is, whether explicitly or implicitly, based on a learning paradigm, a learning model, learning objectives, and learning content.

For reaching an adequate decision what kind of media to use for a certain scenario, all these factors have to be considered.

Learning theory

In any case, learning and teaching is based on a learning paradigm, whether implicitly or explicitly stated by the educator (Baumgartner, 1997). The three major learning paradigms are behaviourism, cognitivism, and constructivism (cf. Section 2.1.1). The inherent learning paradigm directly or indirectly influences the choice of media for learning. Behaviouristic learning models, for instance, require the educator to keep control over the learning process and the chosen media, thus, have to support instruction-orientated elements in such settings. Instruction-orientated elements do, however, not necessarily build on behaviourism but may include cognitivistic elements (Mathes, 2002, p. 8).

Learning objectives

Learning objectives express what the whole learning process or a specific learning activity should result in. Such objectives may or may not be precisely set in advance. While in behaviourist settings, the educator appears to keep control over objectives, objectives in pure constructivist settings are dynamic may vary in the course of a learning process since they are adapted to participants' needs and desires (cf. Bremer, 2001).

Moreover, a learning objective is tightly linked to the specific *subject of the learning content* and outlines what a learner will be able to do differently, resulting in distinct *domains of learning* objectives.

- *Subject of the learning content.* In this context, learning content is viewed as of what has to be learned (from a conceptual perspective) rather than a physical representation of content (e.g., a textbook). A very general way of categorising content is with regard to its corresponding (scientific) discipline and additionally how sophisticated it is. Another completely distinct approach is, for instance, to differentiate between *knowing what*, *knowing how*, *knowing where*, and *to be able to* (e.g., Baumgartner, Häfele, & Häfele, 2002).
- *Domain of learning objectives.* Basically, we can differentiate between cognitive, affective, and psychomotor objectives (cf. Bremer, 2001), although, due to interdependences, it is sometimes difficult to strictly distinguish these from each other. The dependency of media selection on the domain of learning objectives is evident: for example, it seems obvious that learning theoretically how to swim (*intellect*) demands other media than learning how to swim in practice (*skill*). Furthermore, domains can be subdivided into *levels of objectives*. For instance, for the cognitive domain, the *taxonomy of cognitive complexity* by (Bloom, 1972/1973) is widely accepted. From the simplest to the most complex domain this taxonomy describes: knowledge (remembering), comprehension (understanding), application (transferring), analysis (relating), synthesis (creating), and evaluation (judging) (cf. e.g., Berge & Muilenburg, 2002; Bloom, 1972/1973).

Learning phase

Every learning scenario serves a certain purpose within the learning process. Depending on the phase in the process, media have to enable and support the following purposes (e.g., Bremer, 2001):

- representing knowledge (presentation of learning content),
- motivating and activating the learner,
- enabling and supporting communication (between educators and learners or learners among each other),
- supporting learners in processing the learned content and organising their individual learning process,
- supporting reproduction and application of the learned content, as well as
- assessing the learning progress (for learners themselves and by educators).

Appropriate media have to be chosen in accordance to the particular learning scenario in order to provide adequate support of the respective learning phase (e.g., a book will not enable communication between learners).

3.2 Human factors

Learning is all about humans. People involved in learning processes are basically learners and educators which both affect the conditions for media selection. First, variables valid for both learners and educators are outlined. Subsequently, additional variables for learners and educators are dealt with separately.

3.2.1 Variables of both learners and educators

Experience with media

The more experience individuals could have acquired with a certain technology, the better they will be able to make use of it (e.g., Foulger, 1990; Limayem & Hirt, 2000).

Accordingly, learning settings have to be chosen with respect to their participants' media competencies and must not exceed these capabilities. The degree and the selection of e-learning elements in a technology-enhanced learning setting shall therefore be determined by participants' experiences with the respective media (e.g., Albrecht, 2002; Bremer, 2001).

Still, this raises the question when people shall acquire media competence, particularly with *new* media. Considering people's present capabilities, courses could, for instance, be used to further media competence (by using respective media) although it is not the course's actual learning content.

Media acceptance

E-learning is not for everyone. Some individuals are simply not willing to learn or teach in settings other than presence courses as they seem to be convinced to require personal contact and interaction at physical presence (e.g., Duarte & Snyder, 2001). Any attempt to get them working with other media in learning scenarios will run against resistance. As (Hollingshead & McGrath, 1995) point it out,

> "Users may or may not like using the computer. Their attitudes may depend on their expectations before using the system [...] and / or their own experience with the system. This reaction may or may not get more favourable over time."

An educator's media acceptance definitely influences his or her media selection. Additionally, a particular medium's acceptance among participants should clearly be considered for its application in a particular learning setting.

Media preferences

Although interrelated, media preference is not equal to media acceptance. One may accept a medium but prefer a different one, thus yielding way better results with the latter.

When delving into this topic, it has also to be considered that media preference is also affected by a learner's habitual learning place (e.g., Bremer, 2001), since one might prefer different media for learning at home alone or in a crowded lobby when on a business trip.

In order to best support learners and increase their learning outcomes, learners' preferences should dominate educators' preferences in this regard.

3.2.2 Learner specific variables

Learning style (learning habits)

Learning styles are heavily discussed, which gives evidence that this factor renders important. Basically, learning style research aims to find clusters of people who use similar patterns for perceiving and interpreting situations. As media differently support styles, we should use this information for adjusting educational environments in order to make them more effective.

Finding an appropriate model defining learning styles is, though, not an easy task – if not impossible at all at the current state of the art. (Coffield, Moseley, Hall, & Ecclestone, 2004) have undertaken a (non-peer-reviewed) literature review and could identify as many as 71 different theories of learning style. This report criticises most of these theories, as the main instruments used to identify an individual's learning style had – according to their analysis – not proven as appropriate.

(Coffield et al., 2004) provide a detailed overview of the 13 most influential models, providing information about terms and definitions, theoretical origins, and the instruments used to assess types of learning style defined by the respective model. Their in-depth analysis led to the result that none of the most popular learning style theories had been adequately validated through independent research and are, thus, highly questionable.

(Lovelace, 2005), in contrast, provides evidence confirming the validity of Dunn and Dunn's model, which is one of the models that had been criticised by (Coffield et al., 2004) only in the year before. This meta-analysis, though, had been undertaken by one of Rita Dunn's students and does not take account of the previous criticism on the research.

Motive for learning

The issue how to stimulate learner's motivation is widely discussed (e.g., Ames, 1992; Figl & Bauer, 2008a; Schlag, 1995/2004). We agree that media choice has a high impact on motivation.

Beyond, we suggest that a learner's initial motive for learning (e.g., participating in a course) is a relevant factor for the didactical decision on media choice. We hypothesise that a highly motivated person who is extremely interested in a topic will keep motivation for learning at a high level with almost any kind of media. In contrast, someone who is little or not at all motivated to learn (e.g., students who attend a course due to its curricular requirements), media has to be carefully selected in order to increase motivation or at least maintain it at the given level.

3.2.3 Educator specific variables

Beyond competencies that both, educators and learners, need for the appropriate use (application) of media, educators are required to prepare and produce learning material. Consequently, educator's competencies for practical design and implementation are relevant factors for media choice (e.g., Albrecht, 2002).

Pedagogical competencies

It is crucial that the educator is able to put the pedagogical objectives into operation (e.g., Albrecht, 2002) with the media chosen. Appropriate media selection is, thus, dependent on the educator's ability to conceptualise pedagogical issues by using a specific medium.

While for particular activities, tutors may provide assistance (e.g., administrative and technical handling of online peer reviews), for others – especially in synchronous settings – educators are fully dependent on their own.

Production competencies

Regardless whether the educator has some assistance or not, learning material has to be prepared and produced. For instance, introducing a flash video simulation to a course is only an option if there is someone available, who is able to program and implement it.

3.3 Learning environment factors

In any case, learning and teaching need some media, whether technically enhanced or not, to communicate what is to be learned (according to media pedagogy, speech is also a medium!). Consequently, *learning environment factors,* like resources and infrastructure, affect the conditions for media selection in a particular scenario.

Resources and media available

Availability of resources rigorously restricts the possibilities for learning and teaching. For instance, in areas where broadband Internet access is not yet available, it is not a wise choice to stress on high-quality video streaming, which simply overextends connections with little or limited bandwidth.

Principally, we differentiate between resources *on the part of the institution* and *on the part of the learners.*

- *Institutional resources.* For resources on the part of the institution we can further distinguish between human (personnel) resources, technical (material) resources, and budget.
  - *Human (personnel) resources.* The number of people available to support a course or particular pedagogical activity results in a specific ratio of learners to educators (or tutors, technicians for student support, etc.). Put differently, it specifies how many educators (tutors, technicians, etc.) support how many learners (1:1, 1:n, m:n). Depending on this ratio, certain media may be used while others cannot (e.g., web-based trainings may be favoured when a great number of students has to be reached by a small number of personnel in order to ease the burden on the latter).
  - *Technical (material) resources.* Technical resources and infrastructure are not only required for the delivery of e-learning elements but also for developing and deploying learning material (e.g., creating slides for oral presentations) (cf. e.g., Kovacs, 2004). It naturally depends on the availability of resources whether a specific medium may be deployed or not.
  - *Budget.* Last but not least, budget constraints need to be considered when designing pedagogical elements. For example, commercially available e-learning platforms are costly and, thus, not affordable for every institution. On the other hand, open source software exists, which turn out to be an excellent alternative. Special features may require additional infrastructure (e.g., streaming server); the acquisition of such hardware may only be justifiable if it is used

in several courses and / or for a large number of students. However, personnel may be the higher expense factor in most cases. Hence, managers of educational organisation will tend to reduce the number of personnel that support the same or even an increased number of students. In such situations, a thoughtful choice of media may provide educators the chance to keep quality of teaching and learning at an acceptable level. Basically, it is a managerial strategy or a (national) political guideline how available budget is allocated within organisations.

- *Learners' resources.* Particularly when working with technologically advanced features, the learner's technical resources (e.g., broadband Internet access, multimedia PC) are to be considered for the design of technology-enhanced learning setting. If it is foreseeable that learners are not equipped with the necessary resources, it is a good practice that the institution provides adequate infrastructure – or instead other media should be preferred for the setting.

Furthermore, it seems important to consider *when*, *how long*, and *where* resources are available and how easily learners and educators can access them. For instance, if learners have access to the Internet or the chosen e-learning platform for very limited time only (e.g., people who work fulltime and seek further training in their free time) or learn in different time zones, the extensive use of synchronous online conferencing is a poor option.

Reuse of existing learning resources

Due to its significance, learning resources (as a special kind of resource) are treated separately.

Reusability of content is a primary concern of e-learning standardisation (cf. e.g., Advanced Distributed Learning (ADL), 2004). If there is already learning material available for a specific subject in a way that fits the specific learning setting, it can be easily reused. This influences media selection insofar as it might be better to use existing material that is good enough in practice than spending money for developing material that provides only marginal additional benefits.

The following forms of reusable material have been identified so far:

- First, a written representation of content (e.g., a textbook, notes, folios) can be used as it is.
- Second, also electronically available content (e.g., documents, videos, audio files) can be easily used. Attention has to be paid to legal issues

like particularly intellectual property rights, etc.
- Third, educators might invite, for example, an expert for a particular topic; otherwise they have to prepare the topic on their own.

As this example could demonstrate, reusability does not only refer to material sources but also to human sources, a fact that increasingly gains recognition.

4 Promotive, non-directive activities[5]

Learning takes place *inside* persons and cannot be ordered, forced, or even fulfilled by others. Nevertheless, it is possible to further and to facilitate the learning process by providing helpful conditions and resources.

According to the person-centred approach (cf. Section 2.1.3), living and holding the three personal dispositions of congruence, empathy, and acceptance (cf. Section 2.1.3.2) towards and among learners directly induces promotive, non-directive activities. Consequently, when holding all of these dispositions (Rogers variables) and when the other person reciprocally perceives these at least to some degree (e.g., Rogers, 1959), further action or activity will be promotive and non-directive for others (Tausch & Tausch, 1963/1998, pp. 244-245).

Characteristics of such promotive activities driven by these dispositions may be summarised as follows. Promotive, non-directive activities (Tausch & Tausch, 1963/1998, pp. 244-245):

- promote meaningful mental processes and further constructive personality development (e.g., self-respect, openness for experience) in the other person,
- comply with the four psycho-social values of living (self-determination, respect for the person, social order, and mental as well as physical functioning),
- are socially reversible, which means that even young persons may approach adults without being disrespectful,
- facilitate autonomous, self-initiated learning and creativity,
- further the quality of interpersonal relationships, and
- are equally promoting for the *holder* and the *recipient* of the three dispositions.

Integrating such promotive activities in teaching is, though, not sufficient for achieving an adequate learning atmosphere and best learning results. For instance, it may happen that educators – deliberately or not – integrate promotive activities in their teaching although they do not directly follow the person-centred approach or do have not (yet) developed the three Rogers variables to a high degree. In such cases they would rather apply these activities as *techniques* while simultaneously lacking the un-

5 The current Section relies mainly on work published in (C. Bauer, Derntl, Motschnig-Pitrik, & Tausch, 2006).

derlying *attitudes*. While practicing and applying techniques may be effective with respect to learning atmosphere and outcomes, this behaviour has clear limitations compared to teaching driven by the Rogers variables. Applying techniques with the purpose of manipulation may even be a *dangerous* scenario. Consequently, – as already outlined above – it seems necessary that the facilitator holds the dispositions of congruence, empathy, and acceptance at least to some degree and a student is able to perceive them at least to some degree.

Figure 15 gives a general overview of promotive activities and their respective counterparts. While the two columns portray the extremes, a person will usually undertake promotive, less promotive, and non-promotive activities – in varying degrees though. Hence, Figure 15 may be used to reflect a person's style on the promotiveness and non-directivity continuum.

Based on the assumptions and suggestions of the person-centred learning style by (Rogers, 1983), (Tausch & Tausch, 1963/1998, pp. 252-315) identified endeavours that are particularly suited to promote non-directive and self-initiated learning processes. The following provides an overview:

- *Facilitating learning through the provision of resources*. Providing inspiring learning material as well as personnel (human) resources (e.g., experts, the facilitator's time and endeavours) furthers autonomous, self-responsible learning (Tausch & Tausch, 1963/1998, pp. 288-297).
- *Endeavour to design learning material for knowledge transfer in a comprehensible way*. Irrespective of the learning content itself, the way how learning material is designed and structured impacts its level of difficulty. Adhering to the four dimensions of comprehensibility (simplicity, structure, conciseness, and stimulation) helps students in acquiring knowledge from oral or written information resources (Tausch & Tausch, 1963/1998, pp. 266-277).
- *Facilitating thinking processes*. Facilitating creative, autonomous thinking processes is highly promotive and non-directive since such thinking processes tend to be longer-lasting and, thus, induce deeper learning (Tausch & Tausch, 1963/1998, pp. 297-307).
- *Furthering a beneficial working progress*. Basically, this can be achieved in three steps: (1) getting to know the work personally, (2) elaborating and inspecting subtasks, and (3) finalising, exploiting and / or applying the work (Tausch & Tausch, 1963/1998, pp. 307-315).

No promotive activities	Many promotive activities
Not offering opportunities and alternatives, suppressing the other, not providing informative hints.	Offer opportunities and alternatives, stimulate the other, provide informative hints.
Not finding material and resources (e.g., comprehensible texts) and sources of help (e.g., tutors) for someone else and being unavailable to the other.	Find material and resources (e.g., comprehensible texts) and sources of help (e.g., tutors) for someone else as well as to be available to the other.
Not providing feedback and not making agreements, arrangements, or regulations.	Provide feedback, make agreements, arrangements, and regulations.
Not showing the other person promotive conditions to foster self-respect, psycho-social values, and the three interpersonal dispositions.	Provide and show the other person promotive conditions to foster self-respect, psycho-social values, and the three interpersonal dispositions.
Not learning with the other, not creating a promotive learning environment, not doing activities and sharing experiences together.	Learn with the other; create a promotive learning environment, do activities and share experiences together.
Not helping other people to be capable of promotive behaviour toward others.	Help other people to be capable of promotive behaviour toward others.
Overall: activities conflict and do not comply with the three Rogers' Variables.	**Overall**: activities comply and do not conflict with the three Rogers' Variables

Figure 15. Promotive and non-promotive person-to-person activities

Source: (Tausch & Tausch, 1963/1998, p. 247, (adapted))

- *Facilitating temporary work in small teams.* Teamwork is a well-proven method of furthering self-directed learning. (Tausch & Tausch, 1963/1998, pp. 253-266) suggest dividing the class into teams of about 2-5 persons to work on well-defined tasks.
- *Learning contracts.* This approach for defining learning objectives allows students to combine self-initiated learning with responsibility (Motschnig-Pitrik, Derntl, & Mangler, 2003; Rogers, 1983, pp. 149-153). The agreement with the facilitator assures that curricular requirements are met in the face of the provided scope for development.
- *Furthering of helpfully living together in a good group.* For cooperative learning endeavours it is essential that students accept each other and regard the group as coherent. Facilitating the emergence of a good group may be characterised by allowing for autonomous interaction and furthering the exchange of personal feelings and personally important experiences (Tausch & Tausch, 1963/1998, pp. 277-288). Person-centred encounter groups have proved to be a powerful setting to approach this goal (Barrett-Lennard, 1998, 2003; Bozarth, 2005; Motschnig-Pitrik & Nykl, 2005b; Rogers, 1970).

The next Sections (4.1 to 4.7) consider these promotive activities, which have been established and partly proved in traditional (face-to-face) learning settings in class, and transfer them to technology-enhanced environments.

4.1 Facilitating learning by providing resources

As already outlined above, learning processes can be furthered and facilitated by providing helpful conditions and resources. Thereby the appropriateness of resources is essential: they have to be manifold, close to reality, inciting, and available for autonomous exploration and use (Tausch & Tausch, 1963/1998, pp. 288-289).

The term *resource* is often associated with material resources like books or information on websites. However, apart from the fact that material resources are much more than merely books and websites, learning resources go far beyond material resources only and include persons as resources as well.

4.1.1 Material learning resources

Educators who care for their learners in a person-centred way try to organise and provide manifold learning material. These learning resources may, for instance, include books, articles, (official) documents, recordings, experiments, reports, or observations. Not surprisingly, it has been shown that illustrative resources substantially supports understanding of theoretical and rather abstract material (Tausch & Tausch, 1963/1998, p. 289).

Designing and structuring resources in a comprehensible way impacts decisively the material's benefits and promotiveness. Due to this topic's significance, the dimensions of comprehensibility are discussed in a separate Section (cf. Section 4.2).

Besides paying attention to the basic dimensions of comprehensibility, (Tausch & Tausch, 1963/1998, pp. 290-291) could identify techniques related to the provision of material resources that support learners in their striving for solutions:

- *Economic learning methods.* This term basically refers to pedagogical elements, which free the facilitator of some overhead while being capable of supporting students in their learning processes by providing them with options of assessing or training themselves. Well-proven elements are, for instance, self-training, self-examination, or self-evaluation. An alternative method, which seems particularly promotive while freeing the facilitator of some overhead, is to include elements allowing students to assess or train each other. Well proven activities are, for instance, teamwork, peer reviews, or peer evaluation.
- *Transparent goals.* Making goals transparent significantly alleviates work and learning for students. When these goals (e.g., working goals, learning goals, course objectives) are visible and transparent to everyone, it will assist students in adhering to requirements, meeting deadlines, and monitoring their individual learning progresses.

Considering material resources, the Internet (in particular the World Wide Web) offers versatile and almost unlimited options. Considering this broad, fast, and (currently still to a large extent) free offer of material, care must be taken to monitor and assess the quality of information found. In order to ensure quality, careful inspection and comparison with trusted sources appear necessary. However, it is not only the facilitator who selects and filters qualitative resources. Students may engage in searching, comparing, and critically assessing material found on the Internet, which encompasses and furthers valuable thinking processes (cf. Section 4.3). Discussing the quality of material with the whole group will help students to develop a sense for trusted sources and develop skills necessary for assessing the quality of material.

One of the easiest and therefore most widely used ways to deploy technology for teaching and learning is to put lecture notes and presentations on an e-learning platform. This allows for a flexible assembly of material

additionally leveraging motivation and driving learning success. Having assistance by tutors is beneficial in several ways. First, these tutors provide valuable learning aids and coaching for their less experienced peers. Second, tutors are setting an example for other students, which is expected to drive motivation. Moreover, students may perceive a more comfortable learning climate when they are among other students without a professional facilitator nearby. Additionally, tutors draw substantial personal benefits as they tend to be furthered in their own personal developments, particularly with respect to self-esteem and recognising the positive valuing of their personality by others (Tausch & Tausch, 1963/1998, pp. 292-293).

If learning material (e.g., lecture notes) is appropriately offered on an e-learning platform and students are encouraged to elaborate topics independently and in a cooperative way, educators can reallocate some time from the presentation of content to consulting student teams regarding their particular projects, tasks, and interests, inviting experts or drawing attention to the business context related to the elaborated topics.

Additionally, issues raised in face-to-face discussions in class can proceed in online forums. Without technological support cooperative learning processes are naturally interrupted due to the pauses between the course units. The deployment of forums or other means of communication that may involve a larger group effectively contributes to interconnect the presence phases allowing the learning process to continue without halts. On the one hand, the ongoing learning process accelerates the learning progress resulting in a more advanced learning outcome at the end of a semester. On the other hand, the time slots of presence phases dedicated to a retrospect to the prior classes may be held to a minimum since students still have the topics in mind. Instead, this time, which is set free, can be used for other promotive activities.

Furthermore, if appropriate for a course's subject matter, teams of students can be made responsible to relate online discussions to theories found in literature. For example, in courses like, for instance, *Project Management – Communication and Soft Skills* or *Organisational Development*, discussions about motivation to work or to learn can be associated with motivation theories. Students' statements can be related to the particular theories. If participants come up with issues that are not explained by any theory, this can be used for critically assessing the values of theories on complex phenomena like, in our example, motivation. Additionally, this may initiate discussion on the complementation of existing theories. In these and similar ways, personal resources from all participants can be beneficially used.

Following two examples of students' reactions will illustrate the benefits:

- One student wrote in his online reaction sheet, "*I found the elaboration on the topic of motivation very exciting. There are two reasons for that. Firstly, one does not often ask the question, 'Who or what motivates me?' I rarely, if ever, think about who or what motivates me. I found it highly useful to spend some time with directing our thoughts on that, and to acquire some consciousness about this essential issue. Secondly, the way my colleagues responded is an interesting means to learn more about one another. Also, the team working on [the topic] team building can use the results for suggesting how team members can be motivated to cooperate.*"
- Another student commented, "*I was really surprised how much we elaborated cooperatively. In particular, I liked [Paul]'s point on 'trust', it would never have occurred to me on my own. Also, the fact that motivation can be caused by negative experience was a totally new aspect for me, since I associated only positive issues with that term. So far I had often heard about Maslow and Herzberg, but to associate our own terms with these theories allows for a good connection to the theories.*"

Furthermore, students can be strongly integrated as learning resource in the presence phases. For instance, in the course on PROJECT MANAGEMENT – COMMUNICATION AND SOFT SKILLS student teams decide on a soft skills topic, which they prepare. And then they moderate a whole course unit on the respective chosen topic. This scenario has proven to result in highly interactive processes, in which everybody can learn from both the strong and weak features experienced in each setting. In our experience, it turned out to be useful, if students provide the prepared material on the e-learning platform in advance. On the one hand, this allows peers to engage with the topic before the respective course unit and appear better prepared in class. On the other hand, the facilitator gets an impression what to expect in class and also has the opportunity to consult students to revise their work beforehand if important aspects are missing.

Online support also makes it more beneficial to invite external educators or business experts to particular course units. The central face-to-face meeting can be prepared by preceding online phases and / or followed up by online phases dedicated to summarising major issues and discussing open questions (Motschnig-Pitrik & Santos, 2006). For instance, after an encounter group session that was co-facilitated by an external person-centred facilitator, a student submitted online the following reaction sheet, "*The last unit was a very pleasant and interesting one for me as I have learnt that much from [Elisabeth] in terms of speaking and gesticulating. But next to this very positive experience, again I can say that the team works were very productive and inspiring as I have seen other points of view in terms of what active listening is and how I can get a better understanding of this subject. I am looking forward to the next unit.*"

Interestingly, previous research (e.g., Motschnig-Pitrik & Mallich, 2004) indicates that students' motivation to participate in technology-enhanced courses with project work and a high degree of interaction increases if facilitators are perceived as open, respectful, and understanding. We conclude that the facilitator's personal resourcefulness is a key factor in fully exploiting the benefits offered by flexible technology-enhanced learning environments for cooperative whole person learning.

4.2 The four dimensions of comprehensibility

Day in and out we are confronted with content we do not understand. It takes a lot of effort and frequently – due to little success in spite of high effort – self-esteem gets seriously impaired (Tausch & Tausch, 1963/1998, p. 266).

Difficulties in comprehension of information, explanations, laws, etc. are not necessarily to be ascribed to difficulty in the subject matter. In fact, the form in which information is presented (whether in writing or, for instance, in an oral presentation) impacts comprehension, which can be improved by considering straightforward guidelines. According to (Langer, Schulz von Thun, & Tausch, 1974/2002), the comprehensibility of information depends on four basic dimensions – simplicity, structure, conciseness, and stimulation –, which are outlined below:

- *Simplicity*. The simpler an expression, the higher is its comprehensibility. Irrespective whether the content itself is simple or difficult, the wording and phrasing can be simple or difficult either.
- *Structure*. Information needs to be properly structured. Basically, there are two aspects involved: the inner structure and the outer structure.
    - The *inner structure* refers to the logical sequence of sentences and that information is presented in some meaningful order.
    - The *outer structure* refers to the visual representation of structure, which includes the clear arrangement of text parts (e.g., headings, lists for enumerating facts, highlighting of important phrases).

- *Conciseness*. This dimension refers to the language use in relation to the informational aim. Put differently, the length of a text should match the amount of information that it wants to communicate. Neither extremely short explanations nor unnecessarily long presentations are promotive. The optimum level is to be found in the middle. Two aspects are involved in finding a compromise:
  - *Superfluous content*. e.g., unnecessary details, supplementary information, digression from the topic, etc.
  - *Superfluous language use*. e.g., long-winded explanations, repetitions, etc.
- *Stimulation*. Direct speech, examples of everyday life, humorous expression, etc., all contribute to a lively presentation that stimulates the reader's or listener's interest. For comprehension, a medium level of liveliness is appropriate since both extremes, a complete lack of liveliness and long-winded stimulation, seem disadvantageous. A text or presentation that is overwhelmed with stimulating material distracts the reader or listener from the essential information. On the other hand, without any stimulation a text may seem boring and may lack important interlinks that make an issue understandable and easily to memorise.

Figure 17 depicts the ideal rating for texts:

- 0 stands for neutral in the respective dimension (e.g., text is neither simple nor complicated),
- + stands for high in the respective dimension (e.g., simple language),
- + + stands for very high in the respective dimension (e.g., very simple language),
- – stands for low in the respective dimension (e.g., difficult rather than simple language use), and
- – – stands for very low in the respective dimension (e.g., very difficult language).
- The optimum for simplicity and structure lies at + +. These two dimensions are the most important criteria since too complex or unstructured texts always result in bad understanding even when these rate high in the other two dimensions. Concerning conciseness and stimulation the optimum lies in the middle of the scale (0 or +) since neither too concise text nor long-winded explanations raise the comprehensibility of a text.
- The optimum for the criterion stimulation depends on the other dimensions. For well-structured material, additional stimulation in the form of well-chosen examples can be very fruitful. If a text is not optimally

structured, further stimulating material may even increase the confusion. On the other hand, highly stimulating texts can neither be short nor concise. Therefore the optimum lies somewhere in between 0 and + like for conciseness (Langer, Schulz von Thun, & Tausch, 1974/2002).

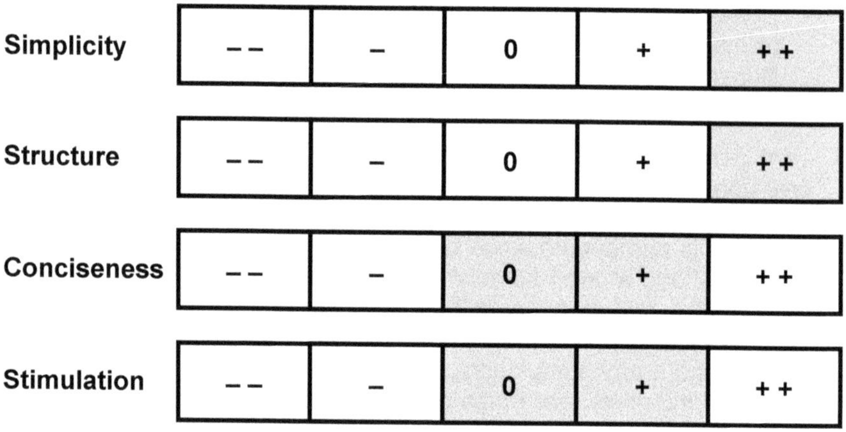

Figure 17. The four dimension in comprehensible writing and optimal ratings

Source: (Langer, Schulz von Thun, & Tausch, 1974/2002, (adapted))

Adhering to these four dimensions of comprehensibility, (Kroop & Mangler, 2006) developed a web-based tool, which allows to learn and train comprehensible writing in a cooperative way. This tool supports two different scenarios for cooperative learning. On the one hand, texts may be rewritten individually and discussed afterwards. In a second scenario, this tool combines the simple Wiki system (Leuf & Cunningham, 2001) and forum discussion, which is more rigid than the common Wiki system but, instead, adds to an overall transparency of the rewriting process.

4.3 Thinking processes

(Tausch & Tausch, 1963/1998, p. 297) observed that thinking processes, such as combining facts, abstraction, or creative problem solving, are rare phenomena in traditional class settings. In order to allow readers to better understand the nature of thinking processes in learning settings, following descriptions of characteristics shall give an idea (Tausch & Tausch, 1963/1998, pp. 298-307).

- Thinking processes occur during the investigation of complex problems with non-obvious solutions. In such cases, people use learned (trained) knowledge and experience.
- Thinking processes follow non-linear patterns and are unpredictable. Hence, they are highly different among persons even for similar problems. Put differently, different people go distinct thinking paths to come to the same solution.
- Talking and thinking are related. It appears that talking makes thinking easier. However, thinking advances can occur without becoming aware linguistically.
- Thinking processes are particularly furthered when problems and solutions of personal interest and significance are tackled. In particular, tackling of complex situations and problems furthers longer-lasting and autonomous thinking processes.
- Combining and structuring are main aspects of thinking processes.
- Comparison, restructuring, and abstraction are thinking processes prevalent in evaluating and valuing of decisions and actions.
- People are often not aware of their thinking processes. The solution evolves almost automatically, without deliberate thinking.

Thinking processes go beyond short-term rote memorisation and foster the re-application and adaptation of knowledge to novel situations. (Tausch & Tausch, 1963/1998, pp. 300-303) provide examples for thinking processes in class:

- comparing phenomena to match similarities or identify differences,
- creating new ideas and finding problem solutions,
- combining, reorganising, and classifying of facts, objects, phenomena, or experiences,
- planning and organising of problem-solving processes,
- abstracting common similarities and characteristics, and
- searching for examples.

Typically, a person's thinking processes cover the whole spectrum from applying learned knowledge to independent thinking. Examples of students' behaviour at these both extremes are shown in Figure 18. Promotive, non-directive activities aim at furthering independent thinking; hence, although a person's behaviour will naturally include the whole spectrum, little by little more behaviour should reflect what is described next to the lower arrow (independent thinking and reasoning).

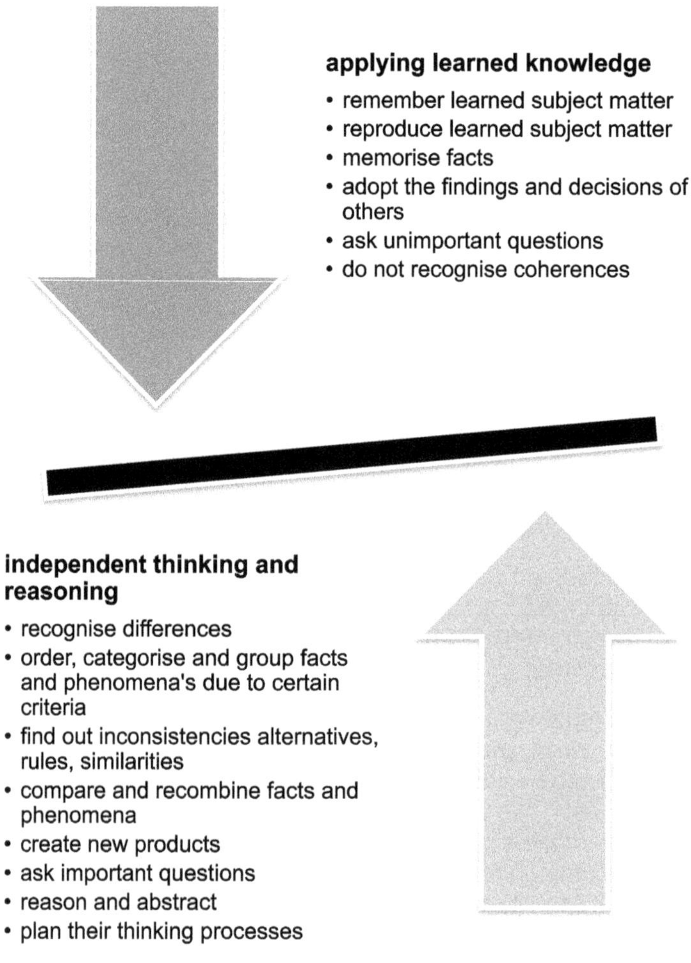

Figure 18. Kinds of thinking processes

Source: (Tausch & Tausch, 1963/1998, p. 305, (adapted))

In person-centred courses, the course objectives and the expectations of students as well as of the facilitator are typically discussed in the beginning of the course. However, after this discussion, other topics are on the agenda and especially in large groups it is not unusual that some goals get forgotten. Speech evaporates, as we already know. In order to keep these goals in mind and to make these transparent to the whole group, it is beneficial to collect each person's goals, expectations, and reservations in an online sequence and to make this collection available to the group on an e-learning platform. Besides being transparent to the whole group, this written account of course goals and group direction can be continuously revisited and potentially revised throughout the course and each participant can take care of following his or her personal targets. This transparency primarily supports the final self-evaluation process, which is aimed at evoking students' (and optimally also the facilitator's) reflection processes. Besides this final reflection, which is a thinking process, the continuous revision of the course goal assembly furthers thinking processes throughout a course. Table 4 illustrates the results of a team-based discussion about learning targets and reservations in a basic course on *PROJECT MANAGEMENT – BASICS AND TECHNIQUES*.

Table 4. Top eight expectations and individual fears in the course on *PROJECT MANAGEMENT – BASICS AND TECHNIQUES*

EXPECTATIONS	NOMINATIONS
learning of planning and management tools	10
project planning / project management	9
team management / work / ability / composition / motivation	9
estimate on effort (time, budget, man hours)	8
risk management / risk assessment	7
crisis management	7
gain practical experience / realise project	6
change management / change request	5

FEARS AND RESERVATIONS
too much programming
only lecture format
having little / no relation to practice
too much documentation work
tight schedule
concurrent use of two different e-learning platforms

Another instance of promoting thinking is the free choice to select a topic according to personal interest or the formulation of project visions by student teams. In project-based courses (e.g., *WEB ENGINEERING* or *PROJECT MANAGEMENT*), the facilitator may provide a list of potential project themes, from which students may select. Additionally, this list may contain an item like *or any other topic to be discussed with the facilitator*. Experience demonstrates that students frequently suggest their own topics or adapt existing ones driven by their particular interests. Once again, it turned out to be useful to provide the initial list of topics on the e-learning platform, as this allows students to think thoroughly before they come to their decisions. As a consequence, thinking processes are longer and also more intense than when they have to reach an ad-hoc decision in class. On the other hand, students are more likely to find topics that are personally meaningful to them when they have enough time to think; with topics they are interested in, motivation is most likely to rise.

Again, the facilitator's attitude plays a key role. Only if it is communicated clearly and honestly that proposing a new topic is highly welcome, students will make use of this offer. In a course on *eBusiness in the Creative Industries* for students of business administration (Master's programme) held in summer term 2008 at the University of Vienna, the facilitator proposed a set of topics and added that any further topic that fits the course objective is welcome. Nobody made use of this offer; only one student team (a dyad) adapted a topic by narrowing down the scope for going into detail. In this course setting, the facilitator did not emphasise the free choice of topics but merely augmented the course by the option that students could involve themselves in proposing topics if they wanted to. Main concern for the facilitator's well thought out topic proposal had been that the most important topics had to be covered by the course. The scope for deviations had been limited although it definitely existed. It appears that students perceived this attitude (maybe even stronger than intended) and stuck to the topics predefined by the facilitator. This example illustrates that the responsibility to foster or restrain thinking processes lies with the facilitator to a great extent. If the facilitator had made her intentions transparent in this course setting, students would probably have made use of the possibility to propose topics themselves in the given scope. Without this transparency of intentions, expectations, and objectives, they could not exploit their freedom of choice since they could not judge the setting accordingly due to the lack of corresponding information.

Besides goals, expectations, and vision statements, cooperative brainstorming processes are well supported by computerised services (C. Bauer, 2002; Mangler & Bauer, 2004). In a technology-enhanced environment, participants can raise their issues independently without being influenced by their peers. Subsequently, ideas can be discussed and elaborated further in the next presence phase. Such a scenario evokes students' individual thinking processes, while in a large face-to-face group brainstorming tends to be narrowed to just a few dominating ideas (C.

Bauer, 2002). Moreover, information about the frequency of topics or ideas mentioned can be easily traced in technology-enhanced environments. This information can give direction on students' perceived importance of the respective topics, and can serve as a guide for further, group-orientated action.

The combination of presence phases and online learning elements is not only useful for brainstorming sessions, but also particularly beneficial for other thinking processes. Following example of a PhD seminar, where all students wished to broaden their view on the topic of their dissertations, will illustrate this proposition. In the presence phase, students and the facilitator elaborated collectively the overlaps of the topics and the facilitator drew a mind map on a flipchart. Thereafter, students used the interactive e-learning platform to present their main themes, raised specific (research) questions, engaged in forum discussions, and shared resources and links. In a follow-up meeting, students and the facilitator collectively agreed on topics to be elaborated based on the participants' expertise and interests. Finally, students gave brief presentations on these topics followed by substantial discussion. Reflecting on the course, one student posted following reaction at the end of the seminar, "*I liked using the e-learning platform very much, because I had the opportunity to gain deeper insight into the topics elaborated by the other participants than in conventional seminars. The idea to have short presentations and long discussions turned out to be very effective. Because of the exchange of viewpoints in the discussions following the presentations everyone could get more into the other topics, contrary to the one-way communication predominant at long presentation sessions.*"

While the above described scenarios highlight the value of technology enhancement, the teaching method *brainstorming and reflection* (Figure 19), which had been implemented as a means for facilitating thinking processes in the course *EBUSINESS IN THE CREATIVE INDUSTRIES* for business administration students in summer term 2008 as well as winter term 2008/2009, illustrates an example that is rather independent from technology as it is a method that is carried out in a presence phase. Still, appropriate media selection may assist educators in keeping record of students' brainstorming results and facilitate comparison of results. With regard to students, the educator's choice of technology will not impact learning, as long as the educator is able to handle the respective medium well.

Basically, the promotive activity *brainstorming and reflection* may be used to introduce new concepts and definitions that seem familiar to stu-

of Microsoft PowerPoint®, allowing for recording the ideas digitally and presenting them in an appropriate way. Having a suitable presentation available that allows for comparing both brainstorming results right after the second brainstorming may not be that easy. Moreover, educators have to make sure that they have the first brainstorming results available at the end of the semester. Although it is not impossible to handle it (even using flip charts would do), a web-based solution may offer certain advantages: providing an easy to use form for registering ideas and a report functionality that allows displaying both brainstorming results next to each other at a click of a mouse button release educators from some preparation overhead. Furthermore, if that well prepared, educators may be relaxed enough to concentrate on moderating the brainstorming and discussion processes. In a nutshell, it may not make any difference for students which alternative the educator selects, for the educator it however does.

Summarising, shared resources and supporting features on an e-learning platform are convenient means of capturing results and reflections from thinking processes. While in presence phases, the actual thinking processes in class prevail, the deployment of technological means enables to capture also thinking processes that proceed outside class. Furthermore, as already stressed in other sections, technology-enhanced environments are capable of extending thinking and learning processes. While processes tend to interrupt between course units in traditional learning settings without technology deployment, learning that proceeds in technology-enhanced person-centred learning settings.

4.4 Furthering a beneficial working process

Involving expertise and personal attitudes, facilitators may further self-directed learning by considering appropriate structuring conditions. (Tausch & Tausch, 1963/1998, p. 307) give examples of activities that may positively affect the working progress in education, which they subsume under three headings:

- learning to know the task personally,
- professional elaboration and investigation of subtasks, and
- finalising, exploiting, and / or applying the work.

Adhering to the same structure, the next Sections discuss the examples given by (Tausch & Tausch, 1963/1998, p. 307) and analyse these promotive activities' eligibility for technology-enhanced learning environments emphasising the particular pedagogical enrichment.

4.4.1 Learning to know the task personally

Basically, there are three components to consider for approaching new tasks in educational settings (Tausch & Tausch, 1963/1998, pp. 308-309):

- confronting students with a task,
- furthering the spontaneous expression of personal thoughts and perceptions, and
- letting students follow their intuitive approaches to a problem.

For each of these components, there exist activities that seem particularly promotive.

Confrontation with the task

In educational settings, a new topic may be introduced by the facilitator, a student, the curriculum itself, or a particular event. (Tausch & Tausch, 1963/1998, p. 308) suggest showing the educational goals and current tasks openly in the learning area. Having these visible throughout a course does not only make goals and tasks transparent but also contributes to keeping them in mind.

At school, the information will mainly be hung-up in the classroom. In higher education, though, many different courses are held in the same room in rotation and students change lecture rooms frequently. Hence, it is difficult to provide the respective information on site. In such cases, the Internet offers an opportunity for making goals and tasks visible as information can be made available on the Internet – presumably on a course's e-learning platform. However, it makes a difference if students have to decide on their own to access the information in the online setting (*pull system*), while in the classroom it does not seem possible to avoid absorbing the information (at least unconsciously) since it is steadily presented within the room (*push system*). Still, the online information is a good complementation to its placement on site and a fairly acceptable substitute in cases where on-site placement is not possible.

Furthermore, (Tausch & Tausch, 1963/1998, p. 308) motivate the importance of the realness and concreteness of professional problems and tasks. The closer tasks are to problems that students face in their current (professional) environment, the more they will perceive the tasks as meaningful, and the more it will facilitate their learning.

In the field of business informatics, activities like communication, gathering information, as well as cooperation via the Internet constitute an immanent part of everyday work. Tasks involving the Internet, hence, represent an environment that students of business informatics and computer science will find themselves in when working after or already during their studies. Therefore, we assume that students will perceive tasks as close to real problems and meaningful when this kind of environment is involved. Subsequently, in the field of computer science, the thoughtful deployment of online working environments is ought to facilitate students' learning.

Spontaneous expression of personal thoughts and perceptions

A further option of approaching a tasks is to encourage students to deal with the subject as well as with their personal perceptions, feelings, and opinions towards the issue (Tausch & Tausch, 1963/1998, p. 308). Both positive and negative feelings should be equally accepted and responded to.

In principle, the expression of personal thoughts and perceptions is possible in any kind of setting as it is mainly an egocentric activity and does not involve others. Primarily, this activity aims at making a student aware of a task's or problem's specific meaning for him or herself. When the individuals are conscious about their relation to an issue, it is beneficial for the whole group since students will be more focussed on the particular tasks.

Spontaneity, though, seems better to be furthered in classroom settings as the online environment allows for thinking processes that go beyond ad hoc reactions (due to a rather high degree of self-attention, expanded time availability, low social presence, etc.). Nevertheless, the submission of online reaction sheets after face-to-face course units proved to be promotive for the expression of thoughts and perceptions. At their own pace, students express their perceptions in written reaction sheets (Motschnig-Pitrik, 2006a), which they submit via the e-learning platform and can be read by the facilitator and – from a predefined point in time – also by all participants. This verbalisation leads to an intense dealing with the subjects dealt with in the course and one's own feelings and perceptions.

(Walther, 1996, p. 26) points out that people may plan, contemplate, and compose comments and reactions more mindfully and deliberately in asynchronous settings than they are able to do spontaneously. Furthermore, people tend to render qualitatively different interpersonal impressions than they might convey in synchronous communication (Walther, 1992, p. 81). This, basically, also reflects our impression in comparing online reaction sheets and the closing sessions at the end of a course unit, in which every student expresses feedback spontaneously and orally. While comments in feedback sessions generally tend to remain superficial and students stick to a few topics, reactions sheets go deeper and address manifold topics and facets of perceptions.

Students' intuitive approaches to a problem

According to (Tausch & Tausch, 1963/1998, p. 309), self-dependent giving a try, intuitive thinking, as well as trial and error learning seem to be meaningful processes that are highly significant in everyday life.

Studies revealed that workers who were given the freedom to autonomously discuss, plan, and try out their ideas for a given assignment showed higher working morale and productivity than workers who had been carefully instructed by their managers (Tausch & Tausch, 1963/1998, p. 309). In educational settings, it seems, hence, necessary that facilitators at least initially hold back their own experience and views and motivate students to express their assumptions and approaches to a certain problem.

A technology-enhanced learning setting can be promotive as regards this aspect. When comparing means of online communication and a face-to-face setting, it can be observed that the latter is dominated by information that is already known by participants. Information and approaches that are not shared have only little chances of being considered. This imperfect exchange is mainly due to the tendency for conformity, which seems to be in high gear in face-to-face situations while lower when communicating by some computer-mediated means (Diehl & Ziegler, 2000, pp. 93-94). Since people tend to produce more ideas of higher quality when collaborating online (Hollingshead & McGrath, 1995, pp. 62, 75), it seems advantageous to initiate tasks in an online setting. So students can start to approach the problem individually and intuitively. In a later phase, they can bring together their ideas and collaborate on their tasks.

4.4.2 Professional elaboration and investigation of subtasks

According to (Tausch & Tausch, 1963/1998, p. 311) it is important that students and facilitators commit themselves to certain subtasks and targets. This learning phase is characterised by self-dependent elaboration in small teams, where students make use of learning material provided. Usually, this phase, in which teams work independently, is followed by interaction of the whole class where information is summarised, structured, and supplemented with professional points of view.

In the scope of having students elaborating and investigating subtasks, (Tausch & Tausch, 1963/1998, pp. 311-313) identified certain promotive activities, which are outlined in subsequent paragraphs:

- providing access to information sources,
- discussing in small teams, and
- providing professional support for work in small teams or individual work.

Access to information sources

According to (Tausch & Tausch, 1963/1998, p. 311), it facilitates learning when students access and elaborate information mainly autonomously and self-dependently. This way of approaching information has substantial similarities with information acquisition with manifold sources that dominates everyday life.

Usually, students' main access point to learning material is via the facilitator. Undoubtedly, the establishment of information material is an essential activity of facilitators (Tausch & Tausch, 1963/1998, p. 312). Collaboration with colleagues may help to improve texts' and presentations' comprehensibility (cf. Section 4.2). According to (Tausch & Tausch, 1963/1998, p. 312), it is easier to prepare comprehensible material in a self-paced manner than spontaneously, for instance, when giving an oral lecture in front of the whole class, frequently without documents (Tausch & Tausch, 1963/1998, p. 312). (Diehl & Ziegler, 2000, p. 94) basically support this idea since self-paced revision (as possible in asynchronous settings) grants the necessary time and ease for dealing with cognitively demanding technologies and thinking processes.

Beyond texts and lectures, the provision of manifold learning sources (e.g., experiments, videos, invitation of experts, visits to museums, etc.) is valuable since students tend to have different learning styles, thus, profiting from different kind of sources. Moreover, the combination of various sources facilitates students in discovering interrelations of topics and views and furthers them to analyse and question presented concepts instead of taking these for granted.

Making material available electronically proved to be helpful since the material can be updated whenever it deems necessary. Furthermore, an e-learning platform may provide support for structuring material adequately and allows for rearranging if necessary at a later point in time.

Moreover, technologies offer valuable opportunities for visualisation. For instance, graphically visualised algorithms contribute effectively to the ease of understanding.

Optionally, students can contribute to searching for material and providing these for the whole class. This explorative, open character is particularly suited to the person-centred learning style since students are free to explore the Internet and learn how to deal with and assess various sources (Motschnig-Pitrik & Derntl, 2002, pp. 4-5).

Discussions in small teams

Team-based learning has proven to be a powerful methodology that can be applied to a variety of disciplines and class sizes. This concept is gaining recognition for being beneficial far beyond facilitating learning on a content level but also furthering social skills and personality (Gomez & Bieber, 2005; Michaelsen, Knight, & Fink, 2002; Steenkamp, 2002). (Tausch & Tausch, 1963/1998, pp. 311-312) suggest work in small teams of two to four persons as promotive team size. Naturally, it is necessary to divide learning targets and content into sub-tasks and sub-targets in order to make these amenable for work in small teams.

Usually, time frames of course units will be dedicated to discussions in small teams. Discussions, however, are not limited to presence phases but may also serve as tie between course units in class. Team members may meet, engage in online discussions (e.g., by using according features of a provided e-learning platform), or even combine both. As experience has shown, self-assigned teams are particularly committed to discussions outside course units.

With additional deployment of electronic communication, we assume that thinking processes are extended and deepened with additional deployment of electronic communication.

Help and professional support for work in small teams or individual work

Previous paragraphs and sections stressed that self-dependent work is highly promotive for students' learning. Therefore, facilitators are ought to encourage students to work independently. Naturally, students will benefit from help and support. In doing so, facilitators may give individual help to particular teams or provide hints to all teams for avoiding difficulties and being able to better manage their tasks (Tausch & Tausch, 1963/1998, pp. 312-313).

The crucial point is that the facilitator is available for support and is willing to provide it.

4.4.3 Finalising, exploiting and / or applying work

Usually, students are occupied with a task for quite some time. By-and-by students delve deeper into the subject, acquire information, and turn it into knowledge. When the information is comprehensive and understandable, one closes work on that topic.

However, occasionally a task will be closed leaving some issues open. Studies revealed that, in real situations, people deal with open problems more often than with closed ones. Artificially closing a problem by completing, summarising, or giving final comments may yield the misleading impression that the field is indeed closed. Time by time, though, almost every topic calls for further learning, development, and progress (Tausch & Tausch, 1963/1998, p. 313).

Before proceeding with a new topic, it seems particularly fruitful if students try to find possibilities for the application of their learning. (Tausch & Tausch, 1963/1998, pp. 314-315) come up with following suggestions:

- Students develop activities that allow them to apply learning in their current environments.
- Students summarise topics and create information sheets for younger students.
- Students think of situations where they recently acquired knowledge that was helpful for the particular topic.

Technology-enhanced learning environments offer versatile options of organising knowledge and structuring learning processes. For project work, for instance, students can use web templates to upload documents needed to fulfil individual project milestones. This predefined, formalised structure of web templates results in a transparent project structure. Finally, students can present parts of these projects in class and discuss documents with the group. Furthermore, students are free to explore the solutions provided by their peers, which augments learning from their own examples and provides further viewpoints.

In courses that require practical skills such as modelling, performing surveys, programming, web design, etc., the provision of additional examples and respective online tools allows students to gain hands-on experience and test their skills based on their own pace. In more theoretical settings, the cooperative construction of a web-based hyperlinked knowledge base that can be reused for subsequent courses may structure thought processes and offers motivation.

A particularly simple but powerful element for a final reflection is the use of transparent online reaction sheets. After each major course unit or topic, students are asked to reflect on their learning and experiences (e.g., likes, dislikes, observations, suggestions, criticism, etc.) such that the facilitator and all peers of a course can read them. Such individual, profound reflections seem to evoke and simultaneously structure thinking processes such that students are ready for closing a topic.

Still, considering the person-centred approach to learning, it seems beneficial to devote the initial minutes of the following face-to-face meeting to discussing students' reactions. Such follow-up discussions with derived consequences for the design of subsequent course units (e.g., emphasising topics that students are currently concerned with) may give students a sense of being respected with all their feelings and concerns.

Online reaction sheets have a quality that cannot be achieved in face-to-face settings. Being influenced by successive statements, rather shy students tend to hold back their viewpoints in face-to-face settings. In an asynchronous online setting, where previous statements cannot be read before submitting a reflection oneself, all participants have the same chance to think about and express their concerns. At the same time, this setting allows facilitators to resonate on the feedback before talking to students. Hence, if taken seriously, reaction sheets are highly effective means of furthering the group process.

4.5 Working in teams

Work in small teams is a proven method for furthering self-directed learning and constructive personality development (Tausch & Tausch, 1963/1998, p. 253; Michaelsen, Knight, & Fink, 2002). In the context of higher education it can be employed to solve complex problems, to work on small-scale projects, or for writing seminar and research papers (Tausch & Tausch, 1963/1998, p. 258).

Beyond acquiring technical knowledge, students develop their team competencies (for details on the development of team competence see (Figl, 2008, 2009)). Team members are in close contact with each other, learn how to organise and make decisions in a team, and learn about the consequences of their own actions (Tausch & Tausch, 1963/1998, p. 260). Promotive facilitators provide teams with relevant content and working resources, coach teams concerning team organisation but also technical issues, and make themselves available to the students on demand (Tausch & Tausch, 1963/1998, p. 259).

Characteristic for team-based learning is that students show supportive behaviour within the team, where both personal and context-specific issues are discussed. In their interactive information exchange and collective elaboration, team members tend to promote each other to reach a higher level. Moreover the contact with other people is perceived as socially and emotionally satisfying (Tausch & Tausch, 1963/1998, pp. 261-262).

In contrast to the traditional approach, students tend to learn more contentedly through social interaction enjoying their freedom to be more creative and act on behalf of their own. Furthermore, they learn to express their feelings and to be less strained but rather motivated. (Tausch & Tausch, 1963/1998, pp. 253, 260-261) summarise that students:

- work and think independently,
- work and think individually as well as cooperatively,
- train their communication skills,
- learn about different points of view,
- learn how to cope with different opinions and conflicts,
- take responsibility for decisions made in teams,
- learn to organise themselves when working with peers,
- develop their own solutions,
- improve their social skills by discussions and mutual help, and
- have more motivation and joy in working and learning.

Corresponding online tools can support work in teams effectively. Amongst other tools, the following features, which are, for instance, implemented in the platform CEWebS (Mangler, 2005), proved very useful.

Web-supported team building

Without technological assistance, an educator may assign students to teams on random. Alternatively, students form teams in class, write down their names on a sheet of paper, which the facilitator collects.

The team-building tool by (Mangler, 2005, pp. 78-79) provides technological assistance that allows students to assign themselves to teams, just by clicking on the respective names in the participants' pool. Once assigned to a team, students can easily change to another team or put themselves back to the participants' pool just by clicking on the respective group heading.

Basically the facilitator's interface allows choosing among different configurations:

- The facilitator sets a maximum number per team. The system does not allow forming teams with more students than allowed. Put differently, when a user tries to switch to a team that has already reached the maximum number of students (or if a student is selected from the pool for such a team), the system does not allow this action.
- Furthermore, the facilitator can lock the service, which is usually done when the team building process is completed. When the system is locked, students can neither switch teams nor move back to the pool.

Students can form teams without pressure in a rather relaxed atmosphere at home. Additionally, time traditionally used for team building in presence phases may be dedicated to other activities. Furthermore, the risks for typing errors (which happens frequently with a pen and pencil team assignment) or overlooking a student are eliminated since all participants are within the system and the team-building process is only finished when the participants' pool is empty. Moreover, the whole process is transparent to both students and facilitator (Mangler, 2005, p. 79).

This very simple and easy to use tool (Figure 20) is widely accepted among students and proved to be very supportive (cf. Mangler, 2005, pp. 78-79).

Workspace for teams

Besides providing workspaces for the whole group or for individual students, e-learning platforms can provide support for work in small teams. Team workspaces provide team members, for example, the possibility to upload and revise material in their space. Students may be allowed to read but not overwrite material in other teams' workspaces. Other pedagogical designs will require that students have only access to their particular team's workspace until a certain event, when interaction of the whole group begins.

In either case, these online workspaces support cooperative work and responsibility for tasks (cf. Derntl, 2005, pp. 292-302).

Online peer reviews

While peer reviews can have assessment character, they can also be used in a formative way giving direction to students for improving their work. In the context of project-based courses (e.g., *WEB ENGINEERING*, *PROJECT MANAGEMENT – BASICS AND TECHNIQUES*), teams may be assigned to partner teams (or they may assign themselves to partner teams) that are responsible for reviewing project documents and consulting teams to improve their results.

Generally, students find this experience with taking on different perspectives helpful and supply constructive comments, which are taken up by the originating teams. Besides supporting the originating teams in improving their work, peer reviews also positively impact reviewer teams' perspectives.

While peer reviews have a long tradition in a pen-and-paper version, the online setting provides certain benefits that reach from the easiness of the handling of forms to major differences concerning the kind and quaility of comments (cf. Section 7).

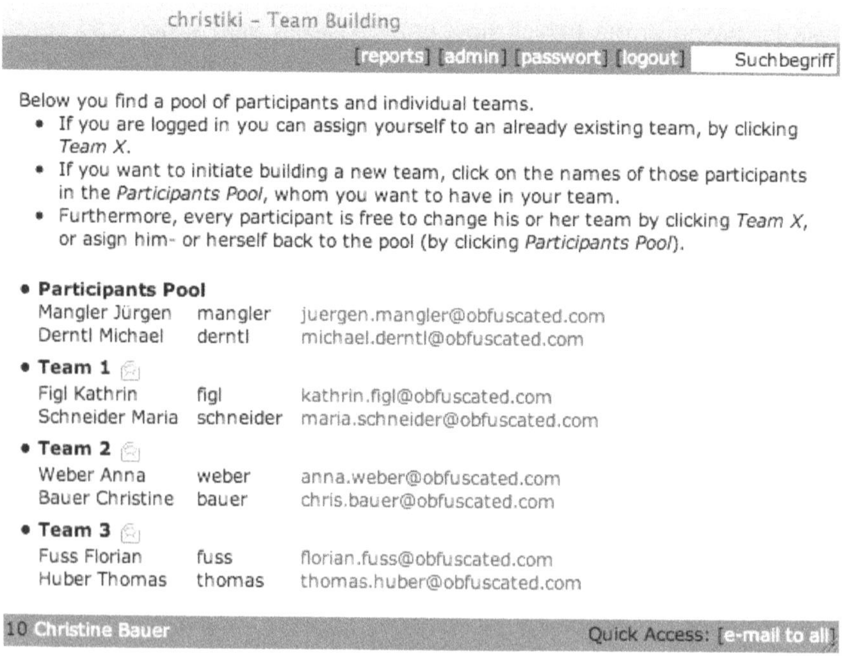

Figure 20. Web-supported team building

4.6 Learning contracts

Combining freedom with responsibility and promoting self-initiated learning, learning contracts have long been recognised as an effective alternative to exams and tests (Rogers, 1983). Basically, facilitator and learners specify learning objectives as well as resources and activities that lead to the achievement of these goals. Then they sign a contract that can be used in the final grading.

This pedagogically highly effective means is, however, time consuming. Consequently, it appears to be applicable for a limited number of students only. With technology support, the number of student teams who work on learning contracts can be increased as experience has shown (Motschnig-Pitrik, Derntl, & Mangler, 2003). Specifically, web services can provide organisational and administrative support, in particular with respect to managing learning contracts as well as peer- and self-evaluation.

For instance, (Motschnig-Pitrik, Derntl, & Mangler, 2003) report on the use of technology-supported learning contracts in a course on *Web Engineering* with no less than 355 participants. Instead of making learning contracts mandatory, they offered students the option to work in small teams of up to four persons on the elaboration of material in the context of their studies (learning contract *Web Engineering Learning License, WELL*) instead of taking a conventional exam. As can be seen from the activity diagram depicted in Figure 21, students deciding in favour of the WELL contract should propose a topic, fill in the agreement (which is outlined in Figure 22), and sign it.

During the semester students had to find resources, plan the table of contents, and define the date for an intermediate version to be checked by the facilitator. Subsequently they elaborated their projects, which they finally uploaded onto the e-learning platform to make it available to be read by all peers. Eventually, 299 out of the 355 students (84%) decided to engage in this kind of constructive work rather than taking the written exam.

The evaluation phase constituted of three parts, combining face-to-face and online elements and including different points of view:

- *Self-evaluation.* Each team had to submit an evaluation of its own work, which had to include a suggestion of grades for each individual team member. These self-evaluations were visible for facilitators only.
- *Peer-evaluation.* Furthermore, each student taking part in the WELL project had to review at least three contributions of peer teams.
- *Discussion with facilitator.* In a final session, students discussed their contributions with the facilitator. This final discussion aimed at checking students' understanding of the subject matter.

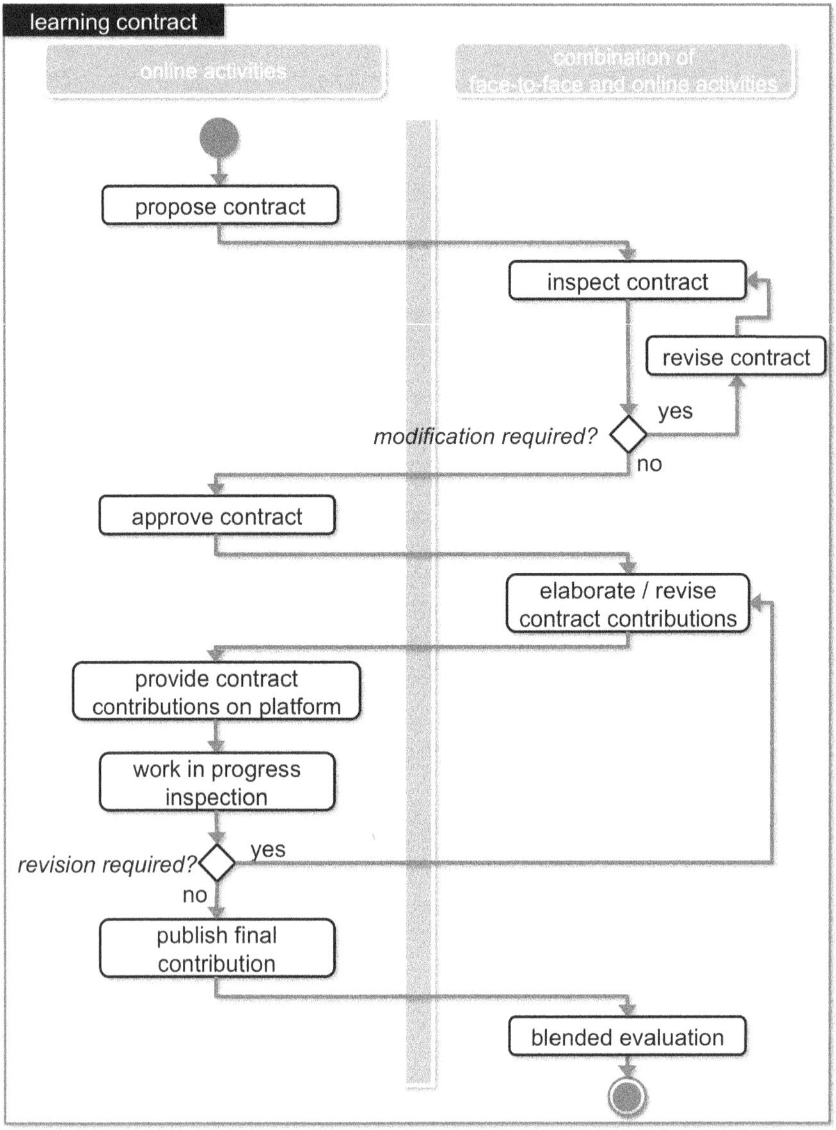

Figure 21. UML activity diagram for WELL learning contracts

Source: (Motschnig-Pitrik, Derntl, & Mangler, 2003, p. 1186; Derntl, 2005, p. 382, (merged and adapted))

Group / team number:

Instructor:

Team members with e-mail address:

Topic:

Goals:

Activities and documents:

Significant changes and their dates:

Intermediate version accepted on:

Final version due:

Signature team representative:

Signature instructor:

Figure 22. Structure of WELL contracts

Source: (Motschnig-Pitrik, Derntl, & Mangler, 2003, p. 1185, (adapted))

Figure 23 provides an overview of the evaluation phase indicating which elements were carried out online or in a face-to-face setting.

The quantitative study of (Motschnig-Pitrik, Derntl, & Mangler, 2003) confirmed that in comparison to taking a conventional exam, 72.8% of the WELL project participants valued their long term learning effect as higher. Additionally, 64% of the WELL participants considered the engagement in the WELL project as more time intensive. Almost equal results were obtained in a subsequent study in 2004 (C. Bauer et al., 2006, p. 32), when the WELL project was repeated. 78.3% of the WELL participants valued the learning effect as higher and 65% considered the required time investment as higher when compared to taking a conventional exam.

The combined qualitative and empirical analyses (Motschnig-Pitrik, Derntl, & Mangler, 2003) indicate that learning contracts are promotive as students were motivated to put extra effort into their project work and felt that their learning effect was deeper when compared with learning for conventional exams.

This example suggests learning contracts as highly promotive activities in higher education. At the same time, we claim that without technology support, an analogous scenario with more than 350 students would have practically been infeasible due to administrative overhead.

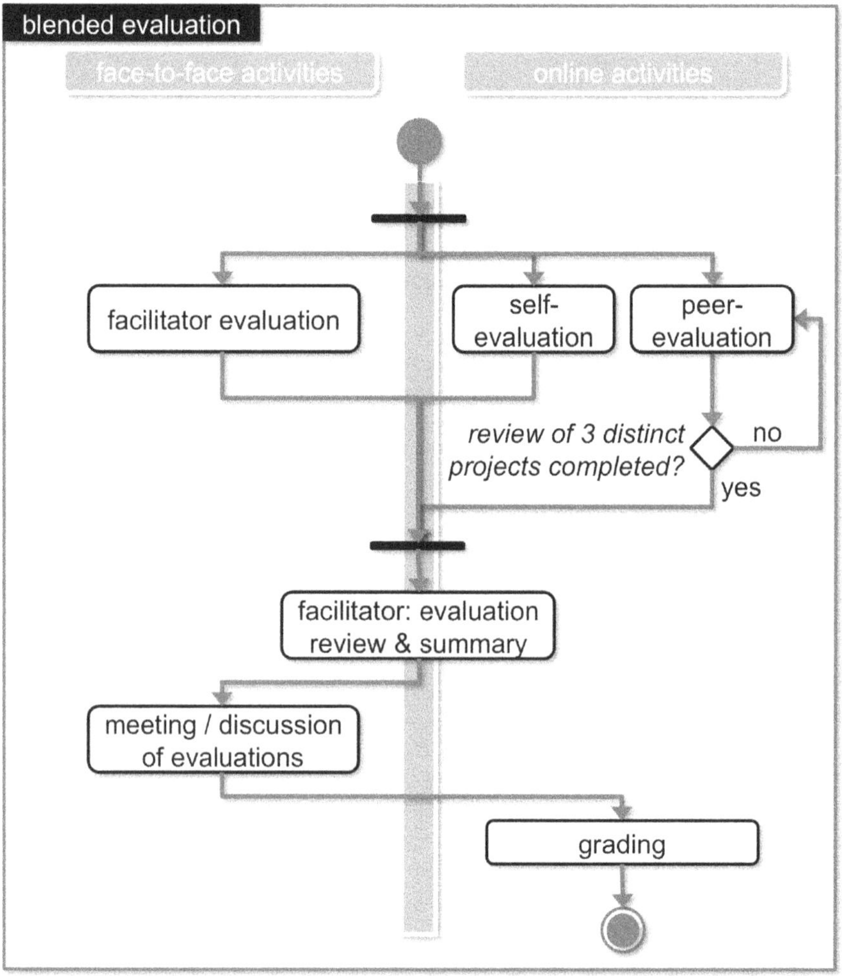

Figure 23. UML activity diagram for the blended evaluation scenario as used for the learning contracts

Source: (Motschnig-Pitrik, Derntl, & Mangler, 2003, p. 1186; Derntl, 2005, p. 187, (merged and adapted))

4.7 Living together in a good group

Last but not least, students consider a positive working atmosphere as one of the top motivational factors. Subsequently, a good working climate significantly contributes to the effectiveness of learning.

Starting with an example, (Motschnig-Pitrik & Mallich, 2004) provides an analysis of individual factors contributing to the course-style cluster. The expected (students' perceptions in the beginning of the semester) and perceived values (evaluation in the end of the semester) of the course-style factors in a course on *PROJECT MANAGEMENT – BASICS AND TECHNIQUES* (held in winter term 2003/2004) are given in Figure 24. This finding clearly illustrates the importance of providing a constructive learning climate. In fact, the positive atmosphere was perceived as highest (mean=4.67 on a five-point Likert scale) among all motivational factors in the course, closely followed by the collegial cooperation among peers (mean=4.53).

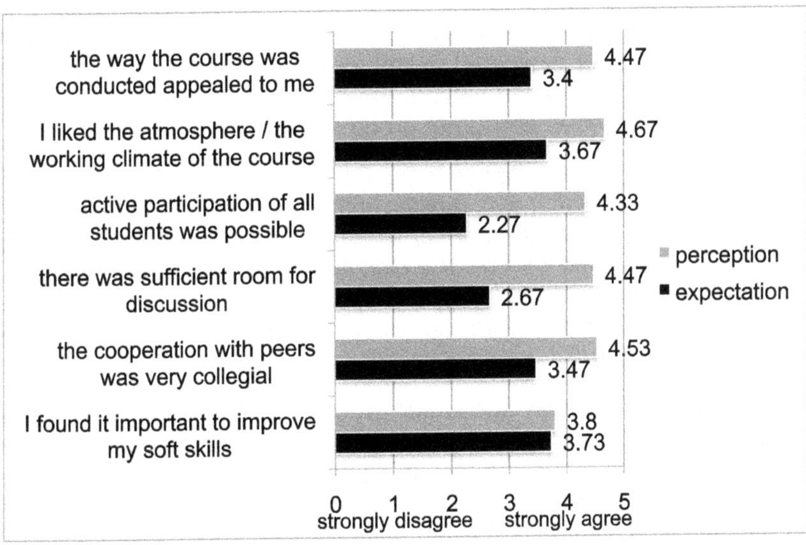

Figure 24. Motivational orientation due to various factors regarding the course style for a typical course (*expectation*) compared with the course on *PROJECT MANAGEMENT – BASICS AND TECHNIQUES* (*perception*), n=15

Source: (Motschnig-Pitrik & Mallich, 2004, p. 185, (adapted))

(Tausch & Tausch, 1963/1998) and (Rogers, 1983) agree that the development towards a *good group* proceeds by allowing for autonomous interaction as well as furthering the exchange of personal perceptions

5 Methods

Although the research field that analyses the use of information and communication technologies in educational settings already exists for some time, it still cannot look back on a long history and has, thus, not yet established its own framework of assessment methods. Rather, as it is interdisciplinary in its core (educational sciences, psychology, computers science, communication science, social science, business administration & economics), it makes use of its related disciplines' methodology.

The Research Lab for Educational Technologies at the University of Vienna pursues the action research approach (cf. Baskerville, 1999). This work is to be seen as part of this action research process. Lessons learned from previous findings are taken into account for this research, as will be this work's findings for future research at the research lab. Hence, although this research project itself does not follow the action research approach, it is to be considered that this methodology plays a prominent role in the broader research field.

Action research consists of a range of research methods, which pursue action and research outcomes at the same time. The discipline of business informatics including information and communication technologies seems to be very appropriate for the use of action research methods. Since communication systems are by no means purely technical but rather social-technical systems, isolation of single variables and keeping them constant (in terms of natural sciences' instruments) may lead to biased results. Action research challenges this aspect. By means of deployment of technology-enhanced learning and collaboration methods, the goals can be approached gradually. Based on students' and facilitators' experiences, reactions, and reflections, the blend will improve towards an atmosphere that enhances learning, improves learning outcomes in the actual setting, and furthers continuous learning for life beyond a particular course.

5.1 Research strategies in social sciences

Research strategies represent different ways of collecting and analysing empirical evidence. And each research strategy has its particular advantages and disadvantages (Yin, 1984/1989, p. 15).

Formerly, the various research strategies were arrayed strictly hierarchically, assuming that case studies were appropriate for the exploratory phase of a research, surveys and histories for the descriptive phase, and that experiments were the only approach qualified for explanatory investigations. However, meanwhile this hierarchical view is regarded as incorrect and replaced by a pluralistic view. This pluralistic view claims that each strategy can be used for all three purposes, whether exploratory, descriptive, or explanatory (Yin, 1984/1989, pp. 15-16). According to (Yin, 1984/1989, pp. 16-20) a research strategy's appropriateness is not based on this hierarchy but rather depends on three other conditions: the type of research question, the extent of control that an investigator has over behavioural events, and the degree of focus on contemporary as opposed to historical events.

Types of research questions (Table 5, column 2)

A basic categorisation scheme for questions is the familiar series: who, what, where, how, and why.

Research questions focusing on what may be of two natures: some types are exploratory (e.g., What are the ways in which a course is performed effectively?), some actually represent a how many or how much line of inquiry (e.g., What have been the outcomes from a particular managerial reorganisation?). The first type of what question is a justifiable rationale for conducting an explorative study aiming at developing hypotheses and propositions for further inquiry. For explorative studies, any of the five research strategies can be used (e.g., exploratory survey, exploratory experiment, exploratory case study) (Yin, 1984/1989, p. 17).

The second type of what questions (which represent a how many or how much line of inquiry), the questions how many and how much, as well as who and where questions, which all target at identifying and / or enumerating outcomes, are more likely to favour survey or archival strategies than others. These strategies are advantageous, when the research aims at describing the incidence or prevalence of a phenomenon or when the investigation is to be predictive about certain outcomes. Typical examples for these strategies are, for instance, the investigation of the incidence of a disease (where an analysis of vital statistics is frequently the favoured strategy) or of prevalent political attitudes (where a survey or a poll might be the favoured strategy) (Yin, 1984/1989, pp. 17-18).

How and why questions, in contrast, have rather explanatory character and will, thus, more likely lead to the use of case studies, histories, and experiments as preferred research strategies. Such questions deal with interdependencies and developments, which need to be traced over time, rather than with mere frequencies or incidence at a certain point in time (Yin, 1984/1989, p. 18). For instance, if you want to investigate why trust in business does not occur under certain conditions, you could design and accomplish a series of experiments.

In a nutshell, how and why questions are likely to favour the use of case studies, experiments, or histories. What questions, on the other hand, may either be exploratory (in which case any of the five strategies could be used) or about prevalence (favouring surveys or the analysis of archival records) (Yin, 1984/1989, p. 19).

Table 5. Relevant situations for different research strategies

	FORM OF RESEARCH QUESTION	REQUIRES CONTROL OVER BEHAVIOURAL EVENTS?	FOCUSES ON CONTEMPORARY EVENTS?
experiment	what (explorative) how why	yes	yes
survey	who what (explorative) what (how many, how much) where how many how much	no	yes
archival analysis (e.g., economic study)	who what (explorative) what (how many, how much) where how many how much	no	yes / no
history	what (explorative) how why	no	no
case study	what (explorative) how why	no	yes

Source: (Yin, 1984/1989, p. 17, (adapted))

Extent of control over behavioural events (Table 5, column 3)

When how and why questions or what questions of explorative character are the focus of study, a further distinction between experiment, history, and case study is the extent of control that an investigator has over behavioural events. The investigators have virtually no access or control when no relevant person is alive to report (even retrospectively) about what occurred. They have to rely on primary and secondary documents or on cultural and physical artefacts as the main sources of evidence. In such cases, histories are the preferred strategy. Accordingly the historical method is characterised by dealing with the *dead past* (Yin, 1984/1989, p. 19).

Besides histories, also the case study is used when the relevant behaviours cannot be manipulated, although in some situations, such as participant-observation, informal manipulation can occur. However, in contrast to the history, this method is preferred in examining contemporary events (Yin, 1984/1989, pp. 19-20).

Experiments need full control over events and are, thus, carried out when investigators can manipulate behaviour directly, precisely, and systematically. In contrast to the widespread misbelief, experiments can occur in laboratory settings or be done in a field setting. Presuming that the laboratory environment can control for all the remaining variables, the laboratory experiment focuses on one or two isolated variables. The term *social experiment* has emerged to cover research in a field setting where investigators treat whole groups of people in different ways (e.g., follow different educational scenarios). However, again the methods overlap and experimental science also includes situations in which the logic of experimental design may be applied although the experimenter can manipulate behaviour (quasi-experimental situations) (Yin, 1984/1989, p. 20).

To summarise, when the investigation (trying to answer how, why, or explorative what questions) allows for manipulation of behaviour, an experiment may be the appropriate research strategy, while histories and case studies are preferred when there is virtually little or no control over behavioural events (Yin, 1984/1989, pp. 19-20).

Degree of focus on contemporary as opposed to historical events (Table 5, column 4)

As already mentioned above, histories and case studies can overlap and rely on many of the same techniques. These strategies mainly distinguish in the focus on the consideration of contemporary and historical events respectively. While histories rely on past events (e.g., primary and secondary documents, cultural and physical artefacts), case studies investigate contemporary events. Although these strategies can overlap, the case study's unique strength is its ability to deal with a full variety of evidence, adding two sources of evidence not usually included in the historian's repertoire: direct observation and systematic interviewing (Yin, 1984/1989, pp. 19-20).

As has been discussed above, some situations do not have a clearly preferred strategy and, thus, all of the five research strategies might be relevant (e.g., exploratory research). In some situations a specific strategy has a distinct advantage. And in other situations two strategies might be considered equally attractive since the strengths and weaknesses of these strategies may overlap (e.g., how and why a certain president got elected). The basic approach is to consider all the strategies in a pluralistic fashion from which researchers draw according to the given situation.

Furthermore, it is possible to use more than one strategy within one study (for instance, a survey within a case study or a case study within a survey) since, to this extent, the various strategies are not mutually exclusive (Yin, 1984/1989, pp. 20, 25).

Contrary to the widely held belief, the contrast between quantitative and qualitative evidence does not distinguish the various research strategies. For instance, experiments (e.g., studies of psychophysical perceptions) or survey questions (e.g., those seeking categorical rather than numerical responses) may rely on qualitative rather than on quantitative evidence. Case studies, on the other hand, can include or even be limited to quantitative evidence (Yin, 1984/1989, p. 24; 1993, p. 3).

5.2 Research strategies in business informatics

Business informatics understands itself as science, which makes use of pluralistic research strategies and methods that are borrowed from theoretical science, real science, and engineering science (Wilde & Hess, 2007, p. 280). The methodical self-conception of business informatics is thereby based on two distinct paradigms – constructivism and behaviourism (Wilde & Hess, 2007, p. 281):

- *Constructivism.* In business informatics, the constructivist paradigm (design science) targets at the development of useful IT solutions, which are developed proactively and researched an evaluated in form of models, methods or systems.
- *Behaviourism.* In contrast to constructivism, the behavioural science is a reactive paradigm and analyses the designs of existing IT solutions and its effects on companies or markets.

Already the divergence of these scientific positions hazards the guess that business informatics makes use of a wide methodical spectrum.

(Heinrich, 2005, p. 110) criticises business informatics for its rarely noticeable methodical advancement. An analysis of 538 scientific articles reveals that researchers in the field of business informatics focus on descriptive methods and design (conceptual design, development, construction, and implementation) but do rarely explain issues. Frequently, papers do not make the methods transparent that were used for descriptions and designs – or researchers may even not act methodically. Business informatics is, thus, characterised by a rather descriptive methodology and particular focus on design.

Besides these aspects that are apparently important in research, the explanatory aspect is also essential in and for research and must not be neglected. Hence, authors need to disclose their perspective and approach to the respective problems and make the methodologies transparent to the scientific community. According to (Heinrich, 2005, pp. 111-112), this aspect is still underdeveloped in the field of business informatics and demands for strong improvement. Furthermore, (Heinrich, 2005, p. 112) claims that researchers in the field of business informatics still lack the appropriate methodical background. Oskar Morgenstern is alleged to have said about his colleagues in economics that they simply do not know what science means. Without being able to cite a personality like Morgenstern, this statement is sometimes also attributed to computer science: *Computer scientists do now know what science means.* Torn between economics and computer science, the statement would nowadays apply for business informatics – provided that it would be true for the one or the other (Heinrich, 2005, p. 112). Obviously, this statement is pure provocation. The fact is, that much research in business informatics lacks in a profound declaration of the applied methods with an appropriate explanation for the choice of methods. Empirical research approaches force researchers more strongly to disclose the applied methods than other – rather theoretical – approaches. Consequently, it is not surprising that empirical investigations explain the applied methodologies in most cases (Heinrich, 2005, p. 112).

In contrast to (Heinrich, 2005), (Wilde & Hess, 2007) could find a scale of methods, which have been explicitly declared by the authors, in a profound analysis of journal articles. They could identify 14 essential methods used in business informatics, which are summarised and described in Table 6:

- formal, conceptual and argumentative-deductive analysis,
- simulation,
- reference modelling,

- action research,
- prototyping,
- ethnography,
- case study,
- grounded theory,
- qualitative as well as quantitative cross-section analysis, and
- laboratory experiment as well as field experiment.

Table 6. The methodical spectrum in business informatics

METHOD	DESCRIPTION
formal, conceptual and argumentative-deductive analysis	Deduction can take place on different levels of formalisation: ▪ within the scope of mathematical-formal models, ▪ in semi-formal models (conceptual; e.g., Petri net), or ▪ on a language level (argumentative; e.g., the non-formal principal agent theory) These three variants are regarded as three separate methods.
simulation	A simulation represents an investigated system's behaviour in a formal model. Environment is represented and determined by model parameters. Both model construction and observations with endogenous model measures, lead to findings.
reference modelling	Reference modelling creates inductively (based o observations) or deductively (e.g., based on theories or models) simplified and optimised representations (ideal concepts) of systems in order to deepen existing insights and, based on this discovery, generate design templates.
action research	A real problem is solved including experts from academia and business. Research pursues several cycles of analysis, action, and evaluation. Each of these deploys low structured instruments like, for instance, group discussion or business games.
prototyping	Prototyping refers to developing and evaluating a preliminary version of an application system. Both steps can lead to new insights.
ethnography	Ethnography is based on participatory observation. It is more extensive than case study since the researcher integration into the investigated social environment. An objective distance is barely existent.
case study	Usually, a case study investigates complex, hardly delimitable phenomena in their natural contexts. Frequently it represents a special form of qualitative-empirical

	methods that research few units of observations intensively. Dependent on the perspective, it focuses the objective as possible investigation of assumptions (behaviourism) or the interpretation of behavioural patterns as phenotypes of the construed realities of the subjects (constructivism).
grounded theory	Grounded theory targets at the inductive generation of new theories by intensive observations. The different processes for coding and analyses of the predominantly qualitative data are exactly specified.
qualitative /quantitative cross-section analysis	These two methods aggregate data collection methods like questionnaires, interviews, Delphi method, content analysis, etc. Data collection is performed once (unrepeated) from several individuals; then data is quantitatively or qualitatively coded and analysed. Findings provide cross-section picture of the sample and typically allows inference to population.
laboratory experiment / field experiment	The experiment investigates causal connection in controllled environment by manipulating a variable in a repeatable manner and measuring the effects of the manipulation. The subject is either researched in the natural environment (field) or in an artificially setting (laboratory); evidently the setting considerably impacts the opportunities to control the environment.

Source: (Wilde & Hess, 2007, p. 282, (adapted))

Frequency analysis reveals that six core methods are used in 91% of the analysed journal articles, while the other methods were rarely used in the sample. The distribution of method use frequency can be seen from (Figure 25). The six core methods are:

- formal, conceptual and argumentative-deductive analysis (total 52%),
- case study (16%),
- prototyping (13%), and
- quantitative-empirical methods (10%).

The argumentative-deductive analysis (35%) does not only head within the scope of deductive methods, but is generally by far most frequently used method of the sample. Case study, prototyping, quantitative-empirical methods, and conceptual-deductive analysis lie rather closer together concerning frequency of use.

The methods profile based on this empirical investigation reveals that research in business informatics focuses on constructive-qualitative methods; argumentative-deductive analysis and prototyping are frequently used and both of these methods show a constructive-qualitative profile (Wilde & Hess, 2007, p. 284).

The case study, which is the second most frequently used method within the sample, is characterised at the borderline the between the constructive and the behaviouristic paradigm. Although (Wilde & Hess, 2007, p. 284) classify the case study as qualitative method, other authors (e.g., Hammersley & Gomm, 2000, p. 3; Merriam, 1988, pp. 16-17; Yin, 1984/1989, pp. 24-25; 1993, pp. 3, 32) highlight case study as being a research strategy making use of varying methods, including both quantitative and qualitative approaches. In either case, the case study's tendency towards a qualitative character supports the whole picture, indicating that business informatics focuses on rather constructive-qualitative methods.

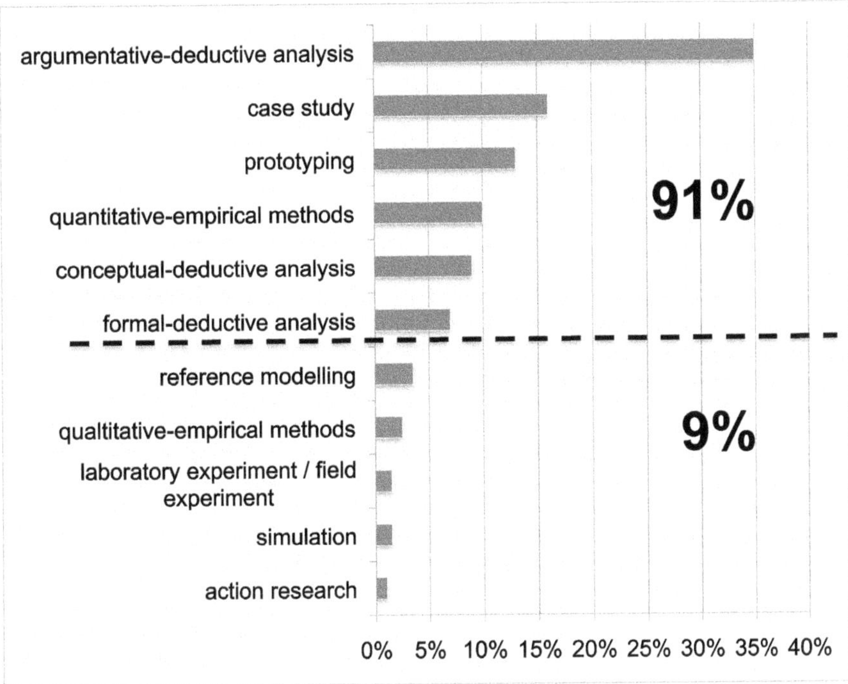

Figure 25. Frequency of research method use in business informatics

Source: (Wilde & Hess, 2007, p. 284, (adapted))

According to (Wilde & Hess, 2007, p. 284), 65% of journal articles report on research making use of quantitative methods, while 35% of articles are based on research using qualitative methods. Due to the ambiguous classification of case studies in the investigation, these figures may not be exact. Still, we may derive that quantitative research prevails in business informatics, although with one third, qualitative methods form a substantive part. Nevertheless, along the time-line we can recognise a slight trend towards quantitative methods (Wilde & Hess, 2007, pp. 284-285). (Frank, 2006, p. 6) ascribes the growing presence of quantitative-empirical methods to the pressure to publish in international journals.

When comparing the profiles of information systems research and business informatics it becomes apparent that case studies, conceptual and formal-deductive analyses are the common denominator. Specific to business informatics are prototyping and argumentative-deductive work; to information systems research, quantitative cross-section analysis and laboratory experiments are specific (Wilde & Hess, 2007, p. 285).

5.3 Quantitative and qualitative methods

There are various ways to gather new insights in empirical research. Two different approaches are quantitative and qualitative methods (cf. Flick, 1995/2002). Table 7 summarises and compares the characteristics of quantitative and qualitative research.

Quantitative research has its roots in positivism and logical empiricism. Phrases frequently associated with these research methods are, among others, empirical, statistical, or experimental. In the form of models, quantitative research tries to describe numeric characteristics and coherences as precisely as possible and make them predictable. The random sample is to be chosen as large and representative as possible. Aiming to keep the same conditions for data generation, quantitative methods are fully standardised and structured (e.g., same questions, same order, same scale, etc.). In most cases, the research setting is, thus, construed artificially or is laboratory. For data collection inanimate instruments, like scales, tests, surveys, or questionnaires are deployed. Quantitative research deploys a deductive mode of analysis making use of statistical methods. The result is objective and independent of the investigator; the researcher is *invisible*. As a consequence, findings are precise, which allows for comparing and interrelating answers and, finally, for generalisation to the population.

In contrast, qualitative research, which has its roots in phenomenology and symbolic interaction, shows much more flexibility. As the focus of interest is the nature or essence of an issue, qualitative methods are rather open or partly structured and have an explorative character. Typically, qualitative research is associated with phrases like fieldwork, ethnographic, or subjective. The choice of the sample is theory-driven, whereby a small group of typical cases for the specific research field is chosen. The investigator's subjectivity is considered and made explicit; the researcher is part of the study. In contrast to quantitative methods, the researcher (as human person) is primary instrument for data collection undertaking observations or interviews. Inductive analysis undertaken by the researcher leads to comprehensive, expansive, often holistic findings, which do not allow for generalisation but give direction for further investigation.

Table 7. Characteristics of quantitative and qualitative research

POINTS OF COMPARISON	QUANTITATIVE RESEARCH	QUALITATIVE RESEARCH
focus of interest	quantity (how much, how many)	quality (nature, essence)
philosophical roots	positivism logical empiricism	phenomenology symbolic interaction
associated phrases	empirical statistical experimental	fieldwork ethnographic naturalistic grounded subjective
goal of investigation	prediction control description confirmation hypothesis testing	understanding description discovery hypothesis generating
design characteristics	predetermined structured	flexible evolving emergent
setting	artificial laboratory	natural conditions fieldwork
sample	large random representative	small non-random theoretical
data collection	inanimate instruments (scales, tests, surveys, questionnaires, computers)	human person (researcher) as primary instrument observations interviews
mode of analysis	deductive (by statistical methods)	inductive (by researcher)
findings	precise narrow reductionist	comprehensive holistic expansive

Source: (Merriam, 1988, p. 18, (adapted))

In principal, the appropriate choice of method depends on four factors:

- the problem (the research question),
- the theoretical background,
- the existing resources, and
- the researcher's level of methodogical knowledge and experience.

In the past, mythological disputes between quantitative and qualitative research haven often been conducted on a very abstract level and only few studies addressed these issues. Nevertheless, strong arguments have been presented polarising quantitative or qualitative research (Gläser-Zikuda & Järvelä, 2008, p. 79).

In contrast, for instance, (Ercikan & Roth, 2006) suggested a continuum in making inferences with both kinds of data. Each research question requires its own methods, which are all imbedded in one single research design (e.g., Flick, 1995/2002, pp. 380-393). Multiple, complementary methods (e.g., content analysis and interviews, survey and focus group discussion, etc.) may enrich the investigation resulting in more meaningful results. After overcoming the controversy regarding quantitative and qualitative research methodologies (e.g., Creswell, 1994/2006), the application of multiple methods for triangulation (cf. Section 5.5.2) is currently well accepted (Flick, 1991/1995; Jick, 1979; Johnson & Onwuegbuzie, 2004; Kaplan & Duchon, 1988; Tashakkori & Teddlie, 1998/2006).

5.4 The research design

Based on the considerations discussed in the Sections 5.1 to 5.3, this Section addresses the choice of the research strategy for addressing the research question (How can promotive activities be implemented in technology-enhanced learning settings in order to enhance cooperative whole person learning with mixing the forms of expression and why?).

As already mentioned above, this research project is carried out at the Research Lab for Educational Technologies at the University of Vienna. Courses used for investigation are associated with the Department of Knowledge and Business Engineering. As this research is imbedded in the research endeavours of this research lab, it is to be regarded as part of the action research process (cf. Baskerville, 1999) that researchers of this lab jointly follow. In the sense of action research, each research cycle's findings interplay with colleagues' further research actions. This work is predominantly influenced by (Derntl, 2005) and strongly interplays with (Figl, 2008, 2009). However, although the dynamics of the action research approach allows for considerable progress in highly dynamic research fields, it does not contribute to narrowing down the complexity of the entire research field as it even augments dynamics – and, thus, complexity – by taking actions. On the other hand, action research suggests a range of research methods (cf. Baskerville, 1999) that consider and handle such dynamics.

The research environment notwithstanding, this work grounds on a very complex field of study as regards content, as Section 3 could demonstrate. The proposed framework (cf. Figure 14, page 88) illustrates that there exists a large scale of influencing factors – some of them known, some of them still unknown. Due to this problem's complexity, it is not feasible to research into all influencing factors for almost unlimited pedagogical scenarios and provide the ultimate answer on a level that allows for generalisation. Instead, it is necessary to focus on promising elements with respect to feasibility, educational success, and pushing research to the next level.

After having discussed the research environment and setting, we can derive the appropriate research strategy on a more formal basis by following the guidelines presented in Section 5.1.

This work's research question is a *how and why* question. Since technology-enhanced learning is still a rather new and dynamic field of research, it is obvious that a contemporary set of events is investigated rather then historical documents and artefacts only. The research involves people in a technology-enhanced learning environment and the control over behavioural events is, thus, restricted. Although there is scope to manipulate the setting to some extent (for instance by introducing various modes of expressions to different groups or by adopting the same modes in different educational settings), the control over behaviour is, due to group dynamics, severely limited.

When how or why questions are being asked about a contemporary set of events and when the investigator has little control over these events, the case study strategy has a distinct advantage (Yin, 1984/1989, pp. 17-20). Due to the constrained control over behavioural events, the possibilities of social experiments are limited in this context.

Nevertheless, as already discussed in the Sections 5.1 and 5.3, the various research strategies are not mutually exclusive. Basically, answering this work's research question demands a thoughtful combination of research strategies as well as quantitative and qualitative methods. Merely combined analysis will deliver the desired insights and will grant an acceptable level of objectivity.

Based on these considerations, this research endeavour follows the case study research strategy[6]. Within every case chosen, different methods will be applied in order to fathom manifold corners of to research in order to enrich results.

5.4.1 The case study as a research strategy

The discussion has progressed without a formal definition of the case study strategy. Indeed, the term *case study* is not used in a clear and fixed sense (Hammersley & Gomm, 2000, p. 2). Given this, let us now attempt to sketch the central components of its meaning and define this strategy.

Often, the term case study is employed to identify a specific form of inquiry, which contrasts with the experiment and the (social) survey in a range of dimensions (Table 8). Two important dimensions, which distinguish the case study from the social survey, relate to the number of cases investigated and the amount of detailed information about each case is studied. Usually – but not exclusively – case study refers to research that investigates a few cases in considerable depth, while surveys typically investigate a large number of cases and gather only a relatively small amount of data from each case. However, experiments, too, involve the investigation of a small number of cases compared to survey work, but what distinguishes it from case study is the fact that it involves direct control of variables. In experiments, the researcher creates the case to be studied while the case study researcher constructs the case out of naturally occurring social situations (Hammersley & Gomm, 2000, pp. 2-3, 14-15).

Some commentators treat the case study as a method to be used – when appropriate – like other methods, depending on the problem under investigation. Many commentators, however, regard case study as more than just a method but consider it as a distinct research paradigm as it involves quite different assumptions about how the social world can and should be studied from underlying approaches. These oppositional views on case study are sometimes formulated in terms of a contrast between

6 Besides best serving the research questions of this work, the case study is a widely accepted and applied research strategy in the field of technology-enhanced learning as well as in the general fields of social sciences and business informatics (cf. Sections 5.1 and 5.2). Consequently, choosing case study as research strategy appears to be also in line with the commonly accepted research practices.

positivism, on the one hand, and naturalism, interpretivism or constructivism, on the other (Hammersley & Gomm, 2000, pp. 3-5). This research follows the positivist view, considering the case study as a strategy.

Table 8. A schematic comparison of case study with experimental and survey approaches

POINTS OF COMPARISON	EXPERIMENT	CASE STUDY	SURVEY
number of cases	relatively small number	relatively small number (sometimes just one)	relatively large number
amount of information per case	small number of features of each case	large number of features of each case	small number of features of each case
setting	case is created in such a way as to control the important variables	naturally occurring case; in action research: study of cases created by the actions of the researcher but where the primary concern is not controlling variables to measure their effects	sample of naturally occurring cases, selected in such a way as to maximise the sample's representativeness in relation to some larger population
focus of interest	quantification of data is a priority	quantification is not a priority; indeed, qualitative data may be treated as superior	quantification of data is a priority
goal of investigation	theoretical inference, development and testing of theory, or practical evaluation of an intervention	understanding the case studied in itself (with no interest in theoretical inference or empirical generalisation; however, there may also be attempts at one or other, or both, of these) alternatively, the *wider* relevance of the findings may be conceptualised in terms of the provision of vicarious experience, as a basis for naturalistic generalisation or transferability	empirical generalisation, from a sample to a finite population (sometimes this is seen as a platform for theoretical inference)

Source: (Hammersley & Gomm, 2000, p. 4, (adapted))

(Yin, 1984/1989, p. 23), an advocate of positivist case study research, defines the case study as "an empirical inquiry that:

- investigates a contemporary phenomenon within its real-life context; when
- the boundaries between phenomenon and context are not clearly evident; and in which
- multiple sources of evidence are used."

With this definition, (Yin, 1984/1989) points to the technically critical features of the case study strategy and distinguishes it from the other research strategies discussed.

The history, for instance, deals – as the case study does – with the entangled situation between phenomenon and context, but usually researches historical events. The experiment, by comparison, divorces a phenomenon from its context since the laboratory environment typically controls the context. And the survey's ability to investigate the context is extremely limited (Yin, 1984/1989, p. 23).

Briefly put, the case study could be the method of choice when the phenomenon under study is indistinguishable from its context. Such a complex interaction between a phenomenon and its (temporary) context is, for instance, given when it is problematic to determine when an activity started or ended (Yin, 1993, p. 3).

In many (e.g., educational) situations the context is extremely relevant. The contextual variables, however, are so numerous that no experimental design can be applied. (Experimental designs typically control the context and focus on a specific variable in isolation from the broader environment.) When introducing the context into a study, the number of variables is likely to exceed by far the number of data points available (Yin, 1993, pp. 31-32). Therefore the case study may also be defined as:

> "An empirical inquiry in which the number of variables exceeds the number of data points" (Yin, 1993, p. 32).

Given the above definition, case study research includes both single- and multiple-case studies. While a single-case study focuses on a single case only, multiple-case studies include at least two cases (within the same study), which are replicating each other (either exact replications or predictably different replications) (Yin, 1993, p. 5). Political science, among other fields, has tried to delineate sharply between these two approaches and has used terms such as *the comparative case method* as a distinctive form of multiple-case studies. Other voices, however, claim that these two approaches are in reality but two of the variations in case study designs (Yin, 1984/1989, p. 24; 1993, pp. 5, 33-34).

In evaluation research, case studies have their distinctive place. They are used (Yin, 1984/1989, p. 25; 1993, p. 5):

- to *explain* the causal links in real-life interventions – especially when those are too complex for the survey or experimental strategies – (explanatory case study),
- to thoroughly *describe* a phenomenon within its real-life context (descriptive case study),
- to *enhance* the evaluation (again in the descriptive mode) by the intervention itself, and
- to *explore* those situations in which the phenomenon being evaluated does not have a clear, single set of outcomes. In those instances, the case study aims at defining the questions and hypotheses for a subsequent study (which does not necessarily have to be a case study) or at determining if the desired research procedures are feasible (exploratory case study).

Case studies should not be confused with qualitative research. As already addressed in Section 5.1, the use of quantitative and qualitative evidence does not distinguish the various research strategies. "The essence of qualitative research consists of two conditions: (a) the use of close-up, detailed observation of the natural world by the investigator, and (b) the attempt to avoid prior commitment to any theoretical model" (Yin, 1984/1989, p. 25). This type of research, however, does not always produce case studies. On the other hand, case studies are not limited to these two conditions; they may be based on quantitative data and do not necessarily include direct observation as a source of evidence (Hammersley & Gomm, 2000, p. 3; Merriam, 1988, pp. 16-17; Yin, 1984/1989, pp. 24-25; 1993, pp. 3, 32).

Interestingly, the history of case study research is characterised by periods of intense use and periods of non-use. The origins of this form of research can be traced to Europe – predominantly to France. In the United States, this research strategy is most closely associated with the Department of Sociology at The University of Chicago, since the Chicago School was pre-eminent in this field for more than thirty years (from the early 1900s until 1935), and contributed therefore a great deal of literature (Tellis, 1997).

5.4.2 The case study design

Every type of empirical study has a research design – if not explicit then implicit. In the most elementary sense, a research design is the logic that links the empirical data to be collected to a study's initial research questions and ultimately, to its conclusions. Colloquially said, a research design is an action plan that guides the investigators in the process of collecting, analysing, and interpreting their observations. It is the logical model that allows researchers to draw inferences concerning causal relations among the variables under investigation and defines the domain of generalisability of the results (Yin, 1984/1989, pp. 27-29).

Once the case study has been selected as the method to be used, following eight issues are especially important for the case study design (Yin, 1984/1989, pp. 29-35; 1993, pp. 32-35):

- defining the research questions,
- outlining the propositions (if there are any),
- identifying the major unit of analysis,
- deciding between single- and multiple-case study,
- selecting the specific cases to be studied,
- defining the relevant data collection strategies,
- indicating the logic linking the data to the propositions, and
- determining the criteria for interpreting the findings.

Defining the research questions

This first component of the research design has already been described in Section 5.1. Although the substance of research questions will vary, the type of the question (who, what, where, how, and why) provides an important clue regarding the most appropriate research strategy to be used. The initial task for the research design is therefore to clarify precisely the nature of the research questions in this regard (Yin, 1984/1989, p. 29).

Outlining the propositions

Besides reflecting an important theoretical issue (which needs to be exposed in any study), an investigation's underlying propositions shed light on where to look for relevant evidence. Legitimate reasons for not having any proposition have studies of explorative character. However, as every exploration should still have some purpose, the design for exploratory studies should therefore state this purpose as well as the criteria by which an exploration will be considered successful (Yin, 1984/1989, p. 30).

Identifying the unit of analysis

The third component of the research design is defining what the case is. While simple designs have single units of analysis, more complicated designs may have multiple units, which are embedded within each other. In the classic case study, an individual person (e.g., a clinical patient or an exemplary student) may be the case being studied, and in such situations the individual would be the primary unit of analysis. In a multiple-case study, information about several relevant individuals (cases) would be collected and included in the study. In other designs, the case might be some event or entity that is less well defined than a single person and may include multiple units, which are embedded within each other (e.g., a university may be the main single case but the students in this university might be an embedded unit of analysis). Frequently, it may be difficult to define the case in terms of the borderlines. For instance, if the unit of analysis is a small group, the persons to be included in the group (and, thus, in the unit) have to be distinguished from those, which are excluded (in context of the case study). For almost any topic, the specific beginning and end of the case have to be defined as regards the timeline (Merriam, 1988, pp. 44-47; Yin, 1984/1989, pp. 31-33; 1993, pp. 32-33).

Deciding between a single case and multiple cases

A single case can serve exploratory, descriptive, or causal purposes. If multiple cases are to be the subject of study, they should follow a replication rather than a sampling logic. A sampling logic would consider the cases as data points representing a larger population, which would be an inappropriate rationale since the results of a case study are not to be generalised to a population but rather to some theory. If the sampling logic is important to a research, the survey or the experimental method are more likely to satisfy the investigation's needs than the case study method would do (Yin, 1993, pp. 33-34).

Selecting the specific case(s)

The selection criteria may include criticality (e.g., some case may be a critical case for the research), topical relevance (e.g., some case is most suitable for the phenomenon being studied), or feasibility and access (e.g., some person or group is disposed to be the subject of the case study). Whatever the criteria, the case selection process may require to collect preliminary information from a large group and to perform a screening analysis in order to determine the final participants (Stake, 1995, pp. 4-7; Yin, 1993, p. 34).

Defining the data collection strategies

Unlike experiments or surveys, the case study does not claim any particular method for data collection. Thus, any method – from testing to interviewing – can be used for gathering data (Merriam, 1988, p. 10). In fact, there is no particular moment when data collection begins; it begins even before there is any commitment to do the study (backgrounding, acquaintance with other cases, first impressions) (Stake, 1995, p. 49). Nevertheless, once researchers have decided to perform a study, they have to choose from different kinds of strategies for data gathering. Investigators may decide for a one-time data collection effort or for a more extended data collection period, or they may even deliberately choose to use both.

With the first strategy the investigator, typically, dedicates a small number of days for every case to be studied. Much of the critical information is collected through interviews and documents (post-hoc data collection). The advantage of the second mode lies in the direct observation, since the investigator spends a longer time period on-site. This mode, however, is more costly and requires special access to the on-site facilities. Furthermore, the investigator does not have any control over whether or not the relevant events will occur in the observed setting. And if they indeed occur, there is still the risk whether the researcher will happen to be at the right place at the right time to observe them (Yin, 1993, p. 35).

Notwithstanding these considerations, evidence for case studies may be based on six types of sources: documents, archival records, interviews, direct observations (with the investigator as observer), participant-observations (with the investigator simultaneously as a participant and an observer), and physical or cultural artefacts.

The principle of case study research is to incorporate at least *two* sources of evidence into the investigation, which will increase the study's quality substantially (Yin, 1984/1989, pp. 84-95).

Indicating the logic linking the data to the propositions

Although the linking of data to propositions can be done in various ways, none of the methods has become as precisely defined as how hypotheses and data have to be connected in psychological experiments. The idea of *pattern matching* described by Donald Campbell (cf. Yin, 1984/1989, pp. 109-113) is one promising approach for case studies. When applying this technique, several pieces of information from within the same case are correlated with some theoretical proposition. For instance, when two or more potential patterns are considered as rival propositions (e.g., an *effects proposition* and a *no effects proposition* regarding the impact of a treatment under study), the pattern matching technique may be used for relating the data to the propositions, even in those cases when the entire study consist of a single case only (Yin, 1984/1989, pp. 33-35).

Determining the criteria for interpreting the findings

In many instances, it is not possible to do statistical tests for making comparisons, especially when undertaking a qualitative research. When, for example, applying the pattern matching technique, the problem arises to define how close a match has to be in order to be considered as a match. Unfortunately, there is no precise way of qualifying the criteria for interpreting these types of data and findings. In fortunate cases, the different patterns will be sufficiently contrasting so that the findings can be interpreted in terms of comparing at least two rival propositions (Yin, 1984/1989, pp. 33-35).

5.4.3 The case study selection

For the purpose of addressing the research question (How can promotive activities be implemented in technology-enhanced learning settings in order to enhance cooperative whole person learning with mixing the forms of expression and why?), case studies will be performed in three different (but not distinct) fields of interest within the area of technology-enhanced cooperative whole person learning. Each selected case will be performed as independent case study. The term independent herby refers to the fact that the three cases are not considered as part of a large-scale multiple-case study, which would demand for a case replication, but each case addresses a slightly different aspect of technology-enhanced cooperative whole person learning.

Selecting three fields of interest within the whole research area allows for going into detail in each field, which would not be feasible if the whole area would be addressed. Simultaneously, this scenario allows keeping a broad picture while narrowing down the investigation to only one field of interest would loose the global perspective that the research question requires.

The three selected fields of interest within the scope of promotive activities in technology-enhanced cooperative whole person learning are:

- motivational aspects in technology-enhanced learning settings,
- the impact of media selection on peer reviews, and
- active listening in technology-enhanced learning settings.

As this work aims at giving a rough direction concerning motivational aspects, this issue could be addressed by a single study with a rather large sample. Each of the other two fields of interest, in contrast, are addressed with two case studies as – for both fields – the results of the respective first case study called for a follow-up study.

Ultimately, the consolidation of the case studies provides a kaleidoscopic picture of the research field due to including different perspectives (see also Section 5.5.2).

5.4.3.1 Case 1. Motivational aspects in technology-enhanced learning settings[7]

Motivation in and for learning is a widely researched topic as it is an important quality that affects performance and success. Promotive activities in educational settings have to be motivational as only then students will perform these activities with interest and tap the full potential of learning.

The research questions

This study aims at identifying motivational elements based on a comparison of a range of courses. Besides driving students' motivation to varying degrees, we expect that the different course designs spark distinct interests and motives.

Consequently, the specific research questions are:

- How do the four courses under investigation differ in motivating students?
- Do these courses differ regarding student's motives for commitment and performance?

The underlying propositions and the study's purpose

This study aims at identifying motivational elements in courses that follow a technology-enhanced cooperative whole person learning approach.

The major unit of analysis

The perception of the individual student is important and contributes to the collective perception. For the comparison of course designs, the unit of interest is, though, a course and not the individual. Consequently the major unit of analysis is a course.

7 Findings of this case study on motivational aspects have been published in (Figl & Bauer, 2008a).

Deciding between a single case and multiple cases

The analysis of a course design for its motivational aspects can provide meaningful insights. The comparison with courses that comprise similar but also a set of distinct pedagogical elements may lead to more relevant results. The availability of an appropriate scale of courses that are appropriate for comparison is a scarce and considerable asset for this research endeavour.

Consequently, multiple cases will be included in order to allow for an empirical comparison of course designs, which goes beyond exploration and description of available motivational factors.

The selection of the specific case(s)

In accordance with the chosen major unit of analysis and the decision for multiple cases alongside with available courses, four specific and particularly interesting courses are selected and compared with a typical course.

In general, all of the investigated courses are part of the curricula of business informatics and are held as technology-enhanced courses. In particular, these courses are: *Web Engineering* (WE), *Project Management – Communication and Soft Skills* (SS), *Person-Centred Communication* (PCC), and *Organisational Development and Business Processes* (OD). Research and data collection took place in the time frame from summer term 2003 to winter term 2006/2007; each course took one term.

Defining the relevant data collection strategies

Since existing measurement instruments did not seem to meet the purpose of this study, we decided to set up a pool of items for measuring motivational aspects. The total of 42 items on motivational aspects was part of an online questionnaire, which also included further items on other issues. Out of the whole set of 42 items, 22 relevant motivational items were selected.

We used five-level Likert-style rating scales (Likert, 1932) as these proved to be highly suitable for measuring attitudes in the context of learning (particularly, when data is collected by means of online questionnaires (Page-Bucci, 2003)).

Indicating the logic linking the data to the propositions and determining the criteria for interpreting the findings

In order to measure students' motivation in the investigated courses, a variance analysis seems the most appropriate choice. However, the precondition of normality was not met for most items (right skewed distributions), such that this method could not be deployed. As the whole set of items was not used for all courses, calculating sum scores did not seem appropriate either for getting insights on motivational aspects.

Finally, a non-parametric procedure – the Chi-Square Test – was calculated for all items, which was significant for 20 out of the selected 22 items.

The results

The results demonstrate that the course design has a significant impact on students' motivation and on the motives that drive commitment and performance. The person-centred course style shows high appreciation and its satisfactory impact on motivation confirms the power of this approach in a technology-enhanced learning setting.

Surprisingly the course *WEB ENGINEERING* scored even lower than a typical course in many motivational items. Unfortunately, clear-cut conclusions cannot be drawn concerning this finding. The study, however, shows that a facilitator's traits and attitudes highly influence students' motivation. Furthermore, results indicate that students see a course's relevance more clearly if content is relevant to their current lives and needs than (only) for future career.

The study will discuss results concerning all 22 items in detail (cf. Section 6).

5.4.3.2 Case 2a. Differences of face-to-face and written online peer reviews[8]

Peer reviews are used in a wide variety of disciplines. Nevertheless research investigating the impact of technology on peer-reviewing mainly derives from the field of language courses and writing classes.

This case presents an experimental study exploring communication and collaboration aspects of the peer review task in an IT project management course, on the one hand, and the quality and kind of feedback

8 Findings of this case studies on peer reviews have been published in (C. Bauer & Figl, 2006) and (Figl, Bauer, Mangler, & Motschnig-Pitrik, 2006).

given in the peer review task, on the other hand. In particular, the study analyses differences between the face-to-face and the online setting.

The research questions

While most research on comparing face-to-face and online peer-reviews focuses on the degree of participation and the number of contributions as well as on the effects on comments and revision, this case additionally analyses collaboration aspects.

Following research questions are addressed:

- Do the online and the face-to-face version show differences in the number of reviews written?
- In which way do reviews differ regarding content?
- How do communication and discussion differ in the online and the face-to-face version?
- How do collaboration within and among teams as well as workload distribution differ?
- Are there differences in the perceived review quality and work efficiency?

The underlying propositions and the study's purpose

As this research is based on the idea of technology-enhanced cooperative whole person learning, this case aims at exploring the effects and drawbacks of peer reviews under the proposition of whole person learning and revealing the potential of technology in the specific pedagogical use of peer reviewing.

The major unit of analysis

Since this case study investigates collaboration and communication aspects, it should include all students of a course participating in peer review tasks. Nevertheless, the perception of the individual is of crucial importance. Due to group dynamics and peer pressure, valuable information would get lost if the unit of analysis would be as big as a peer review team or a whole course. Actually, the results would be biased. As a consequence the major unit of analysis is the individual student participating in a peer review task in a specified course.

Deciding between a single case and multiple cases

In conjunction with the chosen major unit of analysis, this study includes multiple cases. For the same reasons, which have lead to the conclusion that the major unit of analysis has to be broken down to the individual, the research questions demand for the consideration of several perspectives, which implies that multiple cases have to be included in order to provide a picture of the whole and to counteract biased results.

The selection of the specific case(s)

In accordance with the chosen major unit of analysis and the decision for multiple cases, a technology-enhanced course is chosen for the study and considers all of the course's participating students as individual cases. For our research endeavour we deliberately decided to select a course, which includes peer reviews as learning content and course objective in order to provide for an investigation scenario close to reality (field study without laboratory – thus, artificial created – elements).

Consequently, we conducted the study in a course on *PROJECT MANAGEMENT –BASICS AND TECHNIQUES* for computer science students at the University of Vienna in the winter term 2005/2006. This course is part of the Master's programme, which indicates that the participants had already received a Bachelor's degree in computer science.

As this course is held as a technology-enhanced course, it includes both, presence phases in class as well as online elements, which requires students to collaborate online. In the course, students are assigned to create and plan software development projects, which they have to elaborate in small teams of three persons.

For achieving the course goal, students have to elaborate documents like a mission statement of the project, an analysis of status quo and a to-be analysis, use cases and a project proposal, the product and project structure, an IT process model and structure, as well as Microsoft Project® charts.

Since quality assurance and review processes are a significant part of this course's subject matter, the teams practice peer reviewing.

Defining the relevant data collection strategies

Substantial evidence for the peer reviews' quality are the peer reviews' results (i.e. the peer review documents). Therefore the peer review documents constitute a major source of evidence.

Direct observation of team communication would be a sophisticated investigation since multiple cases are involved and, especially in the online version of peer reviewing, the participants do not have any restrictions concerning if, how, and when to communicate with each other. It seems obvious that students cannot be observed all day and night waiting for a communication event to happen. Collecting communication protocols of computer-mediated communication is a possible opportunity for analysis but would be incomplete and risks ignoring crucial information, which did not pass the observed communication channels. Rather it seems appropriate to consult participants about their communication and collaboration behaviour.

Since multiple cases are involved, instead of interviewing some students only, a standardised online questionnaire enables to gather information from all participants. Capturing students' perceptions concerning the online and the face-to-face setting with a combination of closed and open ended questions allows for a direct comparison of the two settings on the one hand, and provides scope for gathering insightful information.

Indicating the logic linking the data to the propositions and determining the criteria for interpreting the findings

This case study makes use of text and qualitative content analysis (Mayring, 1983/2003). The answers to the questionnaire are analysed for each individual student; furthermore the team compositions are taken into account.

The online and the face-to-face peer reviews are analysed regarding type and quality. For a content categorisation, a classification scheme is developed inductively from raw data. To prove its consistency, the fitting of all statements into categories is checked after setting it up and the classification scheme is reformulated if it deems necessary. Categorisation is undertaken by two researchers[9] in order to increase inter-subjectivity. If researchers identify differences in categorisation, best fitting categories are to be chosen after discussion.

Furthermore, the online and the face-to-face-setting are analysed as concerns differences in activities, workload distribution as well as work efficiency and review quality.

The results

The results show that students commented on fewer topics in the online version but described them in more detail than in the paper version. The online version was experienced as time-efficient and easy to fill in, while students found it significantly easier to express feedback in the paper version.

---

9 At this point, I want to express my sincere thanks to Kathrin Figl for her enthusiasm and cooperation. Without her my research would not have been possible.

Furthermore, students highly appreciated many aspects of the online reviewing tool but found themselves constrained by the lack of discussion, which they experienced and valued in the face-to-face process. The case will discuss further results regarding team communication and collaboration and their implications on the specific pedagogical use of online and face-to-face peer reviewing (cf. Section 7.2).

5.4.3.3 Case 2b. Evaluating peer review settings with different media combinations [10]

Based on the insights gained from the first case study on peer reviews (Section 5.4.3.2), this follow-up case study explores the eligibility of different media combinations for peer reviews.

The research questions

Built upon the findings of the earlier case study comparing peer reviews in face-to-face and online settings, this follow-up case study investigates also combinations of media for the peer review activity. As students are the concerned actors in educational peer review settings, this case study aims at analysing students' perceptions about peer review settings.

Following research questions are addressed:

- What perceived impact do written online peer reviews have on students' learning processes?
- What are the benefits and limitations of online peer reviews as a means of cooperative learning, i.e. how can they contribute to learning *from each other*?
- How do students perceive the eligibility of written online peer reviews compared to face-to-face reviewing activities?
- How can the enhancement of these basic settings (online vs. face-to-face peer reviews) with media combinations contribute to the peer review process?

The underlying propositions and the study's purpose

Based on the idea of technology-enhanced cooperative whole person learning, this case aims at revealing the potential (as well as the drawbacks) of media combinations in the specific pedagogical use for peer reviews.

---

10 Findings of this case study on peer reviews have been published in (C. Bauer, Figl, Derntl, Beran, & Kabicher, 2009a) and (C. Bauer, Figl, Derntl, Beran, & Kabicher, 2009b).

The major unit of analysis

As students' individual perceptions are of main concern in this research, the major unit of analysis is the individual student participating in a peer review task in a specified course. Nevertheless, this study pursues to investigate the collective of students' opinions and perceptions rather than of a few students only. Consequently, the case study should include all students of a course participating in peer review tasks.

Specifying the major unit of analysis as small as an individual student is, though, crucial for the study since we would receive biased results with bigger units of analysis due to the effects of group pressure.

Deciding between a single case and multiple cases

In analogy to case 2a (Section 5.4.3.2), this study includes multiple cases, which goes in accordance with the chosen major unit of analysis. The research questions require considering several perspectives, which implies that multiple cases have to be included in order to capture the whole picture.

The selection of the specific case(s)

In accordance with the decision for multiple cases and the chosen major unit of analysis, a technology-enhanced course is chosen for the study and considers all of the course's participating students as individual cases.

For this case study we deliberately decided to select a course, in which peer review activities are learning content and not merely a pedagogical element for assessment or an artificially created element for investigation. As the course on *Basics of Scientific Writing* provides and introduction to scientific processes, it includes peer reviews as a means of quality assurance. As the course was held the first time in summer term 2008, it could be designed from scratch, which allowed implementing peer review activities matching the needs of our investigation. Consequently, this course suggested itself to be selected for this case study.

Hence, the study was conducted in the course on *Basics of Scientific Writing* for computer scientists, which is part of the module *Scientific Principles in Informatics* of the Bachelor's curriculum informatics at the University of Vienna. We conducted the study in summer term 2008, which was actually the first time this course was held. The course was offered in three parallel courses (groups) held by three lecturers who agreed to follow the same course design.

Basically, the course gives an introduction to scientific writing (including scientific presentation techniques) in the discipline of informatics, which is presented in lectures and elaborated with practical exercises. In order to provide students with an authentic picture of scientific writing in informatics, the course schedule resembles the processing of a scientific conference with submissions in writing and oral presentations.

While the course includes presence phases in class with lectures, presentations, and practical exercises, all aspects of knowledge transfer and collaboration aspects (which includes writing papers and the reviewing process) is accompanied and supported by an e-learning platform.

Defining the relevant data collection strategies

Essential elements of this case study are that students practice and experience a scientific peer review process, in order that we can collect data on students' perceptions.

A qualitative approach with open questions seems appropriate in order to meet the explorative character of the research questions. Consequently, we ask students to reflect on the peer review activities using an online questionnaire, which includes items about the peer review process (five-level Likert scale (Likert, 1932)), and open questions about the appropriateness or peer reviews with four scenarios of peer reviews with distinct media combinations.

With the use of a questionnaire with open questions, the study takes advantage of written reflections, which we expect – in this specific context – to deliver deeper insights than oral interviews.

Indicating the logic linking the data to the propositions and determining the criteria for interpreting the findings

For evaluating students' reflections in the open questions, this case study deploys text and qualitative content analysis (Mayring, 1983/2003). The classification scheme is developed inductively from raw data. In order to increase inter-subjectivity, categorisation is undertaken by two researchers[11], who have to agree on a common classification scheme.

For the analysis of the quantitative part of the questionnaire, a mean-standard deviation analysis seems appropriate.

---

11 At this point I want to thank Kathrin Figl for her outstanding support and enthusiasm. Without her, this research would not have been possible.

The results

The analysis demonstrates that students appreciate the deployment of online peer reviews in the course. Results indicate that the peer review activity has a positive impact on the perception of the essential elements of scientific papers. Furthermore, they become (more) aware that they are self-responsible for their own learning processes. However, in this case study, the peer reviews do not seem to have any impact on the learning climate and on students' motivation.

Students highlight that the advantage of written reviews lies in the good documentation of feedback. Furthermore, they emphasise that the opportunity to raise a query is important in order to minimise misunderstandings. The case study will discuss further details on students' perceptions (cf. Section 7.3).

5.4.3.4 Case 3a and 3b. Active listening in technology-enhanced learning settings[12]

Active listening is a widely-know ingredient in a variety of contexts that involve gathering information and solving problems (among others in psychotherapy (e.g., Rogers, 1980), education (e.g., Weissglass, 1990), and business (e.g., Kubota, Mishima, & Nagata, 2004; Mishima, Kubota, & Nagata, 2000; Rautalinko & Lisper, 2004)).

Active listening is a way of listening and responding to another person that improves mutual understanding. It involves both verbal and nonverbal communication skills (Rogers, 1980). Active listeners take care to fully attend the speaker using techniques such as paraphrasing, summarising, or encouraging. For instance, paraphrasing including both factual and emotional information enables the speaker to find out whether the listener really understood (Rautalinko & Lisper, 2004; Robertson, 2005).

Since active listening is a concept for oral communication, studies analyse its effects in such settings. Nowadays, however, written computer-mediated communication plays an important role in many settings, among them in education and in business. Therefore, this case presents an experimental study adopting the concept of active listening in a completely different setting – in an online educational setting using written online communication. The study presents *active listening*'s potential in

12 Findings of the case studies on active listening have been published in (C. Bauer & Figl, 2008) and (Figl & Bauer, 2008b).

written online communication and explores this medium's drawbacks for being capable of fully exploiting the benefits of this concept.

The research question

Transferring the concept of active listening to written online communication is a novel asset. Therefore, this case aims at analysing whether this concept deriving from oral communication is effective in written online communication.

Following research questions are addressed:

- Can the concept of active listening be applied to settings with written online communication?
- Which adaptations in communicating and listening have to be made?
- What is the potential and what are the drawbacks in applying the concept of active listening in written online communication?
- What influence do media (e-mail vs. instant messaging) have on active listening?

The underlying propositions and the study's purpose

As this research is based on the idea of technology-enhanced cooperative whole person learning, this case aims at exploring the effects of the specific pedagogical use of active listening in a technology-enhanced educational setting under the proposition of whole person learning.

The major unit of analysis

Active listening is a dialogical concept involving two persons, one acting as a listener and one as a sender (talker). Despite the importance of the dialog as such, the significant factor is the individual's perception of the communication. Consequently, the major unit of analysis has to be the individual.

Deciding between a single case and multiple case

Active listening is a proven concept in oral communication and this study aims at exploring this concept's potential in written online communication. Due to this study's explorative character it deems necessary to gather as much new ideas as possible. Thus, this study will include multiple cases in order to get a broad insight into the field.

The selection of the specific case(s)

In accordance with the chosen major unit of analysis and the decision for multiple cases, a technology-enhanced course for students of business informatics and computer science will be chosen for the study and will consider all participating students as individual cases. In order to best serve the requirements of the topic active listening, a course on *COMMUNICATION AND SOFT SKILLS* seems appropriate.

The field of active listening is approached in two case studies, which emphasise distinct interests. The first case study (case 3a) aims at exploring *active listening*'s capacity in technology-enhanced learning settings with written online communication. As the results of this study were positive, a follow-up case study (case 3b) addresses issues raised in the first case and investigates the aspect of media choice for active listening activities.

Both case studies were conducted in a course on *PROJECT MANAGEMENT – COMMUNICATION AND SOFT SKILLS* for business informatics and computer science students at the University of Vienna. This course is part of the Master's programme, which indicates that the participants had already received a Bachelor's degree in computer science. While the first case study refers to the course held in winter term 2005/2006, the follow-up case study refers to winter term 2006/2007.

While the first case study was conducted in winter term 2005/2006, the follow-up case study – targeting the more precisely specified aspect of media choice and media competence – was conducted in the same course but one year thereafter (winter term 2006/2007).

This course is held as a technology-enhanced course and included both, presence phases in class as well as online elements, which requires students to communicate and collaborate online in small-scaled project teams and in the whole group respectively.

After having practiced active listening in oral communication in class, students are assigned to exercise online active listening in groups of two (dyad) acting once as the listener and once as the sender. In the first case study (case 3a), students were free to choose any instant messaging tool they liked. In the follow-up case study (case 3b), half of the group were to use instant messaging, the other half were to use e-mail instead.

Every student has to reflect in writing on the online exercise addressing following questions: What happened during the exercise? How did I perceive it as the sender and as the listener?

Both assignments – the active listening exercise as well as writing a reflection – are an immanent part of the course, which targets at theoretical as well as practical aspects of communication, social skills, and (self-)reflection.

Defining the relevant data collection strategies

As already mentioned above, the dialog itself and the individual's perception are substantial in active listening. As a consequence a protocol of the dialogs and students' reflections serve as the main sources of evidence.

Already for the course's (assessment) purposes, the log files of the instant messaging conversations as well as the written reflections on the exercise are to be provided on the course's e-learning platform. Consequently, these sources can easily be used for this study's analysis purposes.

Indicating the logic linking the data to the propositions and determining the criteria for interpreting the findings

Text and qualitative content analysis (Mayring, 1983/2003) are deployed to evaluate students' reflections. The classification scheme is developed inductively from raw data. For reliability reasons, the log files of the communication sequences are used for reflexive interpretation (reference to and rechecking on the original source). Categorisation is undertaken by two researchers[13] in order to increase inter-subjectivity. If differences in categorisations occur, the best fitting categories are to be chosen after discussion.

The results

Training computer scientists in active listening turned out to be a positive learning experience and is a meaningful contribution to improving students' communication skills.

Results reveal that all of the commonly used techniques in active listening (e.g., paraphrasing) are applicable when communication via instant messaging or writing.

Distraction and missing attention are considered as the prevailing drawback of online active listening, although this phenomenon is rather to be attributed to attitude than to a medium. For active listening via e-mail, students most frequently complain about long waiting times for mes-

13 At this point I want to thank Kathrin Figl for her outstanding support and enthusiasm. Without her, this research would not have been possible.

sages. For instant messaging, the main difficulty is that messages get mixed up.

Nevertheless, reflections indicate that students are aware of the analysed media's strength and weaknesses and are able to handle the mentioned difficulties due to having developed the required media competence (cf. Section 8).

5.5 Quality of research

No matter which type of study one is doing, a research design is supposed to represent a logical set of statements and has, thus, to fulfil certain quality criteria. In quantitative research validity, reliability, and objectivity are undisputedly the criteria, which have to hold.

In qualitative studies, in general, the concepts and definitions of validity and reliability become problematic. The primary reason for this lies in the fact that interpretivist research makes it by definition impossible to guarantee reliability in the objectivistic sense (e.g., in laboratory studies every effort is made to restrict the potential for varying effects). Interpretivist studies are often characterised by dynamic interplay of multiple variables. Hence, obvious variations in time, actors, and context will lead to unpredictability (e.g., Sørnes, 2004, p. 87).

Therefore, alternative approaches for qualitative research are still under discussion (e.g., Flick, 1995/2002, pp. 317-319; Mayring, 1990/2002, pp. 140-142; Yin, 1984/1989, p. 40). One way is to concentrate on these three *classic* criteria and to apply or accordingly adapt those to qualitative research. Another way is to develop new quality factors, which are adequate for the methods in qualitative research by taking the theoretical background and the research process into account. A third alternative queries whether the claim for validity of scientific statements is still justifiable in qualitative research. Obviously, this alternative will neither conduce the further establishment of qualitative research nor contribute to it that its results will be regarded as relevant. The fourth alternative claims that a research's quality goes beyond the formulation of criteria, standards, and critical values (cf. Flick, 1995/2002, pp. 394-413), and concentrates on quality management throughout the whole research process (Flick, 1995/2002, pp. 317-319; Mayring, 1990/2002, pp. 140-148).

The following sections introduce the quality criteria in quantitative and qualitative research. Thereafter special attention is paid to the relevant criteria for case studies.

5.5.1 The classic quality criteria in quantitative research

Having their roots in the (natural) sciences, the quality criteria in quantitative research have already become well established due to having a history. Meanwhile they are therefore often referred to as the three *classic quality criteria*: reliability, validity, and objectivity.

Reliability. If a test is reliable, it measures the trait under investigation exactly and yields consistent results (e.g., Kvale, 1991/1995, p. 427; Mayring, 1983/2003, p. 109; 1990/2002, pp. 140-142).

Validity. A test is valid if it measures what it is supposed to measure. It refers to getting results that accurately reflect the concept being measured (e.g., Kvale, 1991/1995, p. 427; Mayring, 1983/2003, pp. 109-110; 1990/2002, pp. 141-142). The empirical concept of validity is complemented by logical concepts of validity. The *internal validity* (content validity), for instance, refers to how good a sample represents the universe. The *construct validity* refers to the degree to which inferences can be made from the operationalisations in a study to the theoretical constructs, on which they were based. For instance, when performing a study on intelligence, the term intelligence first has to be defined in order to reach an acceptable level of construct validity, since the construct intelligence implies correlations to measurements of other elements (e.g., Kvale, 1991/1995, p. 427). Reliability is a prerequisite for measurement validity, which impacts that a valid test must be reliable, but a reliable test need not be valid (e.g., Mayring, 1983/2003, p. 110; Zöfel, 2002, p. 239).

Objectivity. A test is regarded as objective if it is independent of the person who has performed the investigation (in administration, scoring, and interpretation).

Finally, we can summarise that without assessing the reliability and validity of an instrument and the research design, the results from analyses cannot be upheld. Neither can conclusions be drawn from it (e.g., Sørnes, 2004, pp. 86-87).

Additionally to above described classic quality criteria, a study's *relevance* is usually considered for assessing its quality. This criterion may be evaluated from two perspectives (e.g., Sørnes, 2004, p. 87):

- A study may have high practical value but may deliver limited or even lack theoretical contributions.
- A study may be scientifically significant but may be practically irrelevant or useless.

Research of high quality should serve both, scientific and practical needs. We should, however, keep in mind that scientific advancement might stimulate practical desires, which finally leads to innovation having practical relevance. Innovation with practical focus, on the other hand, may drive scientific advancement. These impacts, however, are often not obvious at the beginning of research but do evolve during an investigation or even after its completion when someone else picks up the results for creating something new.

5.5.2 Quality criteria in qualitative research

As regards quality criteria in qualitative research, alternative approaches are under discussion. Based on the second approach (mentioned in the introduction) claiming that the quality factors have to be adequate for the methods used and therefore new method specific factors have to be introduced, (Mayring, 1990/2002, pp. 140-148) consolidated six intermethodic criteria for qualitative research:

Documentation of procedures

Any result is scientifically worthless, if the procedures, which lead to this result, are not documented properly. In quantitative research, it suffices to refer to the used techniques and measuring instruments as these are standardised. In qualitative research, however, methods are more differentiated and often specific to a certain domain or field of research. As a consequence, procedures have to be documented in detail in order to make the research process traceable to others. The need for explication concerns the preconception, the combination of the instruments used for analysis, data collection, and analysis of data (Mayring, 1990/2002, pp. 144-145).

Argumentative backing up of interpretation

In qualitative research, interpretations play a decisive role and, thus, assessing the research's quality has to emphasise the interpretative parts. Since interpretations cannot be recalculated like arithmetic operations, interpretations have to be reasoned argumentatively. First, the preconception for the respective interpretation has to be adequate inducing that explanation is reasonably theory driven. Second, interpretations have to be argued conclusively. Finally, it is important to think of alternative explanations and to disprove them (Mayring, 1990/2002, p. 145).

Rule drivenness

Although qualitative research has to be open towards its field and ready to modify the in advance planned steps of analysis, it may not result in a completely unsystematic (or even chaotic) proceeding. Qualitative research, too, has to follow certain codes of practice and process data systematically (Mayring, 1990/2002, pp. 145-146).

Proximity to the subject under discussion

Instead of getting the test persons into a laboratory, qualitative research tempts to go into the *field* and perform studies in the natural world of the subject under discussion. In contrast to the experiment, which lives on misleading the test persons, qualitative research (in social sciences) aims at doing research with and in favour of the concerned environment. Through the rapprochement of the interests – of the investigator on the one hand and the persons concerned on the other hand – the research process achieves the closest possible proximity to the subject (Mayring, 1990/2002, p. 146).

Communicative validation

A way of validating the interpretations and results is to present the work to the concerned persons (interview partners, persons observed, etc.) and discuss the matters. If they can find themselves in the results and interpretations, this could be a significant argument that backs up the results. Certainly, this must not be the only criterion; otherwise an analysis could never go beyond the subjective meaning of the persons concerned and would be stuck to their myths, stereotypes, and ideologies. Nevertheless, qualitative-orientated research regards the persons under study as more than merely a data supplier and seeks for the dialog in order to gain significant arguments (e.g., Kvale, 1991/1995, pp. 429-430; Mayring, 1990/2002, p. 147).

Triangulation

The concept of triangulation originally derives from trigonometry and elementary geometry: the coordinates and the distance to a point in geometric space may be definitively determined by specifying the intersection of three vectors (given measurements of angles and sides of the triangle formed by that point and two other known reference points) (Downward & Mearman, 2007, p. 80; Yin, 1993, p. 69). Like with a triangle, where only the linkage of the three sticks constitutes the sound, the combination of several strings of analysis may enhance a qualitative research's quality.

Based on these considerations, (Denzin, 1970/1975) first introduced the concept of triangulation to qualitative research in the 1970s. When combining several strings of analysis, triangulation does not aim at achieving completely identical results but makes use of the different perspectives and composes them to a kaleidoscopic picture (Flick, 1991/1995, pp. 431-434; Mayring, 1990/2002, pp. 147-148). This is, by the way, not restricted to qualitative methods, but may combine qualitative and quantitative analysis on an equal footing (Flick, 1995/2002, pp. 385-386; Jick, 1979; Mayring, 1990/2002, p. 148).

Although one distinguishes four types of triangulation (based on what is combined), all these types go back on the idea of combining different kinds of analysis.

- *Data triangulation* refers to collecting data at different points in time, at different places from different persons.
- *Investigator triangulation*, on the other hand, makes use of multiple, rather than single observers or interviewers in order to balance the subjective bias of the individual.
- *Theory triangulation* consists of using more than one theoretical scheme in the interpretation of the phenomenon. In other words, the research field is approached from different perspectives and hypotheses.
- A central concept is, finally, the *methodological triangulation*, which involves using more than one method. When following such a combination of methods, one may further distinguish between a within-method strategy (e.g., different subscales in a questionnaire) and a between-method strategy, when different methods are deployed (Denzin, 1970/1975; Downward & Mearman, 2007, pp. 80-81; Flick, 1991/1995, p. 433; Mayring, 1990/2002, p. 147).

For details on triangulation cf. (Flick, 2004).

(Yin, 1984/1989) argues that qualitative researchers should aim at analytical abstraction rather than statistical treatment of data. Similarly, (G-uba & Lincoln, 1989/2000) conclude that interpretivist research should emphasise on making a study pragmatically useful, lucid, descriptive, and understandable to other people. Naturally, researchers are, though, required to make findings convincing; thus, they have to make their research's underlying conceptualisations, procedures, and choices transparent to the reader.

5.5.3 Quality criteria for case study research

The principle says that the quality criteria have to be adequate to the methods used (e.g., Flick, 1995/2002, p. 391; Mayring, 1990/2002, p. 142).

As already emphasised, case study research may rely on quantitative data, qualitative data, or it may include both. (Yin, 1984/1989, pp. 40-45) names following four criteria (which are summarised in numerous social science textbooks (e.g., Mayring, 1990/2002, pp. 140-148; Yin, 1984/1989, pp. 40-45; 1993, pp. 39-40)) as relevant for case study designs – the construct validity, the internal validity, the external validity, and the reliability – and offers case study specific tactics to meet these requirements (Table 9).

Table 9. Case study tactics for assuring the quality of a research design

CRITERIA	CASE STUDY TACTIC	PHASE OF RESEARCH IN WHICH THE TACTIC OCCURS
construct validity	use multiple sources of evidence	data collection
	establish chain of evidence	data collection
	have key informants review draft case study report	composition
internal validity	do pattern matching	data analysis
	do explanation building	data analysis
	do time-series analysis	data analysis
external validity	use replication logic in multiple-case studies	research design
reliability	use case study protocol	data collection
	develop case study data base	data collection

Source: (Yin, 1984/1989, p. 47, (adapted))

Construct validity

This criterion determines whether the instruments and measures accurately operationalise the concepts being studied, because many instruments and measures are not necessarily as accurate as desired. As Table 9 shows, there are three tactics available for case studies to increase construct validity (Yin, 1984/1989, pp. 40-42; 1993, pp. 39-40). A common strategy is to use multiple sources of evidence. Obviously this tactic is relevant during data collection (Yin, 1984/1989, pp. 23, 42; 1993, pp. 39-40). A second tactic, which is also relevant during the phase of data collection, is to establish a chain of evidence, which allows the reader to follow the derivation of any evidence from the initial research question to ultimate case study conclusions (similar to the notion used in criminological investigation) (Yin, 1984/1989, pp. 41-42, 102-103). The third tactic is to have the draft case study report reviewed by key informants (Yin, 1984/1989, pp. 41-42, 143-146).

Internal validity

This second criterion is a concern for explanatory or causal studies only, where the investigator tries to determine whether event x led to event y. If the study comes to the conclusion that there is a causal relation between event x and event y without knowing that some third factor z may actually have caused event y, then the research design has failed to consider some threat to internal validity. Since studies of descriptive or exploratory nature are not concerned with making causal statements, this logic is not applicable for this kind of research. Principally, internal validity can be achieved through the appropriate specification of the units of analysis and through the development of presumably rival theories, and the corresponding collection and analysis of data in order to test these rivals (Merriam, 1988, pp. 166-170; Yin, 1984/1989, pp. 40, 42-43; 1993, p. 40).

As regards case study research, the concern over internal validity is a part of the overall problem of making inferences. In a case study, basically, every time an event cannot be observed directly, the investigator will infer that a particular event resulted from some earlier event based on interviews or documentary evidence. The research design has to anticipate, whether the inference may be correct, whether all rival explanations and possibilities have been considered, whether the evidence is convergent, whether the inference does appear airtight, etc. When such questions are anticipated in a research design, the investigator has begun to deal with the overall problem of making inferences and, thus, also addresses the specific problem of internal validity (Yin, 1984/1989, pp. 40, 42-43; 1993, p. 40).

Identifying the specific tactics for achieving internal validity is a difficult task, which is especially true in doing case studies. For addressing this issue, (Yin, 1984/1989) suggests in first instance the analytical tactic of pattern matching (cf. Yin, 1984/1989, pp. 43, 109-113) as well as further two related tactics, explanation building (Yin, 1984/1989, pp. 43, 115-120) and time-series analysis (Yin, 1984/1989, pp. 43, 115-120).

External validity

This criterion deals with the problem of establishing a domain of generalisation that goes beyond the immediate study. While survey research relies on statistical generalisation, case studies and experiments rely on analytical generalisation. In statistical generalisation, a correctly selected sample readily generalises to a larger universe. In analytical generalisation, in contrast, a particular set of results is generalised to some broader theory. Critics typically state that single cases do not offer any basis for generalising from a sample to a larger universe. This analogy to samples and universes from survey research, however, is incorrect when dealing with case studies, which rely on analytical generalisation (Merriam, 1988, pp. 173-177; Yin, 1984/1989, pp. 41, 43; 1993, p. 40).

(Yin, 1984/1989, p. 44) presents (Jacobs, 1961) as an illustrative example. This book is based mostly on experiences from New York City. Rather than reflecting the single experiences of New York, the chapter topics cover broader theoretical issues in urban planning, such as the role of sidewalks, the need for small blocks, or the role of neighbourhood parks. In the aggregate, all these issues represent the setting up of a theory of urban planning on a general basis and are, thus, not restricted to New York City.

In terms of research in the field of learning, we can provide following example: One follows a particular learning theory and focuses on a specific field of interest, which will lead to a certain case to be studied. And it is the same learning theory that will help to identify the other cases to which the results are generalisable. For example, if a study focuses on learning at three levels, the procedure of selecting a course for study will identify those types of courses, which follow the approach of learning at three levels. In principle, theories about learning in all of these courses would be the target to which the results could later be generalised. Findings on promotive activities that are not rigorously bound to the three levels of learning could, for instance, be transferred to the design of cooperative course settings in general.

Naturally, such a generalisation is not automatic and a theory needs to be tested through replications of the findings in other cases, for which the theory has specified that the same results should occur. On the one hand, a multiple-case study may follow the replication logic and may therefore test a theory within the same study. On the other hand, a replication may be based on someone else's study approving this prior study's findings. Once such a replication has been made, the results may be accepted for a much larger number of similar courses even without performing any further replication. Summarising, external validity can be achieved through the specification of theoretical relationships, which allow drawing generalisations (Yin, 1984/1989, pp. 44-45).

Reliability

The objective of reliability is to minimise the errors and biases in a study. Therefore it aims at demonstrating that the operations of a study (e.g., data collection procedures, etc.) can be repeated with exactly the same results. To put it differently, if investigator B conducted the same study and followed exactly the same procedures as described by investigator A, investigator B should arrive at the same results and conclusions as investigator A did. For this, the emphasis is placed on doing the same study over again, and does not refer to replicating the results of one study by doing another study (Merriam, 1988, pp. 170-173; Yin, 1984/1989, pp. 41, 45; 1993, p. 40).

One prerequisite for allowing another investigator to repeat an earlier case study is the documentation of the procedures followed. Without such a documentation (or with poor documentation only), even the original investigators themselves could not try to repeat the study. As Table 9 indicates, the specific tactics for achieving reliability in case study research are the use of formal case study protocols (cf. Yin, 1984/1989, pp. 45, 70-80) and the development of a case study database (cf. Yin, 1984/1989, pp. 45, 98-102), which are both associated with the data collection phase. The case study protocol helps to ensure that the same procedures are followed in multiple cases or in a study conducted by multiple investigators. The case study database is a means to differentiate the evidence from the case study report, which are two distinct components that are readily differentiated in other methods (e.g., a survey database is distinct from the survey report) but are often confused in case study research (Yin, 1984/1989, p. 45).

6 Motivational aspects in technology-enhanced learning settings[14]

Motivation in and for learning is a widely researched topic, which is approached from several disciplines (e.g., education, psychology, etc.) and highlights various aspects related to motivation. Studies have clearly illustrated that motivational aspects are fundamental factors that drive a student's performance (e.g., Ames, 1992; Durik & Harackiewicz, 2002; Van der Merwe, 2007). When motivated to learn, people will involve actively in the learning process. Furthermore, they are likely to choose activities that they believe that will help them learn and drive performance. Although these issues have been actively discussed, there is still a lack of empirical evidence on how motivation drives the learning process and interacts with it in different learning contexts (Gläser-Zikuda & Järvelä, 2008, p. 79).

In the early days of e-learning and distance education, people doubted that students could be properly motivated without the physical presence of an educator or peers. As experience with such learning environments increased and further technological facilities for online learning emerged, the scepticism receded and people came up with creative experiments. Finally, the movement towards technology-enhanced learning environments that combine presence phases with online elements gave rise to systematic concepts and models with respect to motivation to learn.

With the ARCS model, (Keller, 1987) has developed a motivation model that provided a systematic process for implementing motivational aspects into a course design (instructional design) (Shellnut, Knowlton, & Savage, 1999, p. 100; Shellnut, Savage, & Knowlton, 1998). Although dating back more than twenty years, this approach still stands out due to its proven validity and reliability (Astleitner, 2000; Shellnut, Knowlton, & Savage, 1999; Shellnut, Savage, & Knowlton, 1998; Vafa, 1999; Visser, Plomp, & Kuiper, 1999). Given its non-prescriptive approach, it is easily implementable according to a course's specific requirements and is, in particular, widely applicable in technology-enhanced as well as in traditional learning settings (Visser, Plomp, & Kuiper, 1999). These consider-

14 Parts of this study on motivational aspects have been published in (Figl & Bauer, 2008a). While (Figl & Bauer, 2008a) focuses on teamwork, this dissertation reconsiders findings with view to promotive activities.

ations, finally, induced to adopt the ARCS model for our course designs and as basement for analysis.

6.1 Theory and background

Etymologically the term motivation derives from the Latin word *movere*, which signifies *moving*. Motives are reasons for action, and motivation consists of a bundle of motives. Observable actions are frequently indicators for motivation but one cannot conclude directly and unconditionally from action to motivation (Siebert, 2006, p. 58).

Traditionally, pedagogy differentiates intrinsic and extrinsic motivation. Intrinsic motivation comes from the inner and people engage in an activity without obvious external incentives. For instance, they learn because they enjoy engaging in a particular topic or due to enjoying pleasure from learning itself. Extrinsic motivation comes from external factors and sources. Important aspects are, for instance, pursuit of achievement, prestige, reward, or ownership. In such cases, the motivating effect does not derive from the activity itself but from the achievement that is accomplished through the activity (Siebert, 2006, pp. 58-59).

Approaches to motivation are manifold (cf. Siebert, 2006, pp. 58-88). Although motivation theories seem to be distinct, we can abstract basic, categorical key concepts (Figure 26) (Siebert, 2006, pp. 88-89):

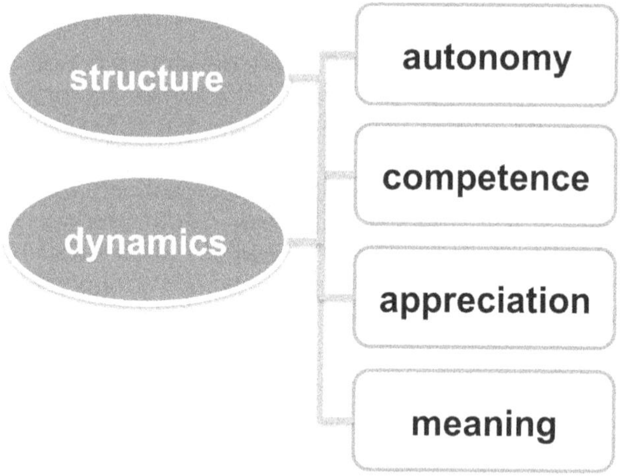

Figure 26. Key concepts for learning motivation

Source: (Siebert, 2006, p. 89, (adapted))

- From an analytic perspective, the key concepts are *structure* and *dynamics*. Motivation to learn is an intra-psychic structure, which follows interpretation and emotion patterns, which have evolved through one's lifetime, and which are integrated in a socio-economic and socio-cultural context. Characteristic for this field of motivation is its dynamics. Consequently, motivation to learn is a psychodynamic process.
- From an intentional perspective, the key concepts are *competence*, *autonomy*, *appreciation*, and *meaning*. Motivation to learn is cognitively and emotionally target-orientated. Adults are motivated to learn, when they expect social appreciation, an increase in autonomy and competence, or when learning seems meaningful to them. These gains are linked to individual feelings of pleasure.

(Siebert, 2006, p. 91) emphasises that educators will not be able to motivate learners directly. Motivation can neither be created pedagogically nor can it be organised since activities that motivate an individual, may make another person feel bored. Motivating people to learn, thus, implies to design a professional and ambitious learning environment, which is experienced as motivating by as many participants as possible. Figure 27 tries to differentiate levels of motivation and rank these (Siebert, 2006, p. 92):

- Basic motivation includes the positive regard of existence, the desire for a happy life and the search for meaning.
- Basic factors of personality are, for instance, extraversion and openness for new experiences.
- The motivation for education aims at the development and the realisation of human abilities directed.
- Generative topics are autonomy, appreciation, justice, and health.
- Thematic interests are related to understanding oneself, other people, and the world.
- Learning styles concentrate reflexive biographical learning, social communicative learning activities, or the acquisition of knowledge and competences.
- Motives for participation may be process-orientated (enjoyment of learning with others), facilitator-orientated (appreciation to a person), or result-orientated (learning results, certificates).

After this brief introduction to motivation, the next Sections are dedicated to motivation models in technology-enhanced learning settings. Essentially there exist three models that relate motivation with instructional design: the ARCS model (Keller, 1987), the time continuum model (Wlodkowski, 1993), and the SuperMotivation model (Spitzer, 1996).

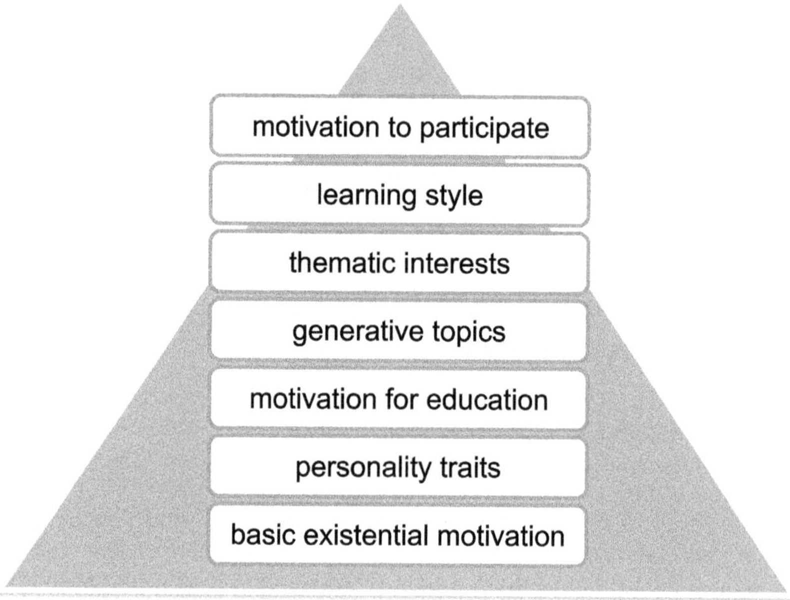

Figure 27. Levels of motivation

Source: (Siebert, 2006, p. 92, (adapted))

As can be read in the next Sections, these models seem to completely reduce motivation to instructional design. It is, however, to be questioned if instructional design is all that influences learning. Particularly when considering Rogers *self-actualising tendency* (Rogers, 1951; Boeree, 1998/2006; Damásio, 1994, 1999), it seems apparent that there are factors (e.g., intrinsic motivation of learners, attitudes of facilitators) that cannot be part of instructional design but are additional forces that drive motivation and learning.

6.1.1 The ARCS model of motivational design

(Keller, 1987) synthesised existing research on psychological aspects of motivation to learn and described a general model of motivational design of instructions, which is referred to as ARCS model. This model has been validated in terms of its application to learning contexts, such as classroom-based instruction, distance learning (Gabrielle, 2003; Huett, 2006; Visser, Plomp, & Kuiper, 1999), web-based learning (Vafa, 1999; Gunter, 2007), multimedia learning (Astleitner, 2000), and computer-aided instruction (D. W. Huang, Diefes-Dux, Imbrie, Daku, & Kallimani, 2004; Song & Keller, 2001).

(Keller, 1987) identified four main categories that help educators to initiate and sustain learners' motivation: attention, relevance, confidence, and satisfaction. The acronym of these four categories gives name to the ARCS model (Figure 28). According to this model, these four categories represent the necessary conditions for fully motivating a person in learning situations. Furthermore, this approach pays particular attention to motivation in e-learning environments and provides practical recommendations for the model's application in technology-enhanced learning environments. The following provides a brief summary of each category.

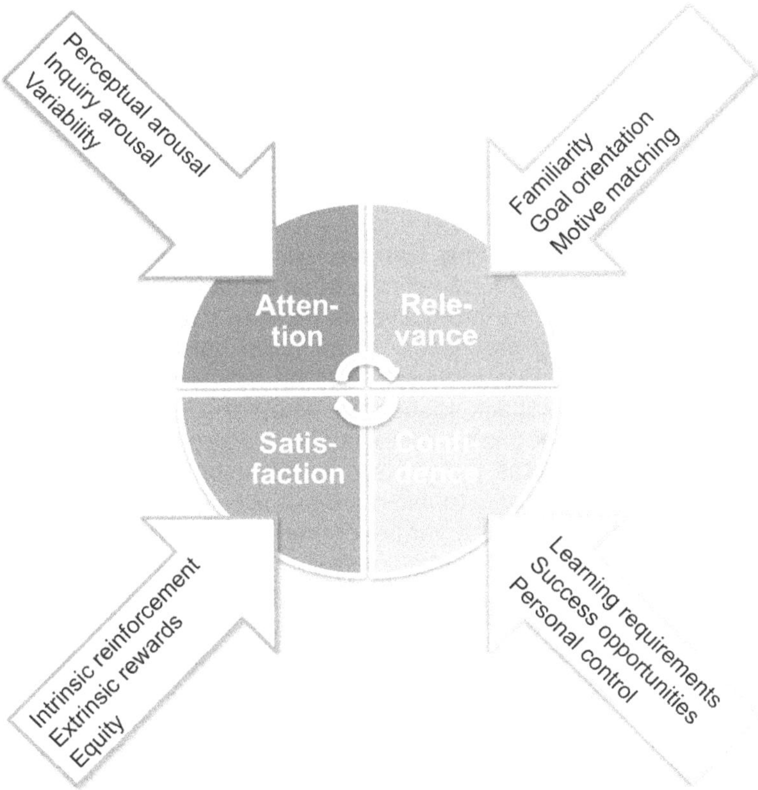

Figure 28. The ARCS model of motivation

Source: (Keller, 1987, (adapted))

[A]ttention

For motivating learners it is crucial to gain and maintain their attention and interest. While it is frequently not too difficult to gain attention in the beginning of a course or lesson, sustaining attention is a challenge. Arousing curiosity and providing stimuli are, thus, key components for maintaining a continuing motivation.

(Keller, 1987) recognises three subcategories for attention: perceptual arousal, inquiry arousal, and variability.

- *Perceptual arousal.* Educators can gain and maintain learners' attention by establishing new, unexpected, and surprising events. In technology-enhanced learning environments this can be achieved by sensory stimuli like, for instance, audiovisual elements (e.g., animated graphics, voices, sounds, etc.). Furthermore, content may be provided in an unusual manner or by making use of provocative statements. It is, however, important to avoid deflection caused by false and excessive use of means for gaining attention; otherwise learners' attention may be affected negatively.
- *Inquiry arousal.* Confronting learners with questions and problems, which have to be solved, can stimulate an attitude of inquiry and curiosity. It turns out to be promotive as regards motivation to provoke and nurture thinking processes. In an online learning environment, such motivating thinking processes can be activated, for instance, by question-answer-feedback sequences, where the learner has to participate actively. Other prominent examples are simulation tools, where the learner manipulates parameters, or other problem-solving situations, which allow learners to explore these actively.
- *Variability.* Making use of a variety of methods and media can be effective for maintaining students' interest. Consequently, throughout a course (or course unit), presentation styles, exercises, assignments, or other activities should vary (e.g., collaborative projects, essays, discussions, chats, etc.). A technology-enhanced learning environment particularly addresses the aspect of variability as, by nature, various media are used. Furthermore, the interplay of presence and online phases in a continuing task or activity may provide a particular value to learners as concerns variability as the specific combination may be new to them and, thus, create a stimulating atmosphere.

[R]elevance

It is crucial that learners perceive a course, training, or activity to have a value for them. Thereby, relevance does not necessarily come from content but from the way of teaching. Accordingly, the benefits of tasks, activities, and a whole course as such should be made transparent for all learners.

Relevance has both, a goal aspect and a process aspect. While the learning content (the learning objective) may be useful and relevant for learners, the learning process itself may also be relevant and motivating (e.g., in the form of group work). In both cases it is, though, crucial that learners perceive relevance – either from a goal-orientated, a process-orientated perspective, or both. The mere existence of relevance does not suffice if learners do not perceive it. Consequently, educators are required to emphasise these aspects and make them transparent to learners.

Relevance can be promoted through familiarity, goal orientation, and motive matching.

- *Familiarity*. The more familiar something is, the more relevant a learner will perceive it to be. Although something to be learned is yet unknown, it can be explained in or with reference to a context that is familiar. When describing abstract and non-familiar terms, metaphors, vivid examples, and images help to make a connection to something familiar.
- *Goal orientation*. In order to motivate learners, it is important to allow them to strive towards a visible goal. Accordingly it is important to clearly present the educational objectives and to highlight the importance and usefulness of the elaborated topics. It is motivating when the course design allows students to set their learning goals individually (within the frame of curricula requirements) such that individual and course objectives go in line.
- *Motive matching*. Since learners follow different motives, it is a good idea to offer several learning strategies, which suit the learners' motivation profiles. In order that students can better match their motives or values when selecting relevant activities, a course should implement a wide range of tasks and activities (e.g., group work, self-study projects, friendly competition, etc.), which also differ in difficulty in order to fit individual levels.

[C]onfidence

Confidence and positive success expectation are the third condition, which have to be fulfilled for motivating learners. Relevant subcategories of confidence are the expectancy for success, challenge settings, and attribution moulding.

- *Learning requirements*. It is obvious that learners will hardly be motivated as long as they do not know what they are in for. Accordingly the learning objectives as well as the required skills and knowledge should be clearly outlined right in the beginning of a course. Additionally, requirements can be illustrated by providing examples of acceptable achievements. Furthermore, requirements will be more transparent if the structure of a course's learning modules are outlined in advance, clearly specifying each module's learning objectives and assessment criteria. For online activities, students should receive an indication of how much time will be required to complete an activity.
- *Success opportunities*. Students will put effort into a course only if they are confident that they are able to achieve the objectives with reasonable effort and time. Consequently, they will be less motivated when they feel that they are rather likely to fail. Furthermore, it is motivational if learners have sufficient opportunities to experience success. This can be achieved by providing different levels of proficiency for individual achievement standards. Accordingly, new subject matters should be presented from the easiest to the most complex in order to meet learners' demands. With the adaptation of learning objectives to individual abilities and knowledge, boredom as well as excessive demand can be avoided. Students' actual knowledge levels can, for instance, be measured and determined by means of an exam in the beginning of a course. Experiencing success when mastering challenging tasks affects students' confidence in their own abilities positively. Furthermore, achievement strengthens self-esteem.
- *Personal control*. Providing feedback supports determinants of success. Learners should know that their success is based upon their own efforts and abilities. Feedback that ascribes success of failure to luck or giftedness is not motivating and should, thus, be avoided. Providing learners with a certain degree of self-determination (e.g., deciding on the order of topics to be learned) furthers personal responsibility and will act as a motivational stimulant.

[S]atisfaction

Learners should be rewarded for their efforts such that they obtain satisfaction from the learning experience. If their accomplishments are not recognised or if the consequences of their efforts differ from the expected outcome, learners would soon be discouraged.

Basically, (Keller, 1987) distinguishes three aspects of learners' satisfaction: intrinsic reinforcement (also called natural consequences), extrinsic rewards (also refered to as positive consequences), and equity, which are outlined below.

- *Intrinsic reinforcement.* Finding new skills immediately useful satisfies learners. Consequently, it is motivating if learners have meaningful opportunities to apply newly developed or acquired skills and knowledge in real or simulated situations.
- *Extrinsic rewards.* Additionally to intrinsic motivation, positive feedback and reward can reinforce learners' motivation and effort dedicated to tasks and learning. Such external rewards could, for instance, be offered as certificates for courses or praise from a facilitator. In technology-enhanced learning environments, self-assessment tests or games could be used to provide learners with additional opportunities to experience success. Providing motivating feedback after each correct answer or using an animation sequence acknowledging a leaner's high score may be further sources of motivating, positive feedback.
- *Equity.* It is crucial that students experience fairness and equal treatment. Tasks and assignments have to be consistent with learning objectives and the evaluation criteria should be made transparent. Furthermore, it is important that learners perceive equal treatment among all students.

The ARCS model of motivation is particularly appropriate for self-directed learning (Gabrielle, 2003, p. 30). As already stated earlier, this model has been tested extensively in a variety of contexts (e.g., Astleitner, 2000; Gabrielle, 2003; Gunter, 2007; Huett, 2006; Song & Keller, 2001; Vafa, 1999; Visser, Plomp, Amirault, & Kuiper, 2002; Visser, Plomp, & Kuiper, 1999) and research supports that the implementation and application of the ARCS model shows improved motivation, satisfaction, and performance. Since (Keller, 1987) emphasised the design and development of instruction, the majority of studies have tested the ARCS model predominantly from this perspective. (Visser, Plomp, & Kuiper, 1999) had been groundbreaking for being among the first who focussed on learner support, finding that the ARCS model positively affects motivation, persistence, and satisfaction of students in distance learning settings (Gabrielle, 2003, p. 30).

6.1.2 The SuperMotivation model

The SuperMotivation model goes back to (Spitzer, 1995, 1996). Basically the concept puts emphasis on activities that are assumed to promote individuals' development, concern, inclusion, engagement, etc. It builds on the core assumption that "any activity can be made highly motivating if a motivating context is added to the basic tasks" (Spitzer, 1996, p. 45). The foundation of this approach is, thus, to build sufficient motivators into an activity.

(Spitzer, 1996) suggests following ten motivating factors (motivators): action, fun, variety, choice, social interaction, error tolerance, measurement, feedback, challenge, and recognition.

- *Action*. In their personal lives, people avoid boredom and monotony. Instead, people want to be active and involved. Consequently, the first motivating factor refers to the active involvement of learners in their learning processes. Activities can thereby be of physical or mental nature. One of the essential aspects is the interactivity of the learning system.
- *Fun*. The fun factor is easily associated with motivation. The deployment of humorous and surprising elements in the learning environment can arouse interest and foster student involvement. Learning games are, for instance, a good example of how to imbed learning activities with fun.
- *Variety*. Variety of media, resources, and instructional materials used, prevent monotony and may boost motivation.
- *Choice*. Learners should have the opportunity to choose from a range of media, resources, and learning activities. This will provide learners with the feeling of a certain degree of power and control of their learning processes, which will be more motivating than feeling powerless over external forces shaping their lives.
- *Social interaction*. As people are social creatures, they like to interact and socialise with one another, although the degree of sociability will vary between individuals. Opportunities for social interaction – like, for instance, group discussions, work in teams, peer tutoring – have, thus, an important motivational function.
- *Error tolerance*. Making mistakes is an important factor in learning processes. Hence, it is important to create a learning atmosphere, in which students feel comfortable to make mistakes and have opportunities to learn from them.
- *Measurement*. When engaging in sports and games, scorekeeping and completion are motivating factors. In learning scenarios, though, people do not tend to look forward to being measured. Basically it is more valuable and motivating if measurement orientates on achievements and improvements rather than on faults and mistakes.
- *Feedback*. Feedback can be motivating if it is provided continuously and in a positive and encouraging way such that it points out the positive and focuses on how performance can be improved.

- *Challenges*. Trivial tasks are not motivating as people strive for an adequate challenge. Self-set goals by the learners are particularly recommended.
- *Recognition*. Recognition is a powerful force that has the capacity to release energy and increase motivation. Consequently, when facilitators and peers provide encouragement and show appreciation, learners' motivation is likely to increase.

This rather pragmatic list of motivators may be used as a guide for motivational instruction design. The model, though, seems to leave out important factors that drive motivation like, for instance, relevance or applicability in real situations.

6.1.3 The time continuum model of motivation

The time continuum model of motivation by (Wlodkowski, 1993) draws on approaches from linguistics, cognitive psychology, and motivation research. It is presented in the rather pragmatic form of a handbook for developing instruction.

Basically this model shares certain aspects with the ARCS model by (Keller, 1987). The time continuum model is, though, a prescriptive solution while the ARCS model has a strategy selection from a set of categories based on a synthesis of concepts in human motivation (Visser, Plomp, & Kuiper, 1999).

According to (Wlodkowski, 1993), there are six motivational components that influence learner's motivation and are the key to a continuous sequential process in the time continuum: attitude, need, stimulation, affect, competence, and reinforcement.

The main contribution of (Wlodkowski, 1993) is the idea that distinct motivational strategies are required at the different stages in the learning process. The time continuum model identifies three critical periods in the learning process where motivation is most important and in which particular motivational strategies will have the most impact: attitude and needs strategies are most relevant in the beginning of an activity, stimulation and affect strategies are most pertinent during an activity, and competence and reinforcement strategies are important when ending an activity.

- *Phase 1 – Attitudes and needs*. In order to meet learners' needs, these have to be identified in the beginning of a course or learning process. For instance, a needs assessment seems appropriate to survey students' particular needs. Based on these insights an educator should consider how to address these requirements and design the course or activity accordingly. If the course design allows for choice and self-direction, learners are able to fine-tune activities to best serve their individual needs. Furthermore, it is crucial to address learners' attitudes right in the beginning of a learning sequence. For instance, icebreaker activities or clearly outlining learning objectives may facilitate that learners develop a clear understanding of what will be required to be successful in the course and may, thus, contribute to a positive attitude. Establishing awareness of contents' relevance is a further strategy to enhance a positive learning climate (Hodges, 2004).

- *Phase 2 – Stimulation and affect.* During the learning process, further stimulation is required to maintain (or even increase) learners' motivation. Stimulation may be achieved through the provision of new learning material. Making the learning experience as personalised and relevant to the learner as possible is a promising strategy in this learning phase. In order to maintain a stimulating learning environment, it is recommended to involve learners via questions, varying presentation styles, or the use of different modes of activities from lecture to group work. Finally, establishing a positive affective experience and emotional learning climate facilitates motivation at this stage of the learning process (Hodges, 2004).
- *Phase 3 – Competence and reinforcement.* At the end of a learning experience, motivation is best achieved by affirming or increasing learners' feelings of competence and providing reinforcement. Frequent feedback and communication of the learning progress are main methods that allow learners to develop confidence in their competences and achievements. Recognising learners' performances could be addressed by providing rewards in any form that seems appropriate (Hodges, 2004). Additionally, at this final stage of the learning process, learners should be made aware of how the newly acquired knowledge and developed skills enable them to do what they have not been able to do before.

The time continuum model of motivation is not based on a scientific theory but draws from a variety of research from various disciplines. It is prescriptive since strategies, which should be used, are precisely defined and presented in the form of a handbook for developing and designing instruction. Put differently, it follows a rather pragmatic approach. The time orientation is, though, an aspect that other motivation models lack.

6.2 Measuring motivation

Only a few scientifically valid test exist to measure motivation in higher education (Siebert, 2006, p. 117). Apart from validation, motivation tests do not seem appropriate in all instances due to being based on differing assumptions as well as distinct definitions and models of motivation. While some test target at the aspect of participation (e.g., Boshier, 1991; Blunt & Yung, 2002), others stress the aspects of active involvement in the learning process (e.g., Chow & Law, 2005).

Consequently, it is not surprising that researchers try to gather items for their questionnaires from various sources in order to meet the specific demands of their research designs.

The following will briefly present measurement instruments that have been validated in several studies. The first portrayed instrument is the *Education Participation Scales (EPS)* as developed by (Boshier, 1991). Thereafter, two instruments that measure ARCS components of motivation will be described: the *Instructional Materials Motivation Survey (IMMS)* and the *Course Interest Survey (CIS)*.

As already mentioned earlier, researchers tend to develop their own instruments for measuring motivation, which fit their specific research design. Although the presented measurement instruments have been validated in scale of studies, still researcher use (approved) modified versions for their studies in order to fit their specific requirements (e.g., D. W. Huang et al., 2004; Kim & Keller, 2008; Marguerratt, 2007).

Education Participation Scales (EPS)

The *Education Participation Scales (EPS)* by (Boshier, 1991) is a 40-item survey with a scale from 1 (no influence) to 4 (much influence). The question to be answered for all items is: To what extent did these reasons influence you to enrol in your adult education class? For analysis, this instrument distinguishes six motive dimensions: social contact, social stimulation, professional advancement, community service, external expectations, and cognitive interest (Siebert, 2006, p. 117).

- *Social contact.* This dimension subsumes needs for variety, activity, relaxation, and avoidance of boredom.
- *Professional advancement.* The desire for occupational advancement, competence enhancement, competitiveness, and formal qualification (e.g., graduation, certificates) dominate this dimension.

- *Community service.* Motives to learn are civic involvement, honorary activities, political tasks on a community level, and political codetermination.
- *External expectations.* Occasions to engage in learning activities may be assignments by employers, encouragement by relatives, loss of employment and social status, or formal – for instance, legal – requirements.
- *Cognitive interest.* This dimension subsumes motives like curiosity, broadening experience, or joy at learning itself.

For each dimension the points for the according items are summed up and divided by the number of items. These calculated average values allow arranging a ranking of learning motives (Siebert, 2006, p. 118).

Course Interest Survey (CIS)

The Course Interest Survey (CIS) is a situational measure to identify motivation in a particular course (Gabrielle, 2003, pp. 17, 31). It is a 34-item survey with five-level Likert-style rating scales, which range from 1 (not true) to 5 (very true). Out of the 34 items, nine are reversed. For each item (statement), participants of a course are asked to indicate how true it is in relation to the particular course. The survey makes use of five subscales: one for each of the ARCS components (attention, relevance, confidence, and satisfaction), and one for the ARCS total score (Gabrielle, 2003, p. 31; Huett, 2006, pp. 38-39).

Instructional Materials Motivation Survey (IMMS)

The Instructional Materials Motivation Survey (IMMS) was developed to measure motivation related to instructional materials and has been tested extensively for reliability, primarily with undergraduate and graduate students (Gabrielle, 2003, pp. 17, 31).

The Instructional Materials Motivation Survey is a 36-item survey with five-level Likert-style rating scales. In analogy to the Course Interest Survey, the response scales range from 1 (not true) to 5 (very true). Out of the 35 items, ten are reverse items. Learners are asked to indicate how true each item (statement) is in relation to the instructional materials they have just studied. Again, there are five subscales: one for each of the ARCS components (attention, relevance, confidence, and satisfaction), and one builds an overall motivation score (Gabrielle, 2003, pp. 31-32; D. W. Huang et al., 2004, pp. TIE-32; Huett, 2006, pp. 39-40).

6.3 The research questions

This study aims at identifying motivational elements based on a comparison of a range of courses. The four courses under investigation have the same background as regards university, faculty, field of study, course co-ordinator, the use of a technology-enhanced learning setting as pedagogical means, and partly even the same students as some students participated in several courses. These courses, however, differ with respect to pedagogical elements that will – according to above-described motivation models – differently affect students' motivation.

This leads to the first research question: How do the four courses under investigation differ in motivating students?

Besides driving students' motivation in varying degrees, we expect that the different course designs spark distinct interests and motives. This hypothesis leads to the second research question: Do these courses differ regarding student's motives for commitment and performance?

6.4 The case design

As is obvious from the theoretical introduction to motivation, this research field is complex and research could already reveal many influencing factors. In terms of experiments, these factors can, though, not be held alike. Rather, studies investigating motivation to learn are bound to field studies, which are strongly limited as regards complexity reduction and the simultaneous isolation of several variables. Consequently, field studies on motivation to learn are very focussed on specific factors of interest. On an eclectic basis, each study contributes to the advancement of this research field.

Based on this work's overall research question towards promotive activities, this study on motivational aspects will, hence, concentrate on instructional designs.

6.4.1 Course designs

This study investigates four courses with differing course designs. The next Section (6.4.1.1) describes the courses under investigation. Thereafter, Section 6.4.1.2 provides a detailed overview over pedagogical elements in these courses.

6.4.1.1 Course descriptions

In general, the University of Vienna – more precisely the Department of Knowledge and Business Engineering – offers all of the investigated courses within the curricula of business informatics. Except for *WEB*

ENGINEERING, which is a compulsory course in the Bachelor's curriculum, all courses are part of the Master's curriculum. A course takes one term each course's workload is about five credit points according to ECTS (European Credit Transfer System). Group sizes are similar as each course group has about 20 participants.

All courses are held as technology-enhanced learning courses and include presence phases in class, which are accompanied by an e-learning platform (Mangler, 2005). Except for *WEB ENGINEERING*, the courses include self-evaluation as well as peer evaluation and employ online reaction sheets after each presence phase.

WEB ENGINEERING *(WE)*

The course *WEB ENGINEERING* is a laboratory course (*Übung*) accompanied by a lecture of the same title. Our investigation refers to the laboratory course only. In contrast to the other selected courses, *WEB ENGINEERING* is a compulsory course in the Bachelor's curriculum and six different facilitators facilitate the groups.

The course *WEB ENGINEERING* aims at providing insights into current concepts and methods of web application engineering and development. The course provides an overview of the technological basis of modern web applications and students learn about methods and processes to plan, model and develop web information systems.

At the beginning of the term, students build teams of three or four persons. Throughout the term each team develops a small web application with XML web services. Teams are free to choose a specific problem for implementation according to personal interests. Depending on their suitability to support the development process of the particular application, student teams have to choose corresponding analysis and design techniques like UML, XML, PHP, or Java.

Since students work on small web projects in teams, they experience team-based cooperative learning as well as project work. The particular design of the course requires students to collaborate online as well as in face-to-face situations.

For their small web applications, students are assigned to create design documents and to model programme parts. For each project phase, students have to provide these artefacts on the e-learning platform. Milestone results are then presented in the laboratory course units (presence phase). For quality assurance of the student teams' projects, partner team evaluation is deployed.

PROJECT MANAGEMENT – COMMUNICATION AND SOFT SKILLS *(SS)*

This course – from now on referred to as *Soft Skills* – is not a compulsory course but belongs to a specific *core subject combination*[15]. It primarily aims at improving students' soft skills competencies as required in project work situations. Particular attention is paid to team communication, ad hoc presentations, and moderation techniques.

The course is based on active, experiential learning (person-centred learning) and accompanied by an e-learning platform (Mangler, 2005) for knowledge intensive inputs and materials.

The facilitator moderates the initial three workshops introducing the basic topics and elaborating moderation skills with students. In the units thereafter, students take over. More precisely, based on their interests, each student team (about three to four persons each) is free to choose a particular soft skills topic, which fits the course content and objectives. Then each team prepares material and moderates its own workshop on the respectively chosen topic.

While a student team is responsible for a course unit, both the facilitator and peers continuously provide feedback during the workshops as well as in online reaction sheets (Motschnig-Pitrik, 2006b).

PERSON-CENTRED COMMUNICATION *(PCC)*

The course *PERSON-CENTRED COMMUNICATION* integrates the person-centred approach to a high degree. Besides the objective to allow students to experience a person-centred atmosphere based on the three Roger variables, this course aims at providing space for unfolding and experiencing their (inter)personal capacities and communication styles in a non-directive, unstructured setting.

While the major part of the course takes the form of unstructured encounter groups (Rogers, 1970), the three initial workshops are dedicated to sensitise students to the issues of the person-centred approach (Rogers, 1983), active listening (Gordon, 1970/1983, 1977/1979; Gordon & Burch, 1974/1977), sharing of ideas in small groups, and the concept of encounter groups (Motschnig-Pitrik, 2006a).

---

15 A core subject combination (Kernfachkombination) is a block of optional courses related to the respective curriculum, which may be chosen from a catalogue of options offered by the university.

Additionally, students prepare seminar papers in teams of three to four persons. For these papers, students can freely choose any topic related to person-centred communication. All seminar papers are peer evaluated and, finally, every student individually evaluates his or her contribution to the course.

ORGANISATIONAL DEVELOPMENT AND BUSINESS PROCESSES *(OD)*

ORGANISATIONAL DEVELOPMENT AND BUSINESS PROCESSES is not compulsory but belongs to a specific *core subject combination*. In this course students experience selected, authentic issues of organisational development and practise to model business processes on the basis of distinctly expressed strategic goals. The course is strongly group-orientated and involves group decision-making procedures, team exercises, and small-scaled team projects around topics that students select from areas amenable to organisational development according students' perceived needs.

In three workshops, the topics and projects are introduced. Students' presentations, detailed discussion, and process reflection take place in four consecutive days moderated by the main educator and co-facilitated by an international facilitator (Motschnig-Pitrik, 2006a).

6.4.1.2 Overview over pedagogical elements

The courses under investigation implement different course designs and, thus, include different pedagogical elements, which are assumed to have a particular impact on motivation and motives to learn. For the purpose of clarity we grouped these elements by following headings: basic elements, teamwork, as well as feedback and evaluation elements. The following briefly describes the elements that have been implemented and why these elements are assumed to drive motivation.

Basic elements

- *Rewarding self-initiative*. Self-initiated learning processes allow students to bear responsibility and positively impact students' involvement and learning (C. Bauer et al., 2006; Rogers, 1983). If the facilitator correspondingly rewards such proactive behaviour (instead of ignoring it), students will be ambitious and motivated.
- *Practical relevance*. Practice-orientated courses immanently accentuate the relevance of issues to be learned. Furthermore, in contrast to a dry theoretical presentation of topics, practical exercises and stressing the links to professional live will spice up a course and, thus, have a motivational effect.

- *Person-centred course style.* The person-centred approach to technology-enhanced learning does not only further deep learning but is expected to improve motivation, as could already be shown in a scale of studies (e.g., Aspy, 1972; Cornelius-White, 2007; Motschnig-Pitrik, 2006a).

Teamwork

As already outlined, work in small teams is a proven method for furthering self-directed learning and is, hence, an effective, promotive activity in learning environments. Through social interaction, students do not only tend to learn more contentedly but are also rather motivated (C. Bauer et al., 2006; Tausch & Tausch, 1963/1998).

- *Free choice of topic.* We assume that motivation rises when students are given the opportunity to choose a topic they like, since a self-chosen topic is typically one that a student is interested in. Moreover, such a topic will usually be one that a student is currently concerned with and for which he or she perceives its relevance (C. Bauer et al., 2006). Still, we should keep in mind that a few students will choose a topic that they think is easy to deal with instead of one they are most interested in.
- *Team seminar papers.* Team based learning creates an atmosphere of mutual stimulation and motivation, such that team members promote each other to reach a higher level. Furthermore, (Tausch & Tausch, 1963/1998) observe supportive behaviour within teams on a technical level, which provides students with a sound basis of knowledge. We conjecture that students are more likely motivated for further learning when having reached such a solid foundation than when they lack the necessary basics.
- *Moderation of course units.* When student teams are given the opportunity to design and moderate course units on their own, they leave the course with a sense of achievement and the feeling of cooperatively having accomplished something that they feel is important for their future professional lives (Motschnig-Pitrik, 2006b). The responsibility for a course unit paired with the relevance for their future professional careers and also with the space for being creative will drive a student's motivation.
- *IT project work.* Project work combines several motivational aspects. First, projects are goal-orientated and have high practical relevance. It most cases, projects will be highly relevant for computer scientists' future professional lives. Furthermore, this pedagogical element includes teamwork and requires commitment.

Feedback and evaluation elements

- *Team peer review.* Team reviews are gaining importance as pedagogical techniques, particularly in courses for computer scientists, since reviews have also technical relevance, for instance, in software engineering. Peer reviews have many positive effects on students' learning, which are described in detail in Section 7.1.5. We assume that, for instance, the effect that students develop awareness of their own work's quality will also have a positive impact on motivation.
- *Self-evaluation.* When introducing self-evaluation to a course, students are assured that their contributions are fairly assessed and are not merely dependent on a facilitator's impression. According to (Keller, 1987), we expect that this transparent and fair evaluation scheme has a positive impact on motivation.
- *Feedback.* Constant feedback throughout a course provides students with an indication about the current states of their performances (Keller, 1987; Tausch & Tausch, 1963/1998). We assume that the facilitator's feedback (not merely on assignments and tests but also on active participation in class or on the e-learning platform) gives students the feeling that all their contributions are worthwhile and taken seriously, which, in turn, will have a positive impact on motivation. Consequently, we expect course designs with regular feedback scoring higher in motivation than courses without.
- *Reaction sheets.* Including online reaction sheets in the course design allows students to express their likes, dislikes, observations, learning, suggestions, etc. The beginning of the next presence unit is then devoted to discussing students' reactions and deriving potential consequences on subsequent activities in the course. Based on this feedback, facilitators may adopt the course design as required by the specific, situational needs in a particular course (Motschnig-Pitrik, 2006b). We expect that this pedagogical element increases motivation since students have the possibility to express themselves and through discussion and tailoring the course setting accordingly, they perceive the feeling of being taken seriously. Additionally, the course is designed to meet their particular needs.

Table 10 provides an overview of the courses under investigation and allocates the pedagogical elements implemented in the corresponding course design.

Table 10. Pedagogical elements potentially influencing motivational aspects

PEDAGOGICAL ELEMENTS		PERSON-CENTRED COMMUNICATION	ORGANISATIONAL DEVELOPMENT	SOFT SKILLS	WEB ENGINEERING
BASIC ELEMENTS	rewarding self-initiative	✓	✓	✓	
	practical relevance	✓	✓	✓	✓
	person-centred course style	✓	✓	✓	✓*
TEAM-WORK	free choice of topic	✓	✓	✓	✓
	team seminar papers	✓	✓		
	moderation of course units			✓	
	IT project work				✓
FEEDBACK AND EVALUATION ELEMENTS	team peer review	✓		✓	✓
	self evaluation	✓	✓	✓	
	feedback	✓	✓	✓	✓**
	reaction sheets	✓	✓	✓	

* only with some facilitators, ** in varying degrees, depending on the facilitator

6.4.2 Implementation of the study

6.4.2.1 Data collection and methods

The research questions are addressed in a scale of questionnaires, for which a posttest-only research design (Grinnell & Unrau, 2008, pp. 194-195) was applied. Research and data collection took place in the time frame from summer term 2003 to winter term 2006/2007, while each course took one term. In the last week of a course, students were asked to fill in an online evaluation questionnaire. Data was collected as reference values for the comparison by asking students to answer questions for the respective course as well as for a typical course in their studies.

Since existing measurement instruments did not seem appropriate for the purpose of this study, a self-constructed pool of items was set up – as part of the dissertation by (Figl, 2008) – for measuring motivational aspects (cf. Appendix 1). Five-level Likert-style rating scales (Likert, 1932) were used as these proved highly suitable for measuring attitudes, particularly in the context of learning and when data is collected by means of online questionnaires (Page-Bucci, 2003). For the rating scales we used verbal labels that were experienced as equidistant (Rohrmann, 1978). The answering format consisted of five verbal labels in German language, the English pendants of which are: *totally disagree*, *somewhat disagree*, *partly / partly*, *somewhat agree*, and *totally agree*.

The whole set of items on motivational aspects includes 42 items (cf. Appendix 1). However, each of the investigated courses adopts an adapted course design, and so some items, which are relevant in one course, are irrelevant in another one. Hence, only a subset of items was included in each course's questionnaire. For this study, we only included items that were part of the questionnaires of at least three courses. Finally, out of the whole set of 42 items, 22 relevant motivational items were selected.

In order to measure whether students are driven and motivated to take part actively in the investigated courses by different reasons, a non-parametric procedure – the Chi-Square Test (T. R. Black, 1999, pp. 585-586; Zöfel, 2002, pp. 152-160) – was calculated for all items (Morgan, Leech, Gloeckner, & Barrett, 2004, p. 134; Zöfel, 2002, p. 89). Since the precondition of normality was not met for most items, a variance analysis could not be calculated (Zöfel, 2002, p. 97). The right skewed distributions were probably caused by the fact that most items were answered in the affirmative. Calculating sum scores did not seem appropriate for getting insights on motivational aspects since the whole set of items was not used for all courses and specific item-related results were of particular interest.

For 20 out of the selected 22 items the Chi-Square Test was significant, which indicates that students ascribe different grades of importance to those aspects in the investigated courses. For the two items I WANTED TO GET A GOOD GRADE and I LIKE TO SOLVE REAL PROBLEMS, no differences between courses could be identified. Although we considered these items as relevant when setting up the item pool, after reflecting on this finding, we assume that these motivational attitudes are independent from the course that students actually attend.

Unfortunately, under the given data quality, a nonparametric test procedure had been the only valid alternative, which is known for being less powerful than comparable parametric tests (T. R. Black, 1993, p. 162; 1999, pp. 581, 585; Peers, 1996, p. 120). One of the main limitations of applying such nonparametric tests is the difficulty of carrying out the analogous to the post-hoc analysis (T. R. Black, 1999, p. 585). Meeting this problem, several procedures and workarounds have been introduced (cf. T. R. Black, 1999, pp. 588-589; Everitt, 1992; Peers, 1996, pp. 120, 152-159; Penfield & Koffler, 1978; Siegel & Castellan, 1956/1988). Post-hoc analysis for the chosen Chi Square Test is, however, severely limited and considered highly problematic (T. R. Black, 1993, pp. 588-589; 1999, pp. 162-163). In the absence of adequate statistical software for post-hoc tests that allowed calculating which courses actually do differ, the most appropriate modality seemed to use answers' means for interpretation (cf. e.g., T. R. Black, 1999, pp. 585-586; Sirkin, 1995/2005, pp. 198-200, 202).

6.4.2.2 The sample

Table 11 illustrates the sample's distribution among courses as well as the response rates. Altogether students filled in 817 questionnaires. The response rates varied among courses; on total it was 88%. Only 17 out of those 817 students filled in a questionnaire for one and the same course twice in different terms since they failed the course and had to repeat it; this only affects the course *WEB ENGINEERING*.

Table 11. Sample size and response rate

	COURSES				OVERALL
	PERSON-CENTRED COMMUNICATION	ORGANISATIONAL DEVELOPMENT	SOFT SKILLS	WEB ENGINEERING	
questionnaires	171	38	79	529	**817**
response rate	96%	83%	90%	81%	**88%**

The majority of questionnaires derive from the course *WEB ENGINEERING* (529) since it is a compulsory course in the Bachelor's curriculum. The high number of questionnaires for *PERSON-CENTRED COMMUNICATION* (171) is due to the fact that this course took place every term. *SOFT SKILLS* and *ORGANISATIONAL DEVELOPMENT* have fewer questionnaires since these courses belong to a specific *core subject combination*. *ORGANISATIONAL DEVELOPMENT* took place only twice within the investigated course design, resulting in the lowest number of questionnaires.

80% of participants were male, 20% female. These percentages are comparable with the general gender ratio in business informatics, which is the curriculum that 95% of the courses' participants study.

6.5 Results

Figure 29 and Figure 30 provide an overview of all results concerning motivational aspects in the investigated courses. For emphasising particular results, relevant data are extracted and illustrated in individual figures (Figure 31 to Figure 34) in order to support discussion of these findings accordingly. As already outlined above, the answers' means were used for interpretation.

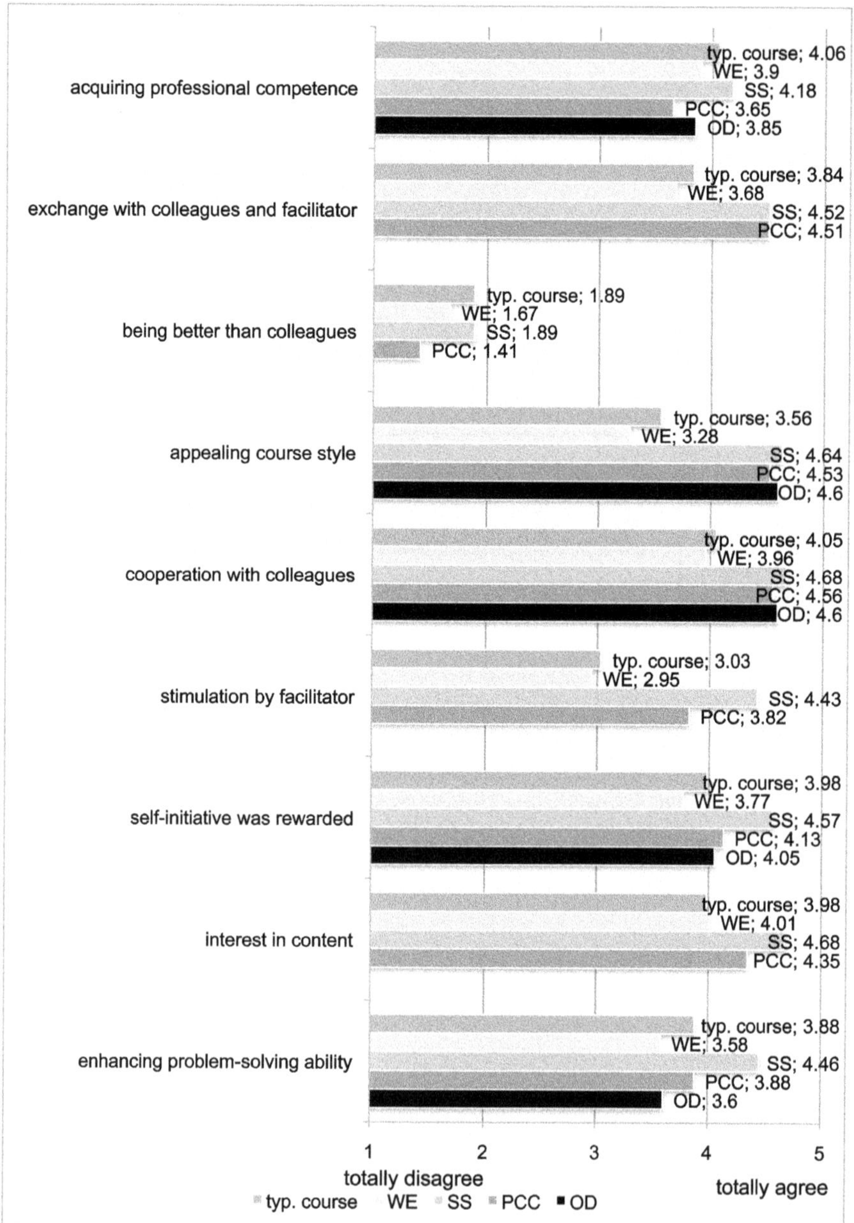

Figure 29. Motivational aspects in various courses (scale from 1 to 5), Part 1

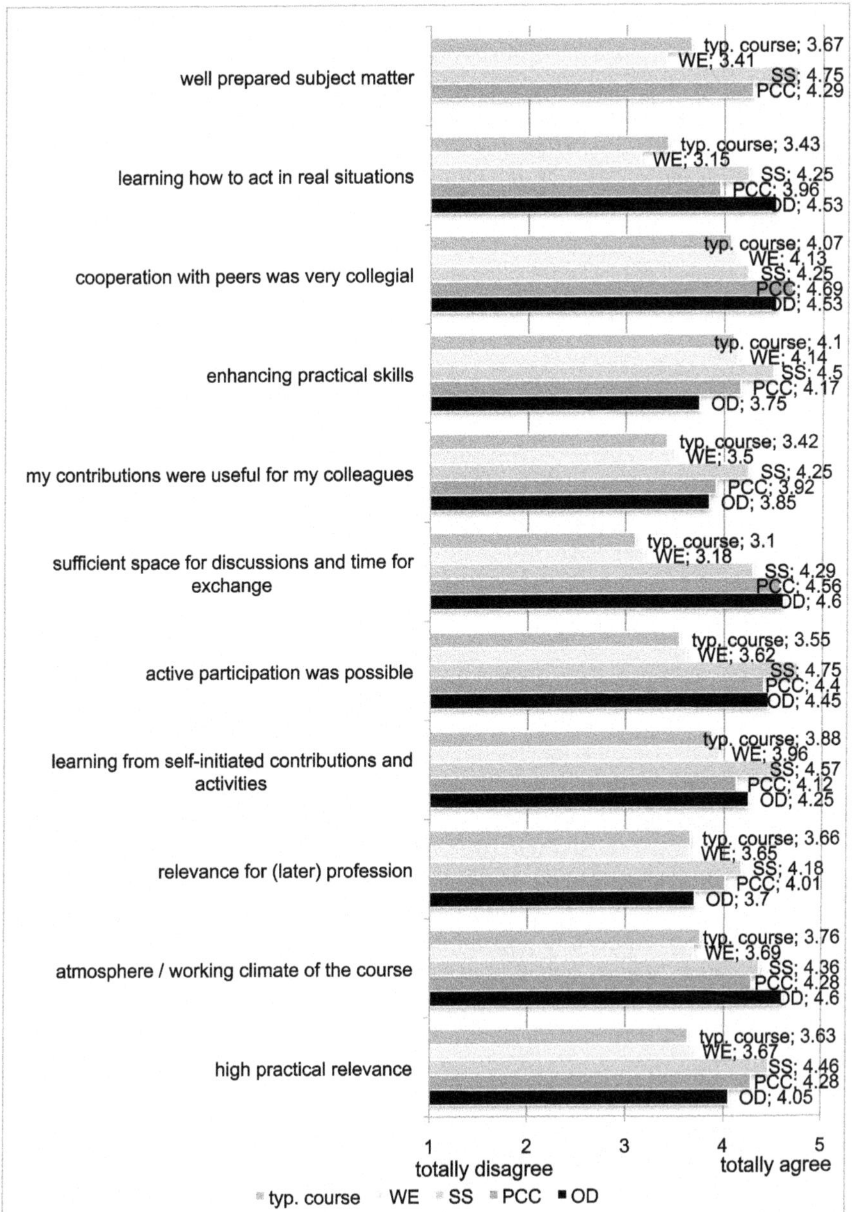

Figure 30. Motivational aspects in various courses (scale from 1 to 5), Part 2

In general, data show in evidence that students judge *WEB ENGINEERING* and a typical course less motivating compared to *SOFT SKILLS*, *PERSON-CENTRED COMMUNICATION*, and *ORGANISATIONAL DEVELOPMENT* with respect to most of the investigated motivation aspects. The only two questions against this trend are BEING BETTER THAN COLLEAGUES and ACQUIRING PROFESSIONAL COMPETENCE (Figure 31). These items do, however, *not* show any *significant* differences among the investigated group of courses.

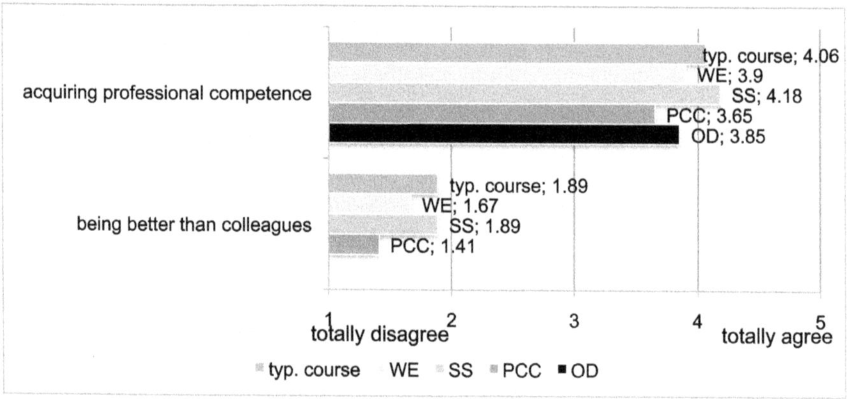

Figure 31. Items without significant differences

As regards the motive of BEING BETTER THAN COLLEAGUES, the answers are rather similar for all these courses. Only *PERSON-CENTRED COMMUNICATION* shows a slightly (but not significantly) weaker agreement concerning the competition aspect. However, this finding that *PERSON-CENTRED COMMUNICATION* scores very low (1.41) concerning competition is not surprising, since this course strongly integrates the person-centred approach and builds on encounter groups, which target personality growth rather than competition. This low level lets conjecture that students developed a sense of community throughout the semester and that they could perceive and enfold the three Rogers variables at least to a certain degree. It is actually more interesting that the other courses (particularly *WEB ENGINEERING*) do not score higher regarding the competition aspect. In fact, all of the investigated courses (including the typical course) score on a very low level (all 1.89 and below) concerning this aspect. On the one hand, we could conjecture that the cooperative learning setting in all courses had a lowering impact on competition. On the other hand, it could be that students' non-competitive attitude enables an ideal atmosphere that allows enfolding the values of cooperative learning. With the given research design, cause and effect are not transparent; accordingly, this issues calls for further investigation.

The only question that students similarly agree for all courses is ACQUIRING PROFESSIONAL COMPETENCE. Since differences could not be identified, striving for professional competence may be related to a pedagogical element, which is inherent in each of the investigated courses, or may have other than pedagogical reasons. Concerning this aspect, further investigation is necessary.

Compared to other courses, *SOFT SKILLS* scores particularly high in following items: ACTIVE PARTICIPATION WAS POSSIBLE, ENHANCING PROBLEM-SOLVING ABILITY, SELF-INITIATIVE WAS REWARDED, LEARNING FROM SELF-INITIATED CONTRIBUTIONS AND ACTIVITIES, MY CONTRIBUTIONS WERE USEFUL FOR MY COLLEAGUES, and ENHANCING PRACTICAL SKILLS (results are displayed in Figure 32).

We conjecture that this is due to the fact that student teams prepare and lead workshops in *SOFT SKILLS*, which affords high self-initiative and is experienced as being more useful to peers than student contributions in other courses. Furthering self-initiative is also an imminent part of the course design in *PERSON-CENTRED COMMUNICATION*; in this course, however, the implication of one's contributions and the effects on fellow students are not immediately apparent. As the internalisation of the person-centred approach's essence takes time to evolve, students may not be able to realise the true value of what they have learned (for instance, their experiences in encounter groups) and the relevance for everyday and professional life at the time when they filled in the questionnaire. Furthermore we have to take care in interpreting the scores concerning the improvement of students' skills (items ENHANCING PROBLEM-SOLVING ABILITY, MY CONTRIBUTIONS WERE USEFUL FOR MY COLLEAGUES, and ENHANCING PRACTICAL SKILLS) as the questionnaire only addresses students' self-perceptions but does neither analyse the respective peers' perceptions, whether these contributions had indeed been useful for them, nor does it measure students' *real* development of skills and abilities in terms of performance.

Furthermore, following items receive higher agreement in *SOFT SKILLS* and *PERSON-CENTRED COMMUNICATION* than in *WEB ENGINEERING* and in a typical course: INTEREST IN CONTENT, STIMULATION BY LECTURER, and WELL PREPARED SUBJECT MATTER. This suggests that participating students are deeply interested in the discussed topics of these courses.

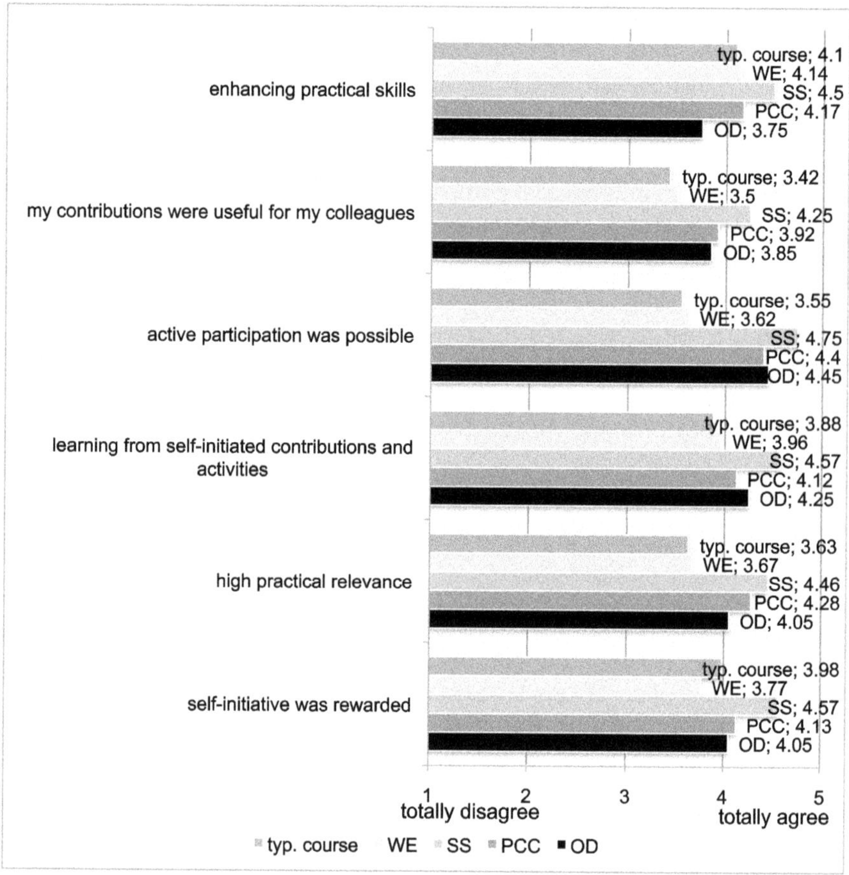

Figure 32. High motivation in the course on *Soft Skills*

Moreover, the results indicate clearly that students experience the person-centred teaching style of *Soft Skills*, *Person-Centred Communication* and *Organisational Development* as being more motivating than the regular style of *Web Engineering* and a typical course (items APPEALING COURSE STYLE and ATMOSPHERE / WORKING CLIMATE OF THE COURSE). In these courses integrating the person-centred style, students experience the high practical relevance (LEARNING HOW TO ACT IN REAL SITUATIONS, HIGH PRACTICAL RELEVANCE), the cooperative learning style (COOPERATION WITH COLLEAGUES and COOPERATION WITH PEERS WAS VERY COLLEGIAL) as well as the scope for discussions and exchange (ACTIVE PARTICIPATION

WAS POSSIBLE, SUFFICIENT ROOM FOR DISCUSSIONS OR TIME FOR EXCHANGE, EXCHANGE WITH COLLEAGUES AND LECTURER) as highly motivating. Figure 33 extracts results emphasising the positive effects of the person-centred style.

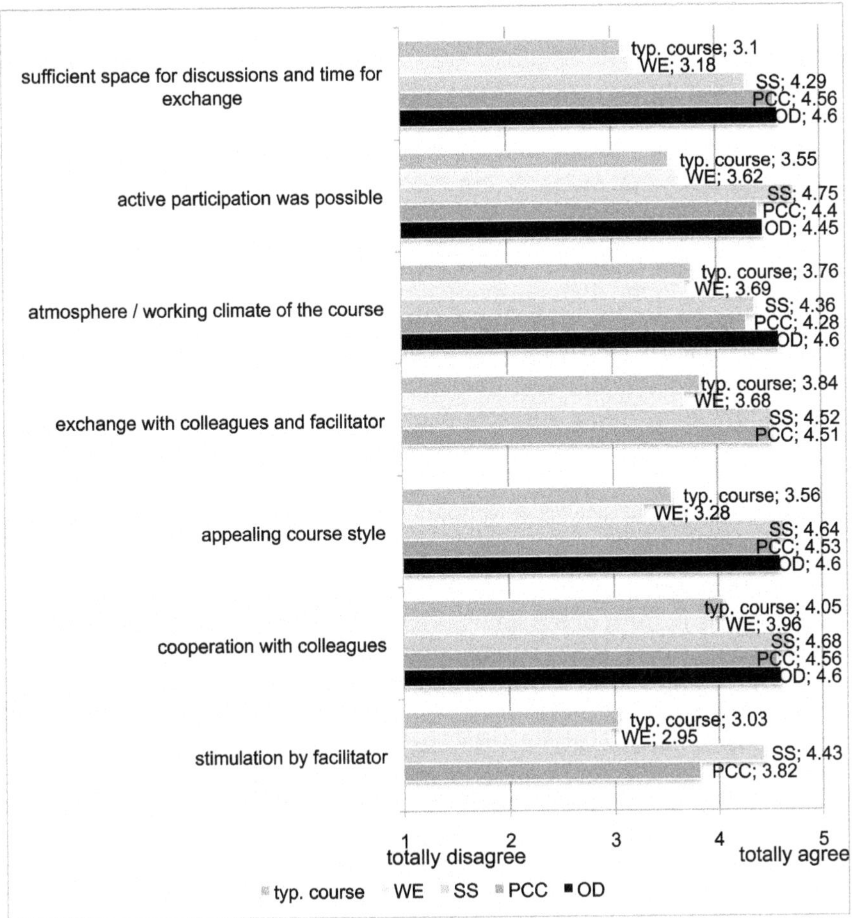

Figure 33. Positive effects of the person-centred style

The fact that *SOFT SKILLS* and *PERSON-CENTRED COMMUNICATION* score higher in the item ENHANCING PROBLEM SOLVING ABILITY than *WEB ENGINEERING* and *ORGANISATIONAL DEVELOPMENT* could arise out of the courses' contents. Students can put new inputs regarding these course's topics immediately, as soft skills and person-centred communication are not bound to specific situations but are relevant in every day life. In contrast, *Web Engineering* and *Organisational Development* concentrate on solving particular problems in professional life. Students with jobs in the field of computer science are more likely to perceive the practical relevance of these courses than students who have not yet entered work live in the IT sector. Additionally, they will immediately profit from the new inputs since they can deploy their learning in their current jobs. This interpretation is also strongly supported by the high score in INTEREST IN CONTENT for *Soft Skills* and Person-Centred Communication since it seems apparent that students are more interested in topics that are relevant in their current lives.

Additionally, *Soft Skills* and *Person-Centred Communication* find more approval in the item RELEVANCE FOR (LATER) PROFESSIONAL LIFE than the other two courses, which is a further indication for the above argument: Students do not perceive the link to their professional lives for topics of *Web Engineering* and *Organisational Development* because in their current lives, these subjects might not yet be highly relevant. Obviously, the practical relevance of topics and learning for their (future) procession needs to be better punctuated in these courses. For instance, the provision of illustrative examples may reveal the link to future but also to current needs.

As already sketched above, *Web Engineering* scores notably lower than other courses in most of the items. Figure 34 extracts the results, illustrating the items where *Web Engineering* scores particularly lower than the other courses and even lower compared to a typical course. Interestingly, these items are strongly linked to the facilitators' traits, abilities, and performances. Most evidently, the item WELL PREPARED SUBJECT MATTER refers to the facilitator's ability and willingness to prepare for the course and his or her actual performance in doing so. While – considered by itself – a score of 3.41 (on a scale from 1 to 5) for *Web Engineering* is not to be considered low, compared to the other courses (scores from 3.67 to 4.75) it however is. Furthermore, students' answers indicate that in contrast to the courses *Soft Skills* and *Person-Centred Communication* they did not feel stimulated by the facilitators in the course *Web Engineering* (item STIMULATION BY FACILITATOR). Additionally the items ATMOSPHERE / WORKING CLIMATE OF THE COURSE and APPEALING COURSE STYLE are closely linked to the facilitators' abilities in creating such an inspiring and appealing atmosphere.

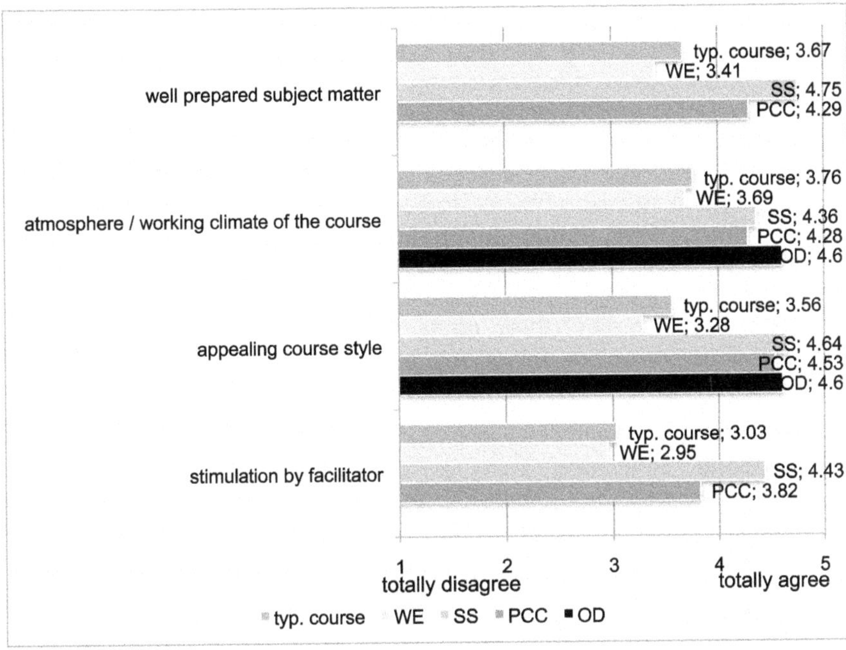

Figure 34. Low scores for *Web Engineering* in motivational items closely linked to facilitators

Keeping this in mind, we should now turn to the course's facilitators. While the courses *Soft Skills*, *Person-Centred Communication*, and *Organisational Development* were held by facilitators who have been dedicated to the person-centred approach to education for a long time[16], the groups of the course *Web Engineering* were held by a scale of different educators with, naturally, varying traits (cf. Figl, 2005). Concerning this aspect, (Figl, 2005) analysed differences between the educators of the course *Web Engineering* with respect to the three Rogers variables and their technical competence as perceived by students in summer term 2004. The most apparent differences were found for empathy and technical competence (Figl, 2005, p. 84). Furthermore, analysis revealed

16 Ratings of facilitators' person-centred attitudes (acceptance, empathy, congruence) as perceived by students are discussed in (Figl, 2005) for the course *Web Engineering* for summer term 2004.

that students of groups of the facilitator whose traits according the Rogers variables as well as technical competence were perceived in high gear, tend to perceive the above-mentioned motivational items (STIMULATION BY FACILITATOR, ATMOSPHERE / WORKING CLIMATE OF THE COURSE, and APPEALING COURSE STYLE) on above-average level. Students of groups of the educator who was perceived significantly lower than all other educators concerning the Rogers variables and technical competence, also valued these three motivational items considerably low for the particular course (Figl, 2005, p. 94). Furthermore, it is the facilitator with the Rogers variables in high gear who could reach high scores in these motivational items for the other three courses (courses *SOFT SKILLS*, *PERSON-CENTRED COMMUNICATION*, *ORGANISATIONAL DEVELOPMENT*).

These findings lead to the founded conjecture that both, the course design as well as the facilitators with their attitudes and traits, highly influence students' motivation. This also supports what the person-centred approach to learning advocates concerning the importance of the three Rogers variables and the principal of reciprocity. Unfortunately the research design does not allow for further analysis and deeper insights concerning this aspect due to the unbalanced distribution of facilitators among the investigated courses.

6.6 Conclusion

Despite the limitations of a posttest-only study, the results could demonstrate that the course design has a significant impact on students' motivation and on the motives that drive commitment and performance. The high appreciation of the person-centred course style and its satisfactory impact on motivation confirm the power of this approach in a technology-enhanced learning setting given highly competent facilitators. Activities following this approach are not only promotive as regards interaction and learning outcomes but also seem to explicitly drive students' motivation.

Surprisingly the course *WEB ENGINEERING*, in which not every facilitator followed the person-centred approach that strongly, scored even lower than a typical course in many motivational items. *WEB ENGINEERING* implements many motivational, pedagogical elements in the course design that other courses include as well. Clear-cut conclusions can, thus, not be drawn and further research is necessary in order to investigate whether those motivational elements that are not implemented in *WEB ENGINEERING* are the determining factors or if other aspects account for the differences. As *WEB ENGINEERING* is part of the Bachelor's curriculum while the other courses belong to the Master's curriculum, it has to be considered that students might have different motives at different stages of their academic career. Moreover, it has to be considered that *WEB ENGINEERING* is a compulsory course within the Bachelor's programme while the other courses may be selected as an elective subject (*core subject combination*[17]). Further research, investigating the reasoning for this finding, is necessary.

More important, *WEB ENGINEERING* involved facilitators that were not active in the other courses under investigation. This could be a further reason for *WEB ENGINEERING*'s distinctiveness compared to other courses. The course design as such is not sufficient for motivation. Our findings strongly support the assumption that facilitators' attitudes and traits highly influence students' motivation. Unfortunately the chosen research design has limitations concerning this aspect as facilitators were unbalancedly distributed among the investigated courses. Although it would be valuable for the research objective to mix facilitators among the courses, we have to admit that it is challenging and due to facilitators' differing knowledge expertises within a university almost – but not completely – impossible to implement such a scenario. Meeting this challenge, study involving similar courses from various universities with distinct facilitators is thinkable, whereby other limitations of field studies (e.g., different contexts) will become effective.

Although motivation theories and models as well as learning theories emphasise that relevance can come from the way something is taught and does not necessarily have to come from content, results indicate that students see the course's relevance more clearly if also perceive the content to be relevant to their current lives and needs. On the facilitator's side, it might also be easier to demonstrate relevance out of a given content, which is a further indication that students perceive relevance more intensely in such cases.

Furthermore, project work is widely regarded as a promotive pedagogical element (e.g., Figl, 2008, 2009; Mills & Treagust, 2003; Okolo & Ferretti, 2000; Tausch & Tausch, 1963/1998; Willard & Duffrin, 2006; Yesildere & Turnuklu, 2006); but this could not be shown in our study. Future research should consider paying special attention to this aspect, which is established but hardly researched. Particularly interesting is research on project work in a course on *PROJECT MANAGEMENT* or the like since

17 A core subject combination (Kernfachkombination) is a block of optional courses related to the respective curriculum, which may be chosen from a catalogue of options offered by the university.

course content, course design, and investigation aims could be ideally combined.

Particularly with respect to the influence of a facilitator's traits, our research illustrates the limitations of learning design patterns. Although design is crucial and gives direction, the implementation of a design is at least equally important. We suggest that particular attention has to be directed to the end users (learners) who have specific requirements and desires, which may be distinct for every user in different settings. Substantially, facilitators' formation is a crucial factor and includes not merely the technical expertise but refers to all three levels of learning and personal growth (intellect, skills, personality).

7 The impact of media selection on peer reviews[18]

While peer reviews have already become a common ingredient in software engineering projects, they also gain recognition as pedagogical techniques in project-based work in learning situations (e.g., Steenkamp, 2002; Tu & Lu, 2004). Particularly in computer science and business informatics courses, students will profit from the pedagogical benefit of peer review activities and simultaneously from its practical relevance as regards their future professional careers. Graduates with a degree in computer science or business informatics will predominantly work in projects. Hence, in this field education with practical relevance needs projects and teamwork to become an intrinsic part of courses (e.g., Meyer, 2001; Steenkamp, 2002) in order to provide graduates with a sound basis. Irrespective of this requirement coming from business, team-based work is regarded as highly promotive as pedagogical element (e.g., Tausch & Tausch, 1963/1998, pp. 253, 258-262).

Peer reviews have been used in a wide variety of disciplines, among them, accounting (e.g., Bailey, Hermanson, & Louwers, 2007), engineering (e.g., Chinn, 2005; Gehringer, 2000; Sitthiworachart & Joy, 2003; Trahasch, 2004; Wolfe, 2004), and social sciences (e.g., Coit, 2004; Dochy, Segers, & Sluijsmans, 1999; Hansen, 2005; S.-Y. Huang, 1998; Lin, Chang, Lee, & Sung, 2002; Tuzi, 2004). Furthermore, the peer review process is widely adopted in the scientific community as a means of quality assurance for papers being published in scientific journals and conference proceedings (e.g., Bailey, Hermanson, & Louwers, 2007; Brown, 2004; Godlee, Gale, & Martyn, 1998; Jefferson, Alderson, Wager, & Davidoff, 2002; Jefferson, Wager, & Davidoff, 2002; Wager & Jefferson, 2001; Ware & Monkman, 2007).

In educational settings, peer review is frequently applied as a means of assessment. Interestingly, although such peer evaluation has been used in many academic fields, it is most often discussed in the context of writing classes, for instance, to improve students' writing skills as well as to learn from reviewing others' work. Mainly, the extensive use of peer reviews in those courses served the purpose to eliminate the need for educators to read hundreds of student essays (Gehringer, 2000).

---

18 Findings of the case studies on peer reviews have been partially published in following four articles: (C. Bauer & Figl, 2006), (Figl et al., 2006), (C. Bauer et al., 2009a), and (C. Bauer et al., 2009b).

However, peer reviewing has benefits far beyond relieving the educator's workload on grading. Although many studies focus on validity and content of reviews (e.g., Derntl, 2006; Dochy, Segers, & Sluijsmans, 1999; Gehringer, 2000; Trahasch, 2004), they do not only elaborate that peer- and co-assessment foster fair grading but also discuss positive effects of peer reviews on students *generic skills* and on educator's workload and teaching. This includes, for instance, development of evaluation skills, increasing reflection abilities, developing awareness of the quality of own work, and learning from peer contributions (e.g., Dochy, Segers, & Sluijsmans, 1999; Trahasch, 2004).

A central concern in this research is to investigate students' perception of online peer review activities and outcomes, as well as to determine how technology influences reviews and students' learning processes. The first case study (Section 7.2) in this field focuses on how the face-to-face and the online setting impact the peer review outcome. As this study's results raised the question whether a combination of media may be appropriate for the peer review activity, we proceeded our research with a follow-up case study (Section 7.3). In this second study, we analyse the appropriateness of diverse peer review settings with different media combinations. As the follow-up study builds on the prior one, findings of the first case study were incorporated into the case design.

7.1 Theory and background

As peer review is used for different purposes in a variety of disciplines, it comes natural that several terms and definitions occur. Peer review, peer evaluation, peer assessment, peer response, peer feedback are only some of them. In order to provide a clear understanding of peer review, the following Sections (7.1.1 to 7.1.5) discuss this concept in the most relevant fields of use (peer assessment, peer review in writing classes and language courses, peer review in scholarship, and peer review in software development). Only after considering the variants of peer review in these domains, the terminology for this work can be specified (Section 7.1.6). Finally, Section 7.1.7 briefly compares the use of peer reviews in online and face-to-face settings.

7.1.1 Peer assessment

Peer assessment is defined as a scenario where students review other students' learning outcomes (artefacts) on the basis of a set of criteria (Trahasch, 2004, p. 16). It is a form of innovative assessment, which is rather seen as a tool for learning than only as a tool for benchmarking knowledge at the end of the learning process (Trahasch, 2004, p. 16).

According to (P. Black & William, 1998), the term assessment refers to all activities undertaken by educators and students that provide information that can be used as feedback to alter subsequent teaching and learning activities. Under this definition, assessment encompasses, for instance, educator observation, classroom discussion, and analysis of student work like assignments and tests (Boston, 2002). Based on how assessment information is used, one traditionally differentiates between summative and formative assessment.

Briefly put, *summative assessment* provides a summary judgment about the learning achieved after some period of instruction (e.g., by grading or scoring a test or paper) (Boston, 2002).

Formative assessment, on the other hand, is a feedback process that uses information about students' performance to close the gap between students' current learning state and the desired state via well-directed pedagogical actions. In other words, assessments become formative, when the information is used to adapt teaching and learning to meet students' actual needs (P. Black & William, 1998; Boston, 2002).

In higher education peer assessment is widely applied both as formative as well as summative assessment. For a generic view on such peer evaluation see (Derntl, 2006).

7.1.2 Peer review in writing classes and language courses

Dating back to the 1970s, writing instruction moved from a *product view* to a *process view* with multiple drafting. Feedback across the various drafts in the writing process gained importance and as a consequence peer reviews have become a significant activity in such courses (Coit, 2004; Hansen, 2005, p. 9). In the context of writing classes, peer reviews are sometimes also referred to as peer response, peer feedback, or peer editing.

When peer reviewing in writing classes, students assume the roles of editors, educators, or tutors and provide feedback on each other's documents either orally or in writing (Hansen, 2005, p. 9). In the last decade, the mode of such peer reviews has shifted from traditional pen-and-paper to the use of information and communication technologies for commenting and discussion (Hansen, 2005, p. 9).

There is a growing body of literature on response to writing, investigating the effects of peer and educator reviews on revisions (e.g., Coit, 2004; Gehringer, 2000; Hansen, 2005; Tuzi, 2004).

7.1.3 Peer review in scholarship

> "Scientific peer review is the evaluation of scientific research findings or proposals for competence, significance and originality, by qualified experts who research and submit work for publication in the same field (peers)" (Brown, 2004, p. 7).

In the scientific community, peer review is the primary method of quality assurance, applied for example by, editors of scientific journals or conference proceedings. On completing a project or stage of work, researchers summarise their experiments, findings and conclusions in a paper, which they send to a journal or a conference to be published. Editors will then ask well-qualified experts to provide written comments and opinions about the research papers that have been submitted for publication. The referees comment on particular criteria (Table 12) and suggest whether the work can be published in the current form or whether it needs minor or major revisions for being published. These peer reviews are used as foundation for the decision whether a paper is finally published in the particular journal issue or conference proceedings (Brown, 2004, p. 7).

The criteria used for evaluating papers are specific to the product (journal, conference) positioning as defined by the particular editorial board. There are, though, several criteria that are commonly accepted (Table 12) and papers generally need to meet these requirements (Brown, 2004, p. 8). First of all, referees assess whether the presented findings are significant to the scientific community. Furthermore, issues have to be presented in an understandable way and an article shall be neither too long nor too short. Relevant current and past research on the topic has to be considered appropriately. It is required that reasoning and evidence are sound and thorough. In order to be relevant, a newly advanced theory has to be preferable to competing (existing) theories. Furthermore, a theory needs to be testable – if not currently then the testability has to be expected by means of future (still to be advanced and developed) methodologies and technologies. Last but not least it is crucial that scholars consider ethical guidelines and practices in their research (cf. H. H. Bauer, 1992).

Peer review can, thus, be seen as a form of *scientific quality control* or an *error detection system*. More than that, the peer review process is considerably more critical and dynamic than many other forms of quality regulation (Brown, 2004, p. 7). Traditionally, peer review has been important mainly for researchers who have to put trust in others' work in order to develop their own (Brown, 2004, p. 2).

Table 12. Common criteria for the scientific peer review

CRITERIA	SPECIFIC QUESTIONS
significance	Are the findings original? Is the paper suitable for the subject focus of this journal / conference? Is it sufficiently significant? (Is the paper predominantly repetitious of previous work, albeit reporting different experiments (me too paper)? Does it seem that the authors divide a corpus of research work between several minimal papers at the threshold of acceptability, rather than presenting it in one (salami slicing)?)
presentation	Is the paper clear, logical and understandable?
length	Does the article justify its length?
scholarship	Does it take into account relevant current and past research on the topic?
evidence	Are the methodology, data and analyses sound? Is the statistical design and analysis appropriate? Are there sufficient data to support the conclusions?
reasoning	Are the logic, arguments, inferences and interpretations sound? Are there counter-arguments or contrary evidence to be taken into account?
theory	Is the theory sufficiently sound, and supported by the evidence? Is it testable? Is it preferable to competing theories?
ethics	For papers describing work on animals or humans: Does appropriate licensing or ethical approval cover the work? (Many biological and medical journals have their own particular guidelines published for such research.)

Source: (Brown, 2004, p. 8, (adapted))

(Ware & Monkman, 2007) recently conducted a study on the use of peer reviews in scientific journals. It provides an international overview and researches into the attitude to and experience with peer review from the angle of the different stakeholders. Despite its wide adoption in scholarship, peer review is not without controversy in the scientific community. (Wager & Jefferson, 2001), for instance, criticise its deployment in the biomedical field.

Many different groups of people (e.g., journalists) comment on scientific issues. Only very few of them, however, refer to whether work has been peer reviewed or not. However, scholars themselves rarely explain to the public what peer review is and fail to demonstrate regard for the distinction. As a consequence, the public cannot develop awareness about the differences in quality and, hence, the social discussion is not very demanding about the quality of scientific information (Brown, 2004, p. xii).

7.1.4 Peer review in software development

Quality assurance plays a significant role in the software development cycle (e.g., Galin, 2004; Harjumaa, Tervonen, & Huttunen, 2005; Iisakka, Tervonen, & Harjumaa, 1999; Tervonen, Iisakka, & Harjumaa, 1998; Wiegers, 2002a). Usually the term *quality assurance* evokes an image of executing software to see whether it functions as intended (Wiegers, 2002b). An alternative, widely practiced form of quality control is to invite colleagues to examine your work in order to detect bugs and faults in software artefacts and code, but also to identify improvement opportunities: a peer review (Mashayekhi, Drake, Tsai, & Riedl, 1993).

While traditional testing is limited to executable code, peer reviews can be applied to any software deliverable, design, or document at any stage of the development process. Even marketing documents, user manuals, or risk management plans may be reviewed (Mashayekhi et al., 1993; Wiegers, 2002a, pp. 11-12). Consequently, peer reviews have long been recognised as a powerful way to improve quality (Mashayekhi et al., 1993; Wiegers, 2002b).

(Wiegers, 2002a, p. 3) points out that the term peer review is often misinterpreted to mean that participants evaluate a colleague's performance. The point of a peer review is, however, to critique a work product, not the individual who worked on it. Furthermore, it is to be highlighted that the goal of reviews is not only to track errors and gather improvement suggestions but also help authors create better work products in the future; in other words, reviews aim at learning something from every review in which one participates either as an author or as a reviewer.

Peer reviews distinguish from formal design reviews in two major aspects: in their participants and authority. While participants of design reviews hold superior positions to the project leader, participants of peer reviews are, typically, members of the project leader's department, members of other units, or project leader's equals (simply put: peers). The other major difference lies in the degree of authority and in the review's objective. Formal design reviews are authorised to approve the design document in order that work on the project's next stage can begin. A peer review's objective lies in detecting errors and deviations from standards and, thus, such an authority of approval is not granted to peer reviews (Galin, 2004, p. 158).

With the appearance of computerised design tools, including Computer-Aided Software Engineering tools (CASE tools) and systems of vast and powerful software packages, some professionals tend to disdain the value of manual reviews. Empirical research findings and software surveys, however, provide convincing evidence that peer review is a highly efficient and effective method (e.g., Galin, 2004, p. 158; Harjumaa, Tervonen, & Huttunen, 2005; Iisakka, Tervonen, & Harjumaa, 1999).

In the context of software quality assurance the term peer review refers to the general activity of peer-reviewing software code and artefacts without regard to precisely how it is conducted. There is a spectrum of peer reviews that range from a very informal to a highly systematic process of inspection. Literature, however, gives conflicting definitions and inconsistent usage for the names of these approaches and activities. Thus, one may sometimes find the terms review, inspection, and walkthrough used interchangeably although they actually represent different methods for performing peer reviews (Wiegers, 2002a, pp. 3, 31).

Adhering to (Wiegers, 2002a, p. 31), who strives for providing a common vocabulary, peer reviews can be classified based either on the degree of formality or on the relative levels of discipline and flexibility (Iisakka, Tervonen, & Harjumaa, 1999; Tervonen, Iisakka, & Harjumaa, 1998). The following paragraphs briefly present both models of classification.

Figure 35 places several common review methods along a *formality* scale. This figure, though, serves only as an exemplification since these are not the only types of peer reviews and multiple variations of many of them exist.

Inspections are the most systematic and rigorous type of peer review and have several characteristics (Wiegers, 2002a, pp. 32-34):

- defined objectives,
- participation by a trained team,
- leadership by a trained moderator,
- specific participant roles and responsibilities,
- a documented review procedure,
- reporting of results to management,
- explicit entry and exit criteria,
- tracking of defects to closure, and
- recording of process quality data.

Informal reviews may well meet one's needs in certain situations. They are quick and cheap, do not require any advance planning nor demand an organisational infrastructure, and can help the authors to proceed their work on an improved course. Ad hoc reviews may be as simple as one programmer asking another to spend a few minutes helping to track down an elusive bug. Nevertheless such spur-of-the-moment reviews are important due to providing a quick way to get another perspective that often finds errors, oneself just cannot see (Wiegers, 2002a, pp. 1, 32, 41).

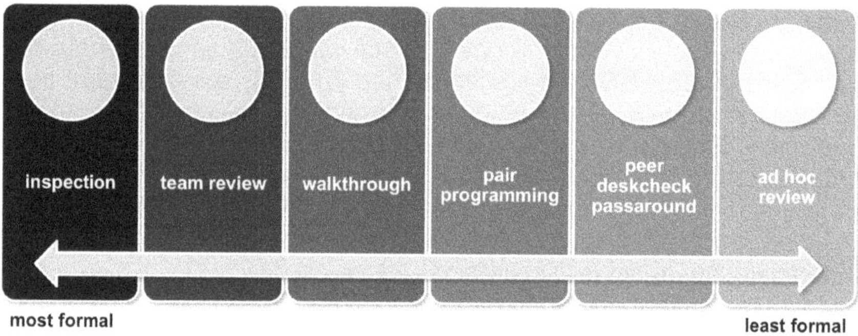

Figure 35. Peer review formality spectrum

Source: (Wiegers, 2002a, p. 32, (adapted))

Combining informal reviews with a formal inspection may provide a powerful quality strategy. A final inspection's effectiveness may be improved when many defects have already been revealed and eliminated in previous informal reviews. Without prior informal reviews some other problems would certainly be overlooked in a defect-riddled specification. Thus, it is good advice to review key project documents early and often, since overall quality is raised and because the cost of finding requirements errors is much lower in the early stages of a project (Wiegers, 2002a, p. 42).

Although the formal inspection plays an import role in the software development process, practitioners see it as being too strict a method. Hence, it is just understandable that organisations tend to find their own ways of adapting the process, which leads to tailored versions of peer reviews, which differ in type and in the degree of formality (Galin, 2004, p. 160; Tervonen, Iisakka, & Harjumaa, 1998). Figure 36 depicts the two dimensions, discipline and flexibility. Based on above considerations, it illustrates the usability of these dimensions by placing conventional inspection and walkthrough as two examples of peer reviews styles in the figure. The arrows present the two roads for proceeding towards tailored peer reviews.

The *discipline* dimension explains the formal aspect of peer reviews with three key words: roles, procedures, and metrics. As already mentioned above, the much-disciplined form of inspection follows prescriptive roles and procedures. (For example, it is suggested that about four to six software engineers should participate in an inspection). Furthermore, if an organisation desires to shift peer reviews from plain error removal to improving quality, effectiveness metrics with goal values are useful for monitoring peer reviews (Iisakka, Tervonen, & Harjumaa, 1999; Tervonen, Iisakka, & Harjumaa, 1998).

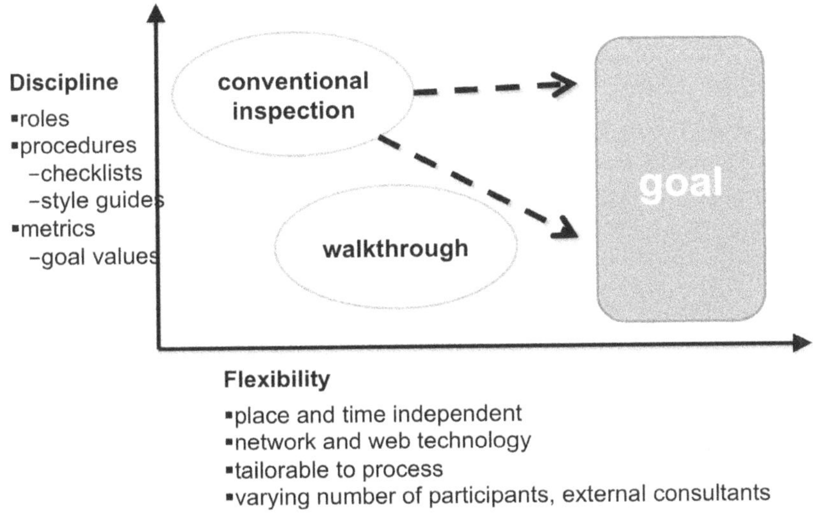

Figure 36. The flexibility and discipline dimensions in peer review

Source: (Tervonen, Iisakka, & Harjumaa, 1998, (adapted))

The *flexibility* aspect comes from the implementation of the peer review process and the deployed supporting tools (Tervonen, Iisakka, & Harjumaa, 1998). A flexibility ratio can be measured with respect to four key items:

- *Place and time independence*. Although face-to-face meetings typically provide a natural way of collecting opinions, it is often difficult to gather the group at the same place at the same time. There is, hence, a need for a shift towards a more flexible implementation of meetings (Iisakka, Tervonen, & Harjumaa, 1999; Tervonen, Iisakka, & Harjumaa, 1998).
- *Network*. Especially web technology provides a base solution for place and time independence (Iisakka, Tervonen, & Harjumaa, 1999).

Peer review tools may provide a set of functions for distributing documents to be inspected, annotating them, searching related documents, and gathering inspection statistics (Tervonen, Iisakka, & Harjumaa, 1998).

- *Tailoring.* The way, how a peer review is conducted, may vary if, for instance, the materials or participants vary (Iisakka, Tervonen, & Harjumaa, 1999).
- *Varying numbers of participants.* Conventional peer reviews have three to eight participants. If it is not possible to gather so many people in a specific situation, another mode of peer review with the available number of participants is to be adopted (Iisakka, Tervonen, & Harjumaa, 1999).

Inspection and walkthrough are the more commonly employed versions of the in Figure 35 mentioned methods. It should, however, be noted that in response to the variability (as illustrated in Figure 36) the borders between the two methods are easily blurred (Galin, 2004, p. 160). Therefore, the differences are not described in detail at this point.

In closing, however, a (very) brief description of typical types of peer reviews shall be given, whereby (Wiegers, 2002a)'s terminology is used (Figure 35):

- *Inspection.* The inspection is the most formal type of peer review, which has been identified as best practice in software industry. It follows a multistage process (e.g., planning, overview, preparation, meeting, rework, follow-up, and causal analysis) with specific roles assigned to participants. Inspections rely on checklists of deficiencies, which are commonly found in various types of software work products, and other analytical techniques used to detect bugs. Apart from being the most rigorous type of review, an inspection is characterised by being lead by participants other then the work product's author (Wiegers, 2002a, pp. 33-34, 50-56).
- *Team review.* A team review is type of *inspection light.* It is planned and structured like an inspection but less rigorous and less formal. A team review allows a group of qualified people to judge whether or not a work product is suitable for use and to identify the parts in which the product does not satisfy its specifications. In contrast to the inspection, which does not allow the author to serve as the moderator, the author might lead a team review. Some participant roles (which are obligatory in the inspection) may be combined and, in contrast to most inspections, the reader role is omitted (Wiegers, 2002a, p. 35).

- *Walkthrough.* The walkthrough is an informal review where a work product's author describes the product to a group of peers and asks them for comments. A walkthrough does not follow a defined structure and records are rarely kept. The author takes the dominant role while other roles are usually not defined. In absence of any defined procedures the way a walkthrough is performed depends on the author and, thus, ranges from casual to disciplined. Walkthroughs do not only aim at finding problems but is also targeted for reaching a shared understanding (Beck, 2000, pp. 58-59; Wiegers, 2002a, pp. 36-38).
- *Pair programming.* It is a component of Extreme Programming (XP) (cf. Beck, 2000), which is a popular agile methodology approach to software development. In pair programming, two developers work simultaneously on the same software on a single workstation. This approach facilitates a continuous, incremental, and informal review of each programmer's ideas and literally applies the saying *two heads are better than one.* Obviously this type of review is informal as it is unstructured and does not involve preparation or documentation. In fact, pair programming is not specifically a review technique but rather a software development strategy. Nevertheless, it cannot be denied that it makes use of basic informal review techniques and some evidence indicates that the synergy of two minds indeed leads to superior product quality (Wiegers, 2002a, pp. 38-39).
- *Peer deskcheck.* A peer deskcheck involves only one person – besides the author – examining a work product. It depends entirely on the reviewer's knowledge, abilities, and self-discipline. Thus, peer deskchecks may be fairly formal if the reviewer employs checklists or other specific analysis methods – or rather informal or not very comprehensively done. Upon completion, the reviewer can simply hand the author the marked-up work product or deliver a thorough defect list. The peer deskcheck may also include a follow-up discussion with the author to explain the reviewer's findings (Wiegers, 2002a, pp. 39-40).
- *Passaround.* In simple terms, a passaround is the defined process of passing around a document and getting feedback on it. More formally expressed, a passaround is multiple peer deskchecks performed concurrently. Instead of asking a single person for comments, the documents are distributed to several peers, which allows for gathering various insights and collating feedback. Instead of distributing physical copies of documents to be reviewed and gathering feedback the same way, an electronic copy of a document may be placed on a shared folder and integrated in an appropriate reviewing tool. This passaround method allows each reviewer to see the comments that other review-

ers have already written, which may in turn minimise redundancy and reveal differences of interpretation (Wiegers, 2002a, pp. 40-41).

- *Ad hoc review.* Ad hoc reviews are as simple as one programmer asking another to take a look at some part of the code in the spur of the moment. Obviously, this kind of review is the most informal type of review, which is a natural part of software team collaboration. It has little impact beyond solving the immediate problem, but is powerful in providing a quick way to get another perspective which allows to continue with the actual task (Wiegers, 2002a, p. 41).

7.1.5 Positive effects of peer reviewing in educational context

Studies reveal that peer reviews have many benefits on students' learning. The main positive effects are summarised below (cf. Dochy, Segers, & Sluijsmans, 1999; Trahasch, 2004):

- "Asking other people to point out errors in your work is a learned – not instinctive – behavior. We all take pride in the work we do. We don't like to admit we make mistakes we don't realize how many we make (or we would correct them ourselves), and we don't like to ask someone else to find them" (Wiegers, 2002a, pp. 13, 22-25). In order to establish a successful peer review programme, people have to overcome this natural resistance to outside critique of their work (Wiegers, 2002a, p. 13). Participating in peer reviews contributes to the process of overcoming this resistance. People familiarise with outside critique and learn that getting a little help from peers can provide benefits both to individuals and to a project as a whole.
- Reviewing peers' work promotes the reflection on a student's own performance, which may increase the awareness of the quality of the student's own work.
- Since students know that both educators and peers will review their work, motivation is likely to rise. And it may contribute to an enhancing atmosphere of positive reciprocal stimulation and competition (for examples see Chinn, 2005; Sitthiworachart & Joy, 2003). As concerns software development, people tend to be more careful to write well-structured, simple and understandable, documented programmes when they know that other people will be checking them (Wiegers, 2002a, p. 8).
- In traditional learning settings, students are often not that interested in their peer's contributions, since they are primarily occupied with managing their own workload. When they have to review their peers, students get the opportunity to learn to learn and benefit from peer contributions (Derntl, 2006).

- Based on insights gained form their peers' feedback, students can improve their own performances (Derntl, 2006; Gehringer, 2000; Wiegers, 2002a, pp. 8, 24), which may finally result in better learning outcomes.
- If carried out in teams as a method of cooperative learning, peer review activities (team peer review) may foster social skills of team members (Wiegers, 2002a, p. 24).
- According to (Sitthiworachart & Joy, 2003), seeing good as well as bad contributions fosters students' learning. Furthermore, students report that they realise mistakes that they made in their own work when reviewing their peers' contributions.

On the educator's side, the deployment of peer reviews may have following impacts:

- Students' comments in peer reviews may provide insights and perspectives on what students expect from each other (Derntl, 2006).
- When peer reviews are used in terms of assessment, they can serve the purpose to reduce or eliminate the need for facilitators to read and grade an immense amount of students' contributions (Gehringer, 2000). The workload of reading and grading is then shared among students and facilitator.
- On the other hand, (Derntl, 2006) draws attention to the fact that the introduction of peer reviews can induce an organisational overhead when it is not being properly dealt with. Particularly in cases with many reviews, it is good advice to have assistance by a tutor and / or the technical support of an adequate e-learning platform.

7.1.6 Terminology

Having these considerations in mind, we favour the term *peer review* over *peer assessment* for following reasons:

- In the courses under investigation, peer reviews are seen as technical content (i.e. practicing the peer review activity) rather than as a means for quality assurance. (Nonetheless, peer review is considered as an essential pedagogical element in the course.)
- The deployment of peer reviews in the investigated courses primarily aims at developing and strengthening students' evaluation abilities, which they will need in their professional lives (either in business or in scholarship).
- Students' peer review reports are not or not exclusively used for grading the reviewed work. Rather the reviewing activity is aimed to foster learning for roles, the reviewer and the reviewed.

- In our course settings, peer review is not intended to give summative judgments on students' contributions but give direction to the authors (originators) and point to shortcomings that can be improved. Thus, the formative aspect is stressed.
- The term peer review is more generic than peer assessment. This reflects the broad orientation of this method's deployment in the respective courses under investigation.

Being aware that the purpose of peer reviews and peer assessments are different, the impacts on learning and teaming are assumed to be similar.

On the other hand, the terms *peer response* and *peer feedback*, which have their roots in language and writing courses, are regarded as similar in their meaning to *peer review*. However, the courses under investigation are intended for computer scientists, and students' assignments aimed at practicing peer reviewing in this domain. Since peer review is, moreover, a technical term in the field of computer science, this term will be used throughout the subsequent sections of this work.

7.1.7 Online versus face-to-face peer reviews

So far, only few studies addressed the comparison of traditional pen-and-paper and online peer reviews. The main part of these comparative studies come from the area of language and writing courses and, typically, concentrate on following aspects (cf. Hansen, 2005):

- students' attitudes towards different settings (modes, tools) of peer reviews,
- the impact of online peer reviews on the degree of participation and the number of contributions, and
- the effects of online peer reviews on the number of comments generated during the peer review activity and on revision.

In a study of (Liu & Sadler, 2003), the face-to-face interaction seemed to be more effective than online communication although the online peer review could count more comments and revisions than the face-to-face peer review. (Bloch & Brut-Griffler, 2001) revealed that students evaluate specific types of tasks differently in the two investigated settings. For instance, students preferred to comment online rather than in the face-to-face setting, while reading online was, though, not highly appreciated.

As concerns participation and interaction among peers, studies show inconsistent results. While, for instance, (Sullivan & Pratt, 1996) report that the degree of participation was much higher in the online peer review than in the face-to-face version, (S.-Y. Huang, 1998) found that the face-to-face peer reviews produced more speech and the whole group participated and contributed more often compared to a synchronous online version.

Regarding the type and quality of reviews, (Bloch & Brut-Griffler, 2001), for example, found that online feedback was more specific than face-to-face peer reviews, where comments were rather general. (Liu & Sadler, 2003) report that comments in online peer reviews were more revision-orientated than those in a paper version. (Hansen, 2005) summarises that research results in the area of English writing classes indicate that online comments are rather focussed on editing and grammatical issues.

Research in this field seems to consist of small puzzle pieces and it is difficult to draw general conclusions. The following case studies and analyses aim to bring up new insights.

7.2 Case 2a. Differences of face-to-face and written online peer reviews

7.2.1 The research questions

The presented case study aims at comparing peer review in a face-to-face and an online setting.

While, most previous studies investigating differences of online and face-to-face peer reviews regarding the type and quality of reviews were undertaken in writing classes and language courses, this study explores peer reviews in a completely distinct context – in an IT project management course.

Existing research notwithstanding, clear results on how comments in peer reviews differ in face-to-face and online settings are still sparse. While most studies comparing face-to-face and online peer reviews focus on the degree of participation and number of contributions as well as on the effects on comments and revision, this case study will, moreover, analyse collaboration aspects.

Therefore following research questions are addressed:

- Do the online and the face-to-face version show differences in the number of reviews written?
- In which way do reviews differ regarding content?
- How do communication and discussion differ in the online and the face-to-face version?
- How do collaboration within and among teams as well as workload distribution differ?

- Are there differences in the perceived review quality and work efficiency?

7.2.2 The case design

As it is a field study and not an experiment in an artificially created environment, we decided to conduct the case study in a course in which peer review is pedagogical element as well as learning content and not merely a means for data collection. A course on PROJECT MANAGEMENT, which required students to work on real projects and to review work – in terms of project management –, seemed particularly suitable for our endeavours. This case design with project work in an educational setting is particularly eligible to deduce findings to project work in business, as the settings are quite similar. Hence, research results will serve a broader scientific community.

7.2.2.1 Description of the setting

The case study was conducted in a course on *PROJECT MANAGEMENT – BASICS AND TECHNIQUES* for business informatics and computer science students at the University of Vienna in winter term 2005/2006. This course is part of the Master's curriculum, which indicates that the participants had already received a Bachelor's degree in computer science or business informatics. The workload is six credit points according to ECTS (European Credit Transfer System). As this course is held as a technology-enhanced course, it includes presence phases in class and is accompanied by an e-learning platform (Mangler, 2005). Cooperation among students is a central component in this course, which requires students to collaborate in both settings, in the presence phases as well as in the online part.

The learning objectives are set as follows:

- practical going through several steps of the two project phases: project initialisation and planning,
- experiencing collaboration in small teams with support of collaborative e-learning technologies,
- practical experience with the use of project management tools like Microsoft Project® for project planning, and
- gaining experience with the scope and limits of support by simple tools.

In the course, students are assigned to create and plan software development projects, which they have to elaborate in small teams of three persons. Each team is free to define a project at its own choice.

For achieving the course goals, students have to elaborate documents for six defined milestones, which are specified as follows:

- project selection (definition) and mission statement,
- an analysis of status quo and a to-be analysis,
- use cases and a project proposal (product structure),
- definition of the procedure structure (project structure),
- IT process model and structure, work breakdown structure, Microsoft Project® charts, and preliminary work for their preparations, as well as
- revised project plans according to required adaptations of the development process.

Since quality assurance and the review process constitute a significant part of this course's subject matter, students practice the procedure by going through a peer review, which allows them to gain experience and strengthen their reviewing abilities. Respectively two (partner) teams are assigned to mutually review their work.

7.2.2.2 Implementation of the case

When working on their projects during the semester, students went through a peer review process twice. Respectively two (partner) teams were assigned to review one another's work. In an early stage of the assigned projects, students reviewed their peers' project documents using a face-to-face (paper) peer review form. In a later project phase, they reviewed their peers' documents using an online version. Both times the peer review – performed in its specificity of computer science – had formative character and was supposed to give teams direction for improving their work.

In the face-to-face version, teams used paper review forms. On these review forms, teams commented about their respective partner team's project documents and noted shortcomings. Both the review forms and the documents, which had to be reviewed, were provided printed out in class. After the forms had been filled in, the partner teams (the reviewer team and the originating team) discussed the review results. Finally, based on these results, the originating team revised its documents accordingly.

The second review, in a later project phase, was carried out by a new combination of partner teams. This time, each team made its documents available on the course platform, such that the reviewer teams had online access to the documents of their respective partner teams. For the peer review, students used a web-based reviewing tool that was designed in accordance with the face-to-face version and the whole peer review process was carried out online.

Based on the terminology by (Wiegers, 2002a), which is described in Section 7.1.3, students followed a passaround with formal rules including a follow-up meeting: documents were delivered to the partner team (three persons), which reviewed the work products; in the face-to-face version the follow-up meeting took place in class, in the online version the partner teams communicated online. The reviewer teams did not have any directives how to perform the review within the team, as it was subject under investigation to which degree and how collaboration took place (cf. Section 7.2.3.4).

Figure 37 illustrates the process of the peer review activities, which holds for the online as well as for the face-to-face peer review version.

After the originating team has elaborated its documents, the reviewer team starts to review this work. Communication within the team is necessary; team members discuss shortcomings and further course of action. Afterwards the review form is filled in according to the team's findings. As long as the review is not considered complete, the team discusses further and completes the review form accordingly. Once the review is completed, the reviewer team hands over the completed review form and discusses the shortcomings directly with the originating team. After this, the origina-ting team proceeds with revising its documents according to its peers' review.

After the first project phase, where the peer review is carried out in a face-to-face setting, the project elaboration continues in a second (final) phase; this time the peer review is carried out with an online review tool.

In both peer reviews (online and face-to-face) the same amount of approximately six documents had to be reviewed.

The case design induces that teams had worked together in this course for different time periods before experiencing the face-to-face and the online peer review. For comparison, this is, though, negligible since all participants in this course already know each other since the beginning of their studies and have already worked together in the same and similar team line-ups in other courses (Figl, Motschnig-Pitrik, & Derntl, 2006).

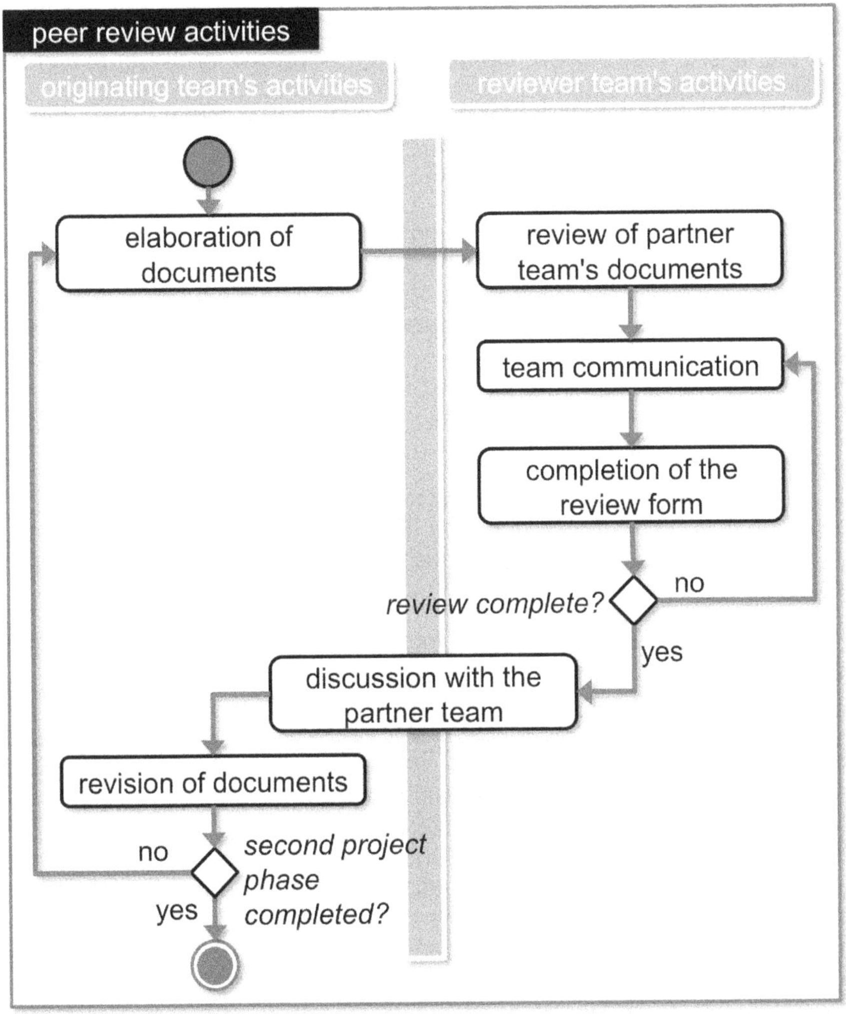

Figure 37. UML activity diagram illustrating the process of the peer review activities

Face-to-face review forms

For the face-to-face review, we used a paper review form. Students had to fill in following information:

- reviewer team's name,
- title of the project that is reviewed,
- documents that are reviewed,
- detailed description of shortcomings that had been identified,
- classification of the shortcomings' severity (according to three categories of importance: C3 – Severe – Rethink whole structure, C2 – Major – Problem that has to be corrected, C1 – Minor – Minor deficiency),
- overall judgment whether a further revision is necessary,
- date of the review, and
- the reviewer team's signature.

Students reviewed their peers' documents in class. Comments had to be noted on the review forms in writing. Furthermore, all teams had the opportunity to discuss the reviews directly with the respective partner team in class.

The structure of this paper review form had been adopted for the online review form, which is described in the next Section.

The online-system for peer reviewing

The web-based reviewing tool that was used for the online peer review was purpose-built in accordance with the paper forms used in the face-to-face peer review.[19] This reviewing tool is loosely modelled after the Bugzilla Software (Bugzilla, 1998-2005) that has been written for tracking errors in software products for quality assurance in software development projects. With the aim to make the whole development progress of each team's project visible to all participants in the course, a simplified system was created that allows registering and managing errors and deficiencies in a cooperative way.

Figure 38 gives a screenshot of the user interface for registering deficiencies. The form contains following input fields, which basically cover the same issues as the paper form in the face-to-face peer review:

---

19 At this point I want to thank Jürgen Mangler for his excellent work and having great powers of endurance in implementing the solution.

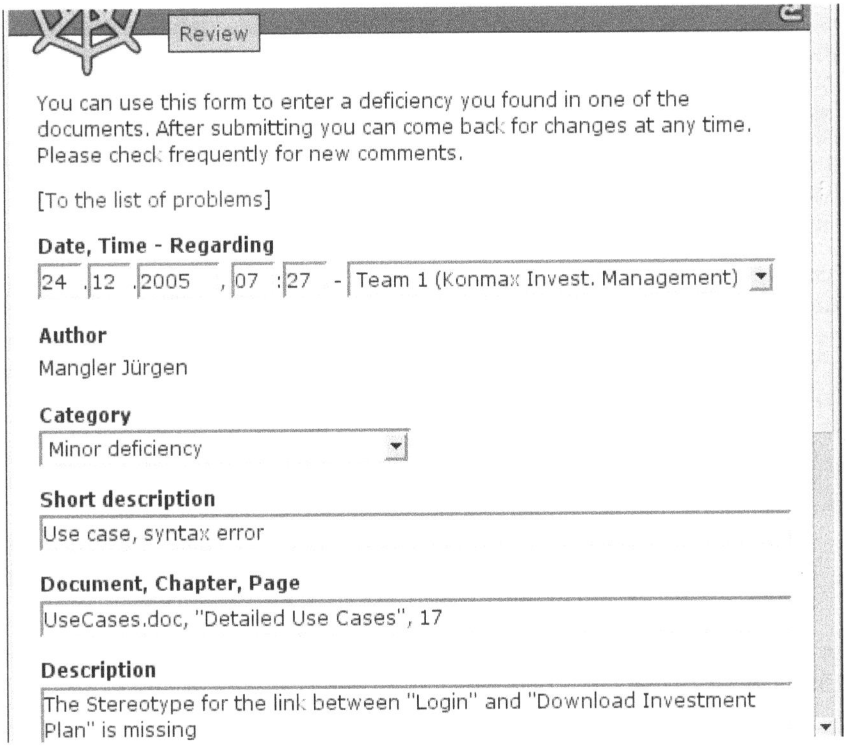

Figure 38. The interface for registering deficiencies

- *Date, Time – Regarding*. Date and time can be set. Under the heading *Regarding*, the student project, for which the error has been detected, can be referred to.
- The *Author* will be set automatically, as only logged-in users can add deficiencies. This field is, thus, immutable.
- *Category* is a drop down menu. Users can categorise the deficiencies according to preset categories, which have been defined by the administrator.
- The *Short description* of the problem that will be shown in the list of shortcomings (Figure 39).
- *Document* name, *Chapter* and *Page* number. Altogether these three details determine and locate the source of the detected deficiency quite accurately.
- A detailed *Description* of the deficiency.
- *Additional Comments* that do not fit any of the above fields.

sign allowed for a direct comparison of the online and the face-to-face version by the students.

Students individually filled in the questionnaire during the last laboratory course unit. The questionnaire (cf. Appendix 2) consisted of five parts. The online and presence version of the peer team review should be compared according to:

- particular reviewing activities (review of the partner team's documents, completion of the review form, communication in the own team, discussion with the partner team, and revision of the documents considering the reviews),
- the workload distribution in teams,
- the work efficiency, and
- the review quality.
- Additionally, students should provide suggestions for improvement for both peer review versions.

The majority of questions were open-ended with the exception of five questions with a bipolar rating-scale for the preference between the online and the face-to-face version (Figure 40). The questionnaire was evaluated mainly quantitatively.

In which version was the quality of the received feedback higher?

paper version	❍	❍	❍	❍	❍	**online version**

Figure 40. Example of questionnaire item

For comparing the online and face-to-face reviews regarding type and content, text and qualitative content analysis (Mayring, 1983/2003) were applied. In Section 7.2.3.2, the formation of categories is described in detail.

7.2.3 Results

7.2.3.1 Differences in the number of words and statements

For the face-to-face and the online version of the peer reviews, we counted the number of words written by students. Results show that students wrote about twice as much in the online version as they did in the face-to-face version (386 versus 194 words). This finding also goes in line with the results of (Liu & Sadler, 2003).

Interestingly, students' comments referred to much more diversified topics (e.g., issues in distinct documents of the partner team) in the face-to-face version compared to the online one (35 versus 19 words). In contrast, the words per statement were much higher in the online version than in the face-to-face review (20 versus 5 words). Furthermore, the range of the numbers of statements per team was wider in the paper version (minimum 3, maximum 11 statements per team) than in the online version (minimum 2, maximum 5 statements per team).

Results are summarised in Table 13. The average number of words per statement is rounded to the next integer.

Table 13. Number of words and statements in peer reviews

	FACE-TO-FACE VERSION	ONLINE VERSION	TOTAL
number of words	194	386	580
number of statements	35	19	54
average number of words per statement	5	20	11

The higher number of words and the higher average number of words per statement in the online version could arise from the fact that the space for writing was – naturally and optically – limited in the paper review form, while the online form provided unlimited character count. In the online version, teams could easily see how many issues other teams reported. In the paper version, instead, the number of comments could not so obviously be recognised. Probably therefore teams submitted about the same number of statements while in the face-to-face version the variance is higher.

This kind of *conformity pressure* notwithstanding, typing is less demanding than handwriting. It is, thus, also very likely that students had been less motivated to provide detailed feedback in handwriting on the paper forms.

Additionally, it has to be considered that the face-to-face setting allowed for discussion with the partner team directly after the review. Accordingly, the anticipation of discussion could be a reason for rather short statements in the forms as students have known that the other team could ask for clarification if the statements had not been precise enough.

Considering learning effects, however, reveals the limitations of the chosen research design. As students went through the online peer review later than the face-to-face version, it could also be that students had learned from the received paper peer reviews. Using a low number of words may indicate a lower level of precision; so they might have tried to explain issues with more words in the later online version. Since students did not address this issue in their answers to the open-ended questions (neither positively nor negatively), we can only broadly conjecture such an influence.

As concerns the total number of words and the average number of words per statement, our findings corroborate (Sullivan & Pratt, 1996) who report of a higher degree of participation in the online review. Regarding the number of statements, however, our results go in line with (S.-Y. Huang, 1998), who observed that students contribute more often in face-to-face settings.

The higher total number of words in the online version would also go in hand with the finding of media choice research that the online setting furthers the free expression of opinion. As the paper forms were filled in within a review team without having the originating team looking over one's shoulder, we, however, assume that the group pressure was not so high that it would have considerably affected the free expression of opinion.

7.2.3.2 Differences regarding the type of peer reviews

Positive and negative feedback

Table 14 provides an overview of the frequency of positive and negative feedback in the reviews. In general, students gave considerably more negative (74%) than positive (26%) feedback. In other words, they rather noted shortcomings of their partner team's project documents instead of praising their work. Even more so, this is to notice in the online version: hardly any positive feedback was given in the online version compared to the face-to-face version (2 versus 12 statements).

The finding that negative feedback predominates does, however, not come surprisingly. Actually it goes in accord with the assignments given by the educator and also with the online and paper forms. As the forms were called *list of shortcomings*, it was probably clear to students that they should rather point out aspects their colleagues should improve. On the other hand, the educator communicated to her students that they could use the forms also for giving positive feedback. Although the low degree of positive feedback may also have other reasons, we assume that this additional comment by the educator had not been sufficient. It is advisable that the forms' titles go in line with the assignment and, furthermore, it should be communicated clearly that any kind of feedback is welcome. Accordingly, we assume that the ratio of positive feedback would have been higher if we would have considered these issues.

As already outlined with the description of the review forms (Section 7.2.2.2), students should categorise shortcomings according to the classification of severity (C3 – Severe – Rethink whole structure, C2 – Major – Problem that has to be corrected, C1 – Minor – Minor deficiency). As can be seen from Table 14, most shortcomings noted were classified as minor (27), followed by major (10), and severe (2). Concerning the rated severity of shortcomings, the online and the face-to-face setting do not apparently seem to differ. The only interesting aspect is that in the online version *none* of the deficiencies were rated as severe. Since only two deficiencies were rated as severe in the face-to-face version, this is, though, not conclusive.

Table 14. Positive and negative feedback

	FACE-TO-FACE VERSION		ONLINE VERSION		TOTAL	
positive feedback	12	34%	2	11%	14	26%
negative feedback	23	66%	17	89%	40	74%
minor (C1)	*14*		*13*		*27*	
major (C2)	*6*		*4*		*10*	
severe (C3)	*2*		*–*		*2*	
missing	*1*		*–*		*1*	
total	35	100%	19	100%	40	100%

... in numbers of shortcomings

Classification of negative feedback

For a content categorisation of the negative feedback, a classification scheme was developed inductively from raw data. After the categorisation scheme had been set up, the fitting of all statements into categories was checked in order to prove the scheme's consistency. In this process, the classification scheme was reformulated several times. Categorisation was undertaken by two researchers[20] in order to increase inter-subjectivity. The inter-rater reliability was high, as more than 90 percent of allocations to categories and judgments were consistent. When the re-

20 At this point I want to thank Kathrin Figl for her outstanding support and enthusiasm. Without her, this research would not have been possible.

searchers identified differences in categorisation, they agreed on the best fitting categories after discussion.

Considering this case study's setting and its particular aims, it seemed reasonable to classify the review statements in two steps.

In the first step, four different types of statements were classified:

- *Shortcomings* and *suggestions* were distinguished from each other, as well as
- statements referring to a *wrong level of detail* and *missing data or files*.

Primarily, we adopted the categorisation model as applied by (Liu & Sadler, 2003) and adhered to a distinction between revision-orientated and non-revision-orientated statements. However, the distinction between shortcomings and suggestions proved to be more adequate for the data of this case study.

In the second step, all identified shortcomings and suggestions were classified into formal and technical ones. For *missing data* and *wrong level of detail*, a further classification did not seem reasonable.

The main categories of review statements, which are the result of going through these two classification steps, are described below:

- *Level of detail.* This category refers to students' judgments claiming that the reviewed documents are either too long or too short, or miss important details. One team wrote for example, "*The technical specifications concerning the project implementation and the goals are quite a bit too short.*" Another team stated about a specific document, "*The only shortcoming ... too extensive, too long ... I would expect two pages at most.*"
- *Missing.* This class includes all statements indicating that documents or parts of documents are missing and can therefore not be reviewed. Examples include "*No description of project structure*" or "*We could not find any document or annotation, where the choice of the process model is mentioned or reasoned*".
- *Shortcomings (formal / technical).* The category *shortcoming* is used for the description of specific shortcomings and deficiencies. Basically we can distinguish formal and technical shortcomings.
    - *Formal shortcomings* refer to the structure, grammar and use of language in documents as well as to aspects of providing documents in the right form (versioning, suitable document format). An

example of a formal shortcoming is, "*No versioning of documents.*" These are circumstantial aspects in contrast to technical shortcomings, which are closely related to project management and documentation skills, which students had to learn in the course.
  - The category *technical shortcomings* includes shortcomings regarding the real content of documents (e.g., correct and plausible project description) and also concerning good planning in project plans or right modelling of Unified Modeling diagrams (UML diagrams). A reviewer team stated, for instance, "*Unified Modeling standard was not followed (arrows, names of relationships).*"

- *Suggestions (formal / technical).* In contrast to shortcomings, suggestions are not mere descriptions of deficiencies but include constructive hints for improvement. They are likely more revision-orientated than *shortcomings*. This category is also used for further suggestions given by students.

  - *Formal suggestion.* In analogy to formal shortcomings, formal suggestions refer to hints that concern formal aspects of documents like structure, use of language, or right file format (e.g., "*Make presentation more colourful: somewhat more colour would give relief to it. But it is not bad because it is only a short presentation and subjective*".).
  - *Technical suggestion.* Analogue to technical shortcomings and in contrast to formal suggestions, technical suggestions consider propositions regarding the technical nature and content of documents (e.g., "*'Logging in' should be connected with 'extends' instead of 'uses'.*").

In general, the major part of negative feedback consisted of shortcomings (38%), followed by suggestions (25%), comments concerning the level of detail (20%) and missing documents (18%). When comparing the face-to-face and the online version, it appears that the percentage of noted shortcomings was lower in the online version (18% versus 52%), while frequency was higher for all other types of negative feedback. Table 15 provides an overview of these figures.

The fact that the face-to-face peer reviews show a stronger focus on shortcomings rather than on other types of feedback, could be due to several reasons. Since students evaluated projects in a later project phase in the online version than in the face-to-face setting, documents were probably already elaborated in more detail. This would also explain that it was easier to give further suggestions in the online version as reviewers already had a concrete picture of the projects. However, the categories *level of detail* and *missing* should also have declined. Another explanation could be that students had the documents printed out in the face-to-face version and could, possibly, therefore concentrate more easily on noting shortcomings.

The ratio of shortcomings to suggestions in both peer review versions could approve the findings of (Liu & Sadler, 2003) that online comments are more revision-orientated. In our case study the online peer review shows more suggestions than shortcomings (revision-orientated) while the face-to-face version other way round (not revision-orientated). The high revision-orientation is not only favourable in educational settings but is also in any kind of project as feedback is constructive and, thus, fosters the learning process and is likely to bring better (learning) outcomes.

Table 15. Types of negative feedback

	FACE-TO-FACE VERSION		ONLINE VERSION		TOTAL	
level of detail	4	17%	4	24%	8	20%
missing	3	13%	4	24%	7	18%
shortcomings	13	52%	3	18%	15	38%
formal	*5*		*1*		*6*	
technical	*7*		*2*		*9*	
suggestions	4	17%	6	35%	10	25%
formal	*0*		*3*		*3*	
technical	*4*		*3*		*7*	
total	23	57.5%	17	42.5%	40	100%

... in numbers of nominations

In our case study, students first went through the face-to-face peer review and then they performed the online review. It would be interesting if, after training constructive feedback in an online setting, reviews are more constructive in face-to-face settings as well. We, however, expect that transferring skills from the online to the face-to-face setting and uniting behaviour and attitudes in both settings is a long-term effect and should, thus, be researched in a long-run investigation.

7.2.3.3 Differences in activities

Review of the partner team's documents

Concerning differences of the online and the face-to-face setting in terms of the reviewing process, four students bring up arguments in favour of the online version whereas four argue for the face-to-face version. Five students do not perceive any differences between the two versions.

One of the arguments appreciating the online version is that particular documents can be analysed more easily in digital form with corresponding software (e.g., Microsoft Project® files) than when certain document views (e.g., detailed work breakdown structure or Gantt chart) are printed out. Students can, for instance, search after key words and do not face paper chaos. On the online platform documents are arranged by milestone, automatically providing an adequate structure of documents. Furthermore, students had access to other teams' documents, which allowed for comparison and better argumentation. Additionally, one student raises the argument that the online version is better suited for teamwork. Unfortunately, this student does not give any reasons for this proposition. Maybe it is the simple fact that students can collaborate as a distributed team. It could also be that this student appreciates that in the online scenario self-attention does not get lost in the team setting as it frequently does in face-to-face situations.

Compared to the face-to-face version, where only one printed out copy of each of the documents was available for a whole reviewer team, students appreciate that each document was available for every team member in the online version and that documents were always up-to-date on the platform. Moreover, students point out that the online setting allows for a rather free disposition of time and wide scope for timing, while in the face-to-face version a rather rigid time constraint was given due to the time slot of the course unit.

A main argument in favour of the face-to-face version is that having the documents printed out was experienced as being more comfortable to read, because a computer display would be tiring for the eyes and too small for that kind of work. Students argue that shortcomings would be recognised more quickly when having documents printed out than when reviewing them online. Interestingly, students had the possibility to print out any of the documents they liked in the form (view) they preferred. Nevertheless, it seems that they did not make us of it. Either they thought that they should entirely stick to the online – which is rather unlikely – or they appreciated the service of having all documents readily delivered.

Furthermore, students bring up that it is easier to comment documents immediately and argue that handling paper documents is easier and quicker. Interestingly enough, students also mention that the paper version was arranged more clearly than the online form although we put effort in designing the web-based reviewing tool in accordance with the paper forms.

Completion of the review form

Results concerning the review forms clearly indicate that students favour the web-based reviewing tool.

Five students prefer the web-based tool due to the fact that they perceived it easier and more comfortable to fill in and liked the guided structure of the form. Furthermore, students appreciate that there is unlimited space for describing shortcomings in the online version, and that it is possible to add an unlimited number of remarks.

Other arguments raised are that completing the web-based review form goes down faster than filling in the paper form due to touch typing, on the one hand, and since there is no difficulty of decoding handwriting, on the other hand. One student, however, dislikes the *clicking through forms* of the web-based tool and regards the handling of the paper version as going down faster.

Team communication

While five students out of three teams did not perceive any differences concerning communication in the two review settings, seven students out of three other teams argue that the face-to-face version is more suited for discussion and communication than the online setting. They explain that it would be "*easier to discuss everything and to write comments together*" in a face-to-face conversation. Reflecting on their communicative behaviour, students perceive that team communication is better in the face-to-face setting. Besides perceiving communication as more *direct* in the face-to-face conversation, students report that more consultation took place within the team in this setting.

While two students, who were members of the same team, report that in the online version no discussion took place at all, others teams communicated via e-mail, voice-over-IP (VoIP), or instant messaging tools.

Discussion with the partner team

Eight students out of three teams indicate that the face-to-face version was better suited for discussing the review with the partner team. Furthermore, students report that discussion with their respective partner teams did not take place online. They also bring up the argument that there was no possibility for discussing online. This, however, is a sign that students are either not self-dependent enough to show self-initiative in finding means to address the respective partner team or an indication that there was no need for discussion.

Other students explain that online discussion had been limited to inserting comments and that a communication system like voice-over-IP (VoIP) or instant messaging should be included in the peer review tool.

In the face-to-face version, in contrast, students appreciate that a positive exchange of opinions had taken place and all shortcomings could have been discussed.

Revision of the documents

Concerning the revision of documents according to review results that teams received from their respective partner teams, most students explain that they had overworked their documents and provide a description on how they had done it. However, the majority of students is not responsive to the question on differences between the online and the face-to-face version. Findings concerning this matter are, thus, limited.

On total, ten students report that they overworked their documents according to the reviews, both in the face-to-face and the online version. Three students do not perceive any difference between the two versions, and two students indicate that it worked out better in the face-to-face setting due to the fact that, in the online version, it was more difficult to ask the partner team when it was hard to understand what the noted shortcomings mean and how to exactly improve the documents.

Overview of results

Students' preferences are summarised in Table 16. The columns with the headings *face-to-face version* and *online version* give the number of students who favour the face-to-face version or respectively the online version for the particular activity, which is given in the first column. The category *indifferent / the same* includes students who brought up arguments in favour of both review versions as well as students who did not perceive any differences. In some cases, it was not possible to match the answers with one of the mentioned categories; these are, thus, consolidated under the heading *no coding possible*.

7.2.3.4 Workload distribution in teams

In their answers, students describe how they divided work into subtasks and distributed those within their teams and which activities they performed conjointly.

Four out of the 16 students consider that the workload distribution had been similar in both peer review settings. Slightly more students report that, in both versions, each team member read all documents (instead of splitting documents into segments and every student just reading the assigned part). In accordance with the answers concerning the differences in activities (Section 7.2.3.3), far more students mention that they discussed and agreed upon what to write in the review forms.

Besides these findings concerning workload distribution in general, one rather noticeable difference between the settings could be identified in the answers: While students filled in the review form together in the face-to-face version, in the online version it occurred more frequently that an individual student filled it in on the team's behalf.

Table 16. Differences of activities in online and face-to-face peer reviews

	FACE-TO-FACE VERSION	INDIFFERENT / THE SAME	ONLINE VERSION	NO CODING POSSIBLE	N
review of the partner team's documents	4	5	4	3	16
completion of the review form	0	5	5	5	15
team communication	7	5	0	4	16
discussion with the partner team	8	3	1	4	16
revision of the documents	2	3	0	9	14

… in absolute numbers of nominations

7.2.3.5 Work efficiency and review quality

For determining which peer review setting students rated better at specific dimensions, one-tailed Student's t-tests (n=16, α=0.025) with the reference value of 3.5 were calculated. The value 1 stands for the preference for the face-to-face version, the value 6 stands for the preference for the online version; therefore 3.5 means that there was neither a preference for the face-to-face nor for the online version.

Exact means, standard deviations (sd), t-values (t), degrees of freedom (df), and the p-values (p) of the results can be found in Table 17.

The calculated t-tests demonstrate that students find it significantly easier to express hints (mean=2.63, sd=1.63, $t_{df=15}$=-2.15, p=0.05) and to give helpful feedback (mean=2.81, sd=1.33, $t_{df=15}$=-2.07, p=0.06) in the paper version. Those students favouring the face-to-face peer review reason their preference with the possibility for discussion and direct communication with the partner team directly after the review in the face-to-face setting.

Table 17. Results of one-tailed Student's t-tests concerning work efficiency and review quality of online and paper reviews

	MEAN	SD	T	DF	P	
easier to express hints	2.63	1.63	-2.15	15	0.05	*
easier to give helpful feedback	2.81	1.33	-2.07	15	0.06	*
higher quality of feedback	3.38	1.41	-0.36	15	0.73	
takes more time to fill in	2.75	1.69	-1.77	15	0.10	
easier to fill in	4.19	1.47	1.87	15	0.08	

The fact that students perceive it easier to express hints in the paper version than in the online one, while the average number of words is lower in the paper version compared to the online review may appear contradictory. However, we conjecture that it may be easier to verbalise feedback in a nutshell in a face-to-face context, while students need more words to express the same issue in an online setting.

Furthermore, the results indicate that filling in the paper review form takes more time (mean=2.75, sd=1.69, $t_{df=15}$=-1.77, p=0.10) than completing the online form. Additionally, students explain that they appreciate the freedom of not being bound to any time constraint in the online peer review since they could work on it at home whereas they are stuck to class hours in the face-to-face version. On the other hand, the online version can be filled in more easily (mean=4.19, sd=1.47, $t_{df=15}$=-1.87, p=0.08), which is also due to the fact that the documents can be better analysed in digital form (e.g., different views in project plans).

These findings are particularly interesting as students state that they appreciate the online version for not having rigid time constraints although it takes less time to fill in the online form than the paper version. Apparently, students had the possibility to dedicate more time to the reviewing activity (reading and analysing) as such than to filling in the form in the online setting. Interestingly, despite the time constraints, they identified and registered more issues in the face-to-face review than in the online version. This could, however, also be due to the fact that projects had already advanced (and improved based on the first review) when students performed the online review.

Finally, results indicate that differences in work efficiency did not impact the reviews' quality as both peer review versions are judged equally with respect to this dimension.

7.2.3.6 Suggestions for improvement

Students were asked to provide suggestions for improvement for both the face-to-face as well as the online peer review. A total of seven suggestions for the face-to-face version and sixteen for the online version could be collected.

For the paper forms, students would rather prefer a questionnaire – similar to a checklist – that is more structured than the version used in the case study. Still, the review form should offer enough space to add further comments. One student states that printed out documents should be sorted chronologically, what contributes to making it easier to find the right documents and avoiding paper chaos at least to some extent. Another student proposes to allow a longer time frame for the task.

For the online review form, ten students suggest a feature making it possible to delete an entry. It is, however, common practice to exclude such a feature in collaborative review tools since the whole reviewing process needs to be transparent to all participants. And deleting an existing entry does obviously not contribute to transparency as it renders impossible to keep track of the revisions and activities. If an entry was submitted by accident, it can be set to *solved* (or *duplicated* if registered multiple times) and the process keeps transparent without requiring participants to pay further attention to the redundant entry. The feature to show only active entries (i.e. hide solved and duplicated entries) supports this practice.

Two students recommend improving the structure in order that it is more clearly arranged (e.g., dividing feedback into different sections for each team). Three students indicate that they would appreciate to have better possibilities to contact and communicate with the partner team.

For both versions, one student argues that reviews should have a stronger focus on positive feedback rather than on shortcomings.

7.3 Case 2b. Evaluating peer review settings with different media combinations

7.3.1 The research questions

As already outlined in the introduction of this Section, most studies consider either face-to-face or online peer reviews but rarely any compare these settings. The results of our first case study, which we dedicated to a comparison of peer reviews in these two settings, suggested a follow-up case study investigating also combinations of media for the peer review activity. Built upon the findings of the earlier case study, this one – again – investigates students' impressions on online peer reviewing in general and in comparison to face-to-face peer reviews. Moreover, this study goes further and investigates students' perceptions about peer review settings that are enhanced with particular media combinations.

Basically, following research questions are focus of interest:

- What perceived impact do written online peer reviews have on students' learning processes?
- What are the benefits and limitations of online peer reviews as a means of cooperative learning, i.e. how can they contribute to learning *from each other*?
- How do students perceive the eligibility of written online peer reviews compared to face-to-face reviewing activities?
- How can the enhancement of these basic settings (online vs. face-to-face peer reviews) with media combinations contribute to the peer review process?

7.3.2 The case design

Also for this follow-up case study we decided to select a course in which peer review activities are not merely a pedagogical element for assessment or a means for data collection but simultaneously learning content. As the course on *Basics of Scientific Writing* for computer scientists was held the first time in summer term 2008, it suggested itself for the case study design as the didactic structure could be formed from the scratch. The introduction to the scientific peer review and the reflection about the peer review process could, thus, be implemented as course content and learning objective. Simultaneously, the peer reviews served as a pedagogical means of collaborative learning and as peer assessment.

7.3.2.1 Description of the setting

The course *Basics of Scientific Writing* for computer scientists is part of the module *Scientific Principles in Informatics* of the Bachelor's curriculum computer science at the University of Vienna. The workload is three credit points according to ECTS (European Credit Transfer System). Under the terms of the curriculum, students should attend this course in the fifth semester of their studies. It was first held in the summer term 2008, in which we also conducted our study.

Due to the expected number of students for this course, the university offered three parallel courses (groups) with about 15 students each. The three educators (one female, two male) agreed to follow the same course design.

Basically, the course gives an introduction to scientific writing (including scientific presentation techniques) in the discipline of computer science. First, the educators present the essential topics and then students elaborate these with practical exercises. The course includes following topics:

- overview about scientific writing and forms of publication,
- literature research and use of (digital) libraries,
- structure of a scientific paper and guidelines for citing and referencing,
- scientific language and comprehensible writing,
- publishing process in journals and conferences, and
- presentations techniques.

In order to provide students with an authentic picture of scientific writing in computer science, the course schedule resembles the complete process of a scientific conference, including paper submissions, peer reviews, and oral paper presentations.

The course includes presence phases with lectures and practical exercises. Furthermore, all aspects of knowledge transfer and collaboration of students and educators in context of the course are accompanied and supported by an e-learning platform (Mangler, 2005). Basically, this platform includes:

- a page with information from the respective educator (schedule, deadlines, instructions, assignments, etc.),
- a tool, which students could use for team-building ((Mangler, 2005, pp. 78-79); cf. Section 4.5) in the beginning of the semester,
- an online workspace, which was used for the submission of all assignments, and
- a forum, which students could use to exchange experiences and information among them or to ask questions.

7.3.2.2 Implementation of the case

As already outlined above, the course design resembled the process of preparing, publishing, and presenting a paper for a scientific conference.

Besides attending the lectures about the essential issues of scientific writing, student teams had to select a topic, write a scientific paper on it, and submit it on the e-learning platform. After the submission deadline, both students and educators reviewed the papers such that each paper was read and evaluated by at least three persons (two students and one educator).

For the reviews, an online form was used, which was structured according to following elements:

- brief summary of the core elements of the paper,
- formal aspects,
- language and presentation,
- content aspects,
- sources and references,
- overall impression,
- comments, and
- suggestions for improvement.

The detailed online peer review form is displayed in Table 18.

After the peer review phase, students prepared their final papers according to the reviews that they received by their peers and the educator. In the final presence block of the course, students presented their articles with laptop and beamer.

Following the peer review phase, there was a face-to-face meeting between the respective educator and each team of authors to discuss issues concerning the reviews outcomes and required paper revisions.

Figure 41 illustrates the chronological order of the individual as well as team tasks and their synchronisation with the presence classes. Horizontally it shows the time line of the semester (from left to right) and vertically it is partitioned into three areas: one for individual tasks (top), one for team task (middle), and one for compulsory presence classes (bottom), which are indicated with triangles.

In addition to the compulsory presence classes, which are drawn in Figure 41, the course offered a LaTeX (LaTeX, 2008) tutorial and an excursion to the magazine of the library of the University of Vienna at midterm, which both were optional.

The topics for the summary of a given article (assignment 1) and for the submission of an own article (assignment 4) orientated on the particular research interests of the respective educator. Several specific topics were offered out of following domains: collaboration in human-human interaction, usability, human-computer interaction, parallel and distributed database systems, grid and cloud computing, and e-learning.

All activities of the peer review process are illustrated in Figure 42. The author's activities are shown on the left side, while the reviewer's activities are drawn on the right.

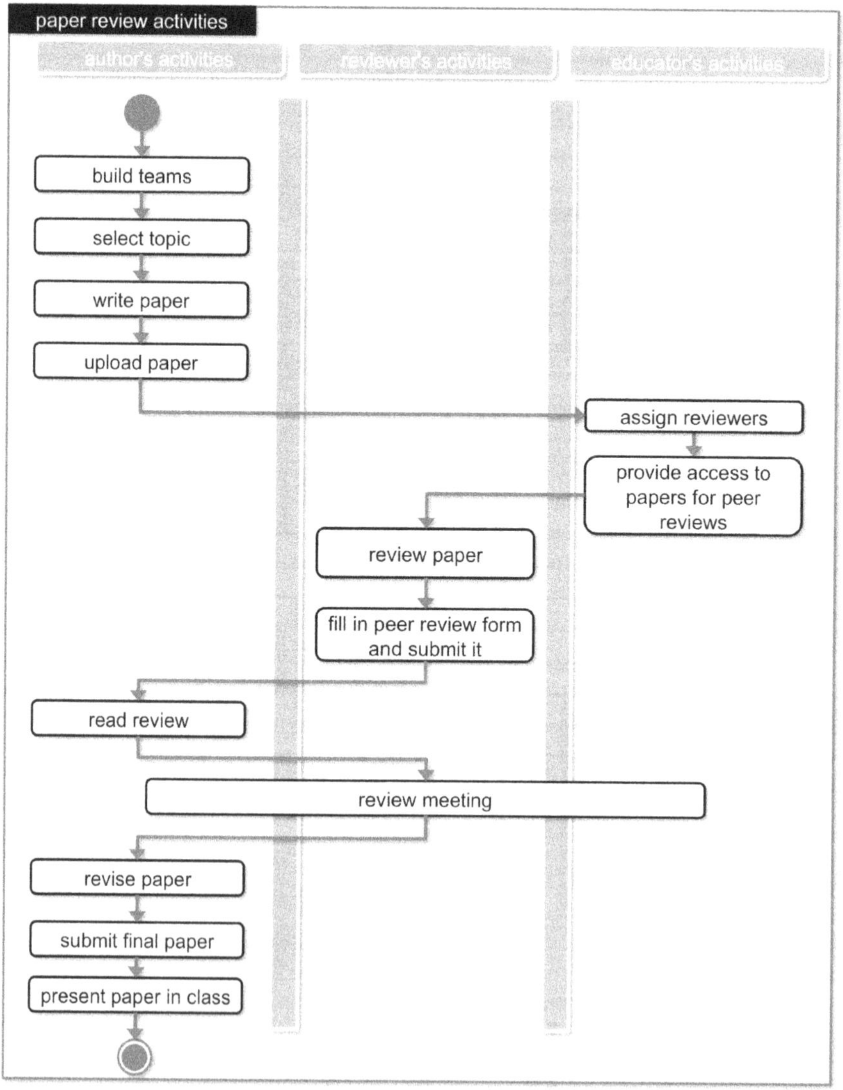

Figure 42. UML activity diagram of the peer review process in the course *Basics of Scientific Writing*

7.3.2.3 Data Collection and methods

As already outlined above, the introduction to scientific peer review was part of the course objective. As a pedagogical element for collaborative learning, students practiced what they learned theoretically by reviewing their peers' papers. Finally, at the end of the course, we asked students to reflect on the peer review activities by administering an online questionnaire, which was provided on the course's e-learning platform (Mangler, 2005).

The questionnaire (cf. Appendix 3) included items about students' perception of the review process and outcome, which had to be scored on a five-level Likert scale (Likert, 1932), and open questions about the appropriateness of peer reviews in face-to-face settings and written online peer reviews. The open questions particularly addressed four scenarios of peer reviews with distinct combinations of media deployment:

- written peer review without any media enhancement,
- oral feedback in a personal conversation (face-to-face peer review) without any media enhancement,
- written peer review providing the author with the possibility to comment or raise a query, and
- oral feedback in a personal conversation (face-to-face peer review) with the provision of a written handout.

The qualitative approach with open questions seemed appropriate in order to meet the explorative character of the research questions concerning online and face-to-face peer reviews.

At the end of the semester, students were asked via e-mail to fill in the online questionnaire, with the indication that the reflection about the peer review process is assessed as active participation in the course.

Of the 53 students who participated in the three parallel groups of the course, 38 students (73%) filled in the online questionnaire.

Results of the quantitative part of the questionnaire are presented in terms of mean values (mean) and standards deviations (sd). For the evaluation of students' reflections in the open questions, we applied a text and qualitative content analysis methodology (Mayring, 1983/2003). A total word count of 1,713 with a total character count of 11,955 could be analysed. The classification scheme was developed inductively from raw data. After setting up the categories, the fitting of all statements into categories was checked in order to prove its consistency. In order to increase inter-subjectivity, categorisation was undertaken by two researchers[21]. In the case that the researchers identified distinct categories or related statements to different categories, the best fitting category was chosen after discussion. Accordingly, the classification scheme was reformulated several times.

7.3.3 Results

On average, reading the papers to be reviewed and writing reviews took students about one and a half hours (mean= 106.77 minutes, sd= 22.86).

In general, students value the online peer review in the course as a very positive experience. As can be seen from Figure 43, they like the idea of having peer review implemented in the course design (mean=4.42, sd=0.76). The reviews that they received are considered helpful (mean=3.82, sd=0.83). Furthermore, students indicate that they have fun doing the reviews (mean=3.81, sd=0.74).

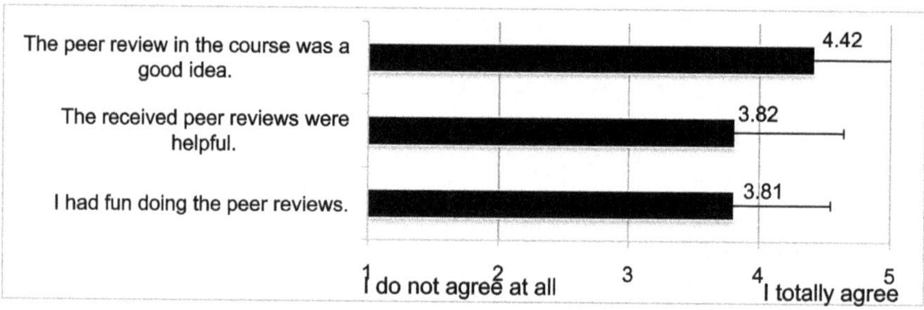

Figure 43. General feedback on the peer review activity (mean +/- sd), n=38

7.3.3.1 Impact of the online peer review activity on students' learning's

Figure 44 provides an overview of students' perception about the influence of the peer review activity on particular learning processes.

39% of students have the impression that reviewing changed their perception of their own paper (mean=3.92, sd=1.01). On the one hand, this leads to better recognition of the quality of their own contributions

21 At this point I want to thank Kathrin Figl and Michael Derntl for their outstanding support and enthusiasm. Without them, this research would not have been possible.

(mean=3.86, sd=0.79; e.g., "*As the paper [I reviewed] was rather badly formatted and also on the content level by far less understandable than ours, I was particularly proud of our paper.*"), on the other hand they receive inspiration on how to improve their papers (e.g., "*As I have read my peers' papers more objectively than my own paper, I noticed what I could change in order to improve my paper.*"). Probably due to the recognition of the quality of their contributions and inspiration for improvement, the reviewing activity strengthened students' confidence in their own performance (mean=3.68, sd=0.87) and stimulated reflection on it (mean=3.61, sd=0.95).

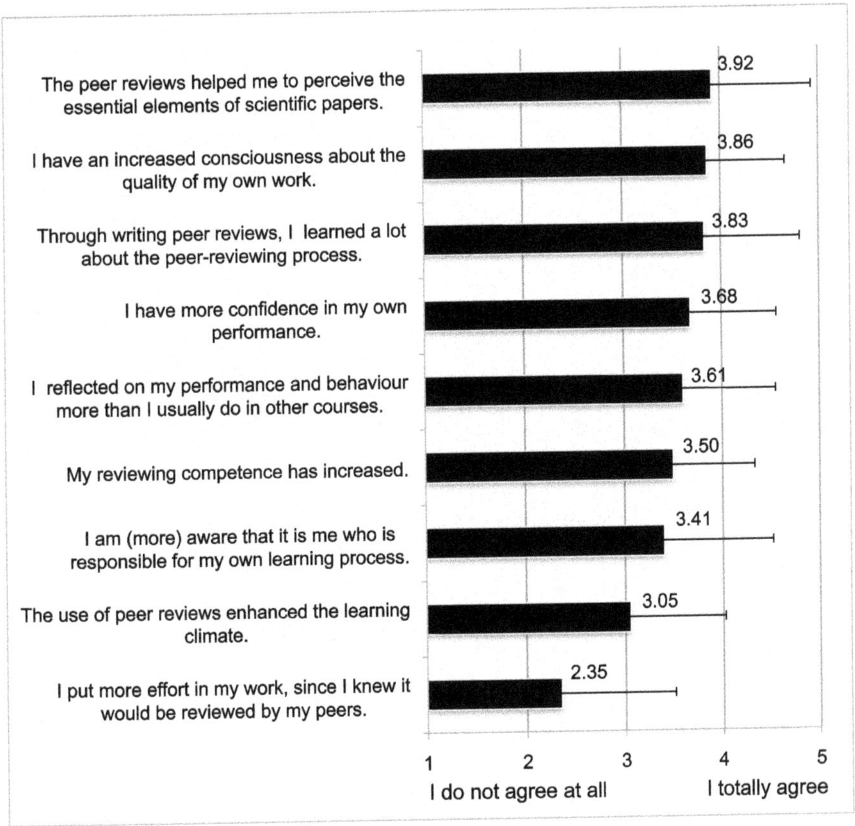

Figure 44. The influence of the online peer review activity on students' learning's (mean +/- sd), n=38

Furthermore, the influence on the responsibility for the own learning process (mean=3.41, sd=1.12), learning about the scientific peer review process (mean=3.83, sd=0.97), and the own review competence (mean=3.50, sd=0.83) are positively valued.

Considerably less agreement reaches the impact of peer reviews on the learning climate (mean=3.05, sd=0.97) and on putting more effort in the task due to knowing in advance that peers will review the paper (mean=2.35, sd=1.16).

As evident from Figure 45, students think that they had thoroughly read their papers assigned for review (mean=4.27, sd=0.65). This could mean that students had taken their task seriously or that they were truly interested in their peers' papers. However, the high score in this item could also be the effect of social desirability response set, in particular if students anticipated that their facilitator would consider the questionnaire results for their grades (which, of course, was not the case).

Besides the papers that they were assigned for review, students did not show a lot of interest in reading additional papers (mean=2.53, sd=1.46). Probably they were not interested in further topics or reading and reviewing the assigned papers thoroughly had already been that time consuming such that they were not eager to take further efforts in reading additional papers. Still, the peer review activity was perceived as a positive experience and students did not only enjoy doing their reviews but even had fun writing them (mean=3.81, sd =0.74).

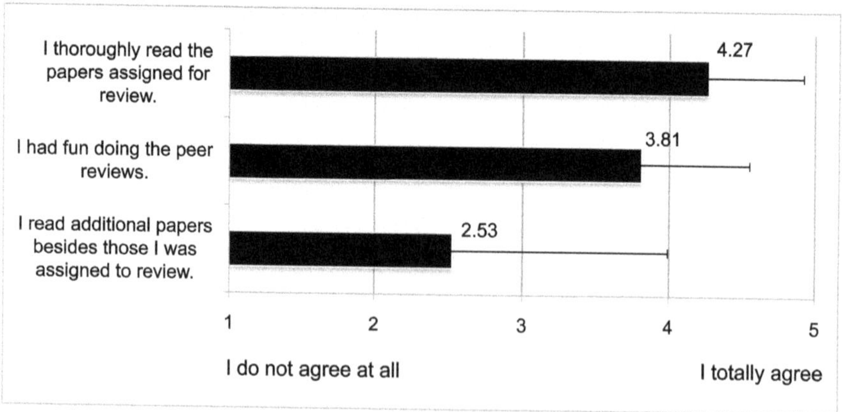

Figure 45. Feedback on writing the peer reviews (mean +/- sd), n=38

7.3.3.2 Difficulties in reviewing other papers

As expected, some of the predefined review criteria (cf. Table 18) were more difficult to assess than others. As displayed in Figure 46, the criteria that are easiest to assess are a paper's language and presentation (mean=4.14, sd=0.84) and its formal aspects (mean=4.00, sd=0.77). We assume that having difficulties in assessing the correct use of sources and references (mean=2.95, sd=0.97) and aspects concerning content (mean=3.34, sd=0.88) arise from the fact that both criteria require considerable subject knowledge and expertise for judgment. In addition, beginners in scientific writing are obviously not yet confident in the correct use of references and citations. Accordingly, it is evident that the mean value for difficulty of grading their peers' work is located somewhere in the middle (mean=3.58, sd=0.84) of the review criteria since this criterion is basically a summative judgement based on other criteria.

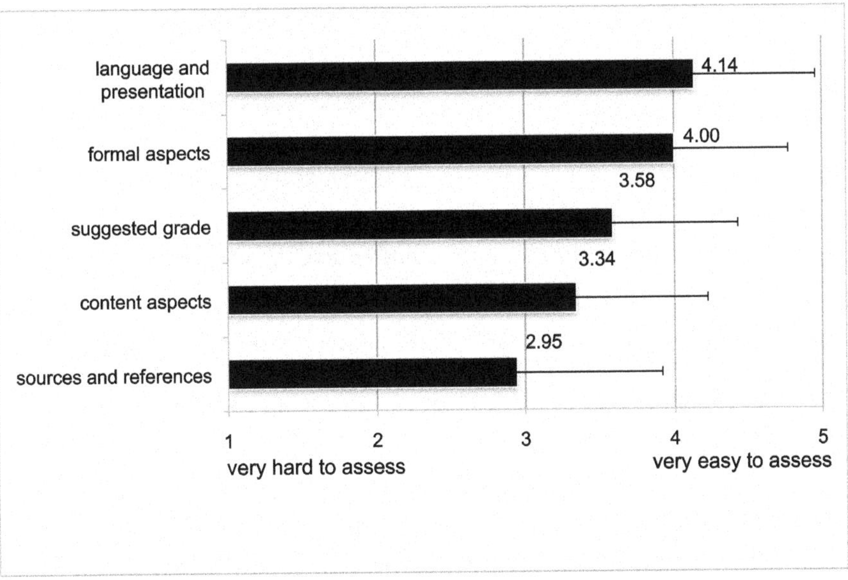

Figure 46. Difficulty of assessing various review criteria (mean +/- sd), n=38

7.3.3.3 Quality of received peer reviews

Figure 47 demonstrates that the received reviews were considered as helpful (mean=3.82, sd=0.83) for paper improvement and overall learning. In particular, students answer that their peers brought up highly justified points for improvement in their reviews (mean=3.95, sd=0.91).

Nevertheless, the impact of the reviews on the revision of the paper is judged highly (mean=2.68, sd=1.06).

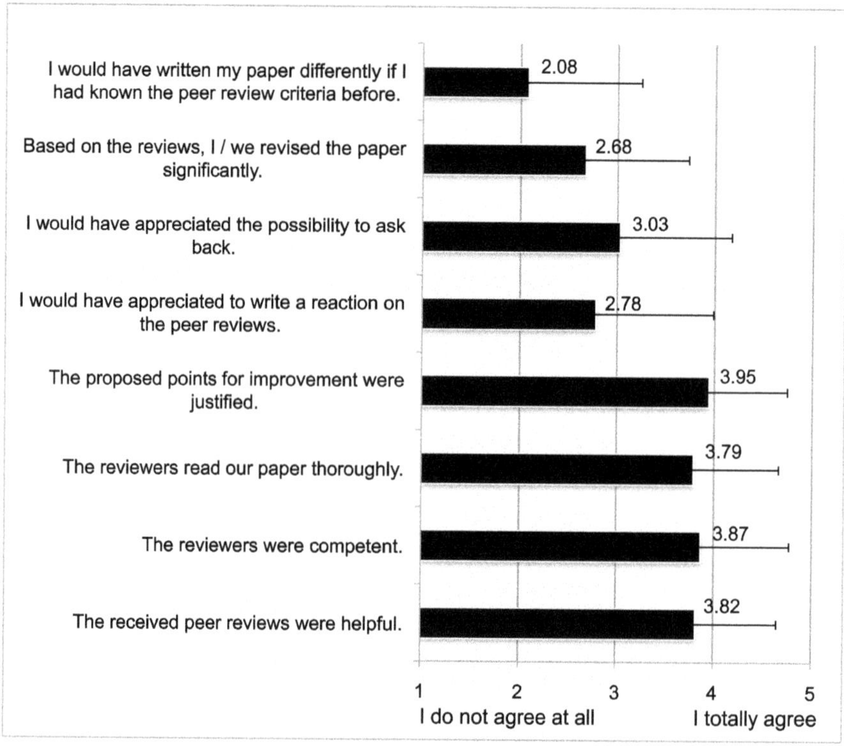

Figure 47. Feedback on receiving the peer reviews (mean +/- sd), n=38

Furthermore, students have the impression that their peer reviewers had been competent in acting in this role (mean=3.87, sd=0.83) and that they had read the papers thoroughly for the review (mean=3.79, sd=0.87). This result is in line with students' answers that they had thoroughly read their assigned papers to be able to write a good review (mean=4.27, sd=0.65). Additionally, this finding is supported by the responses to items regarding the quality of the received peer reviews: Students generally perceived them as being detailed, comprehensible, and consistent (mean=3.36, 3.62, and 3.81, sd=0.81, 0.76, and 1.05, respectively; see Figure 48).

It is also evident from Figure 47 that students would generally not have written their papers differently if they had known the detailed review criteria (cf. Table 18) beforehand (mean=2.08. sd=1.16).

It is particularly interesting that quantitative analysis indicates that there is only moderate appreciation for the possibility to ask questions to their reviewers (mean=3.03, sd=1.14) or to write a reaction on their reviews (mean=2.78, sd=1.20). Detailed qualitative analysis, in contrast, reveals that students bring up a number of arguments that emphasise the significance of the possibility to ask questions or to comment. While this seems contradictory at first sight, considering the formulation of the questions makes transparent that students did not feel that asking questions was necessary for the reviews that they were doing in the course but they generally value having the opportunity to do so whenever they feel that it would help them (cf. Section 7.3.3.4).

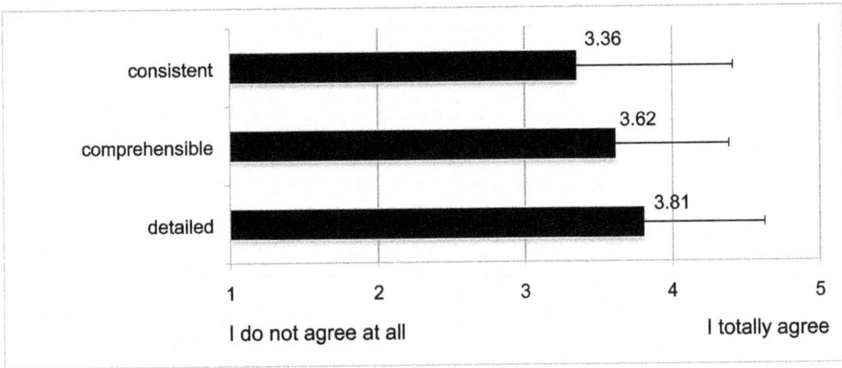

Figure 48. Perception of qualities of received reviews (mean +/- sd), n=37

7.3.3.4 Appropriateness of particular media combinations for peer reviews

The questionnaire introduced four scenarios of peer reviews with distinct combinations of media, for which students were asked to evaluate the suitability:

- written peer review without any media enhancement,
- oral feedback in a personal conversation (face-to-face peer review) without any media enhancement,
- written peer review providing the author with the possibility to comment or raise a query, and
- oral feedback in a personal conversation (face-to-face peer review) with the provision of a written handout.

Table 19 demonstrates that students clearly favour written peer reviews with the possibility to raise a query over the other three introduced review versions (26 nominations). Only five students judge this version as not suitable and two as appropriate with certain reserves. Interestingly, five students describe all of the presented peer review settings as suitable, and for one student none of these seems appropriate. The one who dislikes all of the proposed settings does, however, not indicate which scenario would – according to him – be eligible for peer reviews.

Table 19. Students' perceptions concerning the suitability of different settings of peer reviews

	SUITABLE	PARTLY SUITABLE	NOT SUITABLE
oral peer review	15	5	10
written peer review	17	6	6
written peer review with possibility to raise a query	26	2	5
oral peer review with written handouts	18	3	7

... in absolute numbers of nominations

The high appreciation of the setting with the possibility to ask is, though, not contradictory to the result of quantitative analysis which shows only moderate appreciation for the possibility to ask questions to their reviewers (mean=3.03, sd=1.14). Considering the formulation of the questions in the questionnaire makes transparent that students generally value having the opportunity to ask questions but in the particular reviewing processes in the course they did not come into a situation where they thought it would have been better to have such a possibility.

Considering combinations of answers reveals that eleven out of the 15 students who think that purely oral setting is suitable for peer reviews, also evaluate oral peer reviews with handouts positively. Out of the 17 students who judge purely written peer reviews as appropriate, twelve students also appreciate this setting's enhancement with the possibility to raise a query.

Furthermore, students' answers do not show any explicit opposites between purely written and purely oral peer reviews, as nine students support both of these extremes. Out of the supporters of one of these settings, only an evanescent number of students disapprove the respective other setting (two appreciate oral feedback but reject written peer reviews; four approve written peer reviews but judge oral feedback as inappropriate).

The qualitative analysis of the open questions (overview in Figure 49, detailed figures in Table 20) shows that students highlight more positive aspects (72 nominations) of the introduced settings for peer reviews than negative ones (57 nominations). Written peer reviews with the possibility to raise a query evince most positive nominations (23), followed by statements positively highlighting the oral aspect for peer reviews in general (20 nominations). The ratio of positive descriptions compared to negative ones is particularly high for written reviews in general (82%) and for written peer reviews with the possibility to raise a query (72%).

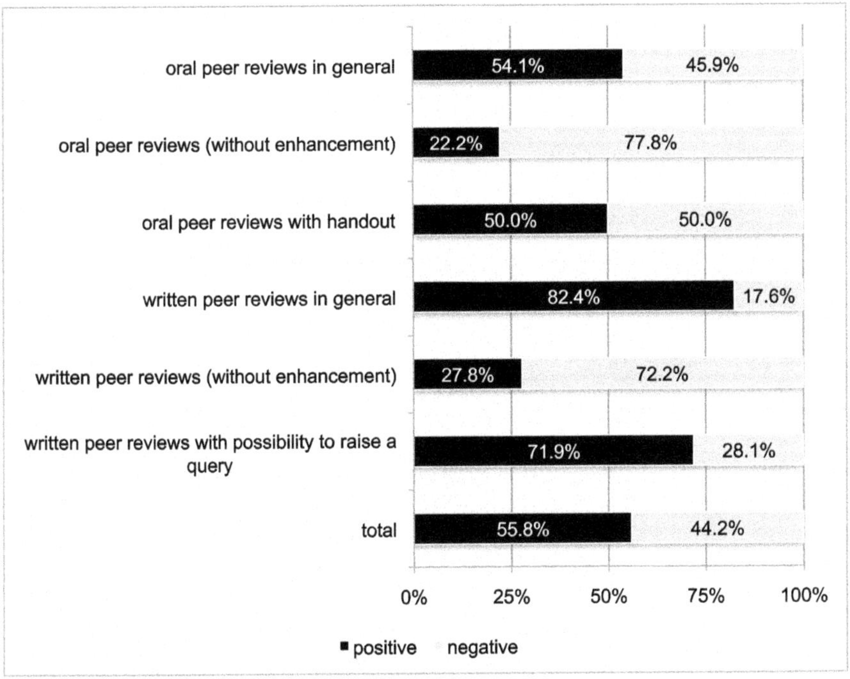

Figure 49. Ratio of positive and negative annotations concerning media combinations for peer reviews

In general, students' answers are rather heterogeneous. In the categorisation process, a multitude of categories with only a few items were found.

Particularly often students mention that in settings with oral elements, misunderstandings can be cleared up more easily or do not even emerge

(19 nominations). As advantage of written reviews, students mention the good documentation (10 nominations). In this context they state that written reviews are detailed and – due to the permanence of the written expressivity – also allow access to feedback at a later point in time (3 nominations). On the other hand, students mention frequently (7 nominations) that the possibility to raise a query is important.

Table 20. Detailed figures on positive and negative annotations concerning media combinations for peer reviews

	POSITIVE		NEGATIVE		TOTAL
	absolute	ratio	absolute	ratio	absolute
oral peer reviews in general	20	54.1%	17	45.9%	37
oral peer reviews (without enhancement)	2	22.2%	7	77.8%	9
oral peer reviews with handout	8	50.0%	8	50.0%	16
written peer reviews in general	14	82.4%	3	17.6%	17
written peer reviews (without enhancement)	5	27.8%	13	72.2%	18
written peer reviews with possibility to raise a query	23	71.9%	9	28.1%	32
total	72	55.8%	57	44.2%	129

... in numbers of nominations

Furthermore, qualitative analysis raises – although only rarely mentioned (3 nominations) – the aspect that students favour written peer reviews because many people do not dare to express critique in oral settings. So they expect that oral reviews will turn out to be milder than written ones and, thus, less constructive and educational (3 nominations). One student, for instance, explains concerning oral peer reviews, "*[...] but it is certainly less objective (automatic, implicit influence by the opponent) [...]*". Another student indicates, "*Good, but difficult to realise because nobody has the heart to say anything*". Probably also due to the already addressed inhibition to criticise, three nominations emphasise that feedback is not objective (e.g., "*Due to sympathy for the author, oral feedback may get biased/useless*").

The combination of the advantages of both methods (oral and written expression) is particularly highlighted positively for written peer reviews with the possibility to raise a query (11 nominations). Five students further emphasise that they credit this alternative best choice. Interestingly, students answer for the combination of oral feedback with handouts that an oral review is sufficient and that handouts are not necessary (5 nominations). One student indicates, "*I think it is needless to combine two kinds since, in my opinion, in an oral review a lot emerges out of the conversation, and if one has a guideline, than these aspects are discussed but not more.*" The differences in students' perceptions for oral peer reviews with written handouts and written peer reviews with possibility to raise a query orally let infer that not only the combination of the deployed media is important; rather also their order and their respective weights in the reviewing process are significant.

Finally it has to be mentioned that two out of the nine negative statements to written peer reviews with the possibility to raise a query can be ascribed to the specific constellation of the participating students in this case study. Concerning the possibility to raise a query they explain: "*Not necessary. Mostly one meets the reviewer at university several times a week, this provides the opportunity to ask.*" and "*I would say that everyone who has a query to raise, will do this via mobile phone or ICQ... we all do know each other.*"

7.4 Conclusion

In the field of peer reviews as a pedagogical element for cooperative learning, we analysed students' perceptions about peer reviewing activities and outcomes. Additionally, we investigated differences of various media combinations – particularly focusing on differences between written online peer reviews and face-to-face reviews.

In the first experimental case study we explored the quality and the kind of feedback given in peer reviews in students' small-scale software engineering projects. Furthermore, we investigated communication and collaboration aspects. In particular, we compared a face-to-face review setting with a scenario using a web-based peer review tool.

In a follow-up case study, we incorporated findings of the first study, which suggested further technology enhancement, in the research design and analysed students' perceptions on the reviewing tasks as well as how media can contribute to peer review activities in higher education. More specifically, we conducted this case study in a course on BASICS OF SCIENTIFIC WRITING. Students were introduced to the scientific peer review and worked on their reviewing competence. Again, differences between written online peer reviews and face-to-face peer reviews were analysed. Additionally, the study addressed peer review settings with combinations of oral and written feedback.

Analysis demonstrates that students generally appreciate the use of online peer reviews in the courses and take the tasks seriously, i.e. they read and analyse their peers' contributions thoroughly and see that their peers also put effort into their reviews. Students indicate that the peer review activity has a positive impact on the perception of the essential elements of scientific papers. Furthermore, due to this pedagogical element they became (more) aware that they are self-responsible for their own learning processes. On the other hand, the peer reviews – as performed – did not seem to have any measureable, statistically significant impact on the learning climate and on students' motivation.

However, we also found that students perceive several review criteria as difficult to assess. They perceive it particularly difficult to evaluate the correct use of sources and references as well as criteria related to content. Further research is required to see if more advanced students (the course is offered to third-semester computer science bachelor students) would have more confidence in assessing these criteria.

Despite those difficulties, students' responses indicate that they are confident that their peer reviewers were acting competently. Basically, they perceive the received reviews as considerably detailed, comprehensive and consistent.

We assume and hope that the positive experience with the peer review will encourage students to implement those review elements and features that they liked in this experimental setting also in work situations after their studies. Given that, we are a step closer concerning the purpose of work life preparation.

Addressing differences in the number of issues raised in the different settings, results indicate that, in our (first) case study, students comment on fewer topics in the online peer review but describe them in more detail than in the paper version.

Interestingly, analysis regarding content (which had been investigated in the first case study) shows that hardly any positive feedback is given in the online version. However, in the paper version the ratio of positive comments was only slightly higher. The generally high frequency of negative feedback was due to the assignment given since deficiencies had to be detected. Students did not perceive the shortcomings' severity differently in the two different settings; both peer review versions showed rather homogenous data. Regarding the quality and kind of reviews, the versions did not differ either.

In the direct comparison of the paper and the online peer review, students prefer the face-to-face setting for communication within their teams and with partner teams. In the online version, there was less discussion with partner teams than in the face-to-face setting. This could be the reason why students found it significantly more difficult to express hints in the online version. Concerning the reviewing activity students' answers are inhomogeneous. While some prefer reading documents on paper, others appreciate the advantages of having the documents in digital form (e.g., searching for keywords, different views of project plans).

Results on collaboration and workload distribution reveal that in the face-to-face setting, students elaborated the reviews in teamwork while they worked individually on subtasks when reviewing online. Interestingly, the teams filled in the review forms in teamwork in the paper version, while usually one student filled it in on the teams' behalf in the online setting.

Qualitative analysis of open questions in the questionnaire and produced reviews brought up following findings:

- Advantages of written reviews are the good documentation and the permanent access to the feedback.
- Students emphasise that the opportunity to raise a query is important, even when they use their personal contact opportunities outside the given options in the reviewing process (e.g., via instant messaging or mobile phone).
- Some students clearly favour written reviews, as they believe that many students do not dare to criticise in a face-to-face setting. They expect that oral reviews are milder than written ones and, hence, not as constructive and educational as they could be.
- Particularly often, students highlight that the oral element in peer review settings helps to clear up misunderstandings and may even contribute that these do not even emerge.
- For oral feedback with written handouts, students mention that the additional handouts would be needless as oral feedback would be sufficient.
- Students perceive it as easier to give helpful feedback in the face-to-face version although they experienced it as more time-consuming.
- Students indicate that they appreciate that documents can be analysed better in the online peer review.
- Students experienced online peer reviews as more time-efficient than reviews in face-to-face settings.
- For following the guidelines and completing the review forms, students prefer the online version. This finding is confirmed in both quali-

tative and quantitative analysis, indicating that filling in the online version is easier than giving feedback in a face-to-face setting.
- While online peer reviews and face-to-face peer reviews were valued equally concerning the reviews' quality, results show differences in the work efficiency how this quality was achieved.

The results of the first case study indicate that online reviews are as valuable as face-to-face reviews. However, although data of this study suggest that there are hardly any differences between these settings, it has to be considered that only written statements were analysed and interactive elements like teamwork in producing reviews and discussion about review results were not a central part of the evaluation. These elements, though, are additional factors, which impact the appropriate choice between the face-to-face and online peer review in a pedagogical setting. Enhancing the online version with communication possibilities allows tapping the full potential of the online version and benefiting from rich discussions among teams.

Based on these findings, we introduced four different peer review settings in a follow-up case study, in order to deepen our research. Out of the four peer reviews settings that were introduced (exclusively written peer review, written peer review with the possibility to raise a query, exclusively oral peer review, and oral feedback with written handouts), students favoured the written peer review with the possibility to raise a query. Despite this preference, students think that all of these settings are basically suitable for peer reviews.

Altogether the results of our case studies in the field of peer reviews encourage that the thoughtful combination of media may increase a review's efficiency. Recent results suggest that not only the combination of the deployed media is relevant; rather the sequence of media's deployment and each medium's weight in the reviewing process are essential factors which impact a peer review's efficiency. In particular, the combination an online written peer review with the opportunity to raise a query in a face-to-face setting seems to be a suitable combination of media for peer reviews.

8 *Active listening* in technology-enhanced learning settings[22]

Day-to-day we are confronted with communication challenges in any kind of interpersonal relationships. Listening to each other is not as easy as it seems. However, listening – real listening – is a key factor. Communication skills are, though, regarded as one of the top generic key skills in higher education (Dearing, 1997; Qualifications and Curriculum Authority (QCA), 2008). Oral communication skills were revealed as the third most important competency required for graduate employment in Europe (Brennan, Johnston, Little, Shah, & Woodley, 2001). Listening abilities, in particular, are regarded as important soft skills for graduates seeking employment in the IT sector (Surakka, 2007).

A highly recognised concept is *active listening*, and so it is no coincidence that communication experts and trainers in soft skills pay attention to it. This concept plays a significant role in a wide variety of disciplines, among them counselling and psychotherapy (e.g., Rogers, 1980), education (e.g., Weissglass, 1990), and business (e.g., Comer & Drollinger, 1999; Kubota, Mishima, & Nagata, 2004; Mishima, Kubota, & Nagata, 2000; Rautalinko & Lisper, 2004).

The concept of active listening has been framed for oral communication. However, nowadays computer-mediated communication – mostly in written form – dominates business and technology-enhanced learning settings. For people who frequently work in distributed teams (e.g., computer scientists), it is important to exploit the full potential of computer-mediated communication. Rather than developing oral or written communication skills independently, it seems crucial to strengthen communicative as well as media competence for being able to fully exploit (inter)personal capacities in each medium's scope and to make appropriate choices regarding the use of media.

For this reason, we studied whether and how the concept of active listening can be applied to written online communication. The first case study (Section 8.4) in this field aimed at exploring *active listening*'s capacity in technology-enhanced learning settings with written online communication.

---

22 Findings of the case studies on active listening have been partially published in following two articles (C. Bauer & Figl, 2008) and (Figl & Bauer, 2008b); (Figl & Bauer, 2008b) has been rewareded with an *Best Research Paper Award*.

Due to the positive results highlighting the concept's benefits, we proceeded our research with a follow-up case study (Section 8.5).

While the first case study focussed on exploring whether the concept of active listening may be applied to written online communication, the second case study goes further and evaluates the issue of media choice for active listening activities. Findings of both case studies highlight the advantages and limitations of online active listening as experienced and reflected by students of computer science.

Although students were newcomers to active listening skills, they delivered insightful responses to key issues such as the possibility to use written online communication for active listening, the fact that some traces of the benefits of active listening can already be observed with students without prior experience with the concept, and the discrepancy between students' attitude towards online active listening (scepticism) and behaviour (acceptance and application).

8.1 Theory and background

When people talk to each other, it frequently happens that they do not listen attentively but are half-listening, half-thinking about something else. In a dispute, people focus on formulating a response and winning the argument rather than paying attention to what the opponent expresses (Rautalinko & Lisper, 2004; Weissglass, 1990).

Active listening is a way of listening and responding to another person that improves mutual understanding by involving both verbal and nonverbal communication skills (Rogers, 1980). Active listeners take care to fully attend the speaker using techniques such as paraphrasing, summarising, or encouraging. For instance, paraphrasing including both factual and emotional information enables the speaker to find out whether the listener really understood (Rautalinko & Lisper, 2004; Robertson, 2005).

Before we can go into detail, we first have to distinguish active listening from other listening modes (Section 8.1.1). After that, Section 8.1.2 outlines the concept in detail, presenting its techniques and discussing benefits and difficulties.

8.1.1 The listening modes

Since listening means different things to different people, this term – or strictly speaking: process – has to be clarified at this point.

Listening requires one person sending a message (talker, sender, originator) and one or more listeners receiving that message (listener, reader, receiver) (Shannon, 1948). We can distinguish several modes of listening. A widely accepted model of differentiation does, however, not yet exist. Hence, several models are to be found in literature (e.g., Comer & Drollinger, 1999; Weisbach, 1999; Weissglass, 1990, pp. 355-356). While, for instance, (Weisbach, 1999) speaks of four modes, (Weissglass, 1990) differentiates in more detail and discusses seven forms of listening.

(Weisbach, 1999) describes following four ways of listening:

- *Pseudo-listening (Pseudo-Zuhören or 'Ich-verstehe'-Zuhören).* Basically it is not a matter of real listening but rather a pick up for one's own talking. Since we regard it as disrespectful to interrupt someone, it has become a habit to use a nice phrase (like e.g., 'I understand...', 'Yes, you are right but...', 'Yes, I am with you. Do you now I...', etc.) to silence the other and take the floor oneself. Often nonverbal cues like nodding, bending forward or straightening up and taking a deep breath precede the speech. The phrase 'I understand' does not implicate true understanding in these cases; rather it is a linguistic break. The involved persons tend to talk at cross purposes, feign to listen but fob one another off with clichés (Weisbach, 1999, pp. 37-38).
- *Assimilating listening (Aufnehmendes Zuhören).* This kind of listening is characterised by keeping silent. The listener dedicates all attention to the sender without saying anything. A nodding does thereby not signify agreement but expresses that the listener's thoughts are with the sender. When eye contact is lacking (e.g., on a phone call), nonverbal cues are usually verbalised by sounds like 'uh-huh', 'mm-hmm', etc. Instead of taking the chance to tell one's own story, the listener uses the nonverbal (and verbalised) cues to encourage the sender to continue. The listener thereby ignores all impulses for a response or question and keeps silent and attentive (Weisbach, 1999, pp. 38-44).
- *Paraphrasing listening (Umschreibendes Zuhören).* The listener paraphrases what the sender said at the level of content (Sachebene (cf. Schulz von Thun, 1981/2003, pp. 26, 47-51)) without adding any opinions, interpretations, judgements, or advices. Paraphrasing points to have understood the content and is an effective means to avoid misunderstandings (Weisbach, 1999, pp. 44-48).
- *Active listening (Aktives Zuhören).* According to (Weisbach, 1999) active listening distinguishes from paraphrasing listening to that extent that the listener does not reproduce the whole statement but tries to put the statement's implicit emotions briefly into words. With this kind of active listening the listener signalises that the sender's feelings came through and emphasises that the listener tries to understand the

point of view and situation (Weisbach, 1999, pp. 48-58). Interestingly, (Weisbach, 1999) does not mention Thomas Gordon's work on active listening (cf. Gordon, 1970/1983; Gordon & Burch, 1974/1977; Gordon, 1977/1979), which passes for the foundation of this concept. Furthermore, his definition is slightly different to the one by Gordon (cf. Section 8.1.2).

As already mentioned above, (Weissglass, 1990) differentiates in more detail and discusses following seven forms of listening:

- *Active (or reflective) listening*. This term was introduced by Thomas Gordon (cf. Gordon, 1970/1983; Gordon & Burch, 1974/1977; Gordon, 1977/1979) for the process developed by Carl R. Rogers (Rogers, 1951) and which was originally referred to as reflective listening. A listener reflects back to the sender of his or her impression of what is expressed without judging (cf. Section 8.1.2).
- *Passive listening*. When listening passively, the listener is genuinely interested in hearing and understanding the other person's point of view and therefore listens intently. Assuming to have heard correctly, the listener does not say anything (i.e. does not verify the message) but indicates interest and attention by nonverbal aspects of communication like by maintaining eye contact and periodically nodding or smiling (Weissglass, 1990, p. 355; Gordon, 1970/1983, pp. 44-46).
- *Inattentive listening*. We speak of inattentive listening, when sound enters someone's ears but there is little chance or even attempt to comprehend or respond. Listening to someone while reading the newspaper would be a good example for this kind of listening mode. Some people claim to be able to listen while reading, although many of their conversation partners do not agree (Weissglass, 1990, p. 355). For other authors (cf. e.g., Imhof, 2004, pp. 6-7; Torralba, 2007, pp. 11-14), however, such situations would be referred to as hearing rather than listening. They claim that the difference between hearing and listening lies in the intention for selection of information, the integration of new information into the existing cognitive structure and in the cognitive as well as the motivational activity of the recipient.
- *Pretend listening*. A scenario of pretend listening frequently happens in classrooms, when students are listening to a lecture but are preoccupied with other concerns. They maintain an interested facial expression but are actually thinking about something else. Unlike inattentive listening, the sender may not even realise that attention is lacking (Weissglass, 1990, p. 355).
- *Conversational listening*. In this listening mode, the roles of sender and listener alternate frequently. The person listening is allowed or

even expected to interrupt the sender to express a point of view (Weissglass, 1990, p. 355).

- *Argumentative listening.* Similar to listening conversationally, the roles of sender and listener alternate continuously when listening argumentatively. Argumentative listening is, however, more passionate and the listener keeps looking for flaws in the sender's argument. Argumentative listening can be beneficial. But unfortunately it frequently degenerates into an attempt to blast the sender's argument and even the sender's self-esteem into bits – a scenario which can be observed in academic and political circles as it can be in personal relationships (Weissglass, 1990, p. 355).
- *Informational listening.* Informational listening occurs when a person attempts to gather information that someone else possesses. The listener may, for instance, ask for advice or help. During a conversation, informational listening may sometimes change to conversational or argumentative listening, when the listener does not agree with the information or point of view. Alternatively, it may change to active listening if the listener wants to user that technique for problem solving. Sometimes it may also change to pretend listening if the listener is overwhelmed by too much information (Weissglass, 1990, pp. 355-356).

Especially when having a look on the description of informational listening, it seems obvious that the differences between the forms of listening are easily blurred. It mainly depends on the conversation partners, their intentions and emotions, as well as the topic, which kind of listening will occur. It may even happen that within a five minute talk all of the above mentioned listening modes come out for a moment: A person may first listen passively without saying a word. Then something comes to the listener's mind and thoughts zone out, resulting in pretend listening. Suddenly a keyword appears and the listener looks in some book nearby for an appropriate chapter – we are in the inattentive listening mode. Then the topic gets more interesting, the roles of sender and listener alternate like in conversational listening. As it gets more emotional, when two points of view clash, argumentative listening is up to rise. In order to calm the situation one person applies the techniques of active listening and finds out that the sender has meaningful things to say and keeps gathering this information (informational listening).

Additionally to above mentioned seven modes, (Weissglass, 1990) introduces a different form of listening: *constructivist listening*. It is based on the principles of constructivism (cf. Glasersfeld, 1987; Watzlawick, 1976) and two further beliefs:

> "First, distress (the accumulation of emotions left from hurtful experiences) is a primary source of unintelligent and uncaring behavior. Second, the natural physiological processes of making expressing emotions contribute to recovery from the effects of distress, making sense of experiences, and thinking more clearly" (Weissglass, 1990, p. 356).

(Weissglass, 1990) argues that constructivist listening is a different form of listening which is for the benefit of the sender (Weissglass, 1990, p. 356). Active listening, though, derives from psychotherapy and counselling and is unambiguously intended in support of the client (the sender) rather than the therapist or counsellor (the listener). Since (Weissglass, 1990) also cites sources about active listening (Weissglass, 1990, pp. 355, 357), which indicates awareness of Gordon's concept, above statement is, hence, questionable and further discussion of the concept of constructivist listening is to be handled with care.

Constructivist listening differs from active listening in that the listener does not interpret the sender's thoughts and feelings. Constructivist listening, though, is not passive listening but, according to (Weissglass, 1990, p. 357), "interpretations by the listener usually interfere with the sender's fully exploring the thought or feeling, expressing emotion, and developing understanding".

In contrast to active listening, in constructivist listening it is not important for the listener to get the senders point as it is based on the assumption that nobody can ever completely understand the thoughts and feelings of another person. Although constructivist listening emphasises the importance that the listener communicates interest, caring and acceptance (Weissglass, 1990, p. 356), which is in accordance with the concept and active listening and also with the personal dispositions of acceptance (Rogers, 1959), the disposition of empathic understanding is, however, disregarded. Moreover, showing interest and caring without understanding the senders thoughts and feelings – or without even attempting to understand – may likely lead to or be a result of insincerity (a breach of the disposition of congruence). Thus, this listening technique does not correspond with the person-centred approach.

Although the terms used in the models by (Weisbach, 1999) and (Weissglass, 1990) are distinct, their meanings show similarities and can, thus, be related to each other. As can be seen from Figure 50, pretend and inattentive listening (Weissglass, 1990) refer to what (Weisbach, 1999) calls pseudo-listening. Assimilating listening and passive listening are equivalents. Although paraphrasing listening (Weisbach, 1999) has no direct counterpart in the model by (Weissglass, 1990), the conversational, argumentative and informational mode seem to show similarities. While both models use the term active listening, the underlying concepts are slightly different. Nevertheless, in a broad sense they refer to similar meanings. This cluster of terms also includes constructivist listening (Weissglass, 1990), which is a derivative of active listening.

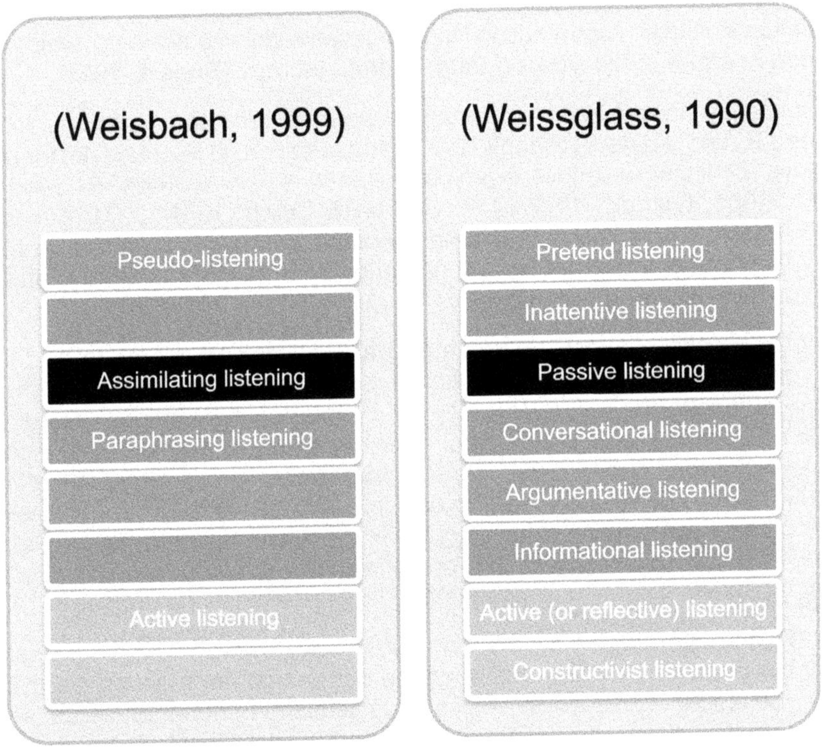

Figure 50. Comparison of listening modes according to the models by (Weisbach, 1999) and (Weissglass, 1990)

8.1.2 Active listening

The concept of *active listening* goes back to the American psychologist Thomas Gordon (cf. Gordon & Sands, 1976/1985; Gordon, 1977/1979; Gordon & Burch, 1974/1977), but has its roots in Carl R. Rogers' client-centred therapy and nondirective counselling (Rogers, 1951).

(Rogers, 1951) believed that listening intently to clients was most effective in allowing a therapist to determine what they needed. In doing this, the reflection of attitudes is crucial, which – once more – asserts the need for empathic understanding with the client. In order to understand a client from his or her frame of reference, the therapist attempts to reconstruct what he or she is thinking and feeling. Simultaneously, the expression of empathy and understanding contributes to the clarification of a client's expression and helps to establish a climate of trust. This communication skill used for reflection Rogers called *reflective listening*, which is a corner-stone of his work on client-centred therapy (Rogers, 1951).

Inspired by his professor and friend's work on reflective listening, Thomas Gordon started to apply the communication skills used in therapeutic settings in rather everyday situations (cf. Gordon & Sands, 1976/1985; Gordon, 1977/1979; Gordon & Burch, 1974/1977). And so the Rogerian reflective listening has become a widely-know ingredient in a variety of contexts that involve gathering information and solving problems (Rautalinko & Lisper, 2004).

The difference between reflective and active listening seems to be tied up only to the setting of application and the primary aim for use. While Rogers spoke of reflective listening in therapeutic settings (Rogers, 1951), Gordon keeps speaking of active listening in everyday situations (e.g., Gordon, 1970/1983; Gordon & Burch, 1974/1977; Gordon, 1977/1979). Thereby, the setting of application tends to go in hand with the primary aim for use since listening in therapeutic settings targets at a client's psychological health and personality development, while in everyday situations it aims for gathering information and solving problems.

In (Rogers & Richard E. Farson, 1957/1987), however, even Rogers speaks of active listening. Although the authors do not mention it explicitly, the article seems so be dedicated to listening in non-therapeutic settings. In this regard the differentiation of terms according to the setting of application, thus, seems reasonable.

(Gordon, 2000) states that he adopted the term active listening from Richard E. Farson, who was a former student of him. Although a clear reference is missing, Gordon presumably refers to above-mentioned article of (Rogers & Richard E. Farson, 1957/1987). This, again, is a good indication that both terms, active and reflective listening, may be used interchangeably. This is further supported by the fact that many sources (cf. e.g., Limbeck, 2005)indeed use these terms synonymously. Hence, this work will adhere to this approach and regards these terms as equivalent.

Basically, active listening requires the listener to capture what the sender is communicating from the sender's frame of reference. More than that, the listener has to convey to the sender that he or she is seeing things from the his or her point of view (Rogers & Richard E. Farson, 1957/1987). Trying to keep distortion at a minimum, the listener has to continuously validate the accuracy of understanding (Gordon, 1977/1979, p. 65), whereby active listening captures also the feelings that come with what is said.

As the model of communication by Shannon/Weaver (cf. Shannon, 1948) (cf. Section 2.2.1.1) describes, messages are encoded by the sender and decoded by the recipient (listener). In active listening, the listener gives feedback on how having decoded the specific message. With this feedback the sender has an indication for how the listener understood the message and can confirm the feedback or set the record straight (Gordon, 1970/1983, pp. 56-57; 1977/1979, p. 64).

The sender's confirmation would then demonstrate that the listener's impression was right (listener's impression = sender's expression), while a rectification would indicate that the impression was not correct (listener's impression ≠ sender's expression). Consequently, both involved persons may be certain that the listener has understood the message (Gordon, 1977/1979, pp. 64-65).

In other contexts, paraphrasing traditionally addresses the level of content (Sachebene (cf. Schulz von Thun, 1981/2003, pp. 26, 47-51)). Active listening goes further and tries to capture what lies beneath – the *feelings that come with what is said.*

According to (Rogers & Richard E. Farson, 1957/1987), to listen actively means that there are several things to do: listening for total meaning, responding to feelings, and paying attention to all cues:

- *Listening for total meaning.* As already outlined in Schulz von Thun's model of communication (cf. Section 2.2.1.4), any message that a person tries to get across is composed of four elements: content, appeal, self-revelation, and the relation between the actors (cf. Schulz von Thun, 1981/2003, pp. 26, 47-51). All of these four are important due to giving the message a meaning (Rogers & Richard E. Farson, 1957/1987).
- *Responding to feelings.* In some instances, the feelings underlying a message are far more important than its content (Rogers & Richard E. Farson, 1957/1987). If, for example, a student would say, "*I'd like to tear this stupid book up and make confetti out of it*", responding to content would be obviously absurd. Instead, responding to the stu-

dent's anger or disgust in trying to work with the book's subject matter recognises this message's meaning.

- *Paying attention to all cues*. Words alone do not tell everything that a sender is communicating. Deep listening requires, hence, including several kinds of communication besides verbal expressions (Rogers & Richard E. Farson, 1957/1987). In particular for finding out about feelings, nonverbal cues are frequently more informative and revealing than words.

Trying to understand the message from the sender's point of view is nothing else than showing empathy. In literature we sometimes come across the term empathic listening. It is stressed at this point that active listening includes empathic listening since empathy is a necessary – though not a sufficient – condition for the former kind of listening. Empathic listening strives for deep (empathic) understanding. The listener, however, does not necessarily have to use active listening for achieving empathic understanding.

Furthermore, it is important to mention that active listening does not require agreement. When listeners, for instance, accept that the sender feels hopeless, they do not necessarily agree that it is good, appropriate, or reasonable to feel hopeless in this specific situation. Accepting someone's feelings is not related to agreement nor is it judgement between good and bad (Gordon, 1977/1979, pp. 79-80; 1970/1983; Gordon & Burch, 1974/1977).In other words, Rogers' disposition of acceptance finds its expression and application in active listening.

8.1.2.1 Techniques in and for active listening

While active listening is rooted in each person's personality and thus, as a whole, is much more than a technique, it encompasses some elements or techniques that have been found to be facilitative in most cases. However, if not applied genuinely and rooted in deep interest in the other person, such pretended usage will soon become evident and the whole listening process will loose its promotive effect. Accordingly the listener will need to hold Rogers' three dispositions (empathy, congruence, and acceptance) at least to a certain degree in order that active listening can show beneficial effects. Simultaneously, when having developed these dispositions to a higher degree, it will be easier for the listener to apply this concept effectively.

Having emphasised this, let us turn to the component techniques commonly used in active listening: paraphrasing (restating), verbalising emotions, asking, summarising, clarifying, encouraging, and balancing (cf.

Decker, 1989). Table 21 provides a brief overview over these techniques' use and purpose, and illustrates these with examples.

Table 21. Active listening techniques

TECHNIQUE	PURPOSE	TO ACHIEVE PURPOSE	EXAMPLES
paraphrasing (restating)	• convey interest • encourage to keep talking	• restate the information just received with one's own words	"So you think this is the safer way but maybe not the best way."
verbalising emotions	• show that one understands • help the speaker to evaluate his or her own feelings	• reflect the speaker's basic feelings and emotions in words	"So you were happy to be there..."
asking	• get more information	• ask questions	"'Are you speaking about yourself?"
summarising	• review progress • pull together important ideas and facts • establish a basis for further discussion	• restate major ideas expressed including feelings	"So your major concern is not being trusted..."
clarifying	• clarify what is said • help the speaker see other points of view	• ask questions for vague statements • restate wrong interpretations to force the speaker to explain further	"You said that you have reacted immediately. Was this still on the same day?"
encouraging	• convey interest • encourage to keep talking	• disagree • use varying voice intonations • offer ideas and suggestions	"That interests me."
balancing	• get more information • help the speaker to evaluate his or her own feelings	• ask questions	"Did you perceive the inconvenience worse than not being taken seriously?"

8.1.2.2 The benefits of active listening

The benefits of active listening are manifold. Learning how to listen actively contributes to the development of personality and therefore furthers the listener to some degree. Predominantly, though, active listening is for the benefit of the sender rather than the listener. The most important positive effects are summarised below (cf. e.g., Gordon & Sands, 1976/1985, pp. 58-60):

- *Avoidance of misunderstandings.* As people confirm that they really understand, active listening effectively contributes to prevent misunderstandings (e.g., Gordon, 1970/1983; Gordon & Burch, 1974/1977; Gordon & Sands, 1976/1985).
- *Disturbing feelings fade.* People believe that they can get rid of feelings by suppressing and forgetting them. Disturbing feelings, however, vanish much earlier when they are expressed openly and active listening furthers the expression of feelings (Gordon & Sands, 1976/1985, p. 58). Moreover, strong negative feelings are often more volatile as they seem. Senders frequently use negative feelings as codes for messages in order to get attention. If the sender is addressed empathically (as active listening does), such strong negative feelings give way for much weaker feelings or even positive ones (Gordon, 1977/1979, pp. 86-87).
- *Feelings get friendly.* Especially in masculine cultures (cf. Hofstede, 2005) emotions are not valued at their best and are hardly accepted in business or educational settings. Ever since childhood we learn to regard feelings as bad or even dangerous. Repressing emotions can harm psychological health, cause psychosomatic symptoms, and impair productivity. With active listening people learn to accept feelings and to loose the idea of emotions being negative or unacceptable (Gordon, 1970/1983, p. 63; Gordon & Sands, 1976/1985, p. 58; Gordon, 1977/1979, pp. 83-86).
- *Increased trust.* The fact that someone listens and understands releases positive feelings, which furthers the relationship between sender and listener and a sense of trust may emerge (Gordon, 1970/1983, p. 63; Gordon & Sands, 1976/1985, p. 58).
- *Increased willingness to listen.* If someone listens to what we have to say, we are more willing to listen to the other's point of view. Persons who are paid attention to are more likely to become good listeners themselves than people who do not get the chance to be heard (Gordon, 1970/1983, p. 64; Gordon & Sands, 1976/1985, p. 58).
- *Demonstrating respect.* It is difficult to convince people that they are respected by telling them so. Rather one is much more likely to get this message across by behaving that way. Active listening gives the sender the feeling of being worth listening and respected (Rogers & Richard E. Farson, 1957/1987; Torralba, 2007, pp. 127-130).

- *Revealing the core of the problem.* People's problems are like onions – they come in layers. Only after peeling off the outer layers one finds the underlying core problem. Sometimes the vital issue is not even apparent to oneself. When someone starts talking about a problem, both, the sender and the listener, tend to notice the ostensible problem only. Active listening helps effectively to advance to the core problem (Gordon, 1977/1979, pp. 88-89).
- *Higher sense of responsibility.* Instead of providing ready solutions for these problems, active listening encourages and stimulates self-dependent thinking and to find solutions oneself. As a result, people get more self-dependent and more responsible (Gordon, 1970/1983, pp. 63-64).
- *Personality development.* Active listening implicates a growth experience both for the sender and the listener. Beside providing the listener with more information than any other mode of listening, active listening tends to alter constructively the attitudes of the listener resulting in an experience of growth (Rogers & Richard E. Farson, 1957/1987). Listening to someone else also implies listening to oneself, which leads to an increased self-awareness (Torralba, 2007, pp. 166-168). On the sender's side, the process of solving a problem independently may contribute to personality development (Gordon, 1970/1983, pp. 63-64). In contrast to having imposed ready solutions on oneself, the process of solving a problem independently may contribute to one's personality development. Especially the awareness of not having had anybody's assistance but having gone it all alone may strengthen self-esteem and self-confidence.
- *Better handling of criticism.* People who are listened to empathically, tend to listen more carefully to themselves and get better aware of their own feelings and thinking (Rogers & Richard E. Farson, 1957/1987), which results in a better understanding of themselves. Furthermore, (Rogers & Richard E. Farson, 1957/1987) point out that active listening reduces the threat of being criticised. With this experience, people are more likely to feel that their contributions are worthwhile.
- *Pleasure to help.* As already mentioned, active listening furthers to find solutions on one's own. Educators and parents report that they take much pleasure in observing that their students or children get self-dependent enough to solve problems on their own. Moreover, this relieves them from the burdening feeling that they would always have to deliver the right solution (Gordon & Sands, 1976/1985, pp. 59-60).
- *Deliberation.* Listening is an act of psychological deliberation, both for the listener and the one who talks. Speaking eases the burden of

thinking. Listening, sincere without disguising oneself, deliberates also the listener from worries (Torralba, 2007, pp. 131-133).

8.1.2.3 Difficulties in active listening

As it is not one of the easiest skills to acquire, active listening demands for continuous practise. Even more important is the fact that learning the skill may require to alter one's basic attitudes, which evolve considerably slowly (Rogers & Richard E. Farson, 1957/1987).

Despite the multitude of benefits that active listening implicates (cf. Section 8.1.2.2), this concept also entails some difficulties, which occur especially in the initial phases of learning and applying it.

- *Initial discomfort.* The idea of reacting to conversation partners totally different than ever before discomfits many people. In early phases, some listeners experience active listening as difficult because it seems not to correspond with their self-perception. Indeed, active listening initially is a mechanical technique, which is applied deliberately (Gordon & Sands, 1976/1985, pp. 62-65). With the development of attitude and personality, active listening may grow to an immanent part of personality and social skills and will then better fit the self-perception. But initially, discomfort is to be observed frequently.
- *Reluctance to talk.* Sometimes a person is just not willing to talk about problems and incidents. Active listening is not always a good door opener. As long as a person does not accept an invitation to talk, active listening will not work (Gordon, 1970/1983, pp. 95-96; Gordon & Sands, 1976/1985, pp. 65-67).
- *In the mood for listening.* Some people get the illusory idea to be obliged to be available to listen at al circumstances when someone has a problem. Experience shows that people simply *cannot* listen if they are not in the mood for it. This is a fact that people have difficulty with to accept. Active listening is a method that implies empathy and acceptance. When someone argues a problem just in the moment the listener is occupied by other urgent concerns and struggles with multitasking, it is obvious that this is an inconvenient point in time for active listening – the listener would not be listening with all possible attention and heart. In such situations, the listener is better off explaining the situation and asking the sender for attending to the issue at a later point in time when both are free to talk (Gordon & Sands, 1976/1985, pp. 67-70; Gordon, 1977/1979, pp. 81-82).
- *Obviousness and resistance.* In the early attempts many people seem to stick to the habit to start all their answers with the same phrases (e.g., 'it seems like...', 'you have the feeling that...', 'you say that...',

'you feel that...', etc.). Using the technique that obviously may seem strange to the listener and frequently leads to resistance (Gordon, 1970/1983, pp. 91-92; Gordon & Sands, 1976/1985, pp. 70-71).

- *Listening without empathy.* It is a real danger when people try to learn active listening from books and do not feel the cordiality and empathy, which have to accompany their endeavours. People do not only want that the listener understands what they express (level of content, Sachebene (cf. Schulz von Thun, 1981/2003, pp. 26, 47-51)) but also the feelings that come with what is said. Sentient persons perceive when their feelings are not understood. Trying to listen actively without empathy may seem mechanic and misses its purpose (Gordon, 1970/1983, pp. 92-94).
- *Exaggeration.* Active listening is not intended to replace other methods that educators use for learning, facilitating, or communicating. In literature about this concept it often comes short that active listening may be inappropriate in certain situations. (Gordon & Sands, 1976/1985) point out that people who learn to apply and internalise the active listening technique tend to overuse it, apply it when there is a problem even so trivial. First, this may lead to frustration on the part of the listener since in these situations active listening does not show effects. Second, senders may be confused about the exaggerated use, especially in inappropriate situations (Gordon, 1970/1983, pp. 94-95; Gordon & Sands, 1976/1985, pp. 72-74).
- *Hidden intent.* Sometimes people want to use active listening to carry their point – and fail. Active listening is intended to help senders find solutions for their own problems. Trying to get one's way does not show acceptance for the sender's feelings (Gordon, 1970/1983, pp. 87-89; Gordon & Sands, 1976/1985, pp. 77-78) and will, thus, not lead to the desired positive effects.
- *Dislike of what one is hearing.* When trying to get someone to express true feelings, we must not be surprised to sometimes hear things that we dislike (e.g., I do not like you, smoking marihuana is great, I cheated on my English exam, etc.). In such critical situations people tend to fall back to their old reaction habits (Gordon & Sands, 1976/1985, pp. 78-82). Acceptance is crucial in this case.
- *Legitimate dependency.* Dependency is *not* an effect of active listening rather it is an obstacle. There are situations of legitimate dependency when the sender needs specific information or the like, which only the listener possesses. Under such circumstances, active listening is not necessary and most frequently inappropriate (Gordon, 1977/1979, pp. 78-79). In such situations the listener cannot further

the sender to find a solution independently but has to provide the necessary information, authority, etc.

8.2 The research questions

As already mentioned above, the concept of active listening is researched and widely accepted in a variety of contexts (for instance, psychotherapy (e.g., Rogers, 1980), education (e.g., Weissglass, 1990), and business (e.g., Comer & Drollinger, 1999; Kubota, Mishima, & Nagata, 2004; Mishima, Kubota, & Nagata, 2000; Rautalinko & Lisper, 2004)). As it is a concept for oral communication, studies analyse its effects in such settings.

This investigation explores active listening in a technology-enhanced educational setting using written online communication. Thereby, transferring the concept of active listening to written online communication is a novel asset. When using written means of expression, the term *active listening* does not exactly verbalise the core of the activity as people do no longer listen but rather read. Derivations like *active reading* or *active communicating* did, though, not seem appropriate either as both may be confused with some vivid activity centralised on oneself rather than the other. Consequently, we decided to stick to the term *active listening* even for settings with written communication as it still seems to best express what the concept stands for.

The presented case studies, thus, aim at analysing whether this concept deriving from oral communication is appropriate and effective in written online communication. With respect to technology-enhanced learning, these studies pay particular attention to this concept's promotiveness in such settings.

Following research questions are addressed:

- Can the concept of active listening be applied to settings with written online communication?
- Which adaptations in communicating and listening have to be made?
- What is the potential and what are the drawbacks in applying the concept of active listening in written online communication?
- What influence do media (e-mail vs. instant messaging) have on active listening?

8.3 The case design

The two case studies in the field of active listening emphasise distinct interests. While the first case study (Section 8.4) aims at exploring *active listening*'s capacity in technology-enhanced learning settings with written online communication, the follow-up case study (Section 8.5) investigates the aspect of media choice for active listening activities.

Although the case's aims are different, the case designs are similar. In order to keep duplicated text at a minimum, this Section describes the case design that applies for both case studies. The parts of the studies that are distinct are clearly indicated.

8.3.1 Description of the setting

Both case studies were conducted in a course on *Project Management – Communication and Soft Skills* for students of business informatics and computer science at the University of Vienna. Students participating in this course did not have any prior training in active listening and were, thus, inexperienced in this domain. While the first case study refers to the course held in winter term 2005/2006, the follow-up case study refers to winter term 2006/2007.

This course is part of the Master's programme, which indicates that the participants had already received a Bachelor's degree in computer science. The workload is six credit points according to ECTS (European Credit Transfer System). This course is held as a technology-enhanced course: it includes presence phases in class and is accompanied by an e-learning platform (Mangler, 2005), which is not only limited to knowledge intensive inputs and materials. In fact, cooperation among students is a central component in both settings, in the presence phases as well as in the online part.

The course primarily aims at improving students' soft skills as required in project work situations, in particular in team communication, ad hoc presentations, and moderation techniques. The course style is based on active, experiential learning and strongly integrates the person-centred approach to education. Besides the objective to allow students to experience a person-centred atmosphere based on the three Rogers variables (congruence, empathy, and acceptance), this course aims at providing space for unfolding and experiencing their (inter)personal capacities and communication styles in a non-directive, unstructured setting.

The facilitator moderates the initial three workshops, and then students take over. More precisely, based on their interests, student teams (about 3-4 persons each) are free to decide on a particular soft skills topic, which they prepare. Each team moderates its own workshop on the respectively chosen topic. Feedback is continuously given during the workshops as well as in online reaction sheets (Motschnig-Pitrik, 2006b).

8.3.2 Implementation of the cases

After a preliminary kick-off meeting, the facilitator introduced the concept of active listening theoretically and then students exercised it practically in class in the first two-day presence phase of the course. For the practical exercise students formed triads consisting of a speaker, a listener, and an observer. One student talked about something he or she wanted to share with the others, one student listened actively, and the third student observed the setting for being able to learn from this passive experience and also to give feedback to his or her colleagues. After approximately ten minutes, students changed roles, so that finally every student had the chance to experience each role. Then, students shared their experiences resulting from the active listening exercise with the whole course community. Referring to the active listening exercise one student for example shared following experience: "*[...] it was very helpful for me. My active listener's listening helped me to take a different view of my own problem, I think about it and I am on the good track to solve that problem.*" Another student explained: "*I really enjoyed this part. I never thought of difficulties I'm having when listening to somebody. I always tend to think about the problem somebody is telling from my point of view which is sometimes horrible because I get often lost in the rest of the matter.*"

After this first presence phase, students built pairs using a web-based team-building tool ((Mangler, 2005, pp. 78-79); cf. Section 4.5) in order to try online active listening in dyads. As suggested by (Weissglass, 1990, p. 359), students had to act once in the role of the listener and once in the role of the sender (talker).

In the first case study, all participants carried out the online active listening exercise with an instant messaging tool. In the follow-up case study, in contrast, half of the class chose instant messaging, while the other half used e-mail instead.

In both cases, students were free to choose any tool or client they liked, as long as they could provide the log files (cf. Section 8.3.3). Furthermore, for the exercise every student could pick up any issue that genuinely mattered to him or her, as the course's facilitator did not impose any topic but recommended to share some personal experience or concern rather than discussing external issues like politics or sports events.

After the exercise, students were asked to reflect (in an online reaction) on the active listening experience addressing following two questions:

What happened during the exercise? How did I perceive it as the talker and as the listener?

Figure 51 illustrates the process of the first case study with instant messaging, including all main activities by the facilitator and the participants; Figure 52 illustrates the activities of the follow-up case study with e-mail and instant messaging. The only difference between the activities of the first and the follow-up case study was that in the follow-up study the medium for online active listening could be freely chosen.

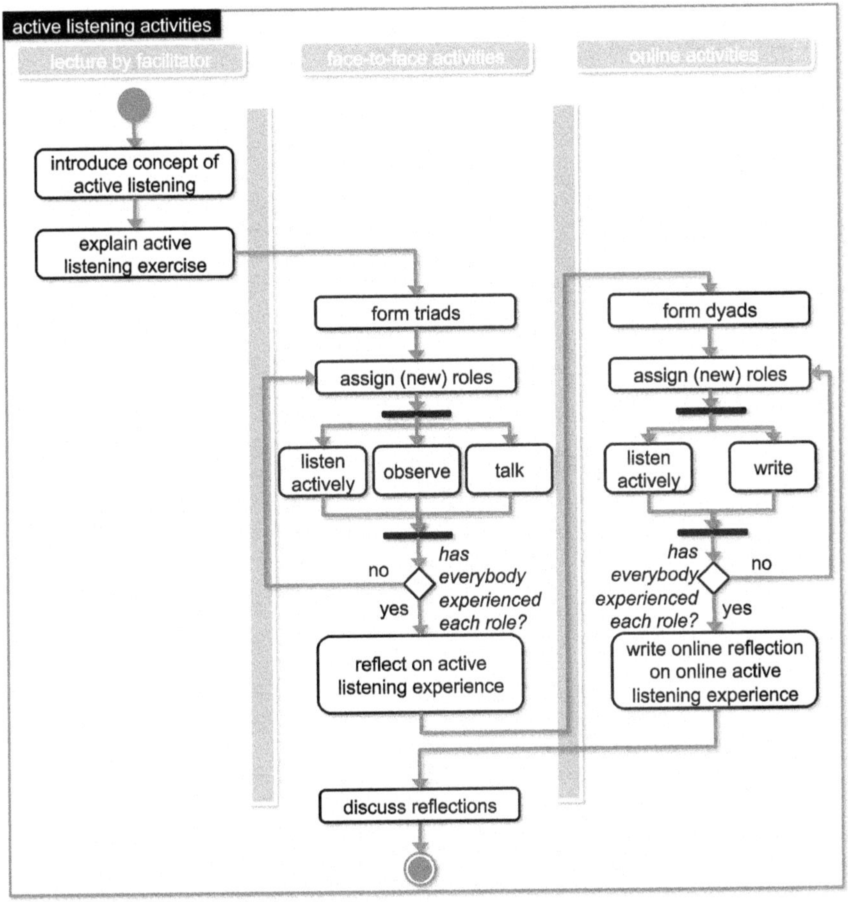

Figure 51. UML activity diagram of the case study *Active listening with instant messaging*

In order to keep track of similarities and differences of the preliminary face-to-face and the subsequent online exercise, both diagrams show comparable activities horizontally on the same level while vertically in different swim lanes (middle face-to-face, right online activity).

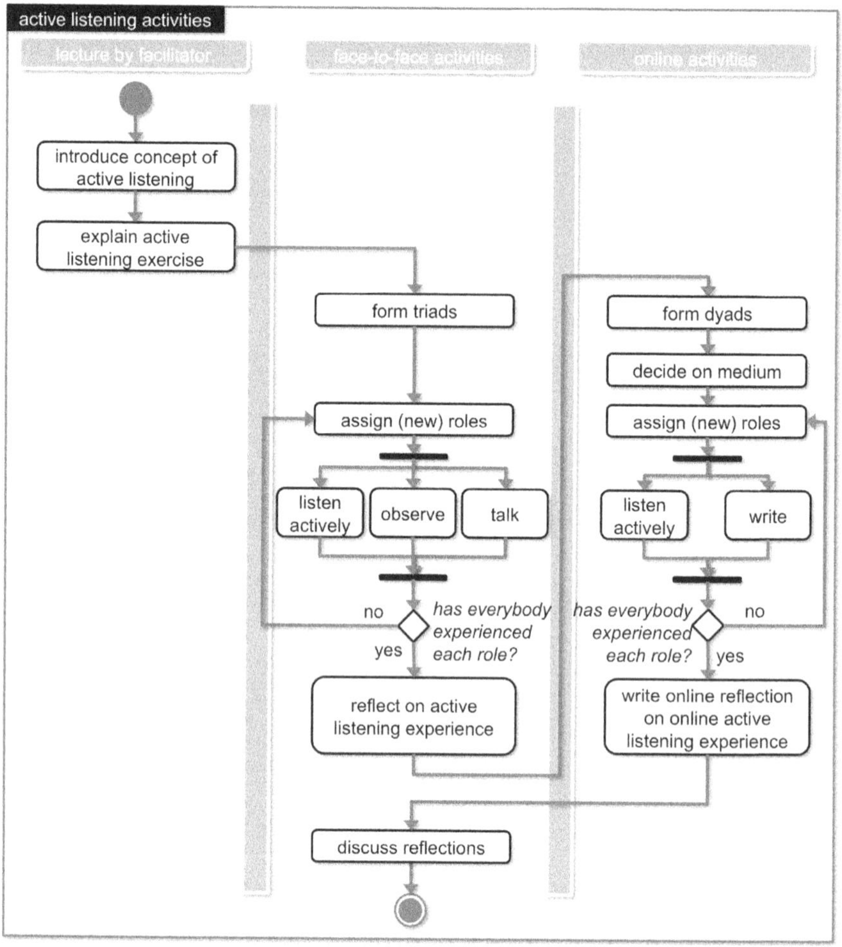

Figure 52. UML activity diagram of the case study *Active listening with e-mail and instant messaging*

8.3.3 Data collection and methods

Students were asked to provide their written reflections on the course's e-learning platform as well as the log files (protocols) of the communication sequences, on which these reflections were based.

We applied text and qualitative content analysis (Mayring, 1983/2003) to evaluate students' reflections. The classification scheme was developed inductively from raw data. For reliability reasons, the log files of the communication sequences were used for reflexive interpretation. Categorisation was undertaken by two researchers[23] in order to increase inter-subjectivity. As more than 90 percent of allocations to categories and judgments were consistent, the inter-rater reliability was high.

8.4 Case 3a. Active listening in written online communication

8.4.1 The sample

Out of the 21 participants in the course, 19 students took part in both exercises (face-to-face and online active listening). Due to the impair number of participants only 16 students could carry out the online exercise in pairs (as suggested by (Weissglass, 1990, p. 359) and intended by the case design). The remaining three students worked in a threesome, including the role of an observer as had been practised in the preliminary face-to-face exercise. Consequently, 19 reflections with a total word count of 3,631 and 10 communication log files (the threesome delivered two log files) could be analysed.

The sample consists of five female (26%) and 14 male (74%) participants, which reflects the average female ratio of 25-30% for computer science students at the University of Vienna.

8.4.2 Results

Formal characterisation of active listening logs

On average students spent 28 minutes with the online active listening exercise (minimum 12 minutes, maximum 44 minutes). Breaks between single statements in the logs took up to six minutes (e.g., one student had to answer the phone during the exercise).

---

23 At this point I want to thank Kathrin Figl for her outstanding support and enthusiasm. Without her, this research would not have been possible.

Characterisation of logs' content

Generally, the conversations cover a wide variety of topics that are often related to what students had experienced on the day of the exercise and what they are usually interested in (e.g., parties, bands, concerts, museums they had visited, problems with cars, fitness training, having a cold, telephone bills, shopping tours, movies, diets, toll charges, politics, soccer matches). As we had expected, university courses (e.g., assignments, Master's thesis, professors, deadlines) had also been among the topics discussed (addressed in four conversations).

Although some conversations seem like small talk at first sight, several students also shared emotions that currently affected them deeply (e.g., one student was very upset and frustrated because she missed an important lecture and had an argument with a course instructor). Probably conversations did not get emotionally deeper since the time frame was rather short. On the other hand, in absence of an instruction concerning time required for the exercise, students themselves deliberately chose how much time they wanted to dedicate to the activity. Furthermore, we assume that sharing deep emotions requires a certain level of trust, which may not have developed yet among the observed teams. Although the degree of prior acquaintance of teams varied to a great extent, most teams knew each other only from their studies, which is a professional relationship rather than a personal one. Moreover, students had been aware that the log files of the conversations were to be provided on the course's e-learning platform and, thus, accessible to all participants. This may have deterred some students from sharing deep feelings. For instance, the introduction of encounter groups in the context of higher education (e.g., Motschnig-Pitrik, 2006a; Motschnig-Pitrik & Nykl, 2005a) could show that some students do not shy away from sharing deep emotions with a large group in oral settings. Once students know that their conversations are conserved in a log file, they are more cautious regarding the sharing of deep feelings. "*Then it is like being carved in stone – especially if up to 23 persons read everything*", one student explains in the reflection on the online active listening task.

Results of reflections

Table 22 gives a brief review of reflections' analysis.

Generally, many students report that they experienced the online active listening exercise as rather easy since they had already been familiar with chatting and instant messaging in other contexts (8 nominations). Only one student surprisingly states, "*I have to say that I have not chat-*

ted before in my whole life because I think it is needless." We expected that students, particularly in the field of computer science, had already gained experience with instant messaging and chatting, so we did not put extra training on the course's agenda. As all other students, though, were already experienced users, we can regard the student without experience as outlier in context of this case study. We can, thus, assume that students could concentrate on active listening instead of learning how to handle the chat client, which implies that the results are not expected to be biased.

Interestingly, many students mention that it had been difficult for them to follow the instructions of the exercise (8 nominations) although the only modifications to the active listening activity in the face-to-face setting had been the deployed medium and the absence of the observer role.

Table 22. Summary of reflections' analysis concerning active listening with instant messaging

		CHAT
GENERAL REACTION ON EXERCISE	exercise was easy because of familiarity with chatting	8
	deviation from instructions	8
	active listening techniques used by students	8
	familiarity with chatting partner	4
	starting problems because of low familiarity with chatting partner	2
DIFFICULTIES OF ONLINE CHATTING	specific difficulties for online active listening	5
	messages get mixed up, parallelism	6
	misunderstandings	5
	distractions and missing attention	9
	easier in f2f to judge attention of partner	2
	missing non-verbal cues and voice	3
	waiting for next message	4
FURTHER CHARACTERISTICS OF ONLINE CHATTING	permanence	3
	emoticons	2
SUITABILITY OF F2F OR CHATTING	chat is useful for exchanging information	2
	f2f is better suitable for important, deeper, complicated or longer conversations	6
	chat is no compensation for f2f meetings	4

... in absolute numbers of nominations

Some students explain that the active listening exercise turned into a common conversation because too many questions appeared (e.g.,

"Hence, we have not really accomplished to listen actively for a longer time because we were simply too curious and could not refrain from counter questions.") As we have already outlined in Section 8.1.2, it takes time until someone fully internalises the concept of active listening. It comes naturally that in the first attempts of applying this concept, people drift off from the initial intention.

In their reflections students also refer to several active listening techniques and describe how they applied them in the online setting (8 nominations). Examples are: "*With clichés like 'I understand' and 'okay, I am with you' he accomplished to create an atmosphere, in which I found myself being understood and taken seriously.*" and "*In the beginning of the conversation, though, I repeatedly wanted to comment on [Peter]'s statements. I have not done that in order to let [Peter] finish his thought and to be able to listen better.*"

Using clichés is, though, not an absolutely certain indication for real understanding as such clichés could also be used for simulating it. Nevertheless, we can derive from the communication logs that something changed in the conversations although students are yet beginners in active listening. Simultaneously, students' reactions referring to finding themselves understood and taken seriously shows that the statements expressing understanding – whether they have been real or just simulated (for similar effects cf. (Weizenbaum, 1966)) – conveyed the inherent feelings and communicative intentions of active listening.

The degree of prior acquaintance of participants varied to a great extent. While, for instance, one student reflected: "*This task was easy for me... naturally the factor was relevant that [Maria] and me frequently communicate with each other via instant messaging*", another student wrote: "*In the beginning of our conversation we both did not know what to talk about, because we knew each other only by sight.*"

In their online reflections students put emphasis on describing difficulties of online chatting, particularly with regard to active listening. The majority of mentioned problems are distractions and missing attention of conversation partners (9 nominations, e.g., "*... of course, one can also deal with other things [while chatting] and thus be distracted. This means for active listening that the narrator is not paid full attention.*"). In face-to-face conversations, people (third persons who are not involved in the conversation) can see that one is occupied and, thus, hesitate to interfere. In online settings, in contrast, communicators have to signalise actively that they do not want to be disturbed. Interestingly only one dyad reports that they arranged for not being disturbed by using the *invisible mode* in their instant messaging tool.

At first glance it may seem that the opportunities for not paying full attention are seductive when being distributed. It, though, is people's attitude, which evokes distraction; those students, who report that they had been distracted, actively engaged with other tasks (e.g., chatting with other people, burning discs, etc.) while accomplishing the active listening exercise. One student, for instance, explains, "*After the exercise I had a look on our log and noticed that I had departed from the task every now and then. The reason for this is simply that I do many things at the same time when I am at the computer and that I am distractible (burning [of disc] completed, download completed, new e-mail...)*". As this exemplary answer illustrates, students blame the online setting for furthering distraction. We, however, attribute it to attitude and the lack of awareness that paying full attention can be controlled.

When using instant messaging, it may happen that conversation inputs overlap as new messages may arrive while someone is still formulating a reply to an earlier message (6 nominations). Sometimes these overlaps can cause misunderstandings (5 nominations, e.g., "*I noticed [...] that misunderstandings occur every now and then. This mostly happens because messages 'get mixed up'.*")

Besides missing non-verbal cues and voice (3 nominations), students give an account of further difficulties for online active listening (5 nominations), which can be best expressed in their own words. Examples are:

- "*With questions, difficulties can easily occur, so that the emerging atmosphere of an empathic conversation is destroyed due to problems of associating messages in their sequence. Active listening is then retarded by the limited possibilities for interaction and coordination.*"
- "*In course of [the exercise] I noticed that it is more difficult for me to communicate in written form that I do not understand something. [...] In face-to-face conversations I usually do not have problems to ask until I understand. But under these circumstances it is more difficult.*"
- "*[...] this way there is somehow missing something. One does not really feel understood when one is deeply emotionally moved.*"

As an advantage of the online setting compared to active listening in the face-to-face setting, students mention its permanence (3 nominations) as one can re-read all messages when using an instant messaging tool. As already mentioned above, permanence may be a barrier for the talker to express and share deep emotions. On the other hand, it may prevent the listener from missing details (as he or she can re-read all messages) and, thus, furthers to be more responsive. It is obvious that the true benefit of the permanence factor does not lie in the opportunity to re-read the conversion some weeks later but in the short-term possibility to recheck statements during a conversation.

As is expected according to the presented media choice theories (cf. Section 2.2.3), students argue that although chatting is useful for the exchange of information (2 nominations), it is no compensation for face-to-face meetings (4 nominations), which are more appropriate for important, deeper, complicated or longer conversations (6 nominations).

Finally it appears interesting that students generally express scepticism concerning active listening by means of instant messaging, while, at the same time, they explain that it worked out well in the exercise, which is also supported by the log files. Where this scepticism originates from deserves further study.

8.5 Case 3b. Online active listening and media competence

8.5.1 The sample

All of the 21 course participants took part in the face-to-face and online active listening exercises. Due to the impair number of participants, only 18 students could carry out the online exercise in pairs. As has been proven in the earlier case study, the remaining three students worked in a threesome including the role of an observer. Prior to the exercise, students chose their preferred online medium. Half of the class (five teams) preferred to use an instant messaging tool (chatting software) for the online activity; the remaining five teams chose to use e-mail instead. Consequently, 21 reflections with a total character count of 45,339 could be analysed.

The sample includes eight female (38%) and 13 male (62%) participants. Compared to the average female ratio of computer science students at the University of Vienna (25-30%), females are slightly overrepresented in the sample. This rather high number of female students in this course may be due to the generally rather high affinity of females for soft skills related topics.

8.5.2 Results

Table 23 provides an overview of reflections' analysis.

Similar to the prior case study, students talked about a variety of topics (e.g., Master's thesis, holidays, attitudes to life, fears, unemployment, ethics, etc.). They report that they made use of several active listening techniques in the online settings (5 nominations; e.g., "*[My communication partner] really put effort into each e-mail to summarise the content of the previous e-mail, and by asking, he also tried to make sure that he had understood my thoughts correctly*").

Students indicate that the active listening exercise was generally easier with communication partners who have already been familiar (6 nominations; e.g., "*Getting to know each other is essential. The chat was pleasant due to the fact that – in the run-up [to the exercise] – we had already met personally many times [...] and, thus, we already knew each other*").

Similar to the reflections in the prior case study, most comments are dedicated to shortcomings of online media – both e-mail and chat. Long waiting time for messages is mentioned particularly often (12 nominations). Interestingly, students do not only criticise the long waiting time for e-mail (8 nominations), which is an asynchronous medium, but also for instant messaging (4 nominations), which should have short-term lag only in a continuous conversation.

Furthermore, students remark that messages get mixed up (in chats) and that they miss non-verbal cues and voice (7 nominations each). It does not surprise that students perceive a lack in non-verbal cues in e-mail conversations more intensely than in chat settings, as the latter allows for immediate response, which conveys a feeling of social presence.

For the chat setting, students also give an account of technical problems and difficulties with distractions and missing attention of communication partners.

Specific drawbacks of e-mailing are the long pauses between sending and receiving. An excessive waiting time leads to insecurities, letting people think and worry why the other does not reply. Furthermore these pauses and interruptions preclude a fluent conversation. The circumstances when sending may be totally different to those when reading a message. Consequently, it is even more difficult to put oneself in the position that the text expresses and may cause misunderstandings. Due to the long waiting time, there is no opportunity for quick questions and queries.

Table 23. Summary of findings concerning active listening with e-mail and instant messaging

		CHAT	E-MAIL	SUM
REACTIONS ABOUT THE ACTIVE LISTENING EXERCISE	active listening techniques used by students	1	4	5
	single nominations: positive start with whiteboard, humour is important, changed my view of the chatting partner			
FAMILIARITY OF COMMUNICATION PARTNER	active listening easier with familiar communication partner	3	3	6
DIFFICULTIES OF ONLINE MEDIUM	waiting for next message	4	8	12
	messages get mixed up, parallelism	5	2	7
	missing non-verbal cues and voice	2	5	7
	difficult to judge honesty and interest		5	5
	technical problems	3		3
	distractions and missing attention	2		2
	identifying relevant themes	1	1	2
	single nominations: exhausting to formulate everything in written form, misunderstandings, even more difficult with more chatting partners, no immediate response of communicators			
APPROPRIATE ISSUES FOR ONLINE MEDIA	**APPROPRIATE FOR**			
	exchange of information	3	1	4
	arranging appointments / organisational tasks	1	3	4
	staying in contact	1		1
	NOT APPROPRIATE FOR			
	no compensation for f2f meetings	2	2	4
	important, complicated or longer conversations	1	2	3
	sharing deep emotions		2	2
FURTHER CHARACTERISTICS OF ONLINE MEDIUM	time to think	2	5	7
	emoticons	1	1	2
	faster flow of communication in chat compared to e-mail	2		2
	exchanging files and documents quickly	2		2
	single nominations: independence of momentarily availability of others, important to see that others are writing, reprocessability			
SUITABILITY FOR ACTIVE LISTENING	difficulties for online active listening / not suitable	5	9	14
	advantages for active listening / suitable	7	1	8

... in absolute numbers of nominations

Moreover, writing e-mails is experienced as more demanding than instant conversation and requires a great deal of concentration since finding the right words is rather central in a setting, which has permanence and does not allow for immediate interaction. This finding supports a row of previous studies (Diehl & Ziegler, 2000, p. 94; Duarte & Snyder, 2001, p. 167; Walther, 1992, p. 61; 1995, p. 189; Walther & Burgoon, 1992, p. 54). Furthermore, students report that it was difficult for them to assess their communication partners' sincerity and interest (5 nominations; e.g., "*In an online conversation you never know whether the e-mail partner is really interested in what you tell him / her; I simply miss the contact to the communication partner.*").

As a positive characteristic of online media, students most frequently mention the additional time to think before answering compared to face-to-face communication (7 nominations).

In general, students think that online media are suitable for exchanging information and arranging appointments (4 nominations each), as well as for staying in contact. For these communicative objectives, however, *ordinary, precise listening* appears to be sufficient. Nevertheless, students reflect that online media are not ready to compensate face-to-face meetings (4 nominations).

Students particularly prefer face-to-face meetings for important, complicated, or long conversations (3 nominations) and for sharing deep emotions (2 nominations, e.g., "*[...] for conversations about private concerns and problems, personal face-to-face communication is better suited*").

Addressing the question whether online media are suitable for active listening, 14 comments describe difficulties of online active listening and raise arguments against the suitability of online media. One student describes, "*'Active reading' demands a lot of time and concentration [...]. For me the question of efficiency arises. Wouldn't I have come to know the whole lot also in a 20 minutes face-to-face conversation?*" Another student explains, "*I have to admit that I preferred the face-to-face conversation because in the online version I missed the affirmative nodding or direct questions, and the conversation dynamics since response times are too long.*"

Fewer (8) – but worthwhile – nominations of advantages of active online listening could be found in the reflections. One student, for instance, reports, "*I was positively surprised by this kind of communication and glad about that experience.*" Another student goes more into detail, "*It was also possible to convey via the medium e-mail that somebody is listening (well) and that I am not alone with that problem. Apparently, enough non-verbal information, which is transported by voice and mimics in a face-to-face conversation, is communicated 'between the lines', for example via phrasing."*

Generally, the reflections indicate that students are aware of the analysed media's strength and limitations. They also seem capable of overcoming difficulties due to their familiarity with these media. Nevertheless, they experience it as very demanding to adapt to the requirements of the respective media. For instance, nonverbal cues like intonation, gestures or facial expressions have to be verbalised in written communication (e.g., with emoticons) in order to transmit this information to the listener. Students are aware of this necessity and are experienced enough to adapt to the medium such that they transform important nonverbal cues into words and emoticons. Nevertheless, they experience this process as cognitively demanding.

All in all, the results described above support the media synchronization theory (Dennis, Fuller, & Valacich, 2008; Dennis & Valacich, 1999; Dennis et al., 1998). They also indicate that to listen actively in an online setting is not possible entirely. However, with conscious intention, experience, and competence as well as additional cognitive effort, it can be approximated to a significant degree. In any case, prior knowledge of your communication partner facilitates online active listening.

8.6 Comparison and Conclusions

Although both case studies in the field of active listening investigate whether this concept can be applied by means of computer-mediated communication, the earlier study analyses communication with instant messaging tools while the follow-up study aims at comparing instant messaging with e-mail communication. Notwithstanding that both case studies originate from the same course (PROJECT MANAGEMENT – COMMUNICATION AND SOFT SKILLS) at the same university (University of Vienna) with the same facilitator, they were conducted in different semesters (winter term 2005/2006 and winter term 2006/2007) with distinct participants. In spite of the fact that both case implementations show extensive similarities, focus of research had been different. While we analysed the suitability of the concept in an online setting in the first case study, we focussed on students' media competence in the second one. In a nutshell, the cases are different, the focus is different, and the data pool is different. Consequently, the implementation does not allow for a direct comparison and a summative conclusion can only be drawn with reservations.

But for all that, we can recognise similarities of both case studies' results and direct attention to aspects that have been identified and particularly emphasised in both studies. The most prominent similarities are summarised in Table 24.

Table 24. Overview of issues raised in both case studies on active listening

		CHAT		E-MAIL	SUM
		case 1	case 2	case 2	
REACTION ABOUT AND STATEMENTS ON THE ACTIVE LISTENING EXERCISE	active listening techniques used by students	8	1	4	13
	active listening easier with familiar communication partner	8	3	3	14
DIFFICULTIES OF ONLINE MEDIUM	waiting for next message	4	4	8	16
	messages get mixed up, parallelism	6	5	2	13
	distractions and missing attention	9	2		11
	missing non-verbal cues and voice	3	2	5	10
	misunderstandings	5	2		7
APPROPRIATE ISSUES FOR ONLINE MEDIA	**APPROPRIATE FOR**				
	exchange of information	2	3	1	6
	NOT APPROPRIATE FOR				
	no compensation for f2f meetings	4	2	2	8
	important, deeper, complicated or longer conversations	6	1	2	9
SUITABILITY FOR ACTIVE LISTENING	difficulties for online active listening / not suitable	5	5	9	19
	advantages for active listening / suitable		7	1	8

... in absolute numbers of nominations

In both case studies, students reported on their own account which active listening techniques they used and how they applied those in the respective online settings (13 nominations). Beyond illustrating that the common techniques of the active listening concept can indeed be applied in settings with written online communication, this finding indicates that students had taken the exercise seriously, engaged with the concept, and learned from the exercises (at least to the extent that they know what techniques may be used).

The perception that active listening is easier with familiar communication partners had been strong in both studies (14 nominations).

Beside scattered nominations of diverse difficulties of communication with an online medium, some are emphasised. The burden that messages get mixed up is frequently mentioned for chat settings (11 nominations). Having to wait for the next message is mentioned particularly often (16 nominations) in all investigated online settings. The complaint about long waiting times, however, derives predominately from the perspective of the active listener. Simultaneously, it can also be regarded as advantage of instant messaging and e-mailing since these media allow extended time to think before responding.

The difficulties with distraction (11 nominations) and the rather frequent occurrence of misunderstandings (7 nominations) had been a widely discussed topic in the earlier case study while in the later one rather not. In contrast, mostly students participating in the e-mail exercise (in the follow-up case study; 5 nominations) had addressed the absence of nonverbal cues and voice as disturbing factor.

Generally we can derive from our studies that distraction and missing attention are considered as the prevailing drawbacks of online active listening. However, while students accuse the online setting for furthering distraction, we attribute it to attitude and the lack of awareness that paying full attention can be deliberately controlled. As the aspect of distraction had been addressed less frequently in the second case study, we assume – and also hope – that our efforts to increase awareness and to alter attitudes had been more fruitful in the follow-up case study due to our growing experience. Nevertheless, further research and specific training seem necessary in this field.

Concerning the appropriateness of settings, both case studies show consistent results. According to both studies, students think that online communication is no compensation for face-to-face meetings (8 nominations), which they particularly prefer for important, deeper, complicated, or rather long conversations (9 nominations). While students' reflections address rather a lot of difficulties (19 nominations) for online active listening, only a few advantages (8 nominations) of online settings are mentioned. Nevertheless, as already discussed above, students were able to overcome these difficulties and managed to adopt the concept of active listening in an online context with written communication.

8.7 Achievements, limitations, and further work

Exploring active listening in an educational setting with students of business informatics and computer science, our case studies present how the concept of active listening can be transferred from traditional face-to-face communication to written online communication, which is a novel asset.

Focusing on the media instant messaging (chat) and e-mail, we analysed whether active listening is effective in written online communication. Interestingly results reveal that all of the commonly used techniques in active listening (e.g., paraphrasing, summarising, or encouraging) are applicable when communicating with the two written online media under investigation. Rather than a concentration of only a few techniques, all of them could be found in almost every of the analysed online conversations.

In our case studies, one of major drawback of online active listening in both online settings was the additional cognitive effort due to diminished social presence. This was even more strongly perceived with using e-mail. Additional disadvantages in the chat setting were distraction and missing attention. Assuming that students are not aware that paying full attention can be deliberately controlled, particular effort should be put in awareness activities and reflection, which we will pursue in courses of upcoming semesters and years. Accordingly, the process of more accurate awareness of the effects (benefits, threats, potentials, etc.) will be accompanied by respective research endeavours.

While students agreed that online active listening was no compensation for face-to-face meetings, they also voiced considerable advantages of the online setting such as leaving control with the person who expresses his or her thought, which allows this person to completely verbalise this thought before responding.

Nevertheless, reflections indicate that students are aware of the analysed media's strength and weaknesses. Consequently, due to being familiar with instant messaging and e-mail, students tend to be able to handle the mentioned difficulties. Students will particularly benefit from specific training towards media competence.

Focus of our research was to identify and evaluate the main characteristics of media with respect to their appropriateness and potential for active listening. While our studies revealed differences between the e-mail and the chat setting concerning most of the analyzed categories, these findings' significance and reasoning have to be further investigated in a direct comparison of these media. In order to get insightful results, the research design should allow subjects to experience both media allowing for a direct comparison. Beyond this, our findings pave the way for upcoming investigations directing the focus of research to the influence of media characteristics on the active listening process. Particularly interesting is the identification of media features that support the promotiveness of active listening.

Generally, we could observe that students' attitude towards online active listening is marked by a touch of scepticism. At the same time students report that it worked out well in the exercise, which is also supported by the exercises' log files. This contradiction calls for further analysis.

Although the participants were beginners in active listening, we could observe traces of the quality of listening in the conversations. The consciousness about these positive effects of active listening was also apparent from students' reflections on the activity. This is particularly precious as Rogers says that it is already promotive if the second person perceived the three Rogers variables at least to some extent. While the study with students at a beginner level of active listening brought valuable insights, further investigations with experienced active listeners are necessary in order to allow drawing general conclusions. Future research should, thus, address communication partners who are more experienced in active listening in face-to-face situations and truly have assimilated or internalised this way of relating to another person. We assume that the prior face-to-face practice of active listening (as we have also implemented in our case studies) influences active listening in an online atmosphere. Furthermore we hypothesise that the online experience will also impact active listening in subsequent face-to-face settings. Future research should address these issues, proving (or rejecting) our hypotheses, and (if approbated) investigate the particular impacts.

Concluding, the introduction of active listening to settings with written means of communication proved to be fruitful regarding several aspects. First of all, our case studies delivered the finding that the concept of active listening is not restricted to oral communication. We can tap this concept's potential and benefits even in online settings. More than that, online active listening constructively contributes to students' media competence, as they learn how to adapt to a medium by overcoming its limitations and making use of its potential. With regard to their future jobs, students will especially profit from a thoughtful combination of active listening in face-to-face and online settings with various media.

9 Conclusions and recommendations

Previous sections could demonstrate that promotive activities as proposed by (Tausch & Tausch, 1963/1998) are not bound to classroom teaching but are equally applicable in technology-enhanced settings in higher education. Particularly the case studies on peer review and active listening could prove that technology enhancement can even intensify positive effects and adds opportunities to introduce promotive activities that would not be possible without media enhancement.

This Section tries to collate findings discussed in earlier sections (Sections 4 and 6 to 8) and derive recommendations for action that can be implemented in technology-enhanced learning environments, particularly in higher education targeted at students of business informatics and computer science.

Figure 53 gives an overview of the most relevant factors to consider for promotive activities in technology-enhanced learning settings. The paragraphs thereafter pick up these keywords and provide handy explanations. Finally, recommendations particularly interesting for peer review and active listening are given.

General recommendations

All of our case studies show that activities and tasks close to reality (real world assignments) are worthwhile. In particular, topics and exercises that are *currently* relevant to students will drive motivation and induce deeper learning than subjects that will be interesting for them only in the future or are not relevant for them at all. Although motivation as well as learning theories stress that relevance may come from the way something is taught, results indicate that students see a course's or concept's relevance more clearly if the content itself is relevant to them. Additionally, it is easier for facilitators to demonstrate relevance out of a given content. Either way, activities that are realistic and relevant for students will drive their motivation and promote their learning – independent from technology.

Furthermore, our investigations confirm that students appreciate the person-centred style. Findings corroborate that this approach to learning drives motivation and has a strong positive impact on the learning climate as well as on interactive aspects. In particular, it furthers active participation, strong cooperation, and lively engagement in group discussions. These effects do not only manifest in face-to-face settings in class but also in online phases, provided that appropriate tools and opportunities for communication and interaction (e.g., integrated chat tool on a central e-learning platform, easy access to students' e-mail addresses or IDs for commonly used instant messaging tools) are offered. In order to achieve these promising effects, it is crucial to offer these resources. Although students would have the possibility to exchange contact details without guidance, such behaviour is not to be expected. Providing those opportunities and resources may be sufficient impulse for using the respective tools and, hence, commit towards a fruitful cooperative learning process.

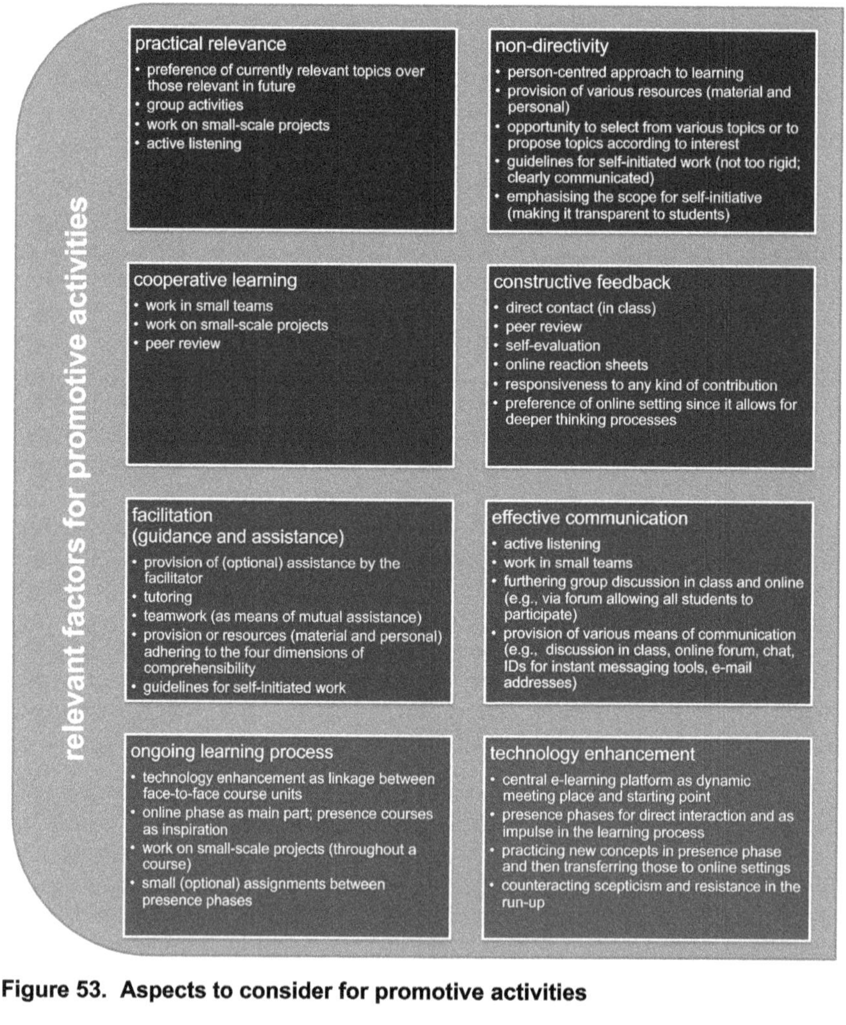

Figure 53. Aspects to consider for promotive activities

Despite the non-directivity of the person-centred approach it proves useful to propose small (optional) assignments, which have to be executed via a central e-learning platform. Such small-scale exercises will keep students at the respective topics between presence phases (course units) and, simultaneously, they offer further opportunities to start or intensify interaction and deepen individual learning processes.

Facilitators should be responsive to exercises, particularly when these are optional – but, in fact, this holds true for any kind of exercise. Such responsiveness may, for example, be expressed in terms of feedback (either specific feedback for individual students or generalised feedback for a whole group), in the form of explanations demonstrating what having fulfilled a respective exercise will enable students to do, or simply by acknowledging students' contributions. On the one hand, constructive feedback is promotive as it provides the basis for (further) improvement. Demonstrating an exercise's value and establishing interrelations between issues, on the other hand, will allow students to perceive an exercise's worth. As we could observe with reaction sheets, dedicating the first few minutes of a presence class for picking up issues from such reactions, demonstrates that their contributions are worthwhile and do not end up in the drawer without being read. As soon as the facilitator is not responsive to reaction sheets, students will loose their interest to contribute any further.

Although students value the non-directive course style and there is evidence that it positively impacts motivation, it is still advisable to offer guides and assistance for those students who – at least initially – need or appreciate it. Although making available relevant resources is an inherent element of the person-centred style, facilitators engaging in this approach to learning and teaching only recently may tend to overstress non-directivity and openness while forgetting to provide necessary guides and resources. For a good facilitation, however, appropriate guides and resources are substantial. The opportunities of the Internet (particularly the World Wide Web) will ease the entrance to this approach concerning the resource aspect since it is rather simple to discover and provide relevant material. Still it is challenging and requires experience to offer qualitative sources and to determine the adequate number of sources.

Recommendations concerning technology enhancement

Despite the versatile offer accruing from technology enhancement of learning settings and the evidence that technology can support the person-centred style and further learning, it is still crucial that students have direct contact (face-to-face setting) with the facilitator and among each other. Yet, it is not that electronic means of communication (e.g., instant messaging, e-mail) would not be able to convey congruence, acceptance, and empathy. In fact they can, as we could particularly demonstrate with our case studies on active listening. In settings with written forms of communication, though, the three dispositions are transported more slowly and students perceive it as more demanding than in face-to-face conversations. Presence phases are, thus, indispensable. The online phases serve as linkage between face-to-face encounters in class and allow for an ongoing cooperative learning process. But for all that, the online phases play a prominent role in the learning process and facilitators should direct particular attention to the online setting. For the very reason that these online phases usually take far more time than the presence units in class[24], it should be evident that this *linkage* is the principal part in the learning process. Instead of considering the online phase as bridge between the course units in class, it is rather more appropriate to regard this phase as main part of the learning process that draws impulses and inspiration from presence units at regular intervals.

From our findings we can conjecture that it is easier for students to apply concepts in the online setting when these are already familiar from presence phases. It is, hence, a good practice to introduce new concepts in a presence phase. It is good advice to provide students with the opportunity to exercise such newly introduced techniques in face-to-face situations first and let then apply or practice these in online settings.

It proved useful to have students reflecting on the comparison of both settings. In doing so, it is important that the facilitator makes key issues transparent in advance. Otherwise it frequently happens that students drift off to clichés, which they do not actually mean and feel but which they were used to read and hear so many times before.

Furthermore, our findings indicate that students gradually adapt to the strengths and weaknesses of media. With this growing media competence they are able to overcome a particular medium's limitations and may finally tap its full potential. In doing so, it is necessary that students are given adequate time to experiment in a given media setting. In order to recognise the differences, we recommend letting students experience various settings for similar tasks.

---

24 Particularly in the university context, classes take place once or twice a week while the rest of the week is assumed to be the *online phase*.

When transferring exercises and promotive activities from face-to-face to online settings, facilitators have to be aware that these cannot be applied exactly the same way in the online context but rather have to be adapted accordingly. It is a mistake to regard everything as homogeneous. Although technology-enhanced settings get more and more important and even though online settings have high potential and render possible much more than people ever thought, we have to point out that each medium and setting requires its particular treatment. General recommendations can, thus, hardly been drawn but are limited to the advice to consider the characteristics of the particular medium and the respective task. Treating diverging media settings exactly the same is a serious mistake as activities that are promotive in one setting may – if not properly adapted – be inefficient in another. Frequently they are not effective and sometimes they may even have negative impact. For details on a rather generic level, we have to refer to Section 2.2.4. More precise recommendations concerning specific tasks and media selection can be found in the course of this Section.

Acceptance and scepticism

Students' reflections on media use and eligibility show scepticism towards written communication in general. Their behaviour, in contrast, reveals high media competence and appropriate use of written communication for many aspects (e.g., active listening, sharing emotions, or discussing complicated and important issues) that they claim these media are not appropriate for.

Being able to anticipate such attitude and behaviour, it is good advice to meet this scepticism in the run-up of tasks that include such communication elements. We may expect that freeing students from their inhibiting attitude towards these tasks may allow for even better learning results and deeper experiences.

Cooperative learning

Work in teams (within small-scale projects) is a convenient pedagogical element with respect to non-directivity and practical relevance (discussed in Section 4.5). The cooperative approach to learning releases a feeling of solidarity and drives the individual's motivation to commit oneself. Furthermore, mutual support and inspiration enhances the learning experience and is likely to lead to overall better learning outcomes.

Group activities are not restricted to presence phases but have high potential in online settings. For instance, small assignments between presence phases may be carried out in dyads or small teams. In such cases, it is advisable to determine the team settings in class and put it down in writing on the respective e-learning platform. Alternatively, students may use a team-building tool (that is provided on the e-learning platform) to assign themselves to teams. When deploying such a tool in a course, it is crucial that the team-building process and the current team settings are transparent to all participants. Otherwise it is likely that some students will allege that they could not have carried out the assignment due to not having known with whom to cooperate. Transparency of the team-building process will easily refute such an argument.

Far beyond such short-time activities, group work is also best suitable for as much as a whole course. Students may work on small-scale group activities in the same line-up throughout a course. Particularly suitable is the work on small-scale projects that last as long as a whole semester.

Irrespective of the duration or kind of group work, it is crucial to provide appropriate assistance and support. Only then, cooperative learning will turn out to be a worthwhile experience. Again, in order to be promotive, it is necessary to provide adequate learning resources, which assist students in fulfilling their tasks. Additionally, it is good advice to provide appropriate tools that support students in their teamwork endeavours. Web-based team spaces for sharing code and other kinds of documents (at best with integrated revision control functionality) have proved to be efficient support. Communication facilities on an e-learning platform or facilitating the use of external communication facilities (for instance, by providing easy access to e-mail addresses or instant messaging IDs, and the like or by making a room available for team meetings) are further well-proven examples for convenient support.

The benefits of team and project work notwithstanding, the effects of cooperative learning are far more extensive as they embrace a whole course group including the facilitator. For instance, group discussions or other forms of interactions in class involve all course participants and influence their learning as students' contributions are shared with the whole group. Enhancing a learning setting with electronic means of communication intensifies the effect of mutual sharing. For instance, if discussions take place in an online forum, all students can participate either actively or – at least – by reading their peers' contributions. In contrast to face-to-face settings, information shared in writing is also available at later points in time and allows rereading whenever deems necessary or appropriate. Accordingly, students will particularly profit from it. Online forums are, though, not the only means for furthering such collective learning. Allowing students to read their peers' elaborations (e.g., seminar papers) is just as promotive as providing space where students can share other kinds of documents (e.g., summaries of particular topics, tutorials for certain technologies, or links to supportive sources on the Internet) or any other means for sharing information. With regard to cooperative learning, the particular benefit of written means of online communication that is accessible for all course participants lies in its transparency and permanence. Students may refer to contributions at later points in time such that they can learn from these when the subject becomes relevant to them or when they are in a mood to learn. They can even pick up a topic to amend statements a later point in time as soon as they have learned sufficiently in order to (better) understand the issues. The face-to-face setting, in contrast, does poorly as concerns these aspects. What a student does not keep in mind right when it is said in a particular situation cannot be taken up at a later point in time. Furthermore, it is rather unlikely that a student deliberately takes up a topic that had been discussed earlier in order to clarify issues; in most cases it will be difficult to find the appropriate opportunity to raise the issue again.

Peer review

Implementing peer review in a course has the potential to positively impact students' learning and their perceptions of the quality of their own contributions. In particular, this activity is promotive as it increases students' awareness that they are self-responsible for their own learning processes.

With respect to learning outcomes, online peer reviews tend to be superior to face-to-face review as the former are more revision-orientated and, hence, more constructive. The advantages of written reviews notwithstanding, the review settings should offer opportunities to raise queries, preferably using oral communication. Students value such a media combination since it allows minimising misunderstandings.

Basically, various media combinations are suitable and not only a particular one. This is good indication for students' flexibility and their readily developed media competence. In cases, where students do yet have to evolve these competencies, peer reviews with media combinations are good opportunities for furthering this development. In consequence of the simultaneous advancement of media competence, learning with respect to peer review or the underlying subject-matter may, however, be decelerated. With respect to learning at three levels this is, though, preferable as learning is expected to be sustainable when all three levels are addressed simultaneously.

Our web-based review tool proved quite adequate. Based on our findings and students' suggestions, following features are particularly recommended to be included in a review tool:

- possibility to upload documents (e.g., project documents, papers) in the original format such that reviewers can analyse these with the corresponding software,
- various sorting and filtering possibilities for the list of deficiencies (at least chronological order and filter by status),
- various sorting possibilities for uploaded documents (at least chronologically by milestone, and by alphabet),
- access to documents of all teams for every student in order to allow for comparison,
- unlimited space for an unlimited number of comments, and
- possibilities to contact the originating team / author.

In order to serve its purpose of furthering students in their learning processes, it is substantial that reviews do not only pinpoint to deficiencies but also highlight positive elements. Accordingly it is good advice that the facilitator emphasises that both aspects, positive and negative feedback, are equally welcome and to be considered. Having learned from our case studies, where we have not been successful in bringing students to give sufficient positive feedback, we recommend highlighting it right from the beginning. At best, facilitators put it down in writing on the e-learning platform in order to make it transparent. Still it is good advice to allude to positive aspects repeatedly while students engage in the review process.

Communication and media competence (active listening)

Applying the concept of active listening in other settings than using oral communication proved to be useful for developing students' media competence while tapping the full potential of this concept, thus, furthering social skills and communication abilities.

Our two case studies indicate that our approach to training students in active listening proved useful. We first introduced the concept on a rather theoretical basis; then students exercised it in triads. Only then the concept was transferred to an online setting using written means of communication. Afterwards students reflected on the exercises. As this training process turned out well, it is advisable to adopt it for similar learning settings. Since introducing the concept of active listening to written online communication is a novel asset, further derivates of training processes do not yet exist. Facilitators and researchers are, hence, highly welcome to experiment with training settings in order to improve efficiency and effectiveness.

Students consider distraction and missing attention as the prevailing drawbacks of online active listening. However, they accuse the online setting for facilitating distraction. Instead we attribute it to the lack of awareness that paying full attention lies within one's own hands and can – at least to a certain degree – be deliberately controlled. As a consequence it deems necessary to put particular effort in awareness activities and reflection concerning behaviour and media in online settings. Since the aspect of distraction had been addressed far less frequently in our second case study on active listening, we assume that our endeavours targeted and increasing awareness and altering attitudes have been fruitful due to our growing experience. At the current state of research we are, however, not able to give detailed instructions concerning this aspect as the precise modification of trainings in the two case studies are – despite documentation – not sufficiently tangible in order to serve as guidance.

10 Summary and outlook

The final Section of this book comprises two parts. First, it provides a summary of research endeavours, and it ends with suggestions for future research.

10.1 Summary

This work presented how promotive activities can be efficiently implemented in technology-enhanced learning settings with respect to whole person learning and cooperative learning endeavours.

In the first Section the motivation was presented based following assumptions:

- Technology-enhanced learning has benefits compared to pure e-learning or pure traditional learning settings in class.
- Learning is most effective in terms of persistency if it addresses the whole person rather than merely the intellect (learning on the three levels: intellect, social skills, and personality).
- Interpersonal qualities can be transformed into promotive actions, in face-to-face as well as in technology-enhanced learning environments.

The second Section presented an overview of the theories and paradigms underlying this research in order to provide the reader with necessary background information. Fundamentally, the approach is based on the integration of two cornerstones, which were elaborated accordingly:

- traditional and current learning theories that are premised primarily on a constructivist point view, in particular the person-centred learning approach and the three levels of learning and personal growth, and
- communication theories respecting interpersonal communication with particular emphasis on media choice theories.

Illustrating the complexity of the research field, the third Section presented a framework considering factors that influence media choice in technology-enhanced learning settings. Basically, the factors identified were subsumed under three headings: learning factors, human factors, and learning environment factors.

As the core contribution of this work, the fourth Section presented promotive, non-directive activities as known from education in class settings and transferred these activities to technology-enhanced learning settings.

Essentially, following activities were considered:

- facilitating learning through the provision of resources,
- endeavour to design learning material for knowledge transfer in a comprehensible way,
- facilitating thinking processes,
- furthering a beneficial working progress,
- facilitating temporary work in small teams,
- learning contracts, and
- furthering of helpfully living together in a good group.

Research strategies that are commonly used in the interdisciplinary field of technology-enhanced learning were presented in the fifth Section. In particular, research methods in social sciences as well as business informatics were elaborated. Based on these considerations, the appropriate research strategy was selected for approaching the underlying research question of this work: the case study approach.

Furthermore, this Section presented the three main fields of interest within the scope of promotive activities in technology-enhanced cooperative whole person learning:

- motivational aspects in technology-enhanced learning settings,
- the impact of media selection on peer reviews, and
- active listening in technology-enhanced learning settings.

For each of these fields the selected case studies were presented with a brief overview of the particular research questions, case design, and results. The subsequent three sections were dedicated to these three fields and presented the respective case studies.

The sixth Section presented a study dedicated to motivational aspects in technology-enhanced learning settings. Four technology-enhanced courses, which implemented similar but, though, distinct course designs, were compared with respect to motivation and motives.

In the seventh Section, two case studies investigating the impact of media selection on peer review were presented. On the one hand, communication and collaboration aspects of the peer review activity were explored. On the other hand, the quality and kind of feedback given in the reviews were analysed. In particular, the study investigated differences between a face-to-face peer review using paper forms and a web-based peer review.

In the eighth Section, two case studies on active listening were presented. Transferring the concept of active listening to written online communication is a novel asset. The Section illustrated how the concept can be applied and exercised by means of instant messaging and e-mail in higher education.

Collating findings from earlier studies and considering the case studies presented in the previous sections, the tenth Section finally presented conclusions and recommendations for non-directive, promotive activities in technology-enhanced learning settings.

10.2 Suggestions for future research

Even though the current state of research presented in this work provides substantial findings that can considerably support one in designing and researching technology-enhanced learning environments, there are still many aspects that require further research. In particular following issues remain unanswered or were raised by recent findings:

- Not only our studies have demonstrated that students appreciate the open, person-centred style. Even students lacking in independence seem to grow in terms of personality and get independent enough to feel comfortable with this learning style and self-direct their learning. However, it is still subject to be researched how people, who show an instruction-driven attitude, handle this rather open learning approach. Even if the person-centred learning style has a positive effect on these persons, it is to be investigated whether the time-effort relation is appropriate. Furthermore, it could not yet be confirmed whether a technical university course is the ideal place to address this issue.
- In particular the study on motivational aspects revealed the limitations of learning design patterns: design is one matter, but the implementation of a design is at least equally important. Based on existing concepts and research on learning design patterns, further investigation may provide new – respectively better – directions concerning implementation.
- Project work is generally regarded as highly relevant as pedagogical means in terms of cooperative learning and closeness to real problems (in business) as both are expected to drive motivation. As this could not have been shown in our study (but neither neglected), we intend to pursue research in this field. Courses on project management seem particularly appropriate for this endeavour since project work can be implemented as both, technical content of the course as well as pedagogical means.

- Students voice reservations concerning the eligibility of active listening by means of written online communication, although their behaviour proves that active listening in writing works out well (i.e. they find appropriate ways to handle it). Maybe it is sufficient to prepare the topic accordingly and open students' eyes in order that they do not respond by clichés concerning media's appropriateness. As students – particularly computer science students – are expected to be rather open-minded to technological advancement and its applicability, this seems rather unlikely. Potentially this sceptical behaviour is contingent on cultural factors. For comparison it should, thus, be analysed in different cultures.
- Findings of our case studies on peer review let infer that not only the combination of deployed media is significant for an effective review but rather also the order and their respective weights in the reviewing process. Further research investigating various media combinations in distinct orders and weights in the reviewing process is necessary in order to allow deducting general statements.
- So far, existing research on social skills and online communication emphasises differences (in terms of behaviour and attitude) between distinct technological settings and investigates how and why these occur. In most cases, the starting point is the conventional face-to-face setting. Interesting would, though, be the issue, whether social skills that people develop in online context have an impact on their behaviour in face-to-face context.
- Furthermore, our studies have shown that online peer reviews are more revision-orientated and, thus, more constructive than a pen-and-pencil version. With regard to this finding it would, hence, be interesting to find out if peer reviews become also more constructive in face-to-face settings in the long run when students are beforehand trained in giving constructive feedback in online settings.
- Limitations of this work are the rather small sample sizes of the case studies on peer reviews and active listening. Still, with respect to the explorative character of this research and the use of case study research with the application of qualitative methods the sample sizes were appropriate to reveal new aspects and perspectives. Thus, despite the small sample sizes, the studies allowed for substantiating further, more precise research questions. Future research should, thus, include larger samples.
- We also have to consider that our studies refer to students that are – naturally – beginners in their fields. Investigations with more experienced participants (e.g., business professionals in continuing educa-

tion) may come to different conclusions. Consequently, further research is necessary in this domain.

- Furthermore, the empirical part of this work concentrates on motivational aspects, peer reviews, and active listening. As elaborated and presented in Section 4, there exist far more promotive activities that proved successful in educational face-to-face settings. Future research should, thus, address activities that go beyond this work, transferring them to technology-enhanced learning settings.

Overall, this work provides insights on what tool designers need to take into consideration when developing tools that support whole person learning. Translating these findings into tangible tool requirements and specifications resulting in supportive tools would be the next steps to be taken.

Our investigations were targeted on students of computer science and business informatics. In these disciplines, students are rather inclined towards technological advancements and know to use the various means of human-to-human communication (e.g., instant messaging, voice-over-IP) and can easily orientate themselves on e-learning platforms. Not only the fact that students had acquired such knowledge and developed the necessary skills prior to our investigations but also that they bring in the respective tendencies and are highly interested in technological aspects, impact the research results. It is open whether the same promotive activities in technology-enhanced settings lead to similar positive effects in courses with less technophile students. We conjecture that some extra training (in the up-front) and tutoring (throughout a course) is necessary in order to ensure that they are comfortable with the respective tools. Still, we have to question whether it is appropriate to claim a high affinity for technology only for educational reasons. In computer science and business informatics (but, for instance, also in business administration or communication science), media competence and team skills are crucial with respect to students' later business lives. There may, however, also exist disciplines where technology-enhanced education demands extra efforts and skills that are not (that) relevant in the respective working world. Nevertheless, concepts like active listening – just to mention one – is effective and highly relevant in everyday life irrespective of the discipline a person works in professionally. Correspondingly, further research endeavours in this field should keep including a wide range of disciplines and fields of application.

As cooperation and interaction is not only important in education, but also in business. In fact, this work is targeted on educating students as preparation for their future jobs as specialists in business informatics and computer science. Emphasising the significance of practical relevance in educational settings, tasks have high practical relevance and, thus, they are very close to real projects and assignments that people encounter in the working world. Findings on media use for peer review and active listening are, thus, predestined for application in business environments. Accordingly, research should not only follow an eventual application in business, but also rather drive application by transferring findings to this different – but though similar – setting.

With respect to life-long learning, it is particularly interesting to investigate whether or how promotive activities have to be adapted if applied for corporate learning processes as means for human resource development. At the current state of research, activities and factors driving motivation in such settings may still be a domain that entrepreneurs and researchers are highly interested in. When working and learning go inseparably with one another, this seems most effective in terms of persistency in learning and may also be favourable in terms of motivation and time efficiency.

In a nutshell, transferring findings to business environments opens a wide scope of perspectives both for application and further research.

11 References

Adams, Lia, Toomey, Lori, & Churchill, Elizabeth (1999). Distributed Research Teams: Meeting Asynchronously in Virtual Space. *Journal of Computer-Mediated Communication, 4*(4). http://www3.interscience.wiley.com/cgi-bin/fulltext/120837772/HTMLSTART [last accessed 22 December 2009].

Advanced Distributed Learning (ADL) (2004). SCORM 2004 3rd. http://www.adlnet.gov/scorm/index.aspx [last accessed 25 July 2008].

Albrecht, Rainer (2002). Kompetenzentwicklungsstrategien für Hochschulen: Was Lehrende wirklich wissen müssen. In: Gudrun Bachmann, Odette Haefeli & Michael Kindt (editors), *Campus 2002: Die virtuelle Hochschule in der Konsolidierungsphase*, pp. 143-157. Münster (Germany): Waxmann Verlag.

Ames, Carole (1992). Classrooms: Goals, Structures, and Student Motivation. *Journal of Educational Psychology, 84*(3), pp. 261-271.

Anderson, Cushing (2000). *eLearning in Practice: Blended Solutions in Action*. (White Paper). Framingham (Massachusetts): IDC. http://whitepapers.silicon.com/0,3800002489,60013383p,00.htm [last accessed 09 January 2003].

Argyle, Michael (1969). Social Skills Training in Education. *Paedagogica Europaea, 5*, pp. 72-79. http://www.jstor.org/stable/150255 [last accessed 22 December 2009].

Aspy, David N. (1972). *Toward a Technology for Humanizing Education*. Champaign (Illinois): Research Press Company.

Astleitner, Hermann (2000). Designing Emotionally Sound Instruction: The FEASP-approach. *Instructional Science, 28*, pp. 169-198. http://dx.doi.org/10.1023/A:1003893915778 [last accessed 22 December 2009].

Attwell, Graham, Dirckinck-Holmfeld, Lone, Fabian, Peter, Kárpáti, Andrea, & Littig, Peter (2003). *E-Learning in Europe – Results and Recommendations* (Vol. 10). Bonn (Germany): Nationale Agentur Bildung für Europa beim Bundesinstitut für Berufsbildung (BIBB). http://european-edupreneural-services.com/pdf/E-Learning_in_Europe.pdf [last accessed 22 December 2009].

Bailey, Charles D., Hermanson, Dana R., & Louwers, Timothy J. (2007). *An Examination of the Peer Review Process in Accounting*. Proceedings of Canadian Accounting Association (CAAA) 2006 Annual Conference, 01 April 2007. http://ssrn.com/abstract=873634 [last accessed 22 December 2009].

Barrett-Lennard, Godfrey T. (1998). *Carl Rogers' Helping System – Journey and Substance.* London (UK): Sage Publications.

Barrett-Lennard, Godfrey T. (2003). *Steps on Mindful Journey: Person-centred expressions.* Ross-on-Wye (UK): PCCS Books.

Baskerville, Richard L. (1999). Tutorial: Investigating Information Systems with Action Research. *Communication of the Association for Information Systems, 2*(19). http://www.cis.gsu.edu/~rbaskerv/CAIS_2_19/CAIS_2_19.html [last accessed 05 July 2008].

Bauer, Christine (2002). *Kommunikation in virtuellen Teams.* Master's thesis, University of Vienna, Vienna (Austria).

Bauer, Christine, Derntl, Michael, Motschnig-Pitrik, Renate, & Tausch, Reinhard (2006). Promotive Activities in Face-to-Face and Technology-Enhanced Learning Environments. *The Person-Centered Journal, 13*(1-2), pp. 12-37.

Bauer, Christine & Figl, Kathrin (2006). *Differences of Online and Face-to-Face Peer Reviews Regarding Type and Quality.* Proceedings of IADIS International Conference Cognition and Exploratory Learning in Digital Age (CELDA 2006), Barcelona (Spain), 08 December 2006, pp. 423-428.
http://www.iadis.net/dl/Search_list_open.asp?code=3216 [last accessed 22 December 2009].

Bauer, Christine & Figl, Kathrin (2008). *Active Listening in Written Online Communication – A Case Study in a Course on Soft Skills for Computer Scientists.* Proceedings of 38th ASEE/IEEE Frontiers in Education Conference (FIE08), Saratoga Springs (New York), 22-25 October 2008, pp. F2C1-6. http://doi.dx.org/10.1109/FIE.2008.4720282 [last accessed 22 December 2009].

Bauer, Christine, Figl, Kathrin, Derntl, Michael, Beran, Peter Paul, & Kabicher, Sonja (2009a). *Der Einsatz von Online-Peer-Reviews als kollaborative Lernform.* Proceedings of 9th International Conference on Business Informatics 2009 (Wirtschaftsinformatik 2009) (WI 2009), Vienna (Austria), 25-27 February 2009, pp. 421-430.

Bauer, Christine, Figl, Kathrin, Derntl, Michael, Beran, Peter Paul, & Kabicher, Sonja (2009b). *The Student View on Online Peer Review.* Proceedings of 14th ACM.SIGCSE Annual Conference on Innovation and Technology in Computer Science Education (ITiCSE 2009), Paris (France), 06-08 July 2009, pp. 26-30. http://dx.doi.org/10.1145/1562877.1562892 [last accessed 22 December 2009].

Bauer, Christine & Kovacs, Michael (2004). *Factors Guiding Your Way to Success in Hybrid Learning.* Proceedings of 4th International Conference on Knowledge Management (I-KNOW'04), Graz (Austria), 30 June 2004, pp. 567-275.

Bauer, Henry H. (1992). *Scientific Literacy and the Myth of the Scientific Method.* Urbana (Illinois): University of Illinois Press.

Baumgartner, Peter (1997). Didaktische Anforderungen an (multimediale) Lernsoftware. In: Ludwig J. Issing & Paul Klimsa (editors), *Information und Lernen mit Multimedia*, 2nd edition, pp. 241-252. Weinheim (Germany): Beltz, Psychologie Verlags Union.

Baumgartner, Peter (1999). Evaluation mediengestützten Lernens: Theorie – Logik – Modelle. In: Michael Kindt (editor), *Projektevaluation in der Lehre – Multimedia zeigt Profil(e)*, pp. 61-97. Münster (Germany): Waxmann Verlag.

Baumgartner, Peter, Häfele, Kornelia, & Häfele, Hartmund (2002, May 2002). E-Learning: Didaktische und technische Grundlagen. *CD Austria, Issue May 2002,* pp. 4-29. http://www.peter.baumgartner.name/material/reference/e-learning_CD_Austria.pdf/?searchterm=E-Learning:%20Didaktische%20und%20technische%20Grundlagen [last accessed 22 December 2009].

Baumgartner, Peter, Laske, Stephan, & Welte, Heike (2000). Handlungsstrategien von LehrerInnen: Ein heuristisches Modell. In: Christoph Metzger, Hans Seitz & Franz Eberle (editors), *Impulse für die Wirtschaftspädagogik: Festschrift zum 65. Geburtstag von Prof. Dr. Rolf Dubs*, Vol. 26, pp. 247-266. St. Gallen (Switzerland): Verlag des schweizerischen kaufmännischen Verbandes (SKV).

Beck, Kent (2000). *Extreme Programming Explained: Embrace Change* (5th edition). Boston (Massachusetts): Addison-Wesley.

Berge, Zane L. & Muilenburg, Lin (2002). Designing Discussion Questions for Online, Adult Learning. In: Allison Rosset (editor), *The ASTD e-Learning Handbook: Best practices, strategies, and cas studies for an emerging field*, pp. 183-189. New York (New York): McGraw-Hill.

Black, Paul & William, Dylan (1998). Inside the black box: Raising standards through classroom assessment. *Phi Delta Kappan, 80*(2), pp. 139-148. http://www.dianelauer.com/Assesslearntool/blackbox.pdf [last accessed 22 December 2009].

Black, Thomas R. (1993). *Evaluating social science research: an introduction*. London (United Kingdom): Sage.

Black, Thomas R. (1999). *Doing quantitative research in the social sciences: an integrated approach to research design, measurement and statistics*. London (United Kingdom): Sage.

Bloch, Joel & Brut-Griffler, Janina (2001). Implementing CommonSpace in the ESL composition classroom. In: Diane D. Belcher & Alan R. Hirvela (editors), *Linking Literacies: Perspectives on L2 Reading-Writing Connections*, pp. 309-333. Ann Arbor (Michigan): University of Michigan Press.

Bloom, Benjamin Samuel (1972/1973). *Taxonomie von Lernzielen im kognitiven Bereich* (2nd edition, Vol. 35). Weinheim (Germany): Beltz.

Blunt, Adrian & Yung, Baiyin (2002). Factor Structure of the Adult Attitu–des Toward Adult and Continuing Education Scale and its Capacity to Pre–dict Participatin Behavior: Evidence for Adoption of a Revised Scale. *Adult Education Quarterly, 52*(4), pp. 299-31421 September 2008].

Boeree, C. George (1998/2006). Personality Theories - Carl Rogers. [Electronic Article]. http://webspace.ship.edu/cgboer/rogers.html [last accessed 20 July 2008].

Boos, Margarete, Jonas, Kai J., & Sassenberg, Kai (editors) (2000). *Computervermittelte Kommunikation in Organisationen*. Göttingen (Germany): Hogrefe.

Borghoff, Uwe M. & Schlichter, Johann H. (1995). *Rechnergestützte Gruppenarbeit: eine Einführung in verteilte Anwendungen*. Berlin (Germany): Springer.

Boshier, Roger (1991). Psychometric Properties of the Alternative Form of the Education Participation Scale. *Adult Education Quarterly, 41*(3), pp. 150-167.

Boston, Carol (2002). The Concept of Formative Assessment. *Practical Assessment, Research & Evaluation, 8*(9). http://PAREonline.net/getvn.asp?v=8&n=9 [last accessed 05 July 2008].

Bozarth, Jerold D. (2005). Non-directive Person-centered Groups: Facilitation of Freedom and Personal Power. In: Brian E. Levitt (editor), *Embracing Nondirectivity: Reassessing Person-centered Theory and Practice in the 21st Century*. Ross-on-Wye (UK): PCCS Books.

Bremer, Claudia (2001). Online Lehren leicht gemacht!: Leitfaden für die Planung und Gestaltung von virtuellen Hochschulveranstaltungen. In: *Handbuch Hochschullehre*, Vol. A 3.34, pp. 1-39. Berlin (Germany): Raabe Verlag. http://publikationen.ub.uni-frankfurt.de/volltexte/2007/3783/ [last accessed 24 July 2008].

Brennan, John, Johnston, Brenda, Little, Brenda, Shah, Tarla, & Woodley, Alan (2001). *The employment of UK graduates: Comparisons with Europe and Japan. A report to the HEFCE by the Centre for Higher Education Research and Information, Open University*. (No. 01/38). London (UK): Open University. http://www.hefce.ac.uk/pubs/hefce/2001/01_38.htm [last accessed 24 January 2009].

Brill, Andreas & de Vries, Michael (1998). Cybertalk: Die Qualitäten der Kommunikation im Internet. In: Andreas Brill & Michael de Vries (editors), *Virtuelle Wirtschaft: virtuelle Unternehmen, virtuelle Produkte, virtuelles Geld und virtuelle Kommunikation*, pp. 266-300. Opladen (Germany): Westdeutscher Verlag.

Brown, Tracey (2004). *Peer Review and the Acceptance of New Scientific Ideas: Discussion Paper from a Working Party on Equipping the Public with an Understanding of Peer Review*. (No. 0-9547974-0-X). London (UK). http://www.senseaboutscience.org.uk/pdf/PeerReview.pdf [last accessed 22 December 2009].

Bugzilla (1998-2005). Bugzilla Bug Tracking System. http://www.bugzilla.org [last accessed 05 July 2008].

Bühler, Karl (1934/1999). *Sprachtheorie: Die Darstellungsfunktion der Sprache* (3rd edition). Stuttgart (Germany): Lucius & Lucius.

Chandler, Daniel (1995/2000). The Transmission Model of Communication: A Critique. [Electronic Article]. http://www.aber.ac.uk/media/Documents/short/trans.html [last accessed 19 July 2008].

Chinn, Donald (2005). Peer Assessment in the Algorithms Course. 10th annual SIGCSE Conference on Innovation and Technology in Computer Science Education (ITiCSE'05), 37(3), pp. 69-73. http://doi.acm.org/10.1145/1151954.1067468 [last accessed 19 July 2009].

Chou, Chien-Tzu Candace (2001). *Model of Learner-Centered Computer-Mediated Interaction for Collaborative Distance Learning.* Proceedings of 24th National Convention of hte Association for Educational Communications and Technology, Atlanta (Georgia), 08-12 November 2001. http://eric.ed.gov:80/ERICDocs/data/ericdocs2sql/content_storage_01/0000019b/80/1a/85/7d.pdf [last accessed 22 December 2009].

Chow, Angela & Law, Nancy (2005). *Measuring Motivation in Collaborative Inquiry-Based Learning Contexts.* Proceedings of Conference on Computer Support for Collaborative Learning, Taipei (Taiwan), 30 May - 04 June 2005, pp. 68-75. http://doi.acm.org/10.1145/1149303 [last accessed 22 December 2009].

Claxton, Guy (1998). *Hare Brain and Tortoise Mind – Why Intelligence Increases When We Think Less.* London (UK): Fourth Estate.

Coffield, Frank, Moseley, David, Hall, Elaine, & Ecclestone, Kathryn (2004). *Learning Styles and Pedagogy in Post-16 Learning: A Systematic and Critical Review.* London (UK): Learning and Skills Research Centre (LSRC). http://www.lsda.org.uk/files/PDF/1543.pdf [last accessed 25 July 2008].

Coit, Caroline (2004). *Peer Review in an Online College Writing Course.* Proceedings of 4th International Conference on Advanced Learning Technologies (ICALT'04), Joensuu (Finland), 30 August - 01 September 2004, pp. 902-903. http://dx.doi.org/10.1109/ICALT.2004.1357712 [last accessed 22 December 2009].

Comer, Lucette B. & Drollinger, Tanya (1999). Active empathetic listening and selling success: A conceptual framework. *The Journal of Personal Selling & Sales Management, 19*(1), pp. 15-29.

Cornelius-White, Jeffrey (2007). Learner-Centered Teacher-Student Relationships Are Effective: A Meta-Analysis. *Review of Educational Research, 77*(1), pp. 113-143. http://dx.doi.org/10.3102/003465430298563 [last accessed 22 December 2009].

Creswell, John W. (1994/2006). *Research Design: Qualitative, Quantitative, and Mixed Methods Approaches* (2nd edition). Thousand Oaks (California): Sage Publications.

Daft, Richard L. & Lengel, Robert H. (1986). Organizational Information Requirements, Media Richness and Structural Design. *Management Science, 32*(5), pp. 554-571. http://dx.doi.org/10.1287/mnsc.32.5.554 [last accessed 22 December 2009].

Damásio, António R. (1994). *Descartes' Error: Emotion, Reson and the Human Brain*. New York (New York): Putnam.

Damásio, António R. (1999). *The Feeling of What Happens: Body and Emotion in the Making of Consciousness*. New York (New York): Harcourt Brace.

Dearing, Ron (1997). *Higher Education in the Learning Society: The National Committee of Inquiry in to Higher Education, Report for the National Committee of Inquiry into Higher Education*. London (UK): HMSO. http://www.leeds.ac.uk/educol/ncihe/ [last accessed 23 March 2008].

Decker, Bert (1989). *How to Communicate Effectively*. London (UK): Page.

Degenhardt, Werner (1986). *Akzeptanzforschung zu Bildschirmtext: Methoden und Ergebnisse*. München (Germany): Fischer.

DeLuca, Dorrie & Valacich, Joseph S. (2005). *Outcomes from Conduct of Virtual Teams at Two Sites: Support for Media Synchronicity Theory*. Proceedings of 38th Annual Hawaii International Conference on System Sciences (HICSS 2005), Big Island (Hawaii). http://dx.doi.org/10.1109/HICSS.2005.481 [last accessed 22 December 2009].

Dennis, Alan R., Fuller, Robert M., & Valacich, Joseph S. (2008). Media, Tasks, and Communication Processes: A Theory of Media Synchronicity. *Media Information Systems Quarterly, 32*(3), pp. 575-600. http://aisel.aisnet.org/misq/vol32/iss3/8/ [last accessed 22 May 2009].

Dennis, Alan R. & Kinney, Susan T. (1998). Testing Media Richness Theory in the New Media: The Effects of Cues, Feedback, and Task Equivocality. *Information Systems Research, 9*(3), pp. 256-274. http://dx.doi.org/10.1287/isre.9.3.256 [last accessed 22 April 2009].

Dennis, Alan R. & Valacich, Joseph S. (1999). *Rethinking Media Richness: Towards a Theory of Media Synchronicity*. Proceedings of 32nd

Annual Hawaii International Conference on System Science (HICSS 1999), Maui (Hawaii), 05-08 January 1999. http://dx.doi.org/10.1109/HICSS.1999.772701 [last accessed 22 December 2009].

Dennis, Alan R., Valacich, Joseph S., Speier, Cheri, & Morris, Michael G. (1998). *Beyond Media Richness: An Empirical Test of Media Synchronicity Theory.* Proceedings of 31st Annual Hawaii International Conference on System Sciences (HICSS 1998), Kohala Coast (Hawaii), 06-09 January 1998, pp. 48-57. http://dx.doi.org/10.1109/HICSS.1998.653082 [last accessed 22 December 2009].

Denzin, Norman K. (1970/1975). *The Research Act: A Theoretical Introduction to Sociological Methods.* Chicago (Illinois): Aldine Publishing.

Derntl, Michael (2005). *Patterns for Person-Centered e-Learning.* Dissertation, University of Vienna, Vienna (Austria). http://elearn.pri.univie.ac.at/derntl/diss/diss-derntl.pdf [last accessed 22 December 2009].

Derntl, Michael (2006). *A Generic View on Online Peer-Evaluation.* Proceedings of World Conference on Educational Multimedia, Hypermedia, & Telecommunications (ED-MEDIA 2006), Orlando (Florida), 26-30 June 2006, pp. 1809-1816. http://elearn.pri.univie.ac.at/derntl/papers/edmedia06peereval.pdf [last accessed 10 May 2007].

Derntl, Michael & Motschnig-Pitrik, Renate (2004). *Patterns for Blended, Person-Centered Learning: Strategy, Concepts, Experiences, and Evaluation.* Proceedings of ACM Symposium on Applied Computing (SAC 2004), Nicosia (Cyprus), 14-17 March 2004, pp. 916-923. http://dx.doi.org/10.1145/967900.968087 [last accessed 22 December 2009].

Derntl, Michael & Motschnig-Pitrik, Renate (2005). The Role of Structure, Patterns, and People in Blended Learning. *The Internet and Higher Education, 8*(2), p. 20.

Dichanz, Horst & Ernst, Annette (2001, 27 June 2001). E-Learning: Begriffliche, psychologische und didaktische Überlegungen zum "electronic learning". *MedienPädagogik – Zeitschrift für Theorie und Praxis der Medienbildung, 00, Issue 27 June 2001.* http://www.medienpaed.com/00-2/dichanz_ernst1.pdf [last accessed 22 December 2009].

Diehl, Michael & Ziegler, René (2000). Informationsaustausch und Ideensammlung in Gruppen. In: Margarete Boos, Kai J. Jonas & Kai Sassenberg (editors), *Computervermittelte Kommunikation in Organisationen*, pp. 89-101. Göttlingen (Germany): Hogrefe.

Dochy, Filip J. R. C., Segers, Mien, & Sluijsmans, Dominique M. A. (1999). The Use of Self-, Peer and Co-assessment in Higher Education: A review. *Studies in Higher Education, 24*(3), pp. 331-350.

Döring, Nicola (1997/2000). Lernen und Lehren im Internet. In: Bernad Batinic (editor), *Internet für Psychologen*, 2nd, revised and expanded edition, pp. 443-477. Göttingen (Germany): Hogrefe.

Downward, Paul & Mearman, Andrew (2007). Retroduction as Mixed-Methods Triangulation in Economic Research: Reorienting Economics into Social Science. *Cambridge Journal of Economics, 31*, pp. 77-99. http://dx.doi.org/10.1093/cje/bel009 [last accessed 22 June 2009].

Duarte, Deborah L. & Snyder, Nancy Tennant (2001). *Mastering Virtual Teams*. San Francisco (California): Jossey-Bass.

Durik, Amanda M. & Harackiewicz, Judith M. (2002). Achievement goals and intrinsic motivation: Coherence, concordance, and achievement orientation. *Journal of Experimental Social Psychology, 39*(4 July 2008), pp. 378-385.

Eco, Umberto (1972/1994). *Einführung in die Semiotik* (Authorised German Edition, 8th, unchanged edition). München (Germany): Fink.

Eco, Umberto (1987/1991). *Semiotik: Entwurf einer Theorie der Zeichen* (2nd, corrected edition). München (Germany): Fink.

Engelberg, Elisabeth & Sjöberg, Lennart (2004). Internet Use, Social Skills, and Adjustment. *CyberPsychology & Behavior, 7*(1), pp. 41-47. http://dx.doi.org/10.1089/109493104322820101 [last accessed 22 December 2009].

Ercikan, Kadriye & Roth, Wolff-Michael (2006). What Good is Polarizing Research Into Qualitative and Quantitative? *Educational Researcher, 35*(5), pp. 14-23.

Everitt, Brian S. (1992). *The analysis of contingency tables* (2nd edition). London (United Kingdom): Chapman and Hall.

Figl, Kathrin (2005). *Evaluation von e-Learning: am Beispiel der Blended Learning Lehrveranstaltung "Web Engineering"*. Master's Thesis, University of Vienna, Vienna (Austria).

Figl, Kathrin (2008). *Developing Team Competence of Computer Science Students in Person Centered Technology-Enhanced Courses.* Dissertation, University of Vienna, Vienna (Austria).

Figl, Kathrin (2009). *Team and Media Competencies in Information Systems.* München (Germany): Oldenbourg.

Figl, Kathrin & Bauer, Christine (2008a). *Motivational Aspects in Technology-Enhanced Courses.* Proceedings of World Conference on Educational Multimedia, Hypermedia and Telecommunications 2008 (ED-MEDIA 2008), Vienna (Austria), 30 June - 02 July 2008, pp. 3701-3710. http://www.editlib.org/index.cfm?fuseaction=Reader.ViewFullText&paper_id=28899 [last accessed 02 August 2008].

Figl, Kathrin & Bauer, Christine (2008b). *Online Active Listening and Media Competence.* Proceedings of IADIS International Conference e-Learning 2008 (eL 2008) (part of MCCSIS 2008), Amsterdam (The Netherlands), 22-25 July 2008, pp. 207-214. http://www.iadis.net/dl/Search_list_open.asp?code=4679 [last accessed 22 May 2009].

Figl, Kathrin, Bauer, Christine, Mangler, Jürgen, & Motschnig-Pitrik, Renate (2006). *Online versus Face-to-Face Peer Team Reviews.* Proceedings of 36th ASEE/IEEE Frontiers in Education Conference (FIE06), San Diego (California), 28-31 October 2006, pp. T1H 7-12. http://dx.doi.org/10.1109/FIE.2006.322469 [last accessed 22 December 2009].

Figl, Kathrin & Motschnig-Pitrik, Renate (2007). *Developing Team Competence in Technology Enhanced Courses.* Proceedings of World Conference on Educational Multimedia, Hypermedia and Telecommunications 2007 (ED-MEDIA 07), Vancouver (Canada), pp. 1798-1806. http://www.editlib.org/index.cfm/files/paper_25615.pdf?fuseaction=Reader.DownloadFullText&paper_id=25615 [last accessed 27 September 2008].

Figl, Kathrin, Motschnig-Pitrik, Renate, & Derntl, Michael (2006). *Team and Community Building of Students of Business Informatics: Influence Factors in Blended Environments.* Proceedings of 5th International Conference on Networked Learning (NLC'06), Lancaster (UK), 10-12 April 2006. http://www.networkedlearningconference.org.uk/past/nlc2006/abstracts/pdfs/09Figl.pdf [last accessed 22 May 2009].

Flick, Uwe (1991/1995). Triangulation. In: Uwe Flick, Ernst von Kardorff, Heiner Keupp, Lutz von Rosenstiel & Stephan Wolff (editors), *Handbuch Qualitative Sozialforschung: Grundlagen, Konzepte, Methoden und Anwendungen*, pp. 432-434. Weinheim (Germany): Beltz Psychologie-Verlags-Union.

Flick, Uwe (1995/2002). *Qualitative Sozialforschung: Eine Einführung* (6th revised edition). Reinbeck bei Hamburg (Germany): Rowohlt.

Flick, Uwe (2004). *Triangulation: Eine Einführung*. Opladen (Germany): VS Verlag für Sozialwissenschaften.

Foulger, Davis Albert (1990). *Medium as Process: The Structure, Use, and Practice of Computer Conferencing on IBM's IBMPC Computer Conferencing Facility*. Dissertation, Temple University, Philadelphia (Pennsylvania). http://evolutionarymedia.com/mediumAsProcess [last accessed 22 December 2009].

Frank, Ulrich (2006). Towards a Pluralistic Conception of Research Methods in Information Systems. [Electronic Article]. *ICB Research-Report*, 7. http://www.icb.uni-due.de/fileadmin/ICB/research/research_reports/ICBReport07.pdf [last accessed 22 December 2009].

Frey, Hartmut (1999). *E-Mail: Revolution im Unternehmen: wie sich Motivation, Kommunikation und Innovationsgeist der Mitarbeiter wandeln*. Neuwied (Switzerland): Luchterhand.

Fühles-Ubach, Simone (2000). Soziale Kompetenzen und ihre Rolle im IT-Bereich. *SPLITTER, 2000*, pp. 15-18. http://www.itdz-berlin.de/dokumente/splitter/splitter_2000_2.pdf [last accessed 22 July 2009].

Gabrielle, Donna M. (2003). *The Effects of Technology-Mediated Instructional Strategies on Motivation, Performance, and Self-Directed Learning*. Dissertation, Florida State University, Tallahassee (Florida). http://etd.lib.fsu.edu/theses/available/etd-11142003-171019/unrestricted/gabrielle.pdf [last accessed 22 December 2009].

Galin, Daniel (2004). *Software Quality Assurance: From Theory to Implementation*. Harlow (UK): Pearson Education.

Gehringer, Edward F. (2000). *Strategies and Mechanisms for Electronic Peer Review*. Proceedings of 30th ASEE/IEEE Frontiers in Education Conference (FIE 2000), Kansas City (Missouri), 18-21 October 2000, pp. F1B/2-F1B/7. http://dx.doi.org/10.1109/FIE.2000.897675 [last accessed 22 December 2009].

Girgensohn-Marchand, Bettina (1992/1996). *Der Mythos Watzlawick und die Folgen: eine Streitschrift gegen syystemisches und konstruktives Denken in pädagogischen Zusammenhängen* (3rd edition). Weinheim (Germany): Deutscher Studien Verlag.

Gläser-Zikuda, Michaela & Järvelä, Sanna (2008). Editorial: Application of Qualitative and Quantitative Methods to Enrich Understanding of Emotional and Motivational Aspects of Learning. *International Journal of Educational Research, 47*(2), pp. 79-83. http://dx.doi.org/10.1016/j.ijer.2007.11.009 [last accessed 22 December 2009].

Glasersfeld, Ernst von (1987). *Wissen, Sprache und Wirklichkeit: Arbeiten zum radikalen Konstruktivismus* (Vol. 24). Braunschweig (Germany): Vieweg.

Godlee, Fiona, Gale, Catharine R., & Martyn, Christopher N. (1998). Effect on the Quality of Peer Review of Blinding Reviewers and Asking Them to Sign Their Reports: A Randomized Controlled Trial. *The Journal of the Americal Medical Association, 280*(3), pp. 237-240. http://dx.doi.org/10.1001/jama.280.3.237 [last accessed 22 December 2009].

Gomez, Elizabeth Avery & Bieber, Michael (2005). *Towards Active Team-Based Learning: An Online Instructional Strategy.* Proceedings of 11th Americas Conference on Information Sytems, Omaha (Nevada), 11-14 August 2005, pp. 725-734. http://web.njit.edu/~bieber/pub/gomez-ais2005.pdf [last accessed 22 December 2009].

Gordon, Thomas (1970/1983). *Familienkonferenz: Die Lösung von Konflikten zwischen Eltern und Kind.* Reinbek bei Hamburg (Germany): rororo sachbuch.

Gordon, Thomas (1977/1979). *Managerkonferenz: Effektives Führungstraining.* Hamburg (Germany): Hoffmann und Campe.

Gordon, Thomas (2000). The Origins of the Gordon Model. [Electronic Article]. http://private.addcom.de/gpb/gordon/go_hist_e.htm [last accessed 05 July 2008].

Gordon, Thomas & Burch, Noel (1974/1977). *Lehrer-Schüler-Konferenz: Wie man Konflikte in der Schule löst* (11th edition). Hamburg (Germany): Hoffmann und Campe.

Gordon, Thomas & Sands, Judith Gordon (1976/1985). *Familienkonferenz in der Praxis: Wie Konflikte mit Kindern gelöst werden.* Reinbek bei Hamburg (Germany): rororo sachbuch.

Grinnell, Richard M. & Unrau, Yvonne A. (editors) (2008). *Social Work Research and Evaluation: Foundations of Evidence-Based Practice* (8th edition). New York (New York): Oxford University Press.

Grove, Cornelius, Hallowell, Willa, & Molloy, Kathy (2001). Protocols Make E-Mail More Effective ... Fortunately! *Focus: Europe, 1*(3). http://www.grovewell.com/pub-email-solutions.html [last accessed 22 December 2009].

Guba, Egon G. & Lincoln, Yvonna S. (1989/2000). *Fourth Generation Evaluation* (12th edition). Newbury Park (California): Sage Publications.

Gunter, Glenda A. (2007). The Effects of the Impact of Instructional Immediacy on Cognition and Learning in Online Classes. *International journal of Social Sciences, 2*(3), pp. 196-202. http://www.waset.org/journals/ijss/v2/v2-3-30.pdf [last accessed 22 December 2009].

Hammersley, Martyn & Gomm, Roger (2000). Introduction. In: Roger Gomm, Martyn Hammersley & Peter Foster (editors), *Case Study Method: Key Issues, Key Texts*, pp. 1-16. London, Thousand Oaks, New Delhi: Sage Publications.

Handy, Charles (1995). Trust and the Virtual Organization. *Harvard Business Review, 73*(3, May-June), pp. 40-50.

Hansen, Jette G. (2005). Cooperative Learning Methods and the Teaching of English Writing: Peer Response. *STETS Language & Communication Review, 4*(1), pp. 9-14. http://www.stets.org.sg/Vol4No1_2005Hansen.pdf [last accessed 22 December 2009].

Harjumaa, Lasse, Tervonen, Iisakka, & Huttunen, Anna (2005). *Peer Reviews in Real Life – Motivators and Demotivators.* Proceedings of 5th International Conference on Quality Software (QSIC'05), Melbourne (Australia), 19-20 September 2005, pp. 29-36. http://dx.doi.org/10.1109/QSIC.2005.48 [last accessed 22 May 2009].

Heinrich, Lutz J. (2005). Forschungsmethodik einer Integrationsdisziplin: Ein Beitrag zur Geschichte der Wirtschaftsinformatik. *NTM Zeitschrift für Geschichte der Wissenschaften, Technik und Medizin, 13*(2), pp. 104-117. http://dx.doi.org/10.1007/s00048-005-0211-9 [last accessed 22 December 2009].

Heist, Alexander (2006). *Seelsorge-Therapie-Menschenbild: Die Rezeptionsweisen des Konzepts von Carl R. Rogers in der deutschsprachigen, protestantischen Seelsorge.* Master's thesis, University of Vienna, Vienna (Austria).

Herrmann, Thomas (1991). Die Bedeutung menschlicher Kommunikation für die Kooperation und die Gestaltung computerunterstützter Gruppenarbeit. In: Horst Oberquelle & Thomas Herrmann (editors), *Kooperative Arbeit und Computerunterstützung: Stand und Perspektiven*, pp. 63-78. Göttingen (Germany): Verlag für Angewandte Psychologie.

Hodges, Charles B. (2004). Designing to Motivate: Motivational Techniques to Incorporate in E-Learning Experiences. *The Journal of Interactive Online Learning, 2*(3). http://www.ncolr.org/jiol/issues/PDF/2.3.1.pdf [last accessed 22 December 2009].

Hofstede, Geert (2005). *Cultures and Organizations: Software of the Mind* (2nd revised and expanded edition). New York (New York): McGraw-Hill.

Hollingshead, Andrea B. & McGrath, Joseph E. (1995). Computer-assisted Groups: a Critical Review of the Empirical Research. In: Richard A. Guzzo & Eduardo Salas (editors), *Team Effectiveness and Decision Making in Organizations*, pp. 46-78. San Francisco (California): Jossey-Bass.

Huang, David Wenhao, Diefes-Dux, Heidi, Imbrie, P. K., Daku, Brian, & Kallimani, James G. (2004). *Learning Motivation Evaluation for a Computer-based Instructional Tutorial Using ARCS Model of Motivational Design.* Proceedings of 34th ASEE/IEEE Frontiers in Education Conference (FIE04), Savannah (Georgia), 20-23 October 2004, pp. TIE-30-36. http://dx.doi.org/10.1109/FIE.2004.1408466 [last accessed 22 December 2009].

Huang, Su-Yueh (1998). A Comparison Between Chinese EFL Students' Peer Response Sessions Held on Networked Computers and Those Held in a Face-to-Face Setting. Proceedings of 6th International NELLE-Conference, Bielefeld (Germany), 27-30 August 1998. http://eric.ed.gov/ERICDocs/data/ericdocs2sql/content_storage_01/0000019b/80/16/ea/79.pdf [last accessed 22 December 2009].

Huett, Jason Bond (2006). The Effects of ARCS-Based Confidence Strategies on Learner Confidence and Performance in Distance Education. Dissertation, University of North Texas, Denton (Texas). http://digital.library.unt.edu/permalink/meta-dc-5268:1 [last accessed 22 December 2009].

Iisakka, Juha, Tervonen, Ikka, & Harjumaa, Lasse (1999). *Experiences of Painless Improvements in Software Inspection.* Proceedings of 10th European Software Control and Metrics Conference (ESCOM-

SCOPE 99), Herstmonceux Castle (UK), 27-29 April 1999, pp. 321-327. http://www.tol.oulu.fi/i3/1999/Iisakka_ESCOM-SCOPE_1999.pdf [last accessed 22 December 2009].

Imhof, Margarete (2004). *Zuhören und Instruktion: Empirische Ansätze zu psychologischen Aspekten auditiver Informationsverarbeitung* (Vol. 44). München (Germany): Waxmann.

Ishaya, Tanko & Macaulay, Linda (1999). The Role of Trust in Virtual Teams. *Electronic Journal of Organizational Virtualness, 1*(1), pp. 140-157. http://www.ejov.org/Projects/264/Issues/eJOV%20Vol1/Ishaya%20-%201999%20-%20eJOV1.1-9%20-%20The%20Role%20of%20Trust%20in%20Virtual%20Teams.pdf [last accessed 22 December 2009].

Jacobs, Jane (1961). *The Death and Life of Great American Cities* (Vol. 241). New York (New York): Vintage Books.

Jank, Werner & Meyer, Hilbert (1991). *Didaktische Modelle*. Frankfurt am Main (Germany): Cornelson Scriptor.

Jarvenpaa, Sirkka L. & Leidner, Dorothy E. (1999). Communication and Trust in Global Virtual Teams. *Organization Science, 10*(6), pp. 791-815. http://dx.doi.org/10.1287/orsc.10.6.791 [last accessed 22 August 2009].

Jefferson, Tom, Alderson, Philip, Wager, Elizabeth, & Davidoff, Frank (2002). Effects of Editorial Peer Review: A Systematic Review. *The Journal of the Americal Medical Association, 287*(21), pp. 2784-2786. http://dx.doi.org/10.1001/jama.287.21.2784 [last accessed 22 December 2009].

Jefferson, Tom, Wager, Elizabeth, & Davidoff, Frank (2002). Measuring the Quality of Editorial Peer Review. *The Journal of the Americal Medical Association, 287*(21), pp. 2786-2790. http://dx.doi.org/10.1001/jama.287.21.2786 [last accessed 22 December 2009].

Jick, Todd D. (1979). Mixing Qualitative and Quantitative Methods: Triangulation in Action. *Administrative Science Quarterly, 24*(4), pp. 602-611. http://www.jstor.org/stable/2392366 [last accessed 22 December 2009].

Johnson, R. Burke & Onwuegbuzie, Anthony J. (2004). Mixed Methods Research: A Research Paradigm Whose Time Has Come. *Education-*

al Researcher, 33(7), pp. 14-26. http://dx.doi.org/10.3102/0013189X033007014 [last accessed 22 December 2009].

Kaplan, Bonnie & Duchon, Dennis (1988). Combining Qualitative and Quantitative Methods in Information Systems Research: A Case Study. *Media Information Systems Quarterly, 12*(4), pp. 571-586. http://www.jstor.org/stable/249133 [last accessed 22 May 2009].

Keller, John M. (1987). The Systematic Process of Motivational Design. *Performance & Instruction, 26*(9), pp. 1-8.

Kim, ChanMin & Keller, John M. (2008). Effects of Motivational and Volitional Email Messages (MVEM) with Personal Messages on Undergraduate Students' Motivation, Study Habits and Achievement. *British Journal of Educational Technology, 39*(1), pp. 36-51. http://dx.doi.org/10.1111/j.1467-8535.2007.00701.x [last accessed 22 August 2009].

King, Frederick B., Young, Michael F., Drivere-Richmond, Kelly, & Schrader, P. G. (2001). Defining Distance Learning and Distance Education. *AACE Journal, 9*(1), pp. 1-14. http://www.editlib.org/index.cfm?fuseaction=Reader.ViewFullText&paper_id=17786 [last accessed 22 December 2009].

Kirschenbaum, Howard & Henderson, Valerie Land (editors) (1989). *The Carl Rogers Reader*. London (UK): Constable.

Köhler, Th. (1999). Sozialwissenschaftliche Theorien und Befunde zur computervermittelten Kommunikation. In: W. Frindte & T. Köhler (editors), *Kommunikation im Internet*, pp. 137-182. Frankfurt am Main (Germany): Lang.

Köszegi, Sabine T. (2000). *Vertrauen in virtuellen Unternehmen*. Dissertation, University of Vienna, Vienna (Austria).

Kovacs, Michael (2004). *Ansatz zur Gestaltung von e-Education an tertiären Bildungsinstitutionen*. Dissertation, University of Vienna, Vienna (Austria).

Kroop, Sylvana & Mangler, Jürgen (2006). *A Cooperative Way to Learn 'Comprehensible Writing'*. Proceedings of 5th International Conference on Networked Learning (NLC'06), Lancaster (UK), 10-12 April 2006. http://www.networkedlearningconference.org.uk/past/nlc2006/abstracts/pdfs/P37%20Kroop.pdf [last accessed 22 December 2009].

Kubota, Shinya, Mishima, Norio, & Nagata, Shoji (2004). A Study of the Effects of Active Listening on Listening Attitudes of Middle Managers.

Journal of Occupational Health, 46, pp. 60-67. http://joh.med.uoeh-u.ac.jp/pdf/E46/E46_1_07.pdf [last accessed 22 December 2009].

Kvale, Steinar (1991/1995). Validierung: Von der Beobachtung zu Kommunikation und Handeln. In: Uwe Flick, Ernst von Kardorff, Heiner Keupp, Lutz von Rosenstiel & Stephan Wolff (editors), *Handbuch Qualitative Sozialforschung: Grundlagen, Konzepte, Methoden und Anwendungen*, 2nd edition, pp. 427-431. Weinheim (Germany): Beltz Psychologie-Verlags-Union.

Langer, Inghard, Schulz von Thun, Friedemann, & Tausch, Reinhard (1974/2002). *Sich verständlich ausdrücken* (7th edition). München (Germany): Ernst Reinhard Verlag.

LaTeX (2008). The LaTeX Project: LaTeX – A document Preparation System. http://www.latex-project.org [last accessed 04 March 2009].

Lave, Jean & Wenger, Etienne (1991). *Siutated Learning: Legitimate Peripheral Participation*. Cambridge (Massachusetts): Cambridge University Press.

Leuf, Bo E. & Cunningham, Ward (2001). *The Wiki Way: Quick Collaboration On The Web*. Boston (Massachusetts): Addison-Wesley.

Lewe, Henrik (1995). *Computer Aided Team und Produktivität: Einsatzmöglichkeiten und Erfolgspotentiale*. Wiesbaden (Germany): Gabler.

Likert, Rensis (1932). A Technique for the Measurement of Attitudes. *Archives of Psychology*(140), pp. 1-55.

Limayem, Moez & Hirt, Sabine Gabriele (2000). *Internet-Based Teaching: How to Encourage University Students to Adopt Advanced Internet-Based Technologies?* Proceedings of 33rd Annual Hawaii International Conference on System Sciences 2000 (HICSS 2000), Maui (Hawaii), 04-07 January 2000. http://dx.doi.org/10.1109/HICSS.2000.926640 [last accessed 22 December 2009].

Limbeck, Sonja (2005). *"Familienkonferenz": Eine funktionale Übersetzungskritik der deutschen Fassung von Thomas Godons "Parent Effectiveness Training"*. Master's thesis, University of Vienna, Vienna (Austria).

Lin, Chen-Shan, Chang, Kuo-En, Lee, Chee-Lung, & Sung, Yao-Ting (2002). *Improving Experiment Project Evaluation Through Web-based Self- and Peer Assessment.* Proceedings of Society for Informa-

Journal of Occupational Health, 42, pp. 111-118. http://dx.doi.org/10.1539/joh.42.111 [last accessed 22 December 2009].

Morgan, George Arthur, Leech, Nancy L., Gloeckner, Gene W., & Barrett, Karen Caplovitz (2004). *SPSS for Introductory Statistics: Use and Interpretation* (2nd edition). Mahwah (New Jersey): Lawrence Erlbaum.

Motschnig-Pitrik, Renate (2001). *Using the Internet with the Student-Centred Approach to Teaching: Method and Case Study.* Proceedings of 4th International Workshop on Interactive Computer-Aided Learning (ICL 2001), Villach (Austria).

Motschnig-Pitrik, Renate (2002). *Supporting Student-Centred Teaching with New Media: Case Study and Experience Report.* Proceedings of 3rd International Conference on Networked Learning 2002 (NLC 2002), Sheffield (UK), 26-28 March 2002, pp. 456-464. http://www.networkedlearningconference.org.uk/past/nlc2002/proceedings/papers/25.htm [last accessed 22 December 2009].

Motschnig-Pitrik, Renate (2003). Person-Centeredness in Cooperative, Blended Learning and Challenges for Organizational Development. Unpublished Presentation (Folios). University of Vienna.

Motschnig-Pitrik, Renate (2004a). Blended Learning in einer großen Informatik-Lehrveranstaltung: Personenzentriert oder Handlungsorientiert? In: Horst O. Mayer & Dietmar Treichel (editors), *Handlungsorientiertes Lernen und eLearning: Grundlagen und Praxisbeispiele*, pp. 219-248. München (Germany): Oldenbourg Wissenschaftsverlag.

Motschnig-Pitrik, Renate (2004b). *Person Centered e-Learning in a Major Academic Course: What are the Results and What Can We Learn from Them?* Proceedings of 4th International Conference on Networked Learning 2004 (NLC 2004), Lancaster (UK). http://www.networkedlearningconference.org.uk/past/nlc2004/proceedings/symposia/symposium12/motschnig_pitrik.htm [last accessed 22 December 2009].

Motschnig-Pitrik, Renate (2006a). *The Effects of a Blended Course Including Person Centered Encounter Groups on Students' Learning, Relationships, and Teamwork.* Proceedings of 5th International Conference on Networked Learning (NLC'06), Lancaster (UK), 10-12 April 2006, pp. S4D-1-6. http://www.networkedlearningconference.org.uk/past/nlc2006/abstracts/pdfs/09Motschnig-Pitrik2.pdf [last accessed 22 December 2009].

Motschnig-Pitrik, Renate (2006b). *Participatory Action Research in a Blended Learning Course on Project Management Soft Skills.* Proceedings of 36th ASEE/IEEE Frontiers in Education Conference (FIE06), San Diego (California), 27-31 October 2006, pp. S4D-1-6. http://dx.doi.org/10.1109/FIE.2006.322467 [last accessed 22 December 2009].

Motschnig-Pitrik, Renate & Derntl, Michael (2002). *Student-Centered eLearning (SCeL): Concept and application in a students' project on supporting learning.* Proceedings of 5th International Workshop on Interactive Computer-Aided Learning (ICL 2002), Villach (Austria), 25-27 September 2002.

Motschnig-Pitrik, Renate & Derntl, Michael (2003). *Cooperative Person-Centered e-Learning: Moving from Exams to a Web-Engineering Knowledge Base.* Proceedings of 6th International Workshop on Interactive Computer-Aided Learning (ICL 2003), Villach (Austria).

Motschnig-Pitrik, Renate, Derntl, Michael, & Mangler, Jürgen (2003). *Web-Support for Learning Contracts: Concept and Experiences.* Proceedings of 2nd International Conference on Multimedia and Information & Communication Technologies in Education (m-ICTE'03), Badajoz (Spain), 03-06 December 2003, pp. 1184-1188. http://www.formatex.org/micte2003/micte2003.htm [last accessed 28 August 2008].

Motschnig-Pitrik, Renate & Figl, Kathrin (2007). *Developing Team Competence as Part of a Person Centred Learning Course on Communication and Soft Skills in Project Management.* Proceedings of 37th ASEE/IEEE Frontiers in Education Conference (FIE07), Milwaukee (Wisconsin), 10-13 October 2007, pp. F2G-15-21. http://dx.doi.org/10.1109/FIE.2007.4417889 [last accessed 22 December 2009].

Motschnig-Pitrik, Renate & Holzinger, Andreas (2002). Student-Centered Teaching Meets New Media: Concept and Case Study. *Educational Technology & Society, 5*(4), pp. 160-172. http://www.ifets.info/journals/5_4/renate.html [last accessed 22 December 2009].

Motschnig-Pitrik, Renate, Karasek, Achim, & Zelger, Markus (2003). getProfile: Anforderungsanalyse an Wirtschaftsinformatiker(innen) aus der Sicht der Wirtschaft. *OCG Journal, 1*, pp. 8-11. http://www.ocg.at/publikationen/oj/pdfs/oj0301.pdf [last accessed 22 December 2009].

Motschnig-Pitrik, Renate & Lux, Michael (2008). The Person-Centered Approach Meets Neuroscience: Mutual Support for C. R. Rogers's and A. Damasio's Theories. *Journal of Humanistic Psychology, 48*(3), pp. 287-319. http://dx.doi.org/10.1177/0022167807306044 [last accessed 22 December 2009].

Motschnig-Pitrik, Renate & Mallich, Katharina (2002). *Learning at Three Levels: Web-support and Experiential Learning in Project Management.* Proceedings of 5th International Workshop on Interactive Computer-Aided Learning (ICL 2002), Villach (Austria), 25 -27 September 2002. http://www.pri.univie.ac.at/Publications/2002/Motschnig_ICL2002_Learning_at_Three_Levels.pdf [last accessed 22 July 2009].

Motschnig-Pitrik, Renate & Mallich, Katharina (2004). Effects of Person-Centered Attitudes on Professional and Social Competence in a Blended Learning Paradigm. *Journal of Educational Technology & Society, 7*(4), pp. 176-192. http://www.ifets.info/journals/7_4/17.pdf [last accessed 22 December 2009].

Motschnig-Pitrik, Renate & Nykl, Ladislav (2005a). Encountergruppen im Rahmen des ganzheitlichen Lernens an den Universitä ten Wien und Brünn – Motivation, Kontext, Prozesse, Perspektiven. *Zeitschrift für Hochschuldidaktik, 4*(2005), pp. 36-62. http://www.pri.univie.ac.at/Publications/2005/Motschnig_ZFHD2005_Encountergruppen.pdf [last accessed 22 December 2009].

Motschnig-Pitrik, Renate & Nykl, Ladislav (2005b). Was hat Carl Rogers Wirtschaftsinformatikern im Zeitalter des Internet zu sagen? *Gruppendynamik und Organisationsberatung, 36*(1), pp. 81-102.

Motschnig-Pitrik, Renate & Santos, A. (2006). The Person Centered Approach to Teaching and Learning as Exemplified in a Course in Organizational Development. *Zeitschrift für Hochschuldidaktik (ZHD), 4.*

Nohr, H. (2002). Elektronische vermittelte Wissenskommunikation und Medienwahl. *Information - Wissenschaft und Praxis, 52*(3), pp. 141-148.

Nykl, Ladislav & Motschnig-Pitrik, Renate (2002). *Uniting Rogers's and Vygotsky's Theories on Personality and Learning.* Proceedings of The Carl Rogers Symposium 2002, La Jolla (California), 24-28 July 2002. http://www.pri.univie.ac.at/Publications/2002/Motschnig_CRC2002_Uniting_Rogers.pdf [last accessed 22 December 2009].

O'Donohue, William & Kitchener, Richard (editors) (1999). *Handbook of behaviorism*. San Diego (California): Academic Press.

Okolo, Cynthia M. & Ferretti, Ralph P. (2000). Preparing Future Citizens: Technology-Supported, Project-Based Learning in the Social Studies. In: John Potter Woodward & Larry Cuban (editors), *Technology, Curriculum and Professional Development: Adapting Schools to Meet the Needs of Students With Disabilities*, pp. 47-60. Thousand Oaks (California): Corwin Press.

Page-Bucci, Hilary (2003). The Value of Likert Scales in Measuring Attitudes of Online Learners. [Electronic Article]. http://www.hkadesigns.co.uk/websites/msc/reme/likert.htm [last accessed 25 May 2007].

Peers, Ian S. (1996). *Statistical analysis for education and psychology researchers: Tools for researchers in eduction and psychology*. London (United Kingdom): The Falmer Press.

Penfield, Douglas A. & Koffler, Stephen L. (1978). Post Hoc Procedures for some k-Sample Nonparametric Tests for Scale. *Journal of Educational Statistics, 3*(3), pp. 265-282. http://www.jstor.org/stable/1164855 [last accessed 22 December 2009].

Picot, Arnold, Reichwald, Ralf, & Wigand, Rolf T. (2001). *Die grenzenlose Unternehmung: Information, Organisation und Management* (4th, completely revised and enhanced edition). Wiesbaden (Germany): Gabler.

Qualifications and Curriculum Authority (QCA) (2008). Key Skills. [Electronic Article]. http://www.qca.org.uk [last accessed 23 March 2008].

Rautalinko, Erik & Lisper, Hans-Olof (2004). Effects of Training Reflective Listening in a Corporate Setting. *Journal of Business and Psychology, 18*(3). http://dx.doi.org/10.1023/B:JOBU.0000016712.36043.4f [last accessed 22 December 2009].

Reichwald, R., Möslein, K., Sachenbacher, H., & Englberger, H. (1998). *Telekooperation, Verteilte Arbeits- und Organisationsformen* (2nd edition). Heidelberg (Germany): Springer.

Reimer, Christian, Eckert, Jochen, Hautzinger, Martin, & Wilke, Eberhard (1996/2007). *Psychotherapie: Ein Lehrbuch für Ärzte und Psychologen* (3rd, completely revised and actualised edition). Berlin (Germany): Springer.

Retter, Hein (2000). *Studienbuch pädagogische Kommunikation.* Bad Heilbrunn / Obb. (Germany): Klinkhardt.

Robertson, Kathryn (2005). Active listening – More than just paying attention. *Australian Family Physician, 34*(12), pp. 1053-1055. http://www.racgp.org.au/Content/NavigationMenu/Publications/AustralianFamilyPhys/2005Issues/afp200512/200512robinson.pdf [last accessed 22 December 2009].

Rogers, Carl Ransom (1951). *Client-Centered Therapy.* Cambridge (Massachusetts): Riverside Press.

Rogers, Carl Ransom (1959). A Theory of Therapy, Personality, and Interpersonal Relationships, as Developed in the Client-Centered Framework. In: Sigmund Koch (editor), *Psychology: A Study of a Science*, Vol. 3. New York (New York): McGraw-Hill.

Rogers, Carl Ransom (1961). *On Becoming a Person – A Psychotherapists View of Psychotherapy.* London (UK): Constable.

Rogers, Carl Ransom (1970). *Carl Rogers on Encounter Groups.* New York (New York): Harper Row.

Rogers, Carl Ransom (1980). *A Way of Being.* Boston (Massachusetts): Houghton Mifflin.

Rogers, Carl Ransom (1983). *Freedom to Learn for the 80's.* Columbus (Ohio): Charles E Merrill Publishing Company.

Rogers, Carl Ransom & Richard E. Farson, Richard E. (1957/1987). Active Listening. [Electronic Article]. http://www.gordontraining.com/artman2/uploads/1/ActiveListening_RogersFarson.pdf [last accessed 21 April 2009].

Rohrmann, B. (1978). Empirische Studien zur Entwicklung von Antwortskalen für die sozialwissenschaftliche Forschung. *Zeitschrift für Sozialpsychologie, 9*, pp. 222-245.

Sarbaugh-Thompson, Marjorie & Feldman, Martha S. (1998). Electronic Mail and Organizational Communication: Does Saying "Hi" Really Matter? *Organization Science, 9*(6), pp. 85-698. http://dx.doi.org/10.1287/orsc.9.6.685 [last accessed 22 December 2009].

Sassenberg, Kai (2000). Räumlich getrennt gemeinsam entscheiden. In: Margarete Boos, Kai J. Jonas & Kai Sassenberg (editors), *Computer-*

vermittelte Kommunikation in Organisationen, pp. 103-114. Göttingen (Germany): Hogrefe.

Schlag, Bernhard (1995/2004). *Lern- und Leistungsmotivation* (2nd revised edition). Wiesbaden (Germany): VS Verlag für Sozialwissenschaften.

Schuler, Heinz & Barthelme, Dorothea (1995). Soziale Kompetenz als berufliche Anforderung. In: Brigitte Seyfried (editor), *"Stolperstein" Sozialkompetenz : was macht es so schwierig, sie zu erfassen, zu fördern und zu beurteilen?* , pp. 77-116. Bielefeld (Germany): Bertelsmann.

Schulz von Thun, Friedemann (1981/2003). *Miteinander reden 1: Störungen und Klärungen: Allgemeine Psychologie der Kommunikation* (Special Edition edition). Reinbek bei Hamburg (Germany): Rowohlt.

Schwabe, Gerhard (2001). Mediensynchronizität – Theorie und Anwendung bei Gruppenarbeit und Lernen. In: Friedrich W. Hesse & Helmut F. Friedrich (editors), *Partizipation und Interaktion im virtuellen Seminar*, Vol. 13, pp. 111-134. Münster (Germany): Waxmann.

Shannon, Claude Elwood (1948). A Mathematical Theory of Communication. *Bell System Technical Journal, 27*(July, October), pp. 379-423, 623-656. http://cm.bell-labs.com/cm/ms/what/shannonday/shannon1948.pdf [last accessed 22 December 2009].

Shannon, Claude Elwood & Weaver, Warren (1949/1963). *The Mathematical Theory of Communication* (1st paperbound edition). Urbana (Illinois): University of Illinois Press.

Sheer, Vivian C. & Chen, Ling (2004). Improving Media Richness Theory: A Study of Interaction Goals, Message Valence, and Task Complexity in Manager-Subordinate Communication. *Management Communication Quarterly, 18*(1), pp. 76-93. http://dx.doi.org/10.1177/0893318904265803 [last accessed 22 December 2009].

Shellnut, Bonnie, Knowlton, Allie, & Savage, Timothy (1999). Applying the ARCS model to the design and development of computer-based modules for manufacturing engineering courses. *Educational Technology Research and Development, 47*(2), pp. 100-110. http://dx.doi.org/10.1007/BF02299469 [last accessed 22 December 2009].

Shellnut, Bonnie, Savage, Timothy, & Knowlton, Allie (1998). *Using the ARCS Model To Design Multimedia College Engineering Courses.*

Proceedings of Selected Research and Development Presentations at the National Convention of the Association for Educational Communications and Technology (AECT1998), St. Louis (Missouri), 18-22 February 1998, pp. 391-399. http://www.eric.ed.gov/ERICDocs/data/ericdocs2sql/content_storage_01/0000019b/80/16/ee/d2.pdf [last accessed 22 December 2009].

Short, J., Williams, E., & Christie, B. (1976). *The Social Psychology of Telecommunications*. New York (New York): Wiley.

Siebert, Horst (2006). *Lernmotivation und Bildungsbeteiligung: Studientexte für Erwachsenenbildung*. Bielefeld (Germany): Bertelsmann.

Siegel, Sidney & Castellan, N. John (1956/1988). *Nonparametric Statistics for the Behavioral Sciences* (2nd edition). New York (New York): McGraw-Hill.

Sirkin, R. Mark (1995/2005). *Statistics for the social sciences* (3rd edition). Thousand Oaks (California): Sage Publications.

Sitthiworachart, Jirihat & Joy, Mike (2003). *Web-based Peer Assessment in Learning Computer Programming.* Proceedings of 3rd IEEE International Conference on Advanced Learning Technologies (ICALT'03), Athens (Greece), 9-11 July 2003, pp. 180-184. http://ieeexplore.ieee.org/stamp/stamp.jsp?arnumber=1215052&isnumber=27318 [last accessed 05 July 2008].

Song, Sang H. & Keller, John M. (2001). Effectiveness of Motivationally Adaptive Computer-Assisted Instruction on the Dynamic Aspects of Motivation. *Educational Technology Research and Development, 49*(2, June), pp. 5-22. http://dx.doi.org/10.1007/BF02504925 [last accessed 22 December 2009].

Sørnes, Jan-Oddvar (2004). *Information and Communication Technologies in Practice: A Study of Advanced Users in the Workplace in Norway and the United States*. Doctoral Thesis, Norwegian University of Science and Technology (NTNU), Trondheim (Norway). http://urn.kb.se/resolve?urn=urn:nbn:no:ntnu:diva-391 [last accessed 22 December 2009].

Spieß, Erika & Winterstein, Hans (1999). *Verhalten in Organisationen: eine Einführung*. Stuttgart (Germany): Kohlhammer.

Spitzer, Dean R. (1995). *SuperMotivation: A Blueprint for Energizing Your Organization from Top to Bottom*. New York (New York): AMA-COM.

Spitzer, Dean R. (1996). Motivation: The Neglected Factor in Instructional Design. *Educational Technology, 36*(3, May-June), pp. 45-49.

Sproul, Lee & Kiesler, Sara (1986). Reducing Social Context Cues: Electronic Mail in Organizational Communication. *Management Science, 32*(11), pp. 1492-1512. http://dx.doi.org/10.1287/mnsc.32.11.1492 [last accessed 22 December 2009].

Stake, Robert E. (1995). *The Art of Case Study Research*. Thousand Oaks, London, New Delhi: Sage Publications.

Steenkamp, Annette Lerine (2002). *A Standard-Based Approach to Team-Based Student Projects in an Information Technology Curriculum.* Proceedings of 17th Annual Conference International Academy for Information Management (IAIM 2002), Barcelona (Spain), 13-15 December 2002, pp. 54-62.

Straus, Susan G. (1999). Testing a Typology of Tasks: An Empirical Validation of McGrath's (1984) Group Task Circumplex. *Small Group Research, 30*(2), pp. 166-187. http://dx.doi.org/10.1177/104649649903000202 [last accessed 22 December 2009].

Sullivan, Nancy & Pratt, Ellen (1996). A Comparative Study of Two ESL Writing Environments: A Computer-assisted Classroom and a Traditional Oral Classroom. *System, 29*(4), pp. 491-501. http://dx.doi.org/10.1016/S0346-251X(96)00044-9 [last accessed 22 December 2009].

Surakka, Sami (2007). What Subjects and Skills are Important for Software Developers? *Communications of the ACM, 50*(1), pp. 73-78. http://dx.doi.org/10.1145/1188913.1188920 [last accessed 22 September 2009].

Tashakkori, Abbas & Teddlie, Charles (1998/2006). *Mixed Methodology: Combining Qualitative and Quantitative Approaches* (9th edition, Vol. 46). Thousand Oaks (California): Sage Publications.

Tausch, Reinhard & Tausch, Anne-Marie (1963/1998). *Erziehungs-Psychologie* (11th edition). Göttingen (Germany): Hogrefe.

Tellis, Winston (1997). Introduction to Case Study. *Qualitative Report, 3*(2). http://www.nova.edu/ssss/QR/QR3-2/tellis1.html [last accessed 25 June 2006].

Tervonen, Ikka, Iisakka, Juha, & Harjumaa, Lasse (1998). *Software Inspection – A Blend of Discipline and Flexibility.* Proceedings of 9th European Software Control and Metrics Conference and the 5th Conference for the European Network of Clubs for Reliability and Safety of Software (ESCOM-ENCRESS-98), Rome (Italy), 29 May 1998. http://www.tol.oulu.fi/i3/1998/Tervonen_ENCRESS_1998.pdf [last accessed 22 December 2009].

The Cognition and Technology Group at Vanderbilt (1990). Anchored Instruction and its Relationship to Situated Cognition. *Educational Researcher, 19*(6), pp. 2-10. http://dx.doi.org/10.3102/0013189X019006002 [last accessed 22 December 2009].

Thorne, Brian (1992/2003). *Carl Rogers* (2nd, revised edition). London (United Kingdom): Sage Publications.

Torralba, Franccesc (2007). *Die Kunst des Zuhörens.* München (Germany): Beck.

Trahasch, Stephan (2004). *From Peer Assessment Towards Collaborative Learning.* Proceedings of 34th ASEE/IEEE Frontiers in Education Conference (FIE04), Savannah (Georgia), 20-23 October 2004, pp. F3F-16-20. http://dx.doi.org/10.1109/FIE.2004.1408638 [last accessed 22 December 2009].

Tu, Yanbin & Lu, Min (2004). *Mechanism Design for Peer and Self Assessment of a Group Project.* Proceedings of 21st Annual Conference for Information Systems Educators (ISECON 2004), Newport (Rhode Island), 04-07 November 2004, pp. 1-5. http://www.isedj.org/isecon/2004/3262/ISECON.2004.Tu.pdf [last accessed 22 December 2009].

Tuzi, Frank (2004). The Impact of E-Feedback on the Revisions of L2 Writers in an Academic Writing Course. *Computers and Compositions, 21*(2), pp. 217-235. http://dx.doi.org/10.1016/j.compcom.2004.02.003 [last accessed 22 December 2009].

Ulijn, Jan M., Lincke, Andreas, & Karakaya, Yunus (2001). Non-face-to-face International Business Negotiation: How is National Culture Reflected in This Medium. *Journal of Professional Communication on Technical Innovation and Global Business Com, 44*(2), pp. 126-137. http://dx.doi.org/10.1109/47.925516 [last accessed 22 May 2009].

Vafa, Shahrzad (1999). *Web-based Instruction and Motivation: Some Useful Guidelines for Educators.* Proceedings of 10th International

Conference of the Society for Information Technology & Teacher Education, San Antonio (Texas), 28 February - 04 March 1999. http://www.editlib.org/index.cfm?fuseaction=Reader.ViewFullText&paper_id=8151 [last accessed 28 January 2008].

Valley, Kathleen L., Moag, Joseph, & Bazerman, Max H. (1998). 'A Matter of Trust': Effects of Communication on the Efficiency and Distribution of Outcomes. *Journal of Economic Behavior & Organization, 34*(2), pp. 211-238. http://dx.doi.org/10.1016/S0167-2681(97)00054-1 [last accessed 22 December 2009].

Van der Merwe, Alex (2007). Using Blended Learning to Boost Motivation and Performance in Introductory Economics Moduls. *South African Journal of Economics, 75*(03), pp. 125-135. http://dx.doi.org/10.1111/j.1813-6982.2007.00109.x [last accessed 22 December 2009].

Visser, Lya, Plomp, Tjeerd, Amirault, Ray J., & Kuiper, Wilmad (2002). Motivating Students at a Distance: The Case of an International Audience. *Educational Technology Research and Development, 50*(2), pp. 94-110. http://dx.doi.org/10.1007/BF02504998 [last accessed 22 December 2009].

Visser, Lya, Plomp, Tjeerd, & Kuiper, Wilmad (1999). *Development Research Applied to Improve Motivation in Distance Education.* Proceedings of National Convention of the Association for Educational Communications and Technology (AECT), Houston (Texas), 10+14 February 1999, pp. 403-411. http://www.eric.ed.gov/ERICDocs/data/ericdocs2sql/content_storage_01/0000019b/80/15/f6/82.pdf [last accessed 22 December 2009].

Vygotsky, Lev S. (1978). *Mind in Society: the Development of Higher Psychological Processes.* Cambridge (Massachusetts): Harvard University Press.

Wager, Elizabeth & Jefferson, Tom (2001). Shortcomings of Peer Review in Biomedical Journals. *Learned Publishing, 14*(4), pp. 257–263. http://dx.doi.org/10.1087/095315101753141356 [last accessed 22 December 2009].

Walther, Joseph B. (1992). Interpersonal Effects in Computer-Mediated Interaction: A Relational Perspective. *Communication Research, 19*(1), pp. 52-90. http://dx.doi.org/10.1177/009365092019001003 [last accessed 22 December 2009].

Walther, Joseph B. (1995). Relational Aspects of Computer-Mediated Communication: Experimental Observations Over Time. *Organization Science, 6*(2), pp. 186-203.

Walther, Joseph B. (1996). Computer-Mediated Communication: Impersonal, Interpersonal and Hyperpersonal Interaction. *Human Communication Research, 23*(1), pp. 3-43.

Walther, Joseph B. (1997). Group and Interpersonal Effects in International Computer-Mediated Collaboration. *Human Communication Research, 23*(3), pp. 342-369. http://dx.doi.org/10.1111/j.1468-2958.1997.tb00400.x [last accessed 22 December 2009].

Walther, Joseph B. (2000). Die Beziehungsdynamik in virtuellen Teams. In: Margarete Boos, Kai J. Jonas & Kai Sassenberg (editors), *Computervermittelte Kommunikation in Organisationen*, pp. 11-25. Göttingen (Germany): Hogrefe.

Walther, Joseph B. & Burgoon, Judee K. (1992). Relational Communication in Computer-Mediated Interaction. *Human Communication Research, 19*(1), pp. 50-88.

Ware, Mark & Monkman, Mike (2007). Peer Review in Scholarly Journals: Perspective of the Scholarly Community – an International Study. [Electronic Article]. http://www.publishingresearch.net/documents/PeerReviewFullPRCReport-final.pdf [last accessed 22 August 2009].

Watson, Julie Abbott, Keats, Damon, & Yoong, Pak (2005). Online Knowledge Sharing and Media Selection in a Community Organisation: An Application of the Theory of Media Synchronicity. Proceedings of 16th Australasian Conference on Information Systems (ACIS 2005), Sydney (Australia), 29 November - 02 December 2005. http://aisel.aisnet.org/acis2005/67 [last accessed 22 December 2009].

Watzlawick, Paul (1976). *Wie wirklich ist die Wirklichkeit?: Wahn, Täuschung, Verstehen*. München (Germany): Piper.

Watzlawick, Paul, Beavin, Janet H., & Jackson, Don D. (1969/2000). *Menschliche Kommunikation: Formen, Störungen, Paraoxien* (10th unchanged edition). Bern (Switzerland): Huber.

Weigle, J. & Krcmar, H. (2000). Zur Funktionsweise Virtualisierter Organisationen. Stuttgart (Germany): Universität Hohenheim, Institut für Betriebswirtschaftslehre, Lehrstuhl für Wirtschaftsinformatik.

Weisbach, Christian-Rainer (1999). *Professionelle Gesprächsführung: ein praxisnahes Lese- und Übungsbuch* (4th revised and expanded edition). München (Germany): Deutscher Taschenbuch-Verlag.

Weissglass, Julian (1990). Constructivist Listening for Empowerment and Change. *The Educational Forum, 54*(4), pp. 351-370. http://ncee.education.ucsb.edu/articles/constructivistlistening.pdf [last accessed 22 December 2009].

Weizenbaum, Joseph (1966). ELIZA — A Computer Program for the Study of Natural Language Communication Between Man and Machine. *Communications of the ACM, 9*(1), pp. 36-45. http://doi.acm.org/10.1145/365153.365168 [last accessed 22 December 2009].

Wendel, Thomas (1996). *Computerunterstützte Teamarbeit: Konzeption und Realisierung eines Teamarbeitssystems.* Wiesbaden (Germany): Gabler.

Wiegers, Karl E. (2002a). *Peer Reviews in Software: A Practical Guide.* Boston (Massachusetts): Addison-Wesley.

Wiegers, Karl E. (2002b). Seven Truth About Peer Reviews. *Cutter IT Journal, 15*(7).

Wilde, Thomas & Hess, Thomas (2007). Forschungsmethoden der Wirtschaftsinformatik: Eine empirische Untersuchung. *Wirtschaftsinformatik, 49*(4), pp. 280-287. http://dx.doi.org/10.1007/s11576-007-0064-z [last accessed 22 December 2009].

Willard, K. & Duffrin, Melani W. (2006). Utilizing Project-Based Learning and Competition to Develop Student Skills and Interest in Producing Quality Food Items. *Journal of Food Science Education, 2*(4), pp. 69-73. http://dx.doi.org/10.1111/j.1541-4329.2003.tb00031.x [last accessed 22 December 2009].

Wlodkowski, Raymond J. (1993). *Enhancing Adult Motivation to Learn.* San Francisco (California): Jossey-Bass.

Wolfe, William J. (2004). *Online Student Peer Reviews.* Proceedings of 5th Conference on Information Technology Education (SIGITE 2004), Salt Lake City (Utah), 28-30 October 2004, pp. 33-37. http://dx.doi.org/10.1145/1029533.1029543 [last accessed 22 December 2009].

Yesildere, Sibel & Turnuklu, Elfi B. (2006). The Effect of Project-Based Learning on Pre-service Primary Mathematics Teachers' Critical Thinking Dispositions. *International Journal of Science and Mathema-*

tics Education, 6, pp. 1-11. http://www.upd.edu.ph/~ismed/online/articles/project/Vol6_The%20Effect.pdf [last accessed 22 May 2009].

Yin, Robert K. (1984/1989). *Case Study Research: Design and Methods* (5th edition). Newbury Park: Sage Publications.

Yin, Robert K. (1993). *Applications of Case Study Research* (Vol. 34). Newbury Park: Sage Publications.

Zimbardo, Philip G. & Gerrig, Richard J. (2004). *Psychologie* (16th, revised edition). München (Germany): Pearson Studium.

Zöfel, Peter (2002). *Statistik verstehen: Ein Begleitbuch zur computergestützten Anwendung*. München (Germany): Addison-Wesley.

Appendix

Appendix 1. Questionnaire concerning motivational aspects

On the right-hand side, you find the items of the original questionnaire, which had been developed in (Figl, 2008, 2009), in German language. On the left-hand side you find the respective English translations.

	There are many reasons to learn course content and to participate actively in lessons. In the following, you will find a row of possible reasons for these learning endeavours. Please consider how these reasons are true for you personally. I participated in [course's title] because:	Es gibt viele Gründe, den Stoff einer Lehrveranstaltung zu lernen und sich am Unterricht zu beteiligen. Im Folgenden finden Sie eine Reihe möglicher Gründe für diesen Lernaufwand. Überlegen Sie bitte, wie sehr jeder dieser Gründe auf persönlich zutrifft. Ich habe mich an [Kurstitel] beteiligt, weil:
1	I wanted to get a good grade	ich eine gute Note bekommen wollte
2	I could enhance my ability to solve real problems	ich dadurch meine Fähigkeit, reale Probleme zu lösen, erhöhen konnte
3	I had great interest in the content provided	ich schätze, wenn Eigeninitiative beim Lernen honoriert wird
4	I appreciate it when self-initiative in the learning process is rewarded	ich es schätze, wenn Eigeninitiative beim Lernen honoriert wird
5	the lecturer stimulated to participate in the lessons	der/die LVA-Leiter/in mich zur Beteiligung am Unterricht angeregt hat
6	I liked to collaborate with the colleagues	ich gerne mit den Kolleg/innen zusammengearbeitet habe.
7	I found the way the course was conducted appealing	ich die Art und Weise, wie die Lehrveranstaltung abgehalten

		wurde, ansprechend fand
8	it was important to me to show that I was better than my colleagues	es mir wichtig war zu zeigen, dass ich besser bin als meine Kolleg/innen
9	I like to solve real problems	ich gerne reale Probleme löse
10	I benefited a lot from the exchange with colleagues and the lecturer	ich durch den Austausch mit den Kolleg/innen und der/dem LVA-Leiter/in viel profitierte
11	I wanted to acquire a high level of competence in the subject area	es mir wichtig war, ein hohes Maß an Fachkompetenz zu Erlangen
12	the subject matter was elaborated considering high practical relevance	der Stoff der Lehrveranstaltung mit einem hohen Praxisbezug erarbeitet wurde
13	I liked the atmosphere / working climate of the course	mir das Arbeitsklima / die Atmosphäre der Lehrveranstaltung gefallen hat
14	tasks' relevance for my (later) professional activity was identifiable	die Relevanz der Aufgabenstellungen für meine (spätere) berufliche Tätigkeit erkennbar war
15	I could learn much from my self-initiated activities and contributions	ich durch meine selbstständigen Aktivitäten und Beiträge viel lernen konnte
16	active participation of all students was possible	die aktive Mitarbeit aller Teilnehmer möglich war
17	there was sufficient room for exchange and discussions	viel Zeit für Austausch und Diskussionen vorhanden war
18	my contributions were useful also for my colleagues	meine Beiträge auch für die Kolleg/innen von Nutzen waren
19	it was important to me to enhance my practical skills	es mir wichtig war, meine praktischen Fertigkeiten zu erweitern

20	the cooperation with peers was very collegial	die Zusammenarbeit bei den anderen Teilnehmer/innen sehr kollegial war
21	it was communicated in the course how I can act goal-orientated in real situations	in der Übung vermittelt wurde, wie ich in realen Situationen zielgerichtet handeln kann
22	the lecturer prepared the subject matter well	der/die LVA-Leiter/in den Lehrstoff gut vorbereitet hat
23	the lecturer designed the course in a lively and engaged way	der/die LVA-Leiter/in den Lehrstoff gut vorbereitet hat
24	I benefited a lot from the exchange with colleagues	ich durch den Austausch mit den Kolleg/innen viel profitierte
25	it was possible to bring in self-initiated contributions	es möglich war, selbstständig Beiträge einzubeziehen
26	the lecturer knew how to make students interested in the course content	der/die LVA-Leiter/in der Lehrveranstaltung es verstand, die Studierenden für den Stoff der Lehrveranstaltung zu interessieren
27	I liked to work out something autonomously	ich gerne selbstständig etwas erarbeite
28	the course atmosphere course encouraged to take part actively	in der Lehrveranstaltung eine Arbeitsatmosphäre herrschte, die dazu ermutigte, sich zu beteiligen
29	the lecturer provided a motivating atmosphere in the course	der/die LVA-Leiter/in für eine förderliche Atmosphäre in der Lehrveranstaltung gesorgt hat
30	the lecturer expected this from me	der/die Lehrveranstaltungsleiter/in das von mir erwartet hat
31	I wanted to achieve a better exam grade than my colleagues	ich bei der Prüfung besser abschneiden wollte als meine Kolleg/innen

32	I wanted to study further in the course's subject matter	ich mich in diesem Unterrichtsfach weiterbilden wollte
33	it was important to me to show that I studied more patiently than others	es mir wichtig war zu zeigen, dass ich fleißgier studiere als andere
34	I wanted to be among the best in the course	ich in der Übung zu den Besten gehören wollte
35	I wanted to avoid getting in trouble with the lecturer	ich vermeiden wollte, dass ich mit dem/der Lehrveranstaltungsleiter/in Ärger bekomme
36	it was important for me to acquire comprehensive expert knowledge	es mir wichtig war, ein umfangreiches Fachwissen zu erhalten
37	I enjoyed to engage with the course's content	mir die Beschäftigung mit den Inhalten der Lehrveranstaltung Spaß gemacht hat
38	I did not want to disappoint the lecturer	ich den/die Lehrveranstaltungsleiter/in nicht enttäuschen wollte
39	I wanted to be considered a good student by the lecturer	ich wollte, dass mich der/die Lehrveranstaltungsleiter/in für einen/eine gute/n Studierende/n hält
40	it was important for me to improve my professional skills	es mir wichtig war, meine fachlichen Fähigkeiten zu erweitern
41	I wanted to prove to myself that I could complete the course extremely successfully	ich mir selbst beweisen wollte, dass ich die Übung mit sehr gutem Erfolg abschließen kann
42	it was important for me to improve my soft skills	es mir wichtig war, meine Soft Skills zu erweitern

Source: (Figl, 2008, 2009)

RESPONSE FORMAT

totally disagree	trifft gar nicht zu
somewhat disagree	trifft kaum zu
partly/partly	teils/teils
somewhat agree	trifft etwas zu
totally agree	trifft völlig zu

Appendix 2. Questionnaire for comparing online and face-to-face peer reviews

On the right-hand side, you find the items of the original questionnaire in German language. On the left-hand side you find the respective English translations.

	INTRODUCTION	EINLEITUNG
	Please recall the peer review task from the course unit on quality assurance (23 November), in which you gave feedback for your partner team!	Bitte versuchen Sie sich an die Übung der gegenseitigen Reviews zu erinnern, in der sie am 23.11. (Einheit Qualitätssicherung) eine Reviewmängelliste für ein Partnerteam erstellt haben!
	Please answer all open-ended questions!	Bitte füllen Sie auch alle offenen Fragen aus!
	Thank you!	Vielen Dank!

	ACTIVITIES FACE-TO-FACE AND ONLINE	ARBEITSSCHRITTE PRÄSENT UND ONLINE
	Please report for every of the following activities whether your noticed differences between the paper and the online version and describe these differences!	Bitte geben Sie zu jedem der Arbeitsschritte an, ob Ihnen Unterschiede zwischen der Papier- und Onlineversion aufgefallen sind, und beschreiben Sie diese bitte!
1	Review of the partner team's documents	Durchgehen der Dokumente des Partnerteams
2	Completion of the review form	Ausfüllen der Mängelliste

3	Communication within your own team	Kommunikation im eigenen Team
4	Discussion with the partner team concerning the reviews	Diskussion mit Partnerteam bezüglich Reviews
5	Revision of the documents (considering the reviews)	Überarbeiten des eigenen Projektes anhand der Reviews

	WORKLOAD DISTRIBUTION IN TEAMS	AUFGABENVERTEILUNG
6	How did you divide and distribute the peer review task in your team in the paper version?	Wie haben Sie sich die Peerreview-Aufgabe im Team bei der Papierversion aufgeteilt?
7	How did you divide and distribute the peer review task in your team in the online version?	Wie haben Sie sich die Peerreview Aufgabe im Team bei der Onlineversion aufgeteilt?

	WORK EFFICIENCY	ARBEITSEFFIZIENZ
8	Which version was easier to fill in? paper version o o o o o online version	Was war einfacher auszufüllen? Papierversion o o o o o Onlineversion
9	Which version was more time-consuming? paper version o o o o o online	Welche Version war zeitlich aufwändiger? Papierversion o o o o o Online-

	version Why? [ ]	version Warum? [ ]

	REVIEW QUALITY AND SUPPORT FOR REVISION	**REVIEWQUALITÄT UND -NUTZEN**
10	In which version was the quality of the feedback higher in terms of its support for revising your project? paper version o o o o o online version	Bei welcher Version war die Qualität des erhaltenen Feedbacks höher in dem Sinne, dass es hilfreicher war Ihr Projekt zu überarbeiten? Papierversion o o o o o Online-version
11	In which version could you provide your partner team with a more helpful feedback? paper version o o o o o online version	Bei welcher Version konnten Sie dem anderen Team ein hilfreicheres Feedback geben? Papierversion o o o o o Online-version
12	In which version could you better express the suggestions for improvement for your partner team? paper version o o o o o online version Why? [ ]	Bei welcher Version konnten Sie Ihrem Partnerteam gegenüber die Verbesserungsvorschläge besser ausdrücken? Papierversion o o o o o Online-version Warum? [ ]

	SUGGESTIONS FOR IMPROVEMENT	VERBESSERUNGSVORSCHLÄGE
13	What would you improve in the paper version?	Was würden Sie an der Papier-version verbessern?
14	What would you improve in the online version?	Was würden Sie an der Online-version verbessern?

Appendix 3. Questionnaire investigating media enhancement for peer reviews

On the right-hand side, you find the items of the original questionnaire in German language. On the left-hand side you find the respective English translations.

	GENERAL QUESTIONS	GENERELLE FRAGEN
1	Brief summary of the core elements of the reviewed papers (3-5 sentences)	Kurzzusammenfassung der Kernelemente der reviewten Papers (3-5 Sätze)
2	How many reviews have your received?	Wie viele Reviews haben Sie erhalten?
3	How many reviews have you written?	Wie viele Reviews haben Sie verfasst?

	ACTIVE DRAFTING OF THE PEER REVIEW	AKTIVES SCHREIBEN DES PEERREVIEWS
	ASSESSMENT	BEWERTUNG
	It had been easy for me to assess following criteria in the review:	Es war für mich einfach, die folgenden Kriterien im Review zu beurteilen:
4	formal aspects of the scientific work	formale Aspekte der wissenschaftlichen Arbeit
5	language, presentation, diligence	Sprache, äußere Form, Sorgfalt
6	content aspects	inhaltliche Aspekte

7	sources and references	Quellen, Sekundärmaterial
8	suggested grade	Note
	PEER REVIEW ACTIVITY	**PEERREVIEWAKTIVITÄT**
9	I had fun doing the peer reviews.	Es hat mir Spaß gemacht, die Peerreviews zu verfassen.
10	I thoroughly read the papers assigned for review.	Ich habe die Arbeiten sehr genau gelesen, für die ich ein Review verfassen sollte.
11	I read additional papers besides those I was assigned to review.	Ich habe auch weitere Arbeiten von Kollegen gelesen, auch wenn ich dafür kein Review verfassen musste.
12	Did the peer review impact the perception of your own paper? yes ☐ no ☐ If yes, how? [ ]	Hat sich durch das Peerreview die Wahrnehmung Ihres eigenen Papers verändert? ja ☐ nein ☐ Wenn ja, wie? [ ]
13	Would you have evaluated the work differently if it had been absolutely anonymous (i.e., if authors would not have been able to conclude who had written the review)? yes ☐ neo ☐ If yes, how? much more positively (++) + ~ - (--) much more negatively	Hätten Sie im Review die Arbeit anders bewertet, falls es komplett anonym gewesen wäre (d.h., wenn die Autoren keinen Rückschluss darauf machen könnten, dass Sie den Review verfasst haben)? ja ☐ nein ☐ Wenn ja, wie? viel positiver (++) + ~ - (--) viel negativer

14	If rated differently, how?	Wenn anders bewertet, wie?
15	How much time (in minutes) did you dedicate to the peer review?	Wie viel Zeit (in Minuten) haben Sie für das Peerreview aufgewandt?

	RECEIVING THE PEER REVIEW	**ERHALTEN DES PEERREVIEWS**
	QUALITY OF THE REVIEWS	**QUALITÄT DER REVIEWS**
	The received peer reviews were…	Die erhaltenen Peerreviews waren…
16	detailed	detailliert
17	helpful	hilfreich
18	comprehensible	nachvollziehbar
19	consistent	konsistent
	QUALITY OF THE REVIEWING PROCESS	**QUALITÄT DES REVIEWPROZESSES**
20	My (student) reviewers were competent.	Meine (studentischen) Reviewer/innen waren sehr kompetent.
21	The (student) reviewers read my/our paper thoroughly.	Die (studentischen) Reviewer/innen haben meine/unsere Arbeit sehr genau gelesen.
22	The proposed points for improvement were justified.	Die vorgeschlagenen Verbesserungspunkte waren gerechtfertigt.
23	I would have appreciated to write a reaction on the peer reviews.	Ich hätte gerne eine Reaktion auf die Peerreviews verfasst.

24	I would have appreciated the possibility to ask back.	Ich hätte gerne die Möglichkeit gehabt, persönlich nachzufragen.
25	Based on the reviews, I/we revised the paper significantly.	Ich/wir habe/n anhand der Reviews noch viel an der Arbeit geändert.
26	As author I/we would have written my/our paper differently, if I/we had known the peer review criteria before.	Ich/wir hätte/n mein/unser Paper als Autor anders gestaltet, wenn ich/wir schon im Vorhinein die Struktur des Peerreview-Fraugebogens gekannt hätte/n.

	PEER REVIEW IN GENERAL	**PEERREVIEWS ALLGEMEIN**
27	The peer review in the course was a good idea.	Das Peerreview in der Lehrveranstaltung war eine gute Idee.
	ELIGIBILITY OF PEER REVIEW SETTINGS	**EIGNUNG DIVERSER PEERREVIEW-SETTINGS**
	How appropriate are following settings of peer reviews? (Please give reasons for your answer)	Wie geeignet halten Sie folgende Konstellationen für Peerreviews? (Bitte begründen Sie Ihre Antworten)
28	comments purely in writing	rein schriftlich verfasste Kommentare
29	oral feedback (in a personal conversation; face-to-face)	mündliches Feedback (im persönlichen Gespräch; face-to-face)
30	written comments providing the athor with the possibility of the author to ask and comment	schriftliche Kommentare mit der Möglichkeit des Autors, nachzufragen bzw. zu kommentieren

31	oral feedback (in personal conversation; face-to-face) with the provision of written handouts	mündliches Feedback (im persönlichen Gespräch; face-to-face), wobei ein schriftlicher Review als "Handout" zur Verfügung gestellt wird
	PERCEPTION	**WAHRNEHMUNG**
	Does the peer review process influence following aspects?	Hat der Peerreviewprozess Ihrer Meinung nach Einfluss auf folgende Punkte?
32	I have more confidence in my own performance.	Ich habe mehr Vertrauen in meine eigene Leistung.
33	I have an increased consciousness about the quality of my own work.	Mir ist die Qualität der eigenen Arbeit stärker bewusst.
34	I reflected more on my performance and behaviour than I usually do in other courses.	Ich habe über meine Leistung bzw. mein Verhalten im Kurs mehr reflektiert als in anderen Kursen.
35	My reviewing competence has increased.	Meine Reviewkompetenz hat sich erhöht.
36	I put more effort in my work, since I knew peers would review it.	Da ich wusste, dass meine (unsere) Arbeit von Kollegen gelesen und beurteilt wird, habe ich mich mehr angestrengt.
37	I got (more) aware of my own responsibility in my learning process.	Mit wurde bewusst(er), dass ich für meinen eigenen Lernprozess selbst verantwortlich bin.
38	The use of peer reviews enhanced the learning climate.	Der Einsatz von Peerreviews hat das Lernklima verbessert.
39	The peer reviews helped me to perceive the essential elements of scientific papers.	Das Ausfüllen des Peerreview Fragebogens hat mir geholfen, die wesentlichen Elemente wissenschaftlicher Papers wahrzu-

		nehmen.
40	Through writing peer reviews, I learned a lot about the peer review process.	Ich habe durch das Verfassen des Peerreviews viel über den Peerreviewprozess gelernt.

RESPONSE FORMAT	
I totally agree (++)	stimme sehr zu (++)
+	+
~	~
-	-
I do not agree at all (--)	stimme gar nicht zu (--)

www.ingramcontent.com/pod-product-compliance
Ingram Content Group UK Ltd.
Pitfield, Milton Keynes, MK11 3LW, UK
UKHW021848100926
8556IPUK00020B/1111

9 783631 588093